The European Sisyphus

The New Europe: Interdisciplinary Perspectives
Stanley Hoffmann, Series Editor

The European Sisyphus: Essays on Europe, 1964–1994
Stanley Hoffmann

France, Germany, and the Western Alliance
Philip H. Gordon

FORTHCOMING

The European Union: Politics and Policies
John Spencer McCormick

Integrating Social Europe: The International Construction
of a Democratic Polity   *Wolfgang Streeck*

THE EUROPEAN SISYPHUS

Essays on Europe, 1964-1994

Stanley Hoffmann

Westview Press

BOULDER • SAN FRANCISCO • OXFORD

The New Europe: Interdisciplinary Perspectives

Copyright © 1995 by Westview Press, Inc.

Published in 1995 in the United States of America by Westview Press, Inc., 5500 Central Avenue, Boulder, Colorado 80301-2877, and in the United Kingdom by Westview Press, 12 Hids Copse Road, Cumnor Hill, Oxford OX2 9JJ

Library of Congress Cataloging-in-Publication Data
Hoffmann, Stanley.
    The European Sisyphus : essays on Europe, 1964–1994 / Stanley Hoffmann.
        p.   cm. — (The new Europe : interdisciplinary perspectives)
    Includes index.
    ISBN 0-8133-2380-0 (HC). — ISBN 0-8133-2381-9 (PB)
    1. Europe—Politics and government—1945–   I. Title.   II. Series:
New Europe (Boulder, Colo.)
D843.H592   1995
940.55—dc20   94-28821
                                                                                CIP

Printed and bound in the United States of America

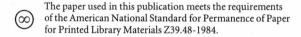

The paper used in this publication meets the requirements
of the American National Standard for Permanence of Paper
for Printed Library Materials Z39.48-1984.

10   9   8   7   6   5   4   3   2   1

Contents

Credits

Permissions to reprint are gratefully acknowledged.

Chapter 1   Reprinted by permission of *Dædalus*, Journal of the American Academy of Arts and Sciences, from the issue entitled "The Contemporary University: U.S.A.," Fall 1964, vol. 93, no. 4 (pp. 1244–1297).

Chapter 2   Reprinted by permission of *Dædalus*, Journal of the American Academy of Arts and Sciences, from the issue entitled "Europe Through a Glass Darkly," Spring 1994, vol. 123, no. 2 (pp. 1–23).

Chapter 3   Reprinted from *Decline or Renewal? France Since the 1930s* (pp. 363–369 and 509–512) by Stanley Hoffmann. Copyright © 1960, 1964, 1968, 1971, 1972, 1974 by Stanley Hoffmann. Used by permission of Viking Penguin, a division of Penguin Books USA Inc.

Chapter 4   Reprinted, with deletions of text, from "No Trumps, No Luck, No Will: Gloomy Thoughts on Europe's Plight," in *Atlantis Lost: U.S.-European Relations After the Cold War*, James Chace and Earl C. Ravenal, eds. (New York: New York University Press, 1976), pp. 1–46. Used by permission of the publisher and the Council on Foreign Relations.

Chapter 5   Reprinted, with deletions of text, from "Uneven Allies: An Overview," in *Western Europe: The Trials of Partnership*, David S. Landes, ed. (Lexington, Mass.: Lexington Books, 1977), pp. 55–110. Used by permission.

Chapter 6   Reprinted, with notes renumbered, by permission of *Dædalus*, Journal of the American Academy of Arts and Sciences, from the issue entitled "Looking for Europe," Winter 1979, vol. 108, no. 1 (pp. 1–26).

Chapter 7   Reprinted from the *Journal of Common Market Studies*, September/December 1982, vol. 21, no. 1–2 (pp. 21–37), by permission. An earlier version of this chapter was presented to the conference of "Europeanists" in Washington, D.C., in October 1980.

Chapter 8   Reprinted from *Foreign Affairs*, the issue entitled "The European Community and 1992," Fall 1989, vol. 68, no. 4 (pp. 27–47), by permission.

Chapter 9   Reprinted, with deletion of the cartoon, from the *New York Review of Books,* January 18, 1990, vol. 36, no. 21–22. Used by permission.

Chapter 10   Reprinted from *Survival,* the issue entitled "Arms Control and the New Strategic Environment," July/August 1990, vol. 32, no. 4 (pp. 291–298), by permission.

Chapter 11   Reprinted from *Foreign Policy,* the issue entitled "The Emerging World System," Winter 1990–91, no. 81 (pp. 20–38). Used by permission.

Chapter 12   Reprinted by permission from *The Shape of the New Europe,* Gregory F. Treverton, ed. (New York: Council on Foreign Relations Press, 1991), pp. 194–220.

Chapter 13   Reprinted, with deletion of cartoons, from the *New York Review of Books,* May 27, 1993, vol. 41, no. 10, by permission.

Introduction

This collection of essays gathers pieces written over a period of thirty years, 1964 to 1994. They comment on the development and difficulties of European integration. First, it was the European Economic Community (EEC), later the European Community (EC); now it is the European Union. It has grown from its original six members to the current twelve, and if the four newly admitted applicants get their electorates to approve their accession, the European Union (EU) will soon have sixteen members—with several more possible: Former members of the late Soviet bloc are knocking at the door. One of my reasons for putting these pieces together is my belief that many of the issues that trouble the EU today have plagued it from the beginning and have not been resolved. It is this continuity in flaws and obstacles that has led me to begin the collection by juxtaposing the oldest essay, written in 1964—an essay that emerged from and reacted to the generally optimistic view of Europe conveyed by the *Daedalus* issue called "A New Europe?" (1963)—and the most recent, which explicitly "revisits" the landscape of 1964. It isn't only European integration that displays the same ambiguities, hesitations, and failings over this long period; the reader will find that my preoccupations and emphases have remained quite constant as well.

A second reason for assembling these pieces is that they provide a view of evolution and change, an examination of the crises and turning points in the history of European integration. The essays fall into three broad clusters: Chapter 1 and 3 were written in the mid-1960s (although the version of Chapter 3 reprinted here was brought up to date in 1973)—at the time of Charles de Gaulle's challenge of both the Jean Monnet conception of functional, supranational integration and the American notion of Atlantic partnership. Chapters 4 to 7 were written during the European Community's "period of stagnation," when the limited recovery that followed de Gaulle's departure from the scene (and entailed a first attempt at moving toward greater economic unity, as well as the enlargement that opened the door to the United Kingdom) was stymied by the combined effects of Henry Kissinger's imperious diplomacy and the oil crises of 1973 and 1979. The remaining chapters were written between 1988 and 1994. They deal with the new recovery that led first to the "1992" single market program and later to the Maastricht Treaty of European Union. They reflect, and brood about, the drastic change in the international context: the collapse of the Soviet empire in Europe (and later of the Soviet Union itself) and the effects on the European Community, or

1

Union, of Germany's unification and the end of the cold war. Those chapters also discuss the effects of the new and prolonged recession of the late 1980s and early 1990s on the construction of a united Europe.

II

Although minor cuts have been made in Chapters 4 and 5, the essays are being reprinted unrevised. In a sense, each later piece amounted to a reconsideration of the earlier ones; I see no reason to conceal from readers (who, in any case, can always examine the original versions in the books and journals where they appeared) the errors, changes of mind, and restatements that have marked my thirty years of analyses. In particular, Chapters 9 to 12, written during the exhilarating turmoil of 1989–1991, show that I overestimated, at first, the "cards" Gorbachev's Soviet Union could still play vis-à-vis Germany, and that I was far from convinced—again, at first—that Germany's unification wouldn't provide Germany's neighbors and partners with good reasons to worry about the return of "the German question" that had dominated Europe, and world politics, from the 1860s to the 1940s. Chapter 9 reflects my initial worries and contains a "plan" for European unification that has almost nothing in common with what actually occurred; it describes a road *not* taken, and it is instructive to ask why. The answer is that it would have required a completely different policy from every one of the major actors as well as a willingness on the part of those actors to act together to impose serious restraints and delays on the Federal Republic. "My" plan represents—if I may presume to say so—an extrapolation from the scheme that de Gaulle had sketched in 1965 (for the twentieth anniversary of Yalta): He had correctly predicted Europe's and Germany's return to unity and the conditions that might bring it about, but he did not predict the way in which these momentous events occurred.[1]

The reader may find some of my remarks in Chapter 6—those that refer to a "growing disconnection from the more distant past" in the publics of Western Europe—at least as weird as my suggestions in Chapter 9. In Chapter 2, written sixteen years after Chapter 6, I revised my analysis and reflected on the considerable change in West European elite attitudes toward the past. "Normalization" (by some historians) of the Nazi past in Germany, combined with the rage of commemorations and studies of national memory in France (a peculiar phenomenon I have discussed elsewhere),[2] are additional danger signals for the believers in the inevitable progress of ever closer European integration: In different ways, both these changes of attitudes reflect a real nostalgia for the days of the sovereign nation-state. The French rediscovery of the past(s)—however fragmented and pluralistic—expresses a deep worry about the erosion and corrosion of national identity, partly caused by integration into a European entity no longer dominated by France.

III

Two of my central concerns that inspired these essays are the connection between Western Europe and the United States and the nature of the European entity. Much has changed with respect to both over the past thirty years. Chapters 1, 3, 4, and 5 emphasize rather relentlessly how much the United States dominated the West European scene in the cold-war period—both as a model of society ("Americanization") and as the hegemonic power in an uneven alliance. I was eager to show why the "American model" would not fully fit West European societies (indeed, if it had, one of the main arguments for the construction of the European entity, the need to preserve a distinct European identity, would have vanished). I wanted also to show how America's predominance and its ambivalence about a "Europe speaking with one voice" (desired by Washington in the abstract, and often resisted in concrete instances) had, in fact, contributed both to divisions among the West Europeans and to their relative impotence and frequent habits of dependence in world affairs. Many of the essays recommended that the United States disengage not from European affairs but from a policy of control over these affairs, and that it recognize that its best interest was a deliberate strengthening of the Europeans' capacity to act autonomously. I was whistling, or sermonizing, in the dark. In 1994, however, I noted in an essay (see Chapter 2) that the weight of the United States on and in Europe had much decreased. The end of the cold war, the collapse of George Bush's vision of a world order in which the USSR would follow America's lead and in which, in effect, the Rooseveltian vision of 1943–1945 would be finally realized, and Bill Clinton's sharp turn toward domestic reforms and policies geared to a U.S. economic renaissance have transformed the U.S.–West European relationship. The recent acceptance by the United States of greater European autonomy within NATO and France's acceptance of this less U.S.-dominated NATO as an at least temporary framework for distinctive European security concerns (even "out of area," as in Yugoslavia) are the result of U.S. policy reorientation and France's belated awareness of and adjustment to it.

As for the nature of the European enterprise, these essays reflect my evolution on two points. First, I have tried to define my own position in the debate between those who saw the EEC, the EC, or the EU as an entity moving toward a kind of Federal Europe under the leadership of partly supranational institutions (Commission, Parliament, Court of Justice) and through the process that Monnet had created and Ernst Haas turned into a theory, and those who believed that it would amount to little more than a *Europe des Etats,* in which the intergovernmental bodies (the Councils of Ministers, the European Council) would dominate. In the beginning, I was eager to show why I didn't share the Federalist vision and Haas's theory. Later, I suggested analyzing the EC as a "strong," indeed unique, international regime (see Chapter 8). With the changes introduced by the Single Act of 1987 and by the Maastricht Treaty, I came to believe that there were features of the EU that went far beyond any other international regime and that we were in the presence of a singular construction: a mix of intergovernmental and federal features that needed to be recognized as *sui generis* and whose final form is far from settled.[3]

A second point concerns the relationship between the nation-states that compose the EU and the European entity. The latter represents a very original attempt at pooling or blending "sovereign" powers, and it also creates central authorities that exert powers transferred to them by the states in a number of important areas: agriculture, external trade, competition policies, and so on. Does this mean a "decline of the nation-state"? Many of these essays emphasize instead the ways in which this relationship is not a zero-sum game and the idea that the European entity has, indeed, helped the restoration and consolidation of its member states. But with the completion of the 1992 program and the further steps envisaged by Maastricht—a planned Monetary Union, in particular—many citizens of these states, especially in France and the United Kingdom, began to feel and resent that many of their sovereign powers had been given away, either to the market or to the Brussels authorities. This is part of the present crisis. Also, many parliamentarians began to realize and resent that the evolution of the European Union strengthened the Executive branch (the commission and, above all, the Council in Brussels, the heads of state and government in the member states) at the expense of a weak Parliament in Strasbourg and of increasingly dispossessed national legislatures.[4]

IV

All these evolutions and revolutions, however, have not altered a few fundamental points, which are highlighted throughout this collection.

First, the theme of, and lament about, the absence of a clear European *projet* or vision of the future remain as justified today as in 1964. If an agreement on a common future had been required (as de Gaulle appeared to demand), the European entity would probably have been incapable of moving ahead. But the lack of an agreement about the destination (and the ultimate institutions) of the European Union is beginning to become more of an obstacle *to* than a condition *of* progress—especially now that the national publics, long left out or standing aside, are awake and mobilized. In the 1980s, "broadening" and "deepening" had been managed simultaneously. The British conception—persistent and relentless—downplays common policies emanating from the Brussels bureaucracy, favors continued broadening, and resists supranationality and the expansion of majority vote; it is in conflict with the conception that insists on a dense network of common policies, opposes the idea that Europe should be little more than a vast free trade zone, and also fears that in a much broader Europe, Germany—rather than the "Franco-German axis"—will become the motor[5] and that the decisive verdict may well be rendered by Germany. The French worry *both* about a joint German-British preference for further broadening and about Germany's potential domination of the common decisionmaking processes. They are ambivalent about the latter, for they want to "contain" the new Germany but not be prevented from exercising what is left of French autonomy.

A second theme is that of the European entity's continuing difficulty to move, on the one hand, from the realm of economic unification and management to a common diplomatic and security policy in world affairs and, on the other, to the creation of a genuine "internal" European political process. The essays collected here try to show why and how the political processes and lives of the members have remained distinct and national and how the diversity of the "national situations," traditions, and interests has impeded the quest for a common foreign and defense policy. These shortcomings are underscored by the multiple postponements of enforcing the Schengen agreements on opening borders to the free flow of people and by the persistence of national sovereignty over the naturalization and integration of foreigners. A recent case study of the European (counter-)performance in Yugoslavia, not included in this collection, glaringly exposes the entity's failure in world affairs.[6]

A third theme concerns not the nature of the European entity and how it is to be conceived, but the nature of international relations and how it needs to be analyzed. If there is any common thread here, it is a critique—often implicit, but explicit in Chapters 10 to 12—of an impoverished realism that focuses almost exclusively on the "structural" factor of the distribution of power and sees in international politics little more than the balancing of power and the fluctuating collusions and collisions of power. The brand of realism that is displayed here is admittedly less parsimonious. An adequate analysis must first embody the idea that state interests are not simply reducible to power and place; that they are constructs in which ideas and ideals, precedents and past experiences, and domestic forces and rulers all play a role. It must also abandon the idea that the theory of international politics can leave aside what happens within the units—which are, after all, the main actors—and live, so to speak, independently and apart from the study of foreign policies. Third, the analysis must consider that the repertory of states is not monotonously limited to balancing or bandwagoning, or the failure to do either; and, finally, that the institutions in which states cooperate have often more than a superficial and ephemeral effect on the way in which they define their interests and calculate their gains or losses.[7] It is true that international politics—in a milieu without central power—is a "game" with a few constant rules; but the actors' capacity to interpret, twist, revise, and add to these rules should not be neglected. The outcome depends, of course, on each actor's position in the game; but it also depends on a factor that is stressed here throughout: the quality of their leadership. It is the interplay between creative leaders and the mass of constraints that results from the configurations of the international system and of the domestic polity that makes the study of international politics so interesting. The progress, and often also the crises, of European integration are largely the products of innovative and willful leaders. The persistent obstacles and limitations are the products of these constraints.

A final word. Although these essays tend to focus on failings and dilemmas and on persistent limitations, they do not ignore the progress that European unity has made. Bouts of expansion both in geographical and functional scope have marked its history, and periods of pessimism and slowdown have—except in the monetary realm—rarely led to regressions. The image of Sisyphus is used only to suggest that the shape of the EU today is quite different from the supranational dream of its founders and that each leap forward brings with it problems as well as reminders of constant handicaps. The prophets of disastrous breakups have been proven wrong again and again. The European Union is now a necessary and permanent part of the European political landscape, and thus a subtle, if often shaky, actor in international affairs. If the idealists of integration have often ignored the difficulties, realists have tended to neglect the reality of the EU. Sometimes something new appears on the stage on which states perform their dangerous ballet.

Notes

1. Cf. "Charles de Gaulle's Foreign Policy." In Gordon Craig and Francis Loewenheim (eds.), *The Diplomats, 1939–1979* (Princeton: Princeton University Press, 1994).

2. Cf. "Thoughts on the French Nation Today," *Daedalus*, Summer 1993, pp. 63–80.

3. Cf. Robert Keohane and Stanley Hoffmann, "Institutional Change in Europe in the 1980s." In Keohane and Hoffmann (eds.), *The New European Community* (Boulder: Westview, 1992).

4. On this point, see Andrew Moravcsik, "Why the European Community Strengthens the State: Domestic Politics and International Cooperation," Center for European Studies, Working Paper No. 52, 1994.

5. Cf. "French Dilemmas and Strategies in the New Europe." In Joseph Nye, Robert Keohane, and Stanley Hoffmann (eds.), *After the Cold War* (Cambridge, MA: Harvard University Press, 1993), pp. 127–147.

6. "Yugoslavia: Implications for Europe and European Institutions," to be published by the Council on Foreign Relations in a volume edited by Richard Ullmann.

7. See the devastating attack on neorealism by Paul Schroeder, "Historical Reality vs. Neorealist Theory," *International Security*, Summer 1994, pp. 108–148.

Part One

Europe's Identity

1

Europe's Identity Crisis: Between the Past and America

Europe today is prosperous and disunited. What it will be like tomorrow remains a mystery—both because disunity results from conflicting assumptions about Europe's future, and because prosperity tends to become an end in itself. Europe today has no clear identity, no profile other than that which a process of industrialization and a process of economic integration have given it. Europe today has no sense of direction and purpose; this essay laments its absence and calls for its rebirth.*

But one cannot be asked to choose his future unless it is first established that freedom of choice exists. The point of this essay is to show that Europe's freedom of choice has been destroyed neither by the advent of industrial society nor by the evolution of world affairs. There is no "determinism" of the economic and social system. Nor has a new "European identity" been fully shaped by the European communities. And yet many Europeans behave as if the future course of Europe had been set, and many Americans believe it too. Whereas the former are divided between happy resignation and bitter protest, the latter show pride and some complacency. There is no justification for either of their attitudes.

One factor is involved in both processes which many see as inhibiting Europe's freedom: Europe's relationship with the United States. This essay is an attempt to explore this relationship. Since 1945 it has been one of double dependence, internal and external. The internal dimension of dependence has been called "Americanization." European societies have been transformed by the eruption of the age

*In this essay, "Western Europe" refers to the so-called Six; the problem of Britain would require a separate analysis. Many of Europe's postwar developments discussed here have affected England also— and yet Britain's absence from the so-called "European experiment," Britain's "special relationship" with the U.S., as well as the important differences between the recent past of England and that of the continental countries (i.e., the illusion of victory vs. the humiliations of defeat) make of Britain's case a special one. Indeed, were "the Six" more capable of defining a new European identity, Britain's painful hesitations about its own might be overcome more easily.

of mass consumption. Of course other terms, such as modernization or industrialization, could be used; but "Americanization" for several reasons applies. It was the United States which preached the gospel of prosperity and which goaded the Europeans into creating the institutions that would usher in the new age. It is the United States which serves as the model for the "new Europeans"—the businessmen back from productivity tours, or the shrewd fabricators of mass culture, or the party propagandists who look for inspiration on Madison Avenue, or the scientists and social scientists who envy, learn and use American theories and techniques. It is in the context of liberal policies, rather than in a framework of totalitarianism and public property, that the economic and social revolution has taken place. The external dimension shows dependence in a less intellectual and far more classical sense. For the first time in modern history, Western Europe has become a stake in the international competition, and its role in the world has been reduced to that of a protectorate of an extra-European power. To be sure the protector has been benevolent, often self-denying and inordinately generous; but this changes only the edge, not the essence, of the relationship. Thus, were it not for America's presence, one could hardly speak of Western Europe as an entity: to the extent to which Europe has a face, it is a borrowed one.

It is therefore not surprising that a mirage should have bloomed in the vision many Americans and Europeans have of Europe's future. It is the picture of a European society increasingly similar in its institutions, behavior and values to the "American model" of industrial society; of a European entity gradually growing into a federation, speaking in world affairs with a single voice, which, because of the very identity of Europe's outlook and interests with America's would use orthodox "Atlantic" language. This essay, in discussing Europe's freedom of choice, tries to show that such a picture may well be a mirage. Internally, an "American" Europe need not be Europe's future. There are enough differences between Europe's and America's industrial societies to feed and to preserve a separate identity—if the Europeans so desire. Externally, an Atlantic Europe is not likely to be Europe's future; but there is a choice between a "European" Europe if the quest for a new European role in the world succeeds and no united Europe at all if it fails. Thus, as much as a call to the Europeans, this essay pretends to be a warning to Americans. Being free, the former ought to think and act for themselves. Being different, the latter should not expect Europe to become America's twin.

I. "Americanization" with a Difference

The "Americanization" of Western Europe is not a mere cliché. It is a fact recently documented by *Dædalus*.[1] Economic expansion, higher wages, a peasantry whose numbers dwindle and whose production grows, classes that are less different from and feel less hostile to each other, a "service class" on the rise, a drive for mass education, the "end of ideology" in political life, intellectuals reconverted from tragedy to expertise, collective bargaining with the participation of "technocrats" instead of deliberations by a political class of leisurely generalists: all of this does indeed make Europe much more like the United States. Had *Dædalus* included in its issue studies of the new public role of the Catholic Church, the transformation of the family, the phenomenal progress of "mass culture," it would have become even more obvious that Tocqueville's prophecy of the democratic age has come true at last. What Tocqueville did not realize was that egalitarian society would triumph in Europe only after the spread of material prosperity. Nor did he see that those voluntary associations without which he thought liberalism would perish from the twin dangers of social conformity and political centralization would in fact grow out of an industrialization that proceeds in the framework of liberal democracy.

And yet industrial society in Europe may remain quite different from America's, for a reason Tocqueville would have well understood. He knew that a single type of society can be ruled by opposite types of regimes. He knew that the face of the polity in the democratic age is shaped by the relations between classes and the state in the predemocratic age. He would have realized that Europe's current emancipation from its past cannot help being shaped by that past—a past entirely different from America's. There are three areas of significant differences. First, there is the problem of the *polity:* America's industrial democracy was a creation; Europe's industrial society involves a conversion of the previous order. Second, there is the problem of *historical conscience:* the United States, on the whole, is at peace with itself; Europe's transformation entails a catharsis. In each of these areas, America's originality is double; not only does the American experience diverge from Europe's as a whole, but America's is single, whereas Europe's is fragmented into separate national experiences. Finally, and as a result, there is the problem of *beliefs.* America's growth is rooted in a creed; Europe's revolution unfolds amidst the repudiation of past creeds.

Creation vs. Conversion

Tocqueville saw the United States long before the age of mass consumption. Yet much in his description remains valid. Obviously, industrial society in America has been affected by the network of pre-existing institutions, laws, customs and values more than it has affected this network. The ideal type of advanced industrial society or that of capitalism tells us little. They are liquids which take the shape of whatever vase they are poured into, although they give their color to the vase. What matters in America's case—it has become a cliché to say so—is that industrialization proceeded in a society already democratic, freed by its revolution not from a previous aristocratic phase but from outside tutelage, and constantly confirmed in its essence by new waves of immigrants. Moreover, industrialization expanded in and benefited from a single national framework, which survived the great test of secession. In both respects Europe's past has been different. It plagues the present and mortgages the future. The industrialization of nations deeply marked, socially and politically, by their "predemocratic" stage and by their rivalries means the laborious breaking down of class barriers and borders. Consequently, on the one hand they are not "like America" *yet*, for the task of conversion still entails both much destruction of the old and the tough resistance of major residues. On the other hand, the new Europe might not be "like America" *ever*, for the task involves innovations which either confirm old differences or create new contrasts with the United States.

What is being destroyed in Europe's social structure would not deserve being mentioned in a study that focuses on what is likely to keep Europe lastingly distinct from the United States, were it not for three reasons. One has to do with the difference in social structure and values; the elimination of various groups whose economic or political function has disappeared has left a residue of bitterness not only among the victims but also among other groups who shared the values if not the social position of those victims. The second reason has to do both with the difference in social structure and with Europe's fragmentation into separate states; the process of elimination has put new strains on already fragile political systems, for it is much more troublesome to deal with angry farmers, displaced miners or depressed areas when they represent a large fraction of the population or of the space of a country than when they occur in the "wide open spaces" of a sparsely settled continent. The last reason has to do with national differences in Western Europe; the destructions and dislocations brought about by economic change have affected these nations unevenly, depending on the degree of development they had reached at the start of the process. Thus Germany, despite the influx of refugees, has suffered least; France has had serious troubles with shopkeepers, peasants and workers made jobless by progress; Italy is the country in which change has entailed not only "the disintegration of agriculture and of traditional rural communities" through a huge rural exodus,[2] but also a problem of regional imbalance of enormous proportions. Despite the common movement toward industrialization and the efforts made by European communities to ease the journey, the fact that each nation has had to deal with its own incidents and its own casualties of progress has strengthened separateness just as it was being undermined.*

It is not only Europe's social structure that is affected by destructions. Partly as a result of those just mentioned the load which Europe's political institutions have had to carry has crushed one vital organ: parliament. The decline of a body that symbolized one important difference between Europe's and America's political systems has, however, not made for any rapprochement. In Europe's cabinet system, parliament was supposedly the fount of all effective and responsible power in contrast with the United States Congress, handicapped by the separation of powers. Today, parliament's share in decision-making and its role in su-

---

*The difficulties encountered in trying to define a common policy on energy for the Six are partly explainable thereby.

pervising the execution of decisions are far smaller than the share and role of Congress. The dispossession of parliament not only by the civil service and interest groups but also by the executive has been much greater. Congress is now protected by the strict separation of powers, by the fragmentation of the bureaucracy, and by the very looseness of American parties. Whenever the party system worked, parliament's decline has occurred because of the control exerted over the majority by the cabinet or by the majority party's ruling organs; where the party system has failed (i.e., in France), parliament has been demoted to a position legally much narrower than that of the United States Congress. Here again, differences among the Europeans compound the difference with the United States. Outside France, parliament, having lost its role, at least preserves its "myth"— that of the body that speaks for the people and that can overthrow the cabinet. In France's hybrid political system, the president plays the part of the people's voice and combines the advantages of a chief executive in a presidential system with those of a cabinet leader in a parliamentary regime—at the expense not only of parliament's position but also of its reputation. Outside France, it is the strength of the parties that has weakened parliament in parliamentary regimes. In France it is the very weakness of the parties which has brought the demise of the parliamentary regime altogether and which is being perpetuated by the practice of so-called "direct democracy."

Destructions and resistance both mark the attempt at transforming the educational system. Nowhere is the difference between the creation of one national industrial society and the conversion of a variety of "old" national societies into a more democratic one so obvious. The need to abandon a system of secondary schools and universities which were the shapers and guardians of societies in which elites were few, access to the elite was restricted and authority was hardly democratic is widely recognized. Most European writers on the subject agree that the new society requires leaders and executives, technicians and bureaucrats in far greater number, that the old curriculums and structures are obsolete, that the new schools ought to be training centers for teamwork and imaginative cooperation. And yet the result of their efforts is not likely to resemble the United States system of education. The United States was able to let its system grow; the Europeans are obliged to let their old one either continue or collapse because they cannot oblige it to adapt. The resistance of the old structures and of the teaching personnel to change is fierce—in the one sector of society where no reform (however much determined from the top, by fiat, or supported from below, by the rising masses) can be adequately carried out without the help of the very men and women whose whole philosophy is being challenged and who are still in charge of training their own successors. Thus the educators try to block reform either by opposing change altogether or through the familiar device of rejecting anything short of perfection. As a result, the reformers are forced either to back down, delay or compromise, or else to try to win by indirection: by undermining that which cannot be persuaded to reform, by initiating new types of school programs or institutes which besiege or submerge the old establishments. The outcome, in either case, is a fearful mess. The *status quo ante* is obviously impossible, but chaos is not necessarily creative. The new structures and the new personnel suffer from a lack of prestige and a frequently makeshift quality. Here again, national differences complicate the matter. There is a great deal of educational planning in France, none in Germany. Resistance to change is greater in Catholic countries, where the religious schools are particularly devoted to the values of the old society. The Belgian problem has been compounded by the Walloon-Flemish split. Thus the prospects of a unified response to the crisis are slim.

Of course, it can be argued that in the United States also there is a crisis, and that the responses and forms of experimentation are multiple. But whereas it is not impossible to improve and diversify the training of elites within a system of mass education, the forceable transformation of a narrow, rigid, coherent and largely successful system of elite education into a democratic one is a heroic and infinitely more controversial enterprise. In mere financial terms it requires extraordinary budgetary transfers and an entirely new attitude on the part of businessmen or foundations, whose role in education has until now been almost nil. Furthermore, there is a major difference between the experiments of a fantastic number of school districts and state and private colleges and universities, and the laborious decisions taken by a small number of ministers of education in the light of their national situations.

The resilience of old patterns of behavior is also visible in the whole area of class relations. The way in which social groups face each other in the new society remains deeply marked by the past history of social and political contests. To be sure, recent European writings show a longing for the "American model" of group politics, democratic authority, face-to-face discussions and compromises. But the model is not really relevant. Whereas America is a fluid society, Europe remains a set of sticky societies. Mobility within each and between them is less practiced and less highly valued. Such viscosity preserves past obstacles to social harmony and even to further economic development (for instance, in keeping the size of enterprise much below the "American model"). Moreover, despite growing prosperity, inequality remains a major social and political issue: first, because everywhere in Europe the differences in living conditions between the rich and the poor are still huge (the access of the latter to higher education and power is far from assured); second, because the underprivileged groups' attitudes toward inequality remain shaped by the European tradition of global protest against and challenge of the "established disorder"; third, because the discontent and the expectations of the underprivileged are far more focused on the state than in the United States; finally, because of considerable variations from nation to nation. Thus, although one can rightly speak of a moderation of the class struggle and of a decline in revolutionary messianism, the long record of contests between the workers and the upper classes and the constant role of the state as a stake and a force in the struggle introduce a lasting distinction between the

American and the European cases. In every European country the workers' organizations—unions or parties—are more concerned with the global economic development of society and with the role of the workers in the management of enterprises than are those in the United States. It may well be that this concern now expresses itself in requests for "participation" instead of the old demands for revolution, but even this points to a difference in scope and temper between America's well-established reformism—more fragmentary and more placid—and Europe's new one.

If one examines not merely the political expression of social grievances in the "new Europe" but political behavior in general, one reaches the same conclusion: despite real changes, old reflexes resist. Ideology in politics (and in the writings of intellectuals on politics) may be declining, in part because of the moderation of the class struggle, in part because of a reaction against the ideological excesses of "secular religions," in part because of the increasing irrelevance of "isms" that grew out of the conditions of preindustrial society. But proneness to ideology (in the sense in which a weak body is prone to diseases) and attachment to old ideological symbols persist, even if the symbols have lost much of their "objective" content. Thus in France and in Italy neither the rise in the standard of living within societies still marked by grave injustice nor the relative decline of groups that provided the bulk of the support of the Communist party (proletarian workers, landless farmers) have seriously reduced the electoral strength of the Communist parties. For where ideology was strong it was never exclusively related to the stage of economic development. There simple discontent still expresses itself in ideological terms, and events unconnected with either the old class struggles or the old stable constellations of political doctrines still provoke ideological reactions. Thus in France the divisions created by the new postwar issues—the Cold War, decolonization, European integration—have been anything but moderate, and the attitudes of the opposed factions anything but pragmatic.[3]

The resilience of old forms of political behavior and traditional styles of political argument explains in large part why the European political problem continues to differ from that of the United States. The American issue is the efficiency of institutions that are stable and legitimate. The issue in the three largest countries of Western Europe is the stability and legitimacy of their institutions. Neither in France nor in Italy nor in Germany are they so secure that they could survive a prolonged period of inefficacy. In none of those three countries could allegiance to the Constitution be the symbol of national integration. Before their alleged death, the ideologies of yesterday left deep scars on the institutions.

Finally, the weakness of representative government, the residues of ideology and the persistence of old habits in class relations all contribute to the preservation of two important differences between Europe's and America's political life. Divided polities in which the state has played a major part in class conflicts and in which a core of efficiency and continuity has been indispensable have produced professional civil services with traditions of their own and also with a natural tendency to persist even if the conditions of their earlier rise and role have changed. The bureaucracy of the European state has preceded the age of democracy; its power and centralization create a problem of control far more acute than in the United States, with its mixture of often rather low-grade professionals and temporary recruits from business or the universities, and its fragmentation of bureaucracy into countless agencies and services. Moreover, the strength and staying power of the civil service continues to limit the scope of representative government, that is, to curtail the chances of what one now calls "participation." Tocqueville is again the more relevant reference: Europe's politics still suffer from that radical distinction between "us" and "them," the subjects and the rulers, the citizens and the state, which has been perpetuated by centuries of absolutism, authoritarianism, and even liberal politics that entrusted the polity to men of knowledge and order only, and thus served the interests of some classes alone.*

Indeed, this is a difference which has been confirmed by one of the major innovations of the new Europe. There has been an increase in the scope of the state. The Europeans' conception of public functions has radically expanded in this century, whereas the Americans' has changed but little—there is a gap between the practices in the two areas, and an even greater one in their "public philosophies." In part because of the differences in the background—greater poverty, the ruins of the war, the need both for reconstruction and for regulation of the sudden boom—Europe has allowed more overt intervention of the state in economic and social affairs, has shown greater concern for welfare and balanced growth, has repudiated uncontrolled laissez faire and has tried to avoid the scandal of public squalor in the midst of private opulence. Although the private virtues have been practiced in Europe so much more fervently than the civic ones, by contrast with the United States, the hold of the state on the individual and the subordination of private gratification to collective requirements have been strengthened. Both the bureaucracy and the interest groups (what the French call *les forces vives*) have received a role in the preparation and execution of state decisions that is both greater and more readily recognized than in the United States. This innovation has not only created a new difference between the United States and Europe; it has also consolidated two old ones. On the one hand, the role and prestige of European parliamentarians has declined even further, whereas United States congressmen cling (and sometimes behave according) to a theory of representation that crowds all public concern within the charmed but occasionally vicious circle of Capitol and White House, and makes of the member of Congress the only legitimate spokesman for his constituents. On the other hand, the expansion of state functions has benefited the public "technocrats" and provoked a

---

*Alain Clément ("Vers l'Amérique," *La Caravelle*, No. 17 [Spring, 1964], p. 6) shrewdly attributes the Europeans' distrust of the official American version of President Kennedy's assassination, and the Americans' almost universal acceptance of this version, to this radical difference in the attitudes of the citizens toward public officials.

renewed demand, often utopian in its scope, for "participation," symbol of a growing gap between "us" and "them."[4] Thus the basic relationship of the American citizen to his officials may well be one of apathy, based both on trust or a sense of identity, and on rather modest expectations; the European's relationship is often a mixture of apathy based on distance or distrust, and hostility due to heavy dependence as well as fear of arbitrariness.

Another area where innovations have both confirmed and added to the contrasts between Europe and America is that of class relations. Both in France and in Germany the structure and the behavior of labor unions have been molded by the past attitudes of the upper classes and the earlier role of the state, as indicated above. Today the circumstances which shaped these French and German unions have disappeared. And yet, on the one hand, the traditional behavior and organization of the workers have been confirmed by the new events. The French workers' pattern of protest and blackmail of the state developed at a time when the bourgeois, who had adopted many features of the French aristocracy in their fight against it, resisted proletarian demands and slowed down economic growth. Today, despite the change in business attitudes, the new and leading part played by the French state in development has perpetuated what Michel Crozier calls the unions' fascination with Power, and has made blackmail even more useful as a way of affecting the distribution of the national income.[5] Moreover, Communist preponderance among the workers provides a new force of protest against inequities in this distribution and a new focus for business and labor hostility to face-to-face discussions. In pre-Weimar Germany, labor unions were more cohesive and less rebellious than in France because of faster economic development promoted by the aristocratic class and by a "Gnaden-bourgeoisie."[6] Today, the influx of refugee labor has contributed both to the numerical strength and to the cautious behavior of the unions. On the other hand, the innovations have sharpened the difference between Europe and America insofar as they have broadened previous differences among the Europeans, thus offsetting the unifying impact of industrialization. The divisions of French unions and the fact that the biggest one is under Communist control oblige the labor movement to concentrate its efforts on the central level—that of Power. German unions are wholly without Communist influence, and their strength allows them to concentrate on the control of the workers in the factory and on relations with business. Moreover, each European nation has created its own network of procedures—ranging from ineffective to quite effective in the Dutch case—for the settlement of social conflicts.

In one area, old differences have been confirmed and a new one has been created not merely by European innovations but by a combination of destructions, resistance and novelties: I refer to the attitude of social groups and nations toward the new industrial society. What is being destroyed is the former bourgeois "sobriety" which once kept the European way of life far below America's splashes of conspicuous consumption, as well as the former reluctance of bourgeois and aristocrats alike to mass production, which meant dependence on the market.

What is, however, resilient is the concern of even hard-working Europeans (businessmen or industrial workers) for "whatever . . . is beyond work": "distraction, pleasure, evasion." There is a desire to put limits on work; there is a determination to preserve "elite cultures" that coexist with but are not submerged by the progress of mass culture and that continue to set standards in the arts. Both show the imprint of the "aristocratic age" in which work was a disgrace for a few, a curse for most, for others a means to rise but not an end in itself, for some a tunnel through which one had to pass before one could cultivate one's inner freedom and fulfill one's deepest aspirations. What is new in the possibility for many more Europeans than in the past to enjoy what is "beyond work"—holidays or paperbacks. As a result an old difference from the United States has been deepened: despite, and even to some extent thanks to, the progress of mass consumption and mass production, Europeans keep "asking more from life" both in terms of an "insatiable demand" for material goods and "in terms of fulfillment" than the Americans, whose society "remains oriented toward and by work."[7]

Moreover, the contrast between America's rather uniform orientation and Europe's has been increased by new differences among the Europeans. The more European societies become alike in their social structures and economic makeup, the more each national society seems to heighten its idiosyncrasies. Recent surveys among young Frenchmen and Germans who have visited each other's country fail to reveal any "homogenization." Clichés about national character live on, and national disparities get stronger: the spectrum extends from Italy, in which the task of economic and social change is least advanced and where the Communists have a powerful intellectual and political hold, to France, whose economic and social transformation has so far made no constructive impact on the party system, and to West Germany, whose values and politics remind observers far more of the United States, for federalism divides its bureaucracy, the disasters brought by past ideologies have singed all who have not been charred, and the ideal of the *Marktwirtschaft* (although it is *Sozial!*) has more than a few illusions in common with American free enterprise. To be sure, there are regional differences in the United States as well, but how pale they look by comparison! The national state, exorcised daily by the prosecutors of its obsolescence, continues to make a difference. Each European country adjusts its "national character" to the new age in its own style, and particularly in its own style of authority.

Pride vs. Purge

It is neither fashionable nor accurate to say that nations have souls. But they do have historical memories—memories of how their citizens behaved toward each other and toward outsiders in moments of stress and crisis. If the concept of industrial society tells us little about the institutions each kind of industrial society will have, it tells us nothing at all about the historical conscience and consciousness of a nation or continent. And yet, since people do not live by economic rationality alone, this is a dimension that cannot be dismissed.

American industrial society has grown in a nation whose rendezvous with history have not been disastrous. It overcame its greatest internal challenge in such a way that its political institutions were strengthened. It survived the depression in such a way that the Presidency emerged as the center of national action and the focus of national expectations. It managed its relations with the outside world, first so as to avoid explicit dependence, and later so that entanglement corresponded with supremacy. Thus it is not surprising that Americans (outside, perhaps, of the South) should feel a special pride in American history, tend to read it—from Wilson to Morgenthau or Niebuhr—in terms of ethical teleology and often indulge, when they speak either of America's development and "purpose" or of the ups and downs of less fortunate nations, in what C. Wright Mills called the national celebration. It is in the literature of the South alone that one finds a deep sense of guilt, resentment, doom and tragedy—and this is of course the literature that appeals to Europeans most.

For however much European societies may have been rejuvenated by postwar changes, their unhappy past clings to them. They may have shed their old skins, but their nerves and blood are still weakened by the diseases of their past. The contrast with the United States is provided not only by a long record of national rivalries and wars that have left traces everywhere, from the history books which are so hard to harmonize this side of expurgation, to the *arière-pensées* of foreign policy. It is also the depressing story of multiple disillusionment and frustration which every major European nation has experienced in this century. Except in the relations between North and South, Americans of different regions can face each other without deep misgivings and look at their past without shame. Their very mobility has loosened the grip of sectional memories. It remains difficult for a Frenchman and a German (even the postwar young ones) to talk to each other as if the past had never happened, or to think of their own nation's recent history with complacency. The only common heritage of the "new Europeans" is one of guilt and shame. Shame, for having produced the biggest record of atrocities in centuries; shame, for having acted in such a way that Europe has become a stake; guilt, for having so often repressed awareness and atonement; guilt, for having again and again turned the national community into an arena for civil war. The plays that describe the European historical condition most adequately are Camus's allegorical *State of Siege,* which uses Spain to express truths of general European relevance, and Sartre's frantic *Condemned of Altona,* which uses Nazism to speak about Algeria. Both are plays of disillusionment and denunciation. The stinkers and the cowards, the politicians of restoration and the practitioners of torture fill the stage. The pure rebels die, and even the self-torturing guilty rebel Frantz, in *Altona,* finds peace in suicide only. This common experience of failure on a massive scale—World War I with its methodical slaughter, the thirties which debased ideologies intellectually but turned them into deadly weapons, World War II with its atrocities, the traumas of dependence and decolonization—all of it opened a gulf between the continent and the United States, and a gap between the continent and England. For although the British and Americans shared some of those experiences, they did it without humiliation and traversed them without much sense of guilt.

True enough the "new Europe," in passionate pursuit of the pleasures of the present, often appears to have digested its past; some of its statesmen talk as if pride, not shame, were its duty; many of its sons behave as if the new generation had been born without parents. The United States is in the midst of a soul-searching act of its own: the civil rights crisis. But the French, two years after the end of the Algerian war, seem to have forgotten what used to be for so long an all-filling tumult. Nor is Nazism a major issue in German politics. And yet suppression is not oblivion; amnesia is no absolution. At least the United States is willing to face its damned spot. Europe wants to remove the smell of blood; but pretending that there is no stench will not make it go away. In every new debate the old lines of division among Frenchmen reappear: Vichy still produces a presidential candidate, and discussions on foreign aid or military policy bring back the sound and fury of Algerian controversies. Trials and scandals show that however much so many Germans may want to think of Nazism as an accident, something like the aberration of another planet, the temporary filling of the German void by a gang of advanced savages fallen from the blue, it was not a fluke but a cancer whose extirpation leaves scars and whose incomplete postoperative treatment leaves doubts as to whether it will recur. What killed Sartre's Frantz was not just the memory of murder but also the discovery of his nation's refusal to remember, and of its abdication to prosperity.

And so the contrast with the United States continues. What sharpens it is the fact that the United States faces its own blotch as one nation (especially since the North realizes that it has its own share of the responsibility), whereas Europe tries to escape from its past as a set of separate nations. Since Europe's recent history has been both one of national hatreds and one of internal strife, each European nation continues to stew in its own sour juice. Each one has tried a different way of coming to terms with itself. The French have been submitted to de Gaulle's psychological massage. They have been told that they all resisted, that their share in victory was great, that their colonial policies were beautiful, grand and generous, that decolonization was their wish and their pride, that the world's eyes were glistening whenever they met France. This heroic effort at restoring self-respect and denying humiliation has had mixed results. The emperor's beautiful clothes do not hide, even from the French, the dirt and the wounds beneath—and there were twelve years during which the emperor was not even around to parade his mantle. Yet mixed with cynicism there is pride, or at least cockiness and self-assertion. Half-believing in pedagogical flattery is more than disbelieving it altogether.

Germany, on the other hand, has been neither flattered by its leaders (how could it be?) nor asked by them to repent (for one hesitates to plunge a whole nation into repentance when one tries both to lead it to its future and to be a democratic politician depending on votes). The result has been what foreigners and many Germans, too, call either the absence of a face or the lack of a national backbone. The French, even and especially when they disagree about the purpose and mission of France, still feel intensely French. They have accepted, indeed some have blessed, the material aspects of Americanization, but they still talk of a "French way" of using it. Many Germans, having passed through the most searing nationalism ever known to the world, now deny having "ever really understood why nations exist."[8] Hence the birth of new misunderstandings which maintain Europe's historical conscience as it always was: fragmented. The French, on the whole, try to exorcise their past by providing their nation with new reasons for hope or pride (this has been true of all their leaders; the drama resides in their miscalculations—Suez!—and in their conflicting assessments). The Germans, on the whole, have tried to do so by exorcising nationalism altogether. There is no pan-European recipe.*

As for Italy, it has come to terms with its past neither in the French nor in the German way. Neither national self-assertion nor "European" good behavior, those two forms of activism, has prevailed. Amnesia, here, has not even tried to be constructive. Hence there exists an intellectual mood of pessimism and protest that reminds one of Germany's twenties or of France's thirties and forties. The nation has neither half convinced itself of its heroic fight against totalitarianism nor acted in such a way that a recurrence of the causes that once produced Fascism becomes unlikely. It is as if Italy had not had its thirties yet. Thus all Europeans have skeletons in their closets, but they are not the same skeletons.

Values vs. Void

Although in the depth of its memories each European nation remains unique, and although the color of its memories makes of the European family an heir to the Atrides, the surface appears much more rosy, more homogeneous and more like that of the United States. The memories, being evaded, do not loom large by daylight. Then too, Americans and Europeans alike celebrate the progress of European pragmatism. Tolerance replaces the clash of ideologies; a concern for concrete issues and practical solutions inspires the politicians and the voters alike. Intellectuals try to contribute to the national discussion and settlement of those issues instead of indulging either in global justification or in a total *mise en cause*. The Europe of "carnivorous idols" has become *l'Europe du dossier*; it celebrates technology and compromise, expertise and empirical research. Does not all this show that American values are sweeping the Old Continent?

In my opinion, it shows nothing of the kind. Europe is converting itself to the functional necessities of a new type of social order—it has not converted itself to

---

*Thus, Gaullism in France means de Gaulle; in Germany it becomes the "Munich group," whose tone and designs send shivers even though French Gaullist spines.

a new set of values. Europe flees from its past because it cannot look at it honestly—not because of a deliberate and mature repudiation. America's pragmatism, pluralism and "engineering approach" rest on a solid bed of beliefs, those of classical liberalism, which the Declaration of Independence and the Bill of Rights embody and a common loyalty to the Constitution symbolizes. Pluralism can be harmonious or cacophonic. America's is harmonious because of a basic consensus: what is never questioned because it is not merely accepted but cherished is always larger and deeper than what is contested. The engineering approach is that of men concerned with the means because the ends are not in doubt. Empirical research is guided by a formidable body of theory, much of which (despite its value-free pretense) conceals or sublimates a firm conviction in the superiority of America's way of political and social life. The school system produces—consciously and enthusiastically—Americans, that is, men and women capable of cooperating because of a common respect for the values of liberal democracy and a common faith in America's purpose. In no society is conflict more universal, and yet its social theory takes consensus, not conflict, as its conceptual framework. There is logic, not paradox, in this apparent contradiction, for conflict flourishes at all levels precisely because it is contained within well-accepted limits and channelled through procedures and institutions to which loyalty is assured. The role of those devices is not to turn conflict into consensus; it is to find for limited conflicts solutions that are inspired by the procedural and substantive consensus which keeps the system going, and which such solutions strengthen in turn. In support of this proposition, we find both the silence of social theory (and the lack of effective procedures) in the one area where consensus was missing—race relations—and the gradual progress of theory and procedures as consensus begins to grow.

None of this is true of postwar Europe. Here there is no agreement on fundamentals. What works in America works because Americans believe in it; what Europeans believe in today is what works. The European consensus is negative: like culture, which a Frenchman defined as "what is left when everything has been forgotten," today's consensus is around "what is left after everything has been discarded." The French who have discovered the virtues of a presidential system, the Germans or Italians who praise liberal democracy often do so not because of any conviction but because everything else has been tried and has failed. The same is true of the intellectuals who repudiate the past tradition of "totalism"; often they do so not because of a deep belief in the intellectual's responsibility as an expert but because of the obvious failure of Grand Intellectuals to bridge the gap between thought and action. There is all the difference in the world between an affirmation and an auto-da-fé. America's intellectual stand has been on the plateau of a democratic *juste milieu;* Europe's road has gone from a mountain range of disparate ideologies to the present naked plain. Intellectuals who believed too fervently and too long that the polity was a battlefield of rival conceptions of good and evil, the *locus sacrus* for saving one's soul, have now fallen into a state of nihilism. It is not a nihilism of despair;* this phase is over. It is a happy nihilism, to be sipped in prosperity after all the great nectars of the past have turned sour. It has, of course, its reassuring charms. But it also brings with it three dangers that can be summed up in two words: Europe's silence.

The first danger is a lack of imagination. The old questions were too big, too vague, too murderous. Today there are no questions. In the past European intellectuals seemed to assume either that the worst was certain or that everything had to be subordinated to the triumph of the best. Today they act as if the worst was certain not to happen, and the best required no choice at all. Not long ago Raymond Aron denounced the ideological opinions which sacrificed the present to the future. Today he wants to investigate how the desire to calculate where one is going has come to replace the desire to ask where one ought to go; his and Camus's plea for modesty, against fanaticism, seems to have been interpreted as an appeal against intellectual probing, for the sacrifice of the future to the present. The accumulation of facts and figures, the extrapolation of trends, the discussion of forecasting and planning as if they involved no fundamental choices but only technical problems—better instruments of detection as it were, or better statistics—as if only the point at which the ball will stop rolling along the slope remained to be discovered, all of this betrays an intellectual fatigue that is excusable, given the past, but hardly encouraging.[9] The fact that in a world *où l'action n'est pas la soeur du rêve* attempts at realizing utopian dreams turned life into a nightmare is no reason for chasing all dreams away. Past questions may have led to the wrong answers, but the avoidance of questions is not likely to prove any better. The man who drives himself into a ditch may get killed; so may the sleepwalker.

The European intellectual who today either borrows American theories, often without questioning their relevance, or else assumes that the questions have been already formulated and answered gives up a role which has been both his glory and the only clean feather in Europe's dirty cap: that of raising the fundamental problems about society—its direction, the ethical validity of its actions, the relative worth of the choices open to it. A society without some judge who frets over its behavior, admonishes, advises, at times indicts and at other times approves, tends all to easily to fall into complacency. America is often charged with it; and yet both in domestic and in foreign affairs the issues are more sharply discussed, the choices more clearly spelled out and more hotly embraced than in present-day Europe. The reader of *Dædalus's* "A New Europe?" cannot find a single European answer to such questions as: What political institutions would be most capable of protecting the individual altogether from excessive bureaucracy, from special interests and from arbitrary executive power? Should Europe's industrial society keep trying to regulate demand so as to give precedence to collective

---

*Except in a few cases, like Sartre's—of all people; he who taught that there are no absolutes has turned politics into the "short change of the absolute."

equipments (if not cathedrals) and to preserve some realm for quality? Should intellectuals accept as good and final the demise not only of verbal efforts to "change the world" but also of their role of overall social critics?

Here lies the second danger. The refusal to ask such questions means the implicit or explicit acceptance of unquestioned illusions. There are three which are quite common. The first is the technological illusion, according to which the progress of the sciences, material expansion and the spread of specialized knowledge will gradually eliminate that residual category, politics. Authoritative answers will at last be given to social problems that have remained unsolved (that is, political, if one accepts Jouvenel's notion that the political is what is insoluble) only because the material and intellectual elements of a solution were missing.[10] Aron once wrote that the day when intellectuals, having discovered the limits of politics, would become indifferent to it was not yet threatening.[11] He may well have been wrong—or rather, having discovered that politics was not all, many intellectuals seem to assert that it could somehow be reduced to nothing. Alas, there are only too many social problems which cannot be erased either through a welfare calculus or through the tidal rise of the learning process, for instance, all those of political philosophy.

A second illusion is the procedural one. It consists in believing that the method for solving problems is to put around a table all the interested parties, informed of course by the spirit of compromise; participation and goodwill shall provide the answers. This is merely a new version of Europe's traditional attitude toward conflict. The recognition of deep-seated cleavages has always been at the core of Europe's social theory, but the practices of European polities—in part because of the prevalence of nondemocratic styles of authority, in part because of the role of state bureaucracies—have always tended toward the settlement of conflicts not through compromise but by acts of authority. Today the old practices are increasingly discredited (although they still abound), but the same desire to eliminate conflict as one removes a spot on a suit shows in the proliferation of suggestions for orderly procedures of settlement, based on the hope that the procedure would transmute conflicts of values and interests into harmony, painlessly and without friction. A kind of *escamotage* at the bottom has replaced the *escamotage* from the top. Once again the parallel with American beliefs is strong, but once again one has to say there is no *escamotage* where the conflicts are marginal, often technical, and steeped in a culture that values agreement for agreement's sake. Where social groups remain divided by memories, suspicions and insecurity, where citizens do not recognize themselves in their public authorities, where interest clashes are made more rather than less ferocious by a dearth of ideological beliefs that lends interests a vicarious fierceness, the situation is not auspicious for procedural solutions. There would be less discussion of "democratic planning" in France if one would at last realize that what is involved in a so-called "income policy" is nothing less than a philosophy of social goals. A coherent policy has little or no chance of resulting from interest compromises and conciliation procedures, for the simple reason that groups and parties disagree drastically on ends and means—the real choice remains (once again) between a decision by fiat and the pluralism of cacophony.

There is a third illusion: believing that Europe's undeniable progress since the twenties in the difficult art of making a society aware of its problems and of its collective responsibility for solving them means an increased capacity to identify the problems of the future or a greater relevance to the concerns of less developed nations. It is true that in the areas of social security, planning, and regulation of the economy, European postwar reforms have carried collective consciousness beyond what exists in the United States. The long battle over medicare seems incomprehensible to many Europeans. But nothing yet shows that the techniques developed in order to solve the problems and allay the fears born out of the thirties will prove equally capable of dealing with the next phase. When it comes to automation and the problems of leisure, to the fate of the aged and to juvenile delinquency, all "societies of plenty" find themselves in the same wasteland. If Europe has been more inventive in battling the scourge of poverty, it is because the pressure was so much greater there. But applied Keynesianism is of little help in the new situation.

What is striking in those areas and in many others as well is the third danger of the void: the absence of a European *projet*—that is, of a European social and cultural design. It is easy to argue that there has never been a European design or that those we find in the past are *ex post facto* intellectual reconstructions. But this is not the way in which Europe appeared to non-Europeans; moreover, whoever reads Europe's doctrines of the past century discovers two sets of convictions. One was the conviction of an over-all movement of mankind. This faith was symbolized by all those philosophies of history that our superior "scientific" knowledge ridicules (but that are still represented in much of America's more sophisticated grand theory of today—*vide* Walt Rostow); the movement was marked not merely by the unfolding of material progress but by political progress as well: the drive toward parliamentarism or imperialism, those summits of human ascent, or at least so they seemed at the time. The other was the conviction of a national purpose, carried at times to incredible chauvinistic lengths but nevertheless of value in unifying national elites often deeply divided on other issues. There is little of either left in today's Europe; smart debunking has replaced rash belief. We should not be surprised; the development of a *projet* requires a sense of stability, a belief in man's capacity to set the course of the journey and to get to the destination through his own means. What prospers instead is either the belief that technological forces will drive one to the end of the road or that the best one can do is hold high the lamp so as to illuminate the next steps.

In no area are the absence of questioning, illusions, and the lack of a *projet* more evident than in education. If the resistance of the old system is so self-righteously strong, if the reforms of the new prophets are so timid and tentative, if the attempts at defining a new curriculum are so groping, if the alternative to the old authoritarian relation between students and teachers so often seems to be the collapse of discipline and structure, if the sum total of national destructions does not amount to a European construction, it is because of the void of values. The old system did not merely dispense knowledge to some. It taught a number of alleged truths and served to shape a society according to those truths. There was a basic conviction: in the value and necessity of elites for the government of society; in the superiority of elites trained in the classics or in pure science, steeped in "general education," made capable of rising above ordinary human mediocrity through the enjoyment of personal freedom (money helped). This freedom was to be achieved through and nourished by the knowledge of essential facts and laws of nature or human nature discovered over time by the wise—facts and laws that did not have to be discovered again by each generation but that could be transmitted authoritatively by those who knew them to those who had to be told and who would later on transmit them in the same way. Neither the purpose or the substance nor the method was in doubt.

In today's enthusiastic rush toward mass education the questions which are not being asked are those about the purpose of the enterprise. Is it to provide the new industrial society with the requisite number of technicians in each branch, or is it to make it possible for a much larger number of men and women to enjoy the kind of knowledge and culture without which liberal values cannot be safeguarded? The choice between economic rationality and a democratic humanism exists, and to avoid stating it may lead to failure on both counts. Nor has one faced the question of whether the plight of the ill-educated is not as sorry as that of the noneducated: surely it is bad to waste talents because of an educational system narrowly reserved to the happy few; but is it any better to waste talents in the quicksands of an ill-conceived mass education whose curriculum is but juxtaposition of unintegrated techniques and whose egalitarianism treats the bright and the stupid alike? The reason for the absence of questions is simple: if the new system of education is to form a new European man, then it cannot be established, because there is no conception of what such a man ought to be. The values which young Americans carry in their school baggage are not universally accepted by the Europeans, since although there may be a drive for mass education, there is no general admiration for a system that puts as much weight on "adjustment" and happiness as on learning. Richard Hofstadter has shown the anti-intellectual basis of much American thinking about education;[12] but in Europe it is still the intellectuals who try to shape the new order, and they do not endorse the creed from overseas, although they like some of its results. Moreover, the American system is linked to the notion of the melting pot—indeed it *is* the melting pot. A nation that tries to make of so many one and has made of mobility a way of life has to place adjustment at the center of its concerns; but there is no school system of pan-European assimilation yet.

Thus there is no clear vision either of the social or of the civic ends of the enterprise. Contrary to Comte's maxim, what is being destroyed is not always being replaced. *L'honnête homme* recedes in the distance and is (rightly) accused of having been merely a rationalization for the harsh old fact of aristocratic and bourgeois leadership, leisure and luxury. But all that we find in his place is the democratic question mark. The new teachers have lost the convictions of their predecessors as to the values that a society needs in order to preserve itself and that a nation needs to keep its place in the world. They have few convictions of their own, for the new society that emerges is born in confusion. They are not familiar enough with it to know what they want it to be, and both in their social and in their national ideals they literally hover between a world already dead and one that is born too recently, too tumultuously and, above all, to *un*deliberately.

In such a void, only illusions bloom. There is the illusion of achieving all the benefits of mass education without any of its disadvantages—the raft of quality miraculously floating on the ocean of quantity, discipline preserved amidst classroom democracy, as if educational systems were machines with interchangeable parts. There is the illusion of social justice through educational reform. It is true that inequality in educational opportunities is at the root of social injustice; it is true that the school system is the social elevator; yet it is a mistake to believe that by forcing the elevator to stop on every floor one will have achieved the breakthrough toward a classless society. Indeed, as long as other obstacles and taboos have not been removed, many people will not even try to catch the elevator. School and university democratization provides a chance to all those who never had one. But whether the chance will be seized depends first on the expectations and on the income of their parents; both have to be raised; otherwise, social structures and values of inequality close up around the reformed educational system, as postwar England shows. Even if the chance is seized, the reform will reach its goals only if the newly educated talents are provided with adequate outlets—an "if" that goes far beyond the educational system itself. Also, even if the outlets are found, whether democratization will lead to genuine mobility over a period of time and not merely to the "rise of the meritocracy," to a new hierarchy along functional lines or to a new disguised inequality shaped by the hierarchy of prestige among allegedly "equal" types of schools remains to be seen.

Finally, there is the civic illusion—the hope that democratization will make good European citizens out of the young. A greater knowledge of the contemporary world, the teaching of and the training for democracy in school, a program less centered on the nation ought to help, but once again America, the example, cannot be the model, for the school or university produces good citizens only when there is a regime, a state, a sense of legitimacy disputed by few. There is none yet in Europe as an entity—nor in all of its main components. Thus if educational reform suffers from so many growing pains, it is because even men who have no particular fondness for the elitist past are not convinced that those pains will lead to growth. It is not wise to treat an anxiety for values and a nostalgia for quality merely as the residue of feudalism or of the bourgeois age.

At this point the tired reader may well inquire: "Granted that today's Europe is not like America in its institutions, in its past and in its values, so what? The differences so laboriously listed are mainly marks of transition: Europe is like a huge disposal that must incinerate its habits and beliefs of yesterday before it can create new creeds and customs, or else those differences will be eliminated as soon as the United States moves in the direction already taken by Europe in the realm of public welfare, and as soon as European integration unites the European nations. At the end, there will be two largely identical industrial societies."

This may well be the case. But it is not at all certain. There comes a moment when the most "agnostic," critical and cautious social scientist must do what Kelsen does with his pure theory of law: he reaches a *Grundnorm* which is a mere hypothesis. We are faced here with a choice of *Grundnormen*. On one side there is the belief in a kind of economic and social determinism—a belief which runs through writings on both sides of the Atlantic, from Marx or Comte to Lipset or Duverger. On the one side there is the belief in a broad and complicated autonomy of the polity: the whole area of man's relation to the overall community and of the relations between the communities is seen certainly not as one where pure chance rules, but as one which is shaped *both* by the economic and social order and by the memories, the cultures, the political institutions and calculations, the ideas and the passions which are so largely independent of the underlying order. The former *Grundnorm* has the merit of simplicity. The latter strikes me as more fertile. As a disciple of Montesquieu, Tocqueville and Aron, I choose the second. It is the one that leaves most room for collective creation and statesmanship. For it shows that there are many forces at work—often at cross-purposes; that none of them determines all the others; and thus that there is room for using them, blending them, shaping them and building a future out of the very contradictions of the present.

There is a first implication from this choice. If the similarity of economic and social orders does not guarantee the similarity of polities, if a certain type of social order does not breed the desired values or obliterate the past all by itself, then the Europeans, supposing they *wanted* to take the United States as the over-all model, would still have to make a special effort of imagination and action. They would still have to overcome residues and resistances the United States never faced; they would have to face their past instead of fleeing it; they would have to adopt American values consciously; they would have to unify Europe less sluggishly and haltingly. They cannot adequately analyze their affairs in American terms, or accept American explanations of Europe in American terms. What is *sui generis* in Europe has to be accounted for; the optimism of various American theories makes sense in and for the United States, but no sense at all if transplanted in Europe. Elections may be the democratic form of the class struggle on this side of the ocean; on the other side both elections and the class struggle remain rather more complicated undertakings. Leaders of private and public bureaucracies who share the values of their subordinates and who rule according to a democratic style of authority may not be dangerous, but when the style and the values of the elites have traditionally not been democratic there is less room for complacency. Even if optimism were justified, Europeans would still have to discriminate. Otherwise the light by which one chooses to be guided could happen to be that of a dead star. The presidential system many Frenchmen admire is that of the Hundred Days, not that of the trench-and-guerilla warfare of recent years; the mass education system which impatient European reformers envy is busy trying to introduce some of the very methods and institutions which those reformers decry. Thus there is a risk of the two cultures crossing each other without ever really meeting or merging.

But there is another and more important implication. If, on the one hand, nothing determines that Europe will be a replica of the United States; if, on the other hand, the past institutions and history of Europe's polities are just as likely to affect Europe's future as the new social order, then the Europeans have no excuse for silence, passivity or complacency. For they are still free to analyze critically America's own experience and to sort the good from the bad so that Europe may be spared the latter. They are still free to make of tomorrow's Europe an industrial society that will have its own profile, not simply because many of the old features will not have been erased by the plastic surgery of industrialization but also because of a deliberate effort to preserve Europe's originality. Nor do the Europeans have any excuse for anti-Americanism. For if they understand that "Americanization" is really just the passage to industrial society, that it has come out of European developments (although the United States encouraged it), that many of the "American" features the process has developed are due either to an almost gleeful European imitation of what is worst in America's industrial society or to the impact of the world's dominant power on a weakened and fragmented continent, but in neither case to any permanent fatality, then they will realize that anti-Americanism is merely an evasion of Europe's own responsibilities. America should be neither imitated nor blamed blindly. Some Europeans are anti-American because they do not want to accept the fact that industrial society has come of age. Denouncing the United States saves them from the difficult task of trying to make a virtue of necessity. Others are anti-American because it is easier to blame the United States for the blemishes of Europe's new society than to trace them back to Europe and to admit how difficult to remove they are. These men are like atheists who, while denying God's existence, never stop making God responsible for man's own plight.

In other words, what is required is Europe's return to a normative attitude. The situation permits it, and moreover *noblesse oblige*. This means, first, that Europeans ought not to act as if all of their social and national past deserved oblivion. Long after Tocqueville, Domenach and Crozier[13] have observed how much the Europeans' concern for the defense of the individual against social pressures and care for the preservation of the intellectual's prestige were linked to the aristocratic age. This is no reason for giving up either. On the contrary, it is a reason for trying to adapt both to the age of democracy. All individuals, not just an elite, ought to be shown how to escape from the alienation of labor, from enslavement to technology, and from the shrill demands of the mass media, of the neighbors or of all sorts of groups. The distance which the intellectual liked to keep between himself and the mass, the irresponsibility to which he often laid claim ought to be abolished, but not his right and inclination to question. *Noblesse oblige* means also that Europeans have no justification for dropping what made Europe great—it was the continent of the examined life. Its spiritual silence of today is as deafening and disheartening as its earlier clamor of despair.

One of the choices Europe still has to make concerns its future role in the world. For in this respect also, there is freedom of choice, but it has not yet been fully used.

II. "Europeanization" with Diffidence

Let us turn from Europe's new social order to Europe's role in the world—from the realm of intellectual dependence to that of dependence in terms of power. Nowhere is the void I have denounced more conspicuous. To be sure, we find an effort toward unity, directly inspired by the example and encouraged by the policy of the United States. Is it not precisely here that the "American model" has been both relevant and useful? Is it not here that the Europeans have succeeded in turning prosperity into statecraft, in breaking with their past without evasion, in shaping a *projet* for Europe? And yet, the answer must be: no. The enterprise has not fully succeeded, because the model was not relevant and the *projet* was not drafted. Aron is right. "It is not sufficient to create a European state. Rather, one must ask: What would be the object of a European state? To have a sense of vocation, Europe would have to discover a goal"[14] It is the search for a common goal which has not yet succeeded. We must therefore examine first to what extent the progress of the European movement has filled the void, then what factors have prevented this void from being filled as yet, and finally what is the margin of choice open to the Europeans.

Delays and Delusions

Let us imagine some European publicist, in a coma since 1914, who suddenly wakes up and looks at the new world picture. He finds the air buzzing with clamors about Europe's new strength and new claims. His curiosity is aroused. What is it that the Europeans have to say? His astonishment begins.

He finds them talking to Americans. They say: "We want to be sure that we will be so effectively protected that we will have to suffer neither invasion nor liberation." They acknowledge dependence in what constitutes the alpha and omega of foreign policy—the area of survival—and merely ask for a greater part in the definition of the mode of protection. The Europeans also say: "Twenty years have passed since the end of the holocaust, and we want to be heard on all the issues that matter." So our publicist listens. But all he hears is a strange cacophony tantamount to silence. On Europe's future relations with what used to be called the Communist Empire in Eastern Europe—on Europe's relations with the new nations—on whether Europe's future is indissolubly linked with that of the United States within some Atlantic community or partnership—on how Europe should be organized so as to find a voice with which to answer such questions—all that he can discover is a few suggestions here and there, which generate neither light nor enthusiasm, but heated rebuttal in other quarters which argue that any talk of a joint European policy is nonsense since salvation lies in huddling under America's umbrella.

To this, the first reaction of our publicist is a sharp flash of familiarity: Isn't it what it has always been? Hasn't Europe always failed to speak with one voice only? But then he sees that there is something abnormal in the situation. Shouldn't the very new fact of dependence for survival incite the dependents to get together and snatch their destinies back? At this point, and with the help of some background briefing, a third reaction sets in: he realizes why there is no European project. It is not just the absence of a precedent, it is also the avalanche of rocks that have battered and buried Europe's pride and ambition. They have not just bruised Europe as a whole; they have bloodied each European state in a different way. A common fate has created a unity of concern in this little "cape of Asia," but there is no unity of reaction. For each nation's fate has been slightly different, and the common fate is not perceived alike.

So the delays in unity are at least explained. Obviously the French have not quite the same interest as the Germans in reunifying Germany. Obviously the Germans pay not quite so much attention to Vietnam—or Algeria—as do the French. Delays and divergences breed confusion. There is a Franco-German treaty of cooperation, but all of France's eggs are in the nuclear basket, labeled independence from the United States, while all of Germany's are in the conventional basket, labeled reliance on the United States. Alice would have felt at home in the European wonderland. Starting from an identical profession of loyalty to self-determination, the Germans move cautiously toward a détente that does in fact consolidate East Germany; they blind themselves by pretending that the détente perforates the wall between the two halves and prepares reunification, whereas the French reject any such move, which they (rightly) see as playing into East Germany's hands—as if their own intransigence were any more capable of undermining the wall.

Our publicist cannot remain discouraged very long. For undoubtedly his eyes will come across the evidence of European integration. Here there is a common enterprise. It has its institutions, it has given Europe a single voice in matters of tariffs and trade, of industry and (soon) agriculture. There *is* one Europe of welfare and wealth—no mean achievement, to be sure. And yet, how much of an achievement is it? It does not amount to a common world design for Europe. There is a striking contrast between the concrete, down-to-earth, toughly bargained results obtained by the economic communities and the often nebulous and usually divergent expectations of the governments and nations engaged in the enterprise. Europe is a divinity which means different things to the different faithful, as well as a business that brings tangible gains to many. For the Germans Europe is both the mast to which they find it wise to tie themselves in order to resist any new siren's temptations, and the new backbone that replaces the cancerous nationalistic one. To the French it is an opportunity for leadership—the only one left. It is the elevator that will lift them to the floor of rank, prestige and power. To the Italians it is a pump of economic development and an alibi for absence on the world scene. Such ambiguity, to be sure, has its merits; indeed, it has its champions. As long, they tell us, as all those divergent aims fasten on the same techniques and institutions, this very diversity of expectations will feed and foster the new entity. As the entity has been endowed with bodies that exploit ably and diligently that convergence of the many on one, it is true that the entity has grown. And yet it is just at this point that our publicist stumbles upon those illusions that abound in the European void. Indeed, it is in the area of integration that illusions have most seductively lulled and dulled European and American minds.

The most potent illusion is of the procedural kind: the "Monnet method." It is a mind-expanding drug which makes those who take it believe that Europe's unity will proceed, thanks to step-by-step, concrete bargains and independent, expert "supranational" therapy. Moreover, the method is not felt to be valid for Europe alone. All interstate problems, all conflicts of purposes and policies could thus be reduced to compromises satisfactory to everyone. The Monnet method, for all its charm, is a fine example of the void I have discussed. For it does not provide an answer to the question: Where do we want to go? In fact, it dismisses the question. It says: It does not matter where we go as long as we go somewhere together. It puts form over content, substitutes procedure for substance, sacrifices direction to motion; hence both its attractiveness and its limits. It attracts all those who want to be in motion, yet have not defined their purpose. But it can succeed only when certain conditions are met, of which the champions of the method are not aware, for those conditions contradict their premises.

The method works only when the question of purpose has already been answered—when the governments have agreed on a goal *and* on a direction, that is, on a policy. Moreover, it works only when the governments are convinced that the procedure will indeed help them stay on the right road and reach the destination. In other words, the method cannot work when each government, however much lip service it pays to the idea of a common goal, actually wants to follow a road of its own, and when the roads the governments propose to travel are so far apart that the statesmen are not willing to entrust their travel plans to an agency that may push them into detours they do not want to take or toward destinations they do not want to reach. This is what the record of European integration shows. The method has worked within the area of welfare alone. Here the governments have been animated by a common will, to maximize wealth; and this common goal has been so to speak, operational, whereas a common desire to maximize security or power would not be sufficient. What has made the enterprise both successful and limited is the essential difference between economic behavior and theory, and political behavior and theory.[15] On one side of the fence we deal with quantifiable interests—capable of being calculated, compensated, bargained in fractions or in toto; it is possible to maximize wealth either without requiring crippling sacrifices from anyone, or by offsetting sacrifices made by someone in one area so that the overall result is still a gain for each. On the other side of the fence we find those intangible interests of state which are of quite another order. For they involve the passions that are the stuff of tragedy: prestige and *hubris*, domination and independence. They concern issues that can hardly be compromised, for they are not divisible and negotiable in such a way that my gain means also your gain, rather than your loss: issues like security, survival, autonomy. On one side of the fence we find a mass of goods which it is easy for all to want to maximize, since they are *instruments* that each can then use either for his own objectives, when there are no joint ones, or for a common enterprise should one emerge. On the other side of the fence there is a small group of men who try to influence each other and who use in the attempt all the instruments at their nation's disposal (including those material goods) in order to reach *ends*. What is at stake here is the possibility for one to impose (through whatever means, including persuasion) his views of the ends on the others, so as to give to the "common end" the face and color of his own desires. Goods can be "integrated" and maximized, so to speak, anonymously; the integration of foreign and military policies, in a world in which security and leadership are the scarcest of values, means what it has always meant: the acceptance by some of the predominance of others. This is why, on the "high politics" side of the fence, a vague "agreement to work together" is not enough. It does not amount to a policy. We must distinguish an intention from a consensus, however fragile; the Monnet method may seize a weak consensus and make it strong, but cannot create it.* In its absence, the recourse to supranational integration by governments means only that they choose to conceal the embarrassment of dissension behind the businesslike façade of supranationality, in which case real consensus remains to be thrashed out.

---

*The case of agriculture is the most interesting. The Treaty of Rome contained only the outlines of a policy, but it went beyond a mere intention, and the institutions of the EEC have turned a weak consensus into a growing one. The treaty stated not merely a common intention—the establishment of a joint agricultural policy—but a common *goal* and a common *direction*: the inclusion of agriculture in the Common Market before the end of the transitional period, with a system of minimum prices and preferential purchasing. Recent difficulties have shown that the transformation of a vague consensus into a strong one is an arduous task, but however vague, the consensus went far beyond a meaningless statement of intentions; and its procedural character (which left the elaboration of the policy to the organ of the EEC) reflects not only the weakness of the consensus but also the previous existence of a substantive consensus on goal and direction.

It is not surprising that this method should appeal so much to Americans. The style of the European entities, with its emphasis on the participation not only of governments but also of interest groups, with its stress on pragmatic steps and functional expertise, its method of bargaining and compromise, corresponds beautifully to the American style of authority. But here we find again the difference I have already mentioned: in the United States this style is the outgrowth of an agreement on fundamentals; in Europe, except in the area of welfare, it would have to be a substitute for such an agreement. The Monnet method is the sleepwalker's way. It works as long as the ground is flat. When the obstacles multiply, the choice for the sleepwalkers is between waking up and hurting themselves. Governments, responsible for their nations, have a way of preferring the former.

A second illusion—a more sophisticated technological cousin of the first—is that which Ernst B. Haas has proposed.[16] He does not pretend that methods which work in the area of welfare, calculus and collective bargaining, are equally applicable elsewhere. He states that the logic of industrial society is to make of this calculus the universal criterion of political choice and of such bargaining the dominant style of political behavior. "There is no longer a distinctly political function." This is not a theory: it is an act of faith. For it to be true, it would be necessary to envisage that very death of politics, that very replacement of the government of men by the administration of things which Saint-Simon predicted a bit prematurely. We are not at that stage. In today's world, industrial society does not assure domestic stability—that is, the death of the internal political function. In today's world, prosperity is not just a goal; it is a means with which states play the same old game (although the stakes are higher and thus the rules less reckless), that of competition in insecurity. The only states which can behave as if the external political function has withered away are those that leave the whole burden of their protection to others—but surely Europe is neither willing nor allowed by its protector to take the veil. For Haas's (or Saint-Simon's) vision to be true, we would have to imagine a united world of plenty, and nothing less. Split it into states again, and international politics is reborn. Introduce scarcity into the distribution of any goods, and domestic politics—the manipulation of men by men for the allocation of what is scarce—re-emerges. Indeed, even in a united world of plenty, authority would remain a scarce good, and there would be a political function still—the competition for the control of the distribution of plenty. There is no escape from politics. There is only the politics of consensus and the politics of conflict. In today's Western Europe, supranationality works where the former prevails, and where the latter rules neither the welfare calculus nor the style of collective bargaining prevails. Therefore even the relatively uniform society of Western Europe hailed by Haas could remain divided into divergent nations, just as a single economic and social system can be harnessed by different regimes.

There is a third illusion: that of the "federating process." Carl Friedrich's conception of such a process is, again, an attractive one.[17] But there is, in my view, a fundamental difference between what I would call the "incipient" and the "federal" stages of the process. As long as the component parts are the masters of the pace, the "federalizing entity" remains a fragile one. It becomes strong—as European federalists have often stated—only when the basis of the entity is not an agreement among the former "sovereign" parts but the will of the people itself. The trouble here is that such a will cannot be created *ex nihilo:* on the one hand, it takes a prior decision of the governments to let the people speak as one; and they are not likely to do so unless they feel sufficiently reassured about the consequences of their auto-da-fé. Even "grass roots" efforts at unification wilt or grow depending on whether the governments turn the hose off or on. On the other hand, should the governments miraculously decide at a very early stage to let the people take over, the result would be at least as likely to hurt the cause of European unity as to help it. For the specific domestic demons of the separate nations would not have been exorcised by such a "leap forward": France's old problem of legitimacy, for instance, would be as likely to weigh on the new European problem of political order as to be alleviated by it; moreover, on matters of the common *projet*—Europe's role in the world—a convention of delegates from all over Western Europe would only pile the national and political divergences among the Europeans upon the flaws and futility shown by any present-day parliament in matters of defense and foreign policy. Thus the problem remains: how to forge a common will out of a clash of wills. Why does it still prove untractable? What are the forces that now prevent the Europeans from agreeing on a direction and a purpose?

Restraints and Recriminations

Limited in its scope, confused in its ambitions, the choice for integration has been based on three factors. First, the Europeans took into account the situation of Europe in the postwar years: the economic collapse of the nations, the felt threat of Communist invasion and subversion. Then there was American policy, determined to unify what had been a zone of wars and what was now a zone of weakness, so as to produce a peaceful and strong entity capable of helping (the French word *seconder* is indispensable here) America carry its world load, as well as of accelerating the hoped-for "thaw" of Soviet policy. Finally there was the "Europeans'" own desire to overcome the poison of nationalism, and to regain a sense of self-respect for Europe. These are well-known factors. Today, if we look at what inhibits Europe's choice of a unified role in the world, we find again three forces, not too different from the first three: the new situation in the world, the policies of the United States and the reactions of the Europeans to General de Gaulle.

The new situation in the world puts money back into the once empty bank account of separate European nations. This is true quite literally: prosperity, although connected with unification, has removed some of the sense of urgency which animated the drive for integration. But it is also true figuratively. On the one hand, individually the nations of Western Europe continue to have population figures, a GNP, a military establishment that may make "realists" scoff: those assets do not amount to power, defined in terms of mobilizable potential. With such a definition of power, the world remains undoubtedly bipolar. If we were still playing the game with all the old stakes and rules, the realists would be right; for in traditional world politics the connection between such power and what one might call "freedom of action and capacity to influence," without ever being a one-to-one relationship, was great and visible. But this was so only because the world competition was a fiduciary operation at the end of which one had to pay cash—war being the actual, likely or expected final test which exposed one's real wealth. Today's world is still dominated by the *risk* of war—hence the role of the superpowers, which in the nuclear age no one can deny. But the *expectation* and *likelihood* of war appear to have decreased, and the very change in the nature of the mobilizable potential has made its actual use in emergencies by its unhappy owners quite difficult and self-defeating. As a result, nations endowed with infinitely less can behave in a whole range of issues as if the difference in power did not matter. The very lightness of their rucksack facilitates their roaming on the world scene, whereas the superpowers are often immobilized by their unwieldy baggage. It is the extraordinary convergence of two quite independent series, the emergence of two poles of power only, and the discovery of nuclear weapons, that has made of a bipolar world a stable one for the first time in history. This stability magnifies the influence of lesser states—which may ultimately impair stability itself.[18] While those developments could help a united Europe, in the meantime they enable the separate European states to avoid or postpone the choice of a goal and role for Europe.

However, there is a difference between national complacency and inter-state discord. In today's Europe, it is discord that exists. Here the responsibility of the United States is real, although—one must be careful—there is a crucial distinction between responsibility and blame. Good intentions often produce unintended consequences. America's relationship to Europe has been and remains dual. On the one hand it is the relation of the leader in a hegemonial alliance to the lesser states—not satellites, given their considerable freedom of external maneuver and domestic action, but nevertheless dependents. On the other hand there is a relation of adviser to client: the United States has supported the kind of supranational integration that Monnet advocates, without ever really expecting that a federating Europe would clash with the United States where it matters, that is, in substantive areas of foreign or commercial or military policy, or over the procedure of decision-making for these areas.

The combination of these two relations has inhibited in three ways the emergence of a new European sense of identity. First, America's relationship of domination has undermined the policy promoted in its capacity as an adviser. For it is of the essence of any relationship of dependence, be it a hegemonial alliance or a genuine empire, not only that the leader be convinced of the broader gauge of his concerns and of his superior understanding of his dependents' true interests, but also that he succeed in so convincing many of the dependents. Through his wealth, his better expertise, his network of official and semiofficial organizations (which in the American case involves the formidable establishment of foundations and centers and councils) the leader is able to develop a perfectly honest and respectable clientele of "friends" who see their nations' interest in exactly the same light and from the same perspective as he. Now, this would not be *necessarily* an obstacle to European unification. But it is *necessarily* an obstacle to the appearance of a united European entity capable of acting in any way but that of a junior partner in the American firm. And it *happens* to be an obstacle to any unification in this particular instance, for two reasons: in matters of diplomacy and strategy the United States has continued to deal with the separate nations of Europe (both a case of responsibility without fault—since the Europeans have not united in those realms—and a self-perpetuating process); moreover, next to the clientele of convinced carriers of America's message, there is a gang of rebellious European urchins who see no point at all in European unity unless it results not in a European echo of American policy but in a European policy (whether it agrees with America's or not being secondary to its being made by Europeans in Europe). Thus domination here is in itself divisive.

Secondly, America's advice and promotion of supranationality have also had divisive and delaying effects on Europe's search for a new mission. Inevitably, people resentful of dependence were bound to be suspicious of any scheme of unit so ardently embraced by the leader: Europeans especially expect no state ever to act selflessly, and Americans tend to be seen as far more cunning and scheming than a careful examination of their policies warrants. This suspicion could not but be strengthened by the fact that the procedure supported by the United States might be legitimately thought of as damaging to European interests if applied prematurely in the sensitive areas of military and foreign policy. Not only the Gaullists happen to note that enthusiasm for such procedures is greatest among those European statesmen for whom dependence on the United States has become a dogma, among those leaders who see in supranationality a cushion to protect them from the direct influence and impact of their more powerful European partners,* and among civil servants and economists with little understanding of the complexities of strategy and diplomacy.

Finally, America's impact on Europe has been inhibiting because of the ways in which the United States reacted when it discovered—in the areas of tariffs, agriculture and strategy—that European unification could lead to conflict, not harmony, in the Atlantic world. American reactions have been fourfold. First, there have been offers of "partnership," but so vague and so circumscribed (since they exclude the military realm) as to disconcert America's friends and to feed fuel to

---

*This role of a cushion between larger and smaller European states is played within NATO by the United States itself.

America's critics. Second, there has been a reassertion of policies designed to consolidate America's domination, even at the cost of undermining the drive toward unification among the Six. The two best examples here are the wooing of West Germany by the United States in economic and military areas, and promotion by the United States of the MLF. This scheme answers none of the Europeans' questions about strategic doctrine; it leaves the solution of the problem of control entirely for the future (that is, preserves United States control in the present) and tries to appease the Europeans with vague promises while reassuring the Soviets with statements about nondiscrimination that are incompatible with the promises. It strengthens America's hold on the other participants, thus tying them to the United States directly in a network of bilateral agreements much like Soviet-satellite agreements after the war. It makes the emergence of a joint European will and policy in the military realm far more difficult, since it diverts the participants' financial resources form such a goal, and even more because it chooses for defense a geographical framework entirely different from that of economic integration.* The third United States reaction has consisted of veiled threats of return to isolationism and unilateral self-protecting or retaliatory action should the Europeans continue to mistake prosperity for power and to harm United States interests. These threats are divisive and regressive because they are used in Europe both by America's friends and by America's critics. The former mention them as reasons why Europeans should be cautious of not docile, and willing to sacrifice some of their ambitions to the overarching need for United States military protection. The latter see in such American arguments merely a form of blackmail that ought to incite all true Europeans to a concerted effort for emancipation.

The final United States reaction, which somehow embraces all the previous ones, consists of stating that as long as Europeans remain divided it is indeed impossible for the United States to share control and to limit its freedom of action. Why bother edifying a common policy for Latin America or Southeast Asia, since Europe either suffers from too many voices or falls back into silence? All that is required, then, is full European backing of America's own position. What could be a goad to unity and identity actually turns into a roadblock, for often in the same breath it is suggested that even were a single voice to emerge, there would be no promise in it for the Europeans. It is asserted either that even though united, Europe would not have sufficient power to go beyond words toward a world role—an argument hardly calculated to discourage those Europeans who put reliance on the United States above unity—or that the only united Europe with which genuine "sharing" could take place would be both fully inte-

---

*Another example would be America's recent request for allied support in Cuba and Vietnam (although during the phase of decolonization it was the U.S. which insisted that NATO covered only the geographical area defined in the North Atlantic Treaty, and that the U.S. could thus not be forced to support France or Holland or Britain outside this zone).

grated *and* docile—again an argument hardly calculated to push Europeans into self-reliant unity, since full integration is not soon a likely prospect, and docility not a very exalting one.* And so among the European recipients of such warnings and promises, the fight continues between those who are hungry for the carrot and those who are angry at the stick.

The fight goes on for another reason as well. Given the political and psychological realities of dependence, the efforts of some Europeans to develop a sense of autonomy and unity, far from succeeding, have had effects exactly as delaying as those of the United States policies that these efforts challenged. And here is the third inhibiting factor: European reactions to de Gaulle. The two facts which stand out today are that the only project for joint European action all over the world and not merely in Western Europe is de Gaulle's, and that his European partners do not accept either his design or his methods. Indeed, nothing appears less likely to galvanize Europe than Zeus's thunderbolts hurled down from Mt. Olympus, the pronouncements that come down from the clouds around the summit, his disdain for mere mortals, and his challenge of that other, bigger Zeus, whose lightning could be thermonuclear, and to whom the mortals still turn for their protection. Whether de Gaulle's ultimate contribution to the cause of European identity will have been positive or negative, we do not know as yet. At present, the case must be argued approximately as follows.

De Gaulle's problem is the creation of a European common will which would rid the Europeans of the sense of international futility fostered by dependence. This has to be done in a world in which the contest of national wills remains the warp and the woof of the fabric. Consequently, in order to provide Europe with the *right* sort of unity—that of relative independence and renaissance—his first duty is to block what he considers the *wrong* kind—the sort of European integration that would produce an entity militarily not only dependent (for this he too recognizes as still inevitable) but subservient, economically docile and politically tied to the United States. Hence, for instance, his veto of Britain and his rejection of the MLF. His second task consists of trying to reach his goal by taking actions that hasten the emergence of the *right* sort of will. This has two implications. First, given both his objective of a Europe that would not be merely an American appendage and his conviction that various trends in world affairs encourage a divergence of interests between the two sides of the Atlantic, he must accentuate those trends (which he does not create), artificially pinpoint existing tensions, rub salt into wounds and turn differences into crises so as to beat into the reluc-

---

*The best example is that of Undersecretary George Ball's speech of May 7, 1964. Nuclear control requires "a very high degree of political unity" among the Europeans, and sharing presupposes their "willingness to accept world responsibilities"; but the latter tends to be equated with support for the U.S. position. Mr. Ball says that the U.S. has few national interests outside its territory; the implication seems to be that whereas "world responsibility" entails no sacrifice of national interests for the U.S., it would have to for the Europeans.

tant and complacent Europeans a sense of distance from the United States. To be sure, the "objective reality" of divergence is partly shaped by him, but his strength lies in his grasping straws that would exist anyhow, and turning them into clubs. Second, while the others hesitate to follow him and wonder whether his conception of Europe is right, he must not only broaden the gap between the two sides of the Atlantic but also take *on his own* irreversible actions that push the others into a difficult choice between stopping the drive for European unity altogether (thus bearing the blame for it) and accepting his terms for unity, his definition of European identity.* His third task consists of writing the new book with the old grammar: to reach the new goal that he deems necessary—a Europe with a sense of mission—he finds only one way possible, the old way of statecraft and leadership. In the battle of wills whose stake is Europe's future face, it must be *somebody's* design that will shape the outcome; it is the true statesman's duty to use the wiles and witchery of his art in order to put *his* vision across, and even a vision of the common good can hardly be expected to omit or deny the peculiar good of the statesman's own *patrie*. Here there is one crucial implication: he must promote French policies designed to increase the position of France. If he succeeds, his united Europe will be one in which France will feel at home; if he fails, if the others refuse to join him and no sense of European mission emerges, he will at least have provided his country with solid assets in the continuing contest. In other words, heads he wins—both as a European and as a Frenchman—tails he still wins, as a Frenchman trying to exploit new opportunities for freedom of action. In either case France would be out of the plush circle, or gilded cage, of Atlantic orthodoxy; it is up to the Europeans to follow France's lead. Thus his intended nuclear force is either a lever with which to pry other Europeans loose from reliance on the American deterrent alone, toward the establishment of a European deterrent in which France's role will be prominent, or a token of France's independence amid European nations that refuse to be shaken out of slumber.

The Gaullist defense presents Europe as a sleeping princess, guarded by the American tutor, whom the Prince Charming tries to awaken. Since she insists on sleeping, his kiss comes pretty close to rape. And it is with rape that his adversaries charge him. The first count in their indictment is that he uses Europe to impose French domination and promote purely French policies. The Gaullist argument—that France is the only nation of Western Europe that can exert leadership anyhow, and that his only choice is between aggressive leadership and a frustrating, futile restraint that would certainly please the others but at the cost of immobility—falls flat with those who point to his disregard of the views of the others and to his constant emphasis on the virtues of the French nation. He says "We, Europe" when he acts as "I, France" in order that tomorrow's "We" should speak with the voice of France; but since today's Europe is far from accepting this voice

---

*See, for instance, his threat to the Germans about agriculture in July, 1963.

as the gospel, and since he himself—in case Europe refuses to be aroused—must have his nation for consolation and fallback, both the abusive "We" and the frequent "I" are denounced as evidence of pure and contagious nationalism. A second charge is that in so doing and in rejecting supranationality he prevents the emergence of the only Europe organically capable of speaking with one voice—a federal one. The Gaullist argument that a premature federation without a policy is far worse than a policy hammered out in con-federation falls flat with those who show that the immediate result is neither confederation, nor federation, nor policy. A final charge is that in his insistence on a separate European policy before anything else, and on an identity shaped through separation from the United States he weakens the unity of the West, which Europe's own unification ought to consolidate, not destroy. The Gaullist argument that the real objective is not to establish a third force but to build a second force in the West, and that ironclad Atlantic solidarity no longer corresponds to the new international reality: a complicated and multiple confrontation instead of the mobilization of two armed camps, falls flat with those who nevertheless would still prefer that Europe's hand be held by the mighty tutor rather than by the haughty Prince Charming.

Thus in the whole realm of world mission and high politics, where common interests are so much harder to discover and upgrade than in the field of prosperity, Europe falls into a dilemma. The mere curbing of the member nations' egos would produce not a common will and ego but a kind of vacuum which could perpetuate silence and dependence; yet the assertion of national egos provokes a tug of war in which Europe, requested to choose between a French face and an American face, may just as well remain faceless. It is a deadlock that prolongs Europe's silence.

Prospects and Projects

Thus the task of filling the void remains. We must examine what choices are open. Here we have to analyze trends, not in order to replace purpose with projection, but as a way of showing both what appears excluded by the trends and how broad a freedom of choice still remains. In every area we shall see that whereas an "Atlantic" Europe, dependent on the United States, is unlikely, the choice between unity and identity on the one hand and on the other a prosperous resignation to national divergence, a complacent abdication from responsibility remains.

An "Atlantic" Europe is unlikely because of different perceptions of interests[*] and genuine divergences of policies between the two sides of the Atlantic. Com-

---

[*]It is easy for the scholar and the propagandist to show that despite the differences in perception, there exists an "objective" or "real" common interest. Indeed, this is often the case. But in the realm of policy—that is, of action and choice—it is the leaders' and elites' perceptions, however faulty, that matter: perceived differences count more than objective convergences.

mon interests abound, and nobody denies them; there is a western interest in monetary stability and in an organization of world trade helpful to the underdeveloped countries; there is a joint interest in deterring Soviet or Chinese provocation and in avoiding nuclear war; there is an interest in a pluralist system of world order that provides the new nations with procedures of peaceful change and that could accommodate even the Communist nations once they are cured of their itch for expansion. And yet once again we find that these common interests are not always operational, for they do not determine identical or similar intermediate goals and directions, and it is these that matter.

Thus, in the case of European economic integration, the very pressures from the United States have pushed the Six into common policies which entail differentiation from and clashes with America. Indeed, each time the EEC has to define its position toward the outside world—the United States, the underdeveloped countries, the Soviet camp—the choice between the kind of agreement that makes of the community a more distinctive force and the fiasco that would result from some members' refusal to accept any other common outcome becomes more loaded in the former direction.

It is in the military area that the transcontinental divergence of interests has been most visible. To be sure, military alliances are always susceptible to tensions: the major power's fear of being dragged into war against its will by its allies, the lesser power's fear of being sacrificed either if the senior ally is trigger-happy or if the senior ally's finger lingers too leisurely on the safety-catch; these strains have been heightened but not created by nuclear weapons. Strains of a radically new kind have appeared only once the United States and the Soviet Union had reached a stage not of nuclear equality but of what might be called peril parity—the capacity of each side to inflict unbearable losses on the other. At this point the Western alliance could not fail to be rocked by the combination of nuclear disparity (that is, America's quasi-monopoly of nuclear weapons and strategy-making in the alliance) and geographical differences. The United States could not help noting that, in case nuclear deterrence did not work, the massive resort to nuclear weapons for the defense of Europe would be suicidal; hence the preference both for a different war strategy and for a different form of deterrence. But the perfectly sound principle that different threats in different places require different strategies means in practice that a direct Soviet attack against the United States (necessarily nuclear) would entail a nuclear response, whereas an attack on Europe (possibly conventional) would provoke a flexible response. The geographical difference happens to correspond not to a distinction among separate portions of one state but to a distinction between separate nations.

Hence a triple conflict. First of all there is a conflict over the strategy of deterrence and war itself. The Europeans do not doubt the wisdom of the idea of flexible response; they question its application to Europe. They would prefer the United States, if not to *treat* any attack on Europe exactly as an attack on the United States, at least to try to *deter* any attack on Europe by making it clear that it would treat it as if it were one on the United States itself. The United States doubts that such a deterrence strategy would be credible, that is, that it would deter. The Europeans doubt that the present United States strategy would deter precisely because it may be only too credible. What is at stake is not the existence of America's commitment to Europe but its nature or its scope. The Europeans would like it to be total; the United States prefers to leave something to chance.

Secondly, there is the problem of control. Even if the Europeans were convinced of the virtues of a flexible response, they would want to be in control of the means of making it. What is at stake is not whether Europe should or should not raise conventional forces for such a response, but whether Europe should or should not have a share in the control of nuclear weapons, that is, the weapons capable of deterring the enemy from provocation and from pushing harder if he has already initiated a limited war. What many Europeans desire is either a finger on the United States trigger or a trigger of their own. The United States thinks in cataclysmic terms: the perspective of the extreme ought to govern all policy, the unlikeliness of Doomsday being judged less relevant than its costs. Hence the United States argues that small nuclear forces not under its control are dangerous, and that should the apocalypse occur, American nuclear weapons would suffice anyhow. Europeans think in different terms and gamble, so to speak, on the unlikeliness of folly. Not only do they believe that a modicum of control of their own would make Armageddon even less likely by complicating the would-be aggressor's calculations; chiefly, they think of all those crises short of but more probable than Armageddon in which he might be tempted to push, pry and provoke unless he feared thereby to drive a European state into using (or threatening to use) its own nuclear weapons and triggering the use (or the threat of the use) of America's own. Thus each side stresses what is in its own interest as well as in its own character: the United States, the situation of all-out war; and Europeans, the familiar situation of less than all-out crises. Last, there is a conflict of interests in the realm of arms control. Europeans are afraid of a bilateral American-Soviet agreement that would either freeze the present relationship of nuclear disparity within the alliance, or even worsen it by, say, some degree of United States nuclear disengagement or some measure to prevent Europeans from developing their own forces.[19]

In the area of diplomatic strategy as well, common interests are somehow pushed back by divergent calculations and concerns. Obviously, all Europeans have an interest in preventing the kind of détente that, while removing some woes and some walls, nevertheless preserves United States predominance in Western Europe and Soviet domination in Eastern Europe. Europe's interest in and concern for the emancipation of Warsaw, Prague or Budapest from Soviet rule are greater than America's. The United States might well be satisfied either with a "Soviet bloc" shorn of its proselytism or with a mere lessening of Soviet control; but a loosening so great that the former satellites could once again behave as Europeans first, that is, a political renaissance of the European continent as a whole, is neither an obvious nor a necessary United States objective. Nor do United States and European objectives in the UN and in the "Third World" coincide. All Europeans have an interest in preserving Europe's influence in the newly independent areas, and in offering them aid and understanding whenever, for any reason, those nations refuse to or cannot turn to the United States. Such a division of labor between the Europeans and the Americans constitutes no more treason of the latter by the former than United States anticolonialism was a betrayal of Europe by America; for the only alternative to such dissociation within the West was then and would remain tomorrow an appeal by the new nations to the "revolutionary models"—Moscow or Peking. Yet precisely because such dissociation is both objectively useful and subjectively resented by those who feel repudiated or abandoned, it points to the unlikeliness of identical policies on the two sides of the Atlantic.

Thus an "Atlantic Europe" would suppose that the Europeans have been capable of overcoming their divisions only by sacrificing Europe's identity to America's mission. In a world that was essentially bipolar—a world in which Europe was still under the surface of the ocean of international affairs, and in which the Soviet-American conflict was the overriding issue which justified Europe's total solidarity with the United States—a case could have been made for such an arrangement. The "polycentric" world of today, in which Europe's nations are again playing with the waves and competing with other swimmers, rules it out despite American desires. But in such a world the very trends that destroy one prospect stop short of dictating another. When the projections are ambiguous, priority to purpose is clear; when the trends point in different directions, it is up to the statesmen to shape them to their goals. Such ambiguity appears in each of the areas we have examined. The choice between unity and dispersion is open.

Thus, economic integration obviously proceeds and the procedures set up by the communities press the governments hard to extend harmonization in all directions. With a common market and a joint external tariff the states cannot afford widely different wage, budgetary and monetary policies. Nations whose prosperity becomes tied to the success of the joint undertaking lose some of their individual freedom of action in the world, for such freedom is limited by the need to keep the concern going. The more eggs are broken into it, the more difficult it is to unscramble the omelet. And yet economic unification still tells us little or nothing about political and military unity. Once everybody is convinced that it is in nobody's interest to break up the concern, each one can go quite far in the pursuit of his own diplomatic or strategic interests without incurring any serious risk of retaliation, as France's veto of Britain showed.* The restraint created by the communities limits each member's capacity to pursue action directly and deliberately aimed at harming his partners; it does not limit his freedom to act in

---

*Those who suggest that the "other five" pursue a policy of isolating France and join the U.S. and Britain in this enterprise thus underestimate France's hold over its partners in the communities.

other respects as he sees fit. Even nations that agree on sound budgets can still distribute their expenditures in very different ways; even nations that agree to spend the same percentage of their GNP on defense or foreign aid can still affect their resources to uncoordinated or conflicting strategies.

The common European interests that separate Europe from the United States in the area of defense serve as the basis of various proposals for a European military organization or a European deterrent. The very smallness of Western Europe's geographical area argues in favor of such schemes. In case of a Soviet provocation against a European nation, the latter cannot be sure about the scope of America's commitment, but it has fewer reasons to doubt that one of its partners and immediate neighbors endowed with nuclear weapons would hesitate to use or to threaten to use them. General Gallois' thesis about the destructive effect of nuclear weapons on alliances is far too blunt and lumps together situations that are politically and geographically distinct. And yet here again the trend is ambiguous. Even if all the nations of Western Europe did agree on the persistence of a Soviet military threat, they would still be able to proceed from common interest to separate policies; the same goal—security—can be pursued through totally different routes. It is here that attempts at unification have been least successful (*vide* EDC) and that separate military programs are most difficult to reverse and to coordinate. The Germans try to still their fears by acting closely with the United States in order to inflect American strategy and gain access to United States decision-making. The French prefer slaps to seduction and challenge to docility; they try to develop their own nuclear force so as to impair the application of America's doctrine and to have something of their own to control. Germany has signed the test ban and hopes to avoid the bad effects of arms control through prior consultation. France continues its tests and boycotts disarmament negotiations altogether. Furthermore, the key to a genuine system of European defense lies probably in England, without whose nuclear force a European deterrent would remain pretty skimpy.

Furthermore, it makes little sense to negotiate a common defense so long as the combined forces would be unable to serve, not merely a common doctrine, but a common foreign policy. Thus the solution to the military problem presupposes an agreement on Europe's role in world affairs. Only then will it be possible to arrange either a coordination of national forces effective enough to give all participants a share in the control if not in the possession of the European deterrent, or a genuine merger of national forces under a single authority endowed with the formidable power to threaten the use of and to use nuclear weapons: a power which presupposes a sense of identity and a certainty about aims and strategy that exist no more today among the Europeans than they exist between them and the United States.

Finally, the task of those who would like to use United States–European military divergences as a reason for reducing intra-European ones is complicated by the détente. True, peril parity, which led the United States to revise its strategy in

Europe, has shocked the Europeans. But this same parity combines with internal Communist dissensions to lessen the risk and the fear of war. Thus, European champions of unity are squeezed between two facts: when the peril is highest, as long as Europe is militarily weak a separate European establishment (by contrast with a specialization of Europe's military contribution as often suggested by the United States) makes no sense. When the peril declines, the sense of urgency recedes and the prevalence of national calculations resumes.

The same reasoning applies in the decisive realm of foreign policy. The divergences between Europe's and America's interests mentioned above obviously suggest the need for European political unity. Only a European organization could be strong enough to affect American policies, or serve as a magnet toward the Soviet satellites so as to awaken a European patriotism among them. For if they should be faced with either an Atlantic bloc or a divided Western Europe in which Germany would be on its own again, they would have little choice but to remain under Moscow's wing, even in case of a loosening of Russia's hold. Only such an organization could fully convince England that its role lies in Europe rather than in trying to cling either to dusty vestiges of power or to the hope of getting the best of both the world inside Europe and the world outside.

And yet the success of the quest for the common new mission is far from certain. The prospect of a détente and the rise of the Third World have evoked at least three conflicting sets of goals and directions in Europe. Some still believe that the best Europe can hope to do is influence American policies from within the alliance; this is the "Atlantic Europe." Others argue for a "European Europe" that would try to keep the détente from harming European interests: Europeans should act as if the Soviet threat had remained constant, but also to emancipate Europe from America's predominance in facing the threat. Others see in the loosening of alliance ties, in the lessening of tensions in Europe, in the decreasing importance of the United States-Soviet Union conflict throughout the Third World, a fishing license for the separate European nations released from the compound of bipolarity. Germany here is a crucial case. As long as the world scene was dominated by the Cold War, West Germany—partitioned and placed next to the Soviet forces—was the European state on which bipolarity weighed most, that is, it was the most dependent on the United States and the one on which United States power could most easily be brought to bear. If the deadlock of the superpowers brings about a détente and "polycentrism," Germany may switch from the direction of an "Atlantic Europe" to that of independent national action. If the United States seeks accommodation with the Soviet Union, why should not Germany pursue its own national aims (which differ from almost everybody else's) by trying for a separate deal with Russia, which holds the key to reunification? The same reasoning can be held by others: Why should not France—tired of beating the reluctant European horse into harness—seek prestige and grandeur in the Third World, and turn what is de Gaulle's fallback objective into the primary one? Why should not Italy opt for nonalignment?

Thus the trends can be interpreted as either suggesting a joint European enterprise or as removing the need for it altogether. There is choice—and a question of will. A joint European undertaking, at this point, is not likely to be supranational or federal, for all the reasons mentioned before. There is not yet any agreement on goals and directions; such an agreement would take time to emerge. But the enterprise out of which such agreement should come presupposes at least a common *intention* to find the goals and the directions. In other words, the prerequisite to common policies (and to institutions capable of carrying them out and of sharpening them) is a determination to define a new role in the world for Europe; behind such a determination there is a *postulate:* that Europe is not only a geographical expression but an entity capable of overcoming its divisions and of bringing its own contribution to world affairs. Out of the postulate of a possible European identity would gradually arise the *policies* realizing this identity. Should the European statesmen of the near future behave in such a way, two consequences would follow. First, the European entity would obviously be playing the game of world politics. Here and there some writers suggest that it should not behave as a superpower; this can mean only that it either ought to behave like someone else's dependent, or that it ought to give the world the example of abnegation or of observance of the Golden Rule (or the Rule of Law). Europe, alas, can hardly define its identity either as subservience or in what amounts to self-sacrifice. The alternatives to a sort of collective European nationalism are a set of separate ones or a kind of despondency, not a world government or a world ruled by love and charity. Second, the European entity, if it becomes a going concern, is likely to pursue policies closer to de Gaulle's than to those of the United States. The precedent of the realm of welfare indicates this, as well as the divergence of interests discussed before. Moreover, any definition of common policies entails of necessity a deliberate distinction between the new entity and the powerful senior ally.

Should the common determination fail to appear, there would be no dearth of "miserable consolers." The prosperity of Europe's separate parts and the opportunities for influence and maneuver would provide good alibis. However, the business and busyness of individual European nations is no substitute for a joint European project. Acting separately, the European states could certainly complicate the task of the superpowers—and nuisance value matters, as de Gaulle has often demonstrated. But they could neither contribute to the solution of the world's main problems nor share responsibilities with the superpowers, for although there are new rules in the game of world politics, some of the harsh old ones are still in force or in reserve. Even in a world of nuclear deadlock the threat of force remains an essential instrument of diplomacy, and power defined as mobilizable potential remains the *ultima ratio.* Separate European nations could not hope to acquire enough of such strength. Should the détente prosper, they could make it more difficult, but they would not be major actors in the decisions that would give it depth. Should the détente vanish, they would again be merely a collection of minor partners of the United States, with concerns too parochial and forces too slender to be taken seriously. In either case their division would leave to others—China for instance—the transformation (and the benefits of the transformation) of a bipolar world into one where more than two superpowers detain the *ultima ratio* and where, perhaps, the influence of the nonpowerful might again drastically decline. In international relations, the possession of power is to be sought not only for the sake of prestige or domination but also because only the mighty create; the influential can maneuver and advise, convince or set examples; they can dig in and defend their place in the sun, but the mighty alone set the course of the sun. De Gaulle has understood this well. This is why, should no European common will emerge, he may remain in history, not as the grave-digger of a unity that was never there to bury (had it been there, he would not have tried or succeeded), but as the last European statesman with a world-wide vision. The "new Europe" would then fall back into the habits of its past, but in the context, both happier and more bitter, of an economic intertwining that would limit its self-destructive atavism, and of a world in which the relative importance of the European nations would—for all their possible freedom of action—be far less considerable than in the past.

A case could be made for a European choice of unity and purpose in world affairs even if Europe's industrial society became the twin of America's—precisely because the social order does not determine foreign policy and because the divergence of interests would persist. Indeed, one could argue that the more European society comes to resemble America's, the more Europeans ought to save their originality by taking hold of their fate in the world. A case could also be made for the proposition that even if it were in Europe's interest or fate to become "Atlantic Europe," it still ought to seek its identity by using its freedom of creation in the internal realm of social and political affairs. But the two problems of choice are connected. For Europe to regain not just a concern for but a voice and a policy in Southeast Asia, Latin America or Eastern Europe, it is not only the habit of external dependence but also the complacency of prosperity that must be overcome. For Europe to design a project of social, educational, political accomplishments, it must realize not only that there is room for creativity within its borders but also that the effort is justified by the role Europe can play again and the example it can still set beyond them.

In both the external and the internal realms, the forces that affect Europe's present and future are so complex that they afford opportunities for statesmanship: they are limits and chances, not constraints and commands. In both realms the existence of such opportunities raises both a question of imagination and a question of self-respect: to believe falsely that one is the master of one's fate when one is not is dangerous, but to act as though one were not when one is—at least in part—is a singularly debasing form of behavior. In both realms there is today a shrinking from originality, a diffidence toward normative ambitions; the happy submission to industrialization, the mistaking of a procedure of integration for a purpose of action are two sides of the same coin.

In both realms, America somehow provides Europe with an alibi. In one realm, the identification of Europe with the United States (whether for the purpose of hailing it or of deploring it) is a mistake, for it is industrial society, not America, that is the force at work; what is distinctively American in the industrial society of the United States need not be transplanted in Europe unless the Europeans deliberately choose to do so, in which case they would be exercising their freedom of choice. In the other realm, Europe's relative decline has been the outcome of Europe's own behavior. Dependence on the United States need not be permanent and total unless the Europeans continue to behave in such a way as to perpetuate a relationship which no law of history imposes.

America has been the social model and the political leader. It is time for the students to emancipate themselves—which means transcending both servility and defiance, the two forms of slavish behavior. For identity can be found in neither. It can be found in separateness. The differences between American and European societies, and between American and European interests, ought indeed to be saluted by Americans and Europeans alike. Their very existence allows the latter to test once again their inventiveness. As for the former, they should realize two facts. First, those differences make it possible for the Europeans to behave as self-respecting actors and thus to make a contribution of their own—something that a nation unaccustomed to imperial domination and unwilling to bear all burdens alone should appreciate, for domination breeds both among those it convinces and among those who resist it a sense of irresponsibility that justifies domination anew, but at an increasing psychological and political cost. Second, those differences are in no way so fundamental as to justify anxieties. In the case of people so closely linked, separateness means neither total divorce nor necessary hostility; it means merely autonomy, the sense of being the author of one's own fate as far as impersonal and uncontrollable forces allow. It is America's mistake often to interpret the request for autonomy as a suit for divorce or a sign of hostility, and it is de Gaulle's shock tactics that justify confusion—although the apparent creation of antagonism, or the apparent plea for divorce, may be the only way of ever reaching autonomy.

In order to reach it, Europe must overcome much of its past: in its distant past, all the legacy of national divergences, but not that of diversity; in its recent past, the passive absorption of American lessons, but neither the drive for prosperity nor the concern for unity. The fruits of industrialization and of a common market ought to keep growing, but so that they can be used for purposes chosen by the Europeans rather than for mere enjoyment. Physical and biological vitality is not missing. It is spiritual vitality that is in question. Under Roman rule the Greek cities, satisfied with the peace and order brought from the outside, saw no reason to coalesce, and congratulated themselves on the degree of rationality they had achieved in the mastery of social problems, for internal complacency and dependence breed and feed each other. In that fertile desert of Europe, which now spurns adventures and savors the delights of production and consumption, and which wavers between a cursed past, a protection increasingly less adequate, and a future so far more happening than chosen, how long will one have to wait until economic vigor is matched by political and intellectual inventiveness—long the chief glory and the only pride of the Old Continent?

Notes

1. See the special issue "A New Europe?" Winter, 1964.

2. See Manlio Rossi-Doria, *Dædalus, op. cit.*, p. 341. It is interesting that the two articles by Mr. Rossi-Doria and Mr. Pizzorno are the most pessimistic of the pieces written by Europeans about Europe's social changes, and Mr. Cavazza's the most impatient.

3. The two previous paragraphs are intended to qualify the conclusions developed by Seymour Lipset, *Dædalus, op. cit.*, pp. 271–303.

4. In the French context, I have discussed this problem in my contribution to *In Search of France* (Cambridge, 1963). See also "La démocratie à refaire," *France Forum* (Paris, 1963) and "Démocratie aujourd'hui," *Action Populaire* (Paris, 1963).

5. See the analysis by Michel Crozier in his very important book *Le phénomène bureaucratique* (Paris, 1964), pp. 315 ff.

6. See the analysis by Ralf Dahrendorf in "Demokratie und Sozialstruktur in Deutschland," *Archives européennes de sociologie*, Vol. I, No. 1 (1960), pp. 86–120.

7. All these quotes are from Alain Clément, *op. cit.*

8. Hans Magnus Enzensberger in *Encounter*, April, 1964, p. 16.

9. See the interesting discussion by Jean Meynaud, "A propos des spéculations sur l'avenir," *Revue Française de Science Politique*, Vol. XIII, No. 3 (Sept., 1963), pp. 666–688.

10. For an example, see Louis Armand et Michel Drancourt, *Plaidoyer pour l'avenir* (Paris, 1961).

11. Last page of *The Opium of the Intellectuals*.

12. See his *Anti-intellectualism in American Life* (New York, 1963), Part V.

13. See J. M. Domenach, "Le modèle americain," *Esprit*, July-August, September and October, 1960; Crozier's article in *Dædalus, op. cit.*, pp. 514–542.

14. *Dædalus, op. cit.*, p. 66.

15. See Raymond Aron, *Paix et Guerre* (Paris, 1962), intro.; also, my comments in "Minerve et Janus," *Critique*, January, 1963, pp. 51–67, and "Discord in Community," in F. Wilcox and H. F. Haviland, Jr. (eds.), *The Atlantic Community* (New York, 1963), pp. 3–31.

16. Ernst B. Haas, "Technocracy, Pluralism and the New Europe," in Stephen R. Graubard (ed.), *A New Europe?* (Boston, 1964), pp. 62–88.

17. See *Man and his Government* (New York, 1963), Chapter 32.

18. The argument is designed to qualify that of Kenneth N. Waltz in "The Stability of a Bi-polar World," *Dædalus*, Summer 1964, pp. 881–909.

19. These points are well covered both in Raymond Aron's *Le Grand Débat* (Paris, 1963) and in various unpublished papers prepared by Hedley Bull for the Council on Foreign Relations.

2

Europe's Identity Crisis Revisited

I

Almost thirty years ago, I wrote an essay about Western Europe which began by calling it prosperous and disunited. I then stated: "Europe today has no clear identity, no profile other than that which a process of industrialization and a process of economic integration have given it. Europe today has no sense of direction and purpose."[1] In 1994, this judgment remains valid, even though so much has happened in the past ten years alone: the *relance* of the mid-1980s, the end of the Cold War and of Europe's division into two armed camps, and the longest recession since the Great Depression. In 1964, my opening paragraph ended bravely: "This essay laments its absence" (i.e., the absence of a sense of direction and purpose) "and calls for its rebirth." I am more sober now: I only propose an analysis.

It is ironic that the crisis of the European Community (EC, now called the European Union [EU]) appears to have begun immediately after the signing of the Maastricht Treaty on European Union, which seemed to promise a major leap forwards. A monetary union, with a single central bank and a single currency, was going, within less than ten years, to crown the enterprise of economic integration begun in 1957 and expanded by the "1992" program of the mid-1980s (the so-called Single Act). The Community's jurisdiction was going to extend to areas beyond the economic realm: social affairs, police matters, immigration—areas close to the core of domestic sovereignty—as well as to diplomacy and defense. A year and a half later, deep pessimism prevails. The French nation endorsed the treaty by the most niggardly of margins. The Danes first said no, and then yes only after having obtained from their partners exceptions that almost amount to exempting Denmark from the Maastricht stipulations. The European Monetary System (EMS) established by a Franco-German initiative in the late 1970s, and only recently joined by the British, was badly shaken by a colossal crisis in September 1992, which drove the British out, and almost wrecked by a second onslaught in July 1993, which obliged the members to enlarge enormously the margins within which their currencies are allowed to fluctuate. The date of the future monetary union is uncertain and who will be in it is also in doubt. As for diplomacy and defense, the Community's fiasco in Yugoslavia has been deeply demoralizing. What went wrong?

Two suggested explanations can be rejected outright. The lofty and persistent chorus of European Federalists puts much of the blame on the governments that failed, in Maastricht, to reform the institutions of the Community in a direction that should have been more democratic and more federal. It is true that the treaty, while marginally increasing the powers of the elected European Parliament, consolidated the preeminent position of the Council—composed of governmental representatives—especially because many of the new areas of the EU's jurisdiction shall be dealt with only by unanimity. But the Federalist answer raises a fundamental question. Why have the governments been so timid, why—more than twenty years after the disappearance from the scene of the arch anti-Federalist, General de Gaulle, and three years after the removal from power of that other fierce foe of "supranationality," Margaret Thatcher—does the progress toward more effective and powerful central institutions remain so slow and halting, despite the efforts of a European Court of Justice that has sometimes sounded as if it wanted to imitate the American Supreme Court in the early decades of the United States' existence? The Supreme Court succeeded because it was interpreting a Federal Constitution; the European Court of Justice's attempt to blow Federalist air into the weak lungs of a community based not on a constitution but on a series of treaties could not, by itself, suffice.

The second explanation that does not take us very far is that the current crisis is, as the French would say, *conjoncturelle*. Recession, so goes the argument, is always bad for the Community: remember the years of the oil shocks, during which the governments tried to find national solutions to their countries' problems and "Europessimism" became fashionable. It is true that despite the creation of a single market for goods, capital, services, and (more or less) people, the same causes have tended to produce the same effects. The "convergence criteria" set at Maastricht to prepare for monetary union are promises for the future; until now, state policies have diverged sufficiently to produce a broad spectrum of deficits, inflation rates, and interest rates. It is also true that matters have been made worse at a crucial moment by the unanticipated costs of Germany's unification—the combination of an industrial and ecological disaster whose proportions exceeded all fears, and of imprudent political decisions about the rate of exchange between the Western and Eastern mark and about financing the rehabilitation of the East by loans rather than by taxes. The independent Bundesbank's decision to combat the inflationary implications of these policies by high interest rates has wreaked havoc on the economies of the countries whose currencies are tied to Germany's, and thus has aggravated the recession. It is also true that the Yugoslav tragedy, which the Community could not prevent or resolve, has proved too complex and too burdensome for the United States and the United Nations as well.

Recessions eventually end. The absorption of Eastern Germany into the new

Federal Republic of Germany (FRG) is under way (and the German government has seen the need for greater fiscal rigor) and the ferocity of ethnic conflict in Yugoslavia is not likely to be reproduced elsewhere (foretold disasters in the rest of the Balkans have not occurred—so far—and Serbian bellicosity may well have been dented, if not daunted, by the costs of the wars in Croatia and Bosnia and of international sanctions). There have been other setbacks and crises in the history of the Community, but its march has always resumed; no crisis ever led to an unraveling.

There is some truth in that argument. The Community overcame the paralysis caused by the conflict between de Gaulle and the "Europeans," it came out of the economic troubles of the 1970s and the long battle over Britain's terms of membership, and it may well triumph over the new sources of division and despair. Nobody wants to undo what has been achieved: insofar as it is a construction built on common interests—let us call them peace and prosperity (among the partners)—there are very few voices that express the thought that each member, or even any one of them, would be better off if the edifice collapsed. The EMS did unravel, but if the key members make an effort to coordinate their economic policies and to adopt the same priorities—the fight against unemployment and recession rather than, as in the Bundesbank's case, high interest rates to prevent inflation, and, as in France's case since the mid-1980s, financial rigor and a strong currency—the EMS might be restored and the march toward monetary union might resume.

However, *conjoncturel* factors do not explain everything. The failure to coordinate economic policies predates the recession and explains why a monetary system that tried to preserve narrow margins of fluctuation among currencies, and whose dominant currency was ruled by a *national* central bank intent on following its understanding of a purely national interest, was bound to run into storms once the national situations and policy priorities began to diverge significantly. Even in less troubled times, an attempt by several of the members (such as Italy) to meet the "criteria of convergence" would have imposed enormous strains upon their habits and practices. And while Yugoslavia may well be exceptional, the European performance in the Gulf crisis was not much more edifying. In those two instances, as in the days that followed the loosening of the EMS, the spokesmen for the governments have congratulated themselves on the Community's ability to avoid fatal splits. But if the criterion of success becomes the ability to put in common a good face on retreats and fiascoes, then the European ambition must have fallen rather low.

II

We must look deeper than the circumstances of the late 1980s and early 1990s, to a number of factors that would hamper the Community's march even if *la conjoncture* improved. They can be divided into two groups: some concern Western

Europe's relations with the rest of the world, some concern its internal situation. In both categories, thirty years ago, Western Europe's relation to American society and to America's world role was the heart of the matter. Today, this relation is far less central, although it remains important.

In the first group, we need to distinguish between two kinds of problems: issues of foreign economic and financial policy, a domain which is either predominantly (trade) or largely (money) within the Union's jurisdiction, and issues of diplomacy and security which are still essentially national, despite the halting "European political cooperation" initiated in the 1970s and the promise of Maastricht (but even after the treaty enters into force, unanimity will be the rule here).

The monetary dramas of 1992–1993 have taught two lessons—both of which are damaging to the Union. The first is that as long as there is no single central bank and currency, a large number of private individual and corporate investors (what the French call "speculators" and Americans "the market") will play the game of attacking those currencies they deem overvalued, and they have financial resources far superior to those the national central banks can provide to defend the threatened currencies. These speculative runs point simultaneously to the need for a single currency and to the enormous difficulty of getting one. They undermine the transitory system—the EMS—that is the preliminary and prerequisite to the final monetary union, and they aggravate the distortions among the members' financial situations. The only ways in which the governments can try to thwart the "speculators" are by widening the margins of fluctuations (which defeats the very purpose of the EMS) or by revaluing undervalued currencies and devaluing overvalued ones. But the political costs, and the feared economic ones, of such manipulations deter democratically elected governments. Moreover, when faced with private capital's offensive against public currencies, the elites of the Union's nations have reacted divergently (and predictably) along familiar national lines. In the United Kingdom (as in the United States) currency tends to be seen as a commodity like any other, whose value it is the function of the market to determine: paper barriers are not going to prevail over the wishes of private actors (especially when they seem encouraged by their governments).[2] In Germany, and even more in France, currency is seen as the symbol, instrument, and attribute of the sovereign state, and not as an ordinary good. But until there is a united Europe, Germany's way of protecting that instrument is shaped by the Bundesbank's definition of the German national interest (and therefore it defended the franc but not the pound and the lira in September 1992, and limited its defense of the franc in July 1993), and France's itch to get its partners to agree on sets of regulations and controls that could restrict the operations of outside speculators is not shared by anyone else. Thus, it is not just the *conjoncture* of 1992–1993 that puts the EU at a disadvantage in this realm, by comparison with the United States or Japan. It is its very unfinished nature, its being a halfway house between a group of formally independent states and a genuine union or federation; and the storms to which it is therefore exposed keep it in this unhappy position.

The divergences among the members are just as apparent in trade policy. The difficulties that emerged during GATT's interminable Uruguay Round may have been made more intense, but they have not been created by the recession. What happened is familiar. In the case of agriculture, as in the case of "cultural services" (movies and television programs), the Community had painfully succeeded in putting together policies that reflected, in the former instance, France's attachment to the original Common Agricultural Policy (which had done so much to boost France's export capacity) and, in the latter instance, France's resistance to the "invasion" of American programs. But when the United States began to exert very strong pressure on both fronts, the surface consensus of the EU cracked and divergent combinations of foreign policy traditions and national policy dispositions reasserted themselves: the French being more protectionist, statist, and anti-American; the British being at the completely opposite end; and the Germans riding the middle line, somewhat closer to the British (and to the Americans) while trying not to break up with the French. The split was reflected even in the EU Commission, where French President Jacques Delors and the British commissioner in charge of external trade, Sir Leon Brittan, were not on the same wavelength at all. The French, at the end, skillfully retreated from the brink just enough to get their partners to support most of their demands, but the compromises to which the United States agreed in December 1993 do not resolve the issues once and for all: the showdown was postponed, and surface consensus within the EU was thus restored, for the time being.

Differing reactions to the pulls and pushes of the outside world—in this instance the United States—had already divided the Community in the 1960s. This is precisely what we find when we turn to the realm of diplomacy and defense. Even though the Community set up by the Treaty of Rome in 1957 had no formal powers in those areas, membership in the EC became a major component of each participant's definition of its national interest. Here, as in NATO, each one, and especially the main actors—France, Germany, England, and Italy—had worked out a specific position during the Cold War, around which grew not only a rationale (partly public, partly sotto voce) but what might be called a cobweb of interests and relationships (hence the remarkable continuity of these positions, despite changes of governments). But the basis for these calculations and policies was the situation in which the West European states found themselves during the Cold War: a divided Europe with a formidable Soviet threat and the necessity of American protection. On this basis the French devised a policy that tried to combine the maximum of possible independence and the development of a European entity that would "contain" West Germany, as did NATO, but also would become capable of resisting American supremacy. France would offset the FRG's economic dynamism with its independent nuclear force and its unique capacity to lead the Community, given the inhibitions that handicapped Bonn in this respect: Germany's past and Germany's division. The Germans saw in the Community a way back to respectability, an avenue of influence, and a provider of support for Germany's legitimate national aspirations. The British, latecomers, also endorsed it as a field of influence (now that decolonization was over and the Commonwealth had faded) and as an instrument for the containment both of Germany *and* of France's anti-American thrusts and leadership ambitions. For Italy it was a highly desirable alternative to the failed nationalism of fascism and, along with NATO, a way of keeping out of power a Communist Party whose own gradual embrace of European integration was deemed incompatible with its support of Soviet policies.

All these calculations have been put in question by the shock of 1989 and the end of the Cold War. To be more precise, the situation in which they grew has been wiped away. The cobwebs are still there but the walls on which they hung are not. At the heart of the matter is the change in the relative power and situation of France and Germany. Despite its current difficulties, the FRG is the main beneficiary of the recent events: it has regained unity and full sovereignty, its main potential enemy, the Soviet Union, has disintegrated, its need for American protection has shrunk, and, at a time when economic clout matters at least as much as military might, it is the predominant economic and financial power in Europe. The weight of the past gets lighter as the past recedes. And while its political elites remain committed to European unity as insurance against the temptations of adventurism and as reassurance toward the rest of Europe, the FRG now has the opportunity to become the Union's leader and no longer needs to be in almost all circumstances its main source of funds for aid to its weaker members and poorer regions. Europe is less a willingly chosen cage and more a tool for influence and for the securing of a favorable environment.

The shocks that have benefited Germany have damaged France's position. Today, for the satisfaction of their national interests, the French need Germany and Brussels far more than before; the would-be leader has become a quasi-dependent. To be sure, constitutional and moral inhibitions curtail Germany's involvement in military operations outside of NATO's domain, but in these areas France's nuclear advantage is almost useless, and its non-nuclear forces have been sacrificed to the nuclear mirage. As a result—and this is the second transformation in France's position—the rather soft but broad consensus on the European policy described above has split and the gap is widening between those who cling to the Union as the best way to limit and supervise Germany's new influence—but from a position of weakness, no longer of strength—and those who, fearing that Germany would dominate the Union and would become a cage for France, would like to regain some of the independence they see as having been frittered away. Both sides remain convinced that America, the sole remaining superpower, is still, or indeed more than ever, a threat (as well as a now less indispensable protector), but one side still hopes to infuse the Union with the proper spirit of resistance, a calculation which the other side mocks as a pipe dream.

England is, of course, also concerned with containing the new German giant, whose advent it greeted with unconcealed dismay. But the present Union does not seem to the British any more capable of performing such a role than it does to the Séguins and the Chevènements of France. Both would like a much looser Europe, extending much farther East. But whereas the French doubters crave greater national independence as a way of resisting real and imaginary American encroachments, the British simply pursue with renewed vigor their old design of a loose European grouping that would be little more than a free trade area, incapable therefore of becoming a counterweight to the United States. If anything the end of the Cold War and the signs of America's temptation to turn inward have made the British more eager than ever to behave as the most faithful and privileged allies of the United States so as to prevent it from disengaging too much from a continent still teeming with dangers, both to the East and—because of Germany's new might—in its heart.

As for Italy, the embrace of European unity lost its anti-Communist function long ago, and its position has been affected less by the events of 1989 than by the domestic avalanche that threatens its political and economic elites. What this cascade of changes in situations, of forced new calculations, and of difficult and incomplete adjustments explains is the continuing difficulty of the states in the Union to agree on a common diplomacy and security policy. What could not be achieved when they were all together in the "Western" cauldron of the Cold War—because their dispositions toward their own pasts, toward the United States, and toward the Soviet Union diverged—is even harder to accomplish now that the lid is off, and the cauldron abandoned.

The disappointing performance of the Union in the two major post-1989 crises in which it nevertheless tried to speak with one voice—the Gulf war and Yugoslavia—is the result of both the divisions or divergent calculations mentioned above and of another phenomenon observed by several people,[3] namely the inadequacy of the Union in geopolitical enterprises. The Community, for many of its enthusiasts, including the disciples of Jean Monnet, was going to be an exemplary civilian power, a fine example of supernation building over an economic foundation. As a result, security was left to NATO (i.e., the United States) and diplomacy to the member states. The latter, either because their forces were tied to NATO, or, as in France's case, because their trump card was nuclear deterrence, or because of varieties of pacifism, lost the habit of external military action, except for limited operations to safeguard bits of an empire or a former empire, as in the Falklands, or in Chad. Large-scale military expeditions not caused by a direct threat to physical security have tended to be dismissed as belonging to a distant past.

This explains why, in the Gulf crisis of 1990–1991, the contribution of most of the Community's members was either symbolic or, in Germany's case, reluctant and predominantly financial. The two states that participated far more actively— England and France—saw in the crisis a way of reasserting their rival claims to "global middle power" status and also a wedge for reintroducing themselves into the old diplomatic game of Arab–Israeli negotiations. None of these calculations bore fruit. In the case of Yugoslavia, two facts are most striking: First, the unwillingness of *any* of the Union's members to intervene militarily except as a participant in a peace*keeping* or humanitarian operation[4]—an unwillingness whose first expression had been the early reluctance to take the breakup of Yugoslavia seriously enough. Second, the range of policies was wide. In the beginning, there was a gulf between France and Britain's preference for preserving a Yugoslav state and Germany's push for early recognition of Slovenia and Croatia. Germany dragged its reluctant partners along: they joined Bonn in order to prevent a unilateral German recognition, which occurred anyhow. When Bosnia became the center of the drama there was still an ample gap between Britain's attitude off prudent (some would say disdainful) nonintervention and Germany's awkward combination of anti-Serb feelings and constitutional impotence, with France playing Hamlet in the middle. The Union's own distinctive contribution—Lord Owen—displayed in successive peace plans a bizarre mix of wishful thinking and resignation to the inevitable and a characteristic reluctance to envisage the military means needed to achieve political ends.

What the "external" part of this story shows is simple. With economic integration largely accomplished, two further tasks assumed increasing importance: monetary union, to consolidate the economic enterprise both within Western Europe and in the world, and a common defense and diplomatic policy so that the new economic giant would cease being a geopolitical dwarf. But the outside world's turbulence and the widely different reactions of the key states of the EU have made it impossible to overcome the obstacles. Not the world's turmoil but the same divisions have thwarted a third advance beyond economic integration: the reform of the EU's institutions. But before we examine this failure, we must turn to the internal part of the story.

III

The West European malaise and the crisis of the Union stem largely from the internal developments of the 1980s and early 1990s. One is, again, a factor of division; others are common to most of these nations.

If one examines the attitudes and statements of members of the political and cultural elites, one is struck by the way in which their relation to their country's past and to its future has changed over the past thirty years. In the early 1960s, the FRG was still uncertain about its future: the Wall had just been built, cementing the nation's division, and the superpowers' grip on the two halves of Europe was firmer than ever. The West Germans were still engaged in a painful exploration of their "unmasterable past." The need to repudiate it and to avoid anything that smacked of it was the lodestar of the new regime; the "embourgeoisement" of the new society and concentration on economic performance were methods of atonement as well as attempts to overcome the dangerous and delirious romanticism of the past. Today, the past is being "normalized": that is what the *Historiker-*

streit of the late 1980s was about. Those who, like Habermas, vigorously opposed the attempt to put Nazism in perspective and to look at it as an episode in a continuous history were waging a noble but rearguard fight. The consternation produced by the first serious recession since the end of World War II and the material and psychological obstacles to the integration of the Eastern *Länder* should not obscure this fact: Germany's future in Europe and in the world is brighter than ever before, and the very challenge of that integration provides Germany with a *projet* that transcends economic performance.

In the early 1960s, especially after the end of the Algerian war, France under de Gaulle's exhortatory leadership was turning away from the past, toward a future that he described in grandiose terms. The view propagated by Gaullists, Communists, and other former *Résistants* that the nation had behaved, on the whole, admirably during World War II was rarely challenged, and as soon as the French pulled out of Algeria and the *pieds noirs* had settled on metropolitan soil a veil of silence and voluntary ignorance fell on the colonial past and on the bloody wars of decolonization. But since 1968 (despite the uninformed clichés spread by the American media) the French have been relentlessly exploring and scratching the wounds of the Occupation, putting the spotlight first on collaborationism, then on anti-Semitism; more recently, the Algerian war has ceased being taboo. But the presence of the past has not only taken the form of a confrontation with shame. There is also a wave of longing for the days of French grandeur. The heated debates on the French Revolution showed both sides of this fascination with the past: for some the Revolution, and especially its Jacobin paroxysm, was the forerunner of modern totalitarianism; for others the revolutionaries were, if not holy, at least to be admired for having created and tried out the ideology and institutions of *La République,* which the Third Republic was going to perfect. Republicanism, with its Rousseauistic emphasis on the general will and on the guiding role of the state, is widely presented as a very different and better formula than "Anglo-Saxon" liberalism. It is also a yardstick used to judge, and deplore, the performance of the Union. The past engages and fascinates; it is the future that appears dim.[5]

Across the Channel there has been less of a reversal, but this is only because postwar Britain has been more often bitterly savoring the memories of its past glories and "finest hour" than facing the future with confidence and a sense of direction. The Thatcher episode was an exception. She, like de Gaulle, tried to provide a seamless vision of grandeur linking the future to the past. But, unlike de Gaulle, her internal policies were too fiercely divisive and the results too mixed for the attempt to succeed. If in present-day France the invocation of the Republican past becomes an incentive to criticize a technocratic and bureaucratic Union, nostalgia for Britain's past is a weapon for resisting any increase in the Union's effective powers. British and French nationalism are essentially defensive, aimed at safeguarding whatever can be preserved of the past. If we leave aside the extreme Right in Germany, which rabidly displays an exaggerated version of the same nostalgia, the German elites are not "renationalized," partly because of the need not to repeat the past, but also because the Union today so largely satisfies German interests and endorses German policies.

If we move from elite attitudes to the evolution of societies, we find greater uniformity—but of a kind that contributes to the widespread unhappiness of the moment. In 1964 I wrote about "Americanization with a difference," placing emphasis on difference. Much has happened since. Many of the hopes of the early 1960s have turned out to be illusions. Technological progress did not usher in an age of ever-growing opulence ad did not resolve the major social problems. Indeed, the spread of such progress to much of the rest of the world is one of the sources of today's industrial difficulties and of Western Europe's relative decline. The creation of elaborate procedures for the conciliation of interests (what has sometimes been called corporatism) neither succeeded in turning politics into a mere process of group adjustment nor survived the shrinking of the pie that was to be distributed by the state. Planning, the most celebrated perhaps of these procedures, has become both impossible (in an integrated and open Western Europe) and obsolete at the national level and unfeasible (because of a lack of power, resources, and will) at the Union level. The great dream of "mass education without any of its disadvantages—the raft of quality miraculously floating on an ocean of quantity"[6]—has turned into a nightmare: except for a very small elite, quality has declined and quantity has produced masses of young unemployed. The loss of illusions has reinforced a feature that had struck me in 1964: the absence of any new set of values underlying the conversion to the "functional necessities of a new kind of social order."[7] With these necessities now often under fire, the "solid bed of beliefs" provided in the United States by liberalism is even less visible, despite a brief moment of liberal euphoria during the days when communism fell and the single market rose. The bizarre "events" of 1968 had many aspects: one was a protest against the vacuum of beliefs, or, with regard to communism, against the ossification and sterilization of the creed. But the attempt to spread new values failed: it was a revolt, not a revolution. In 1964 I wrote that the European consensus was negative; I do not think that there is one today.

Many West Europeans, especially those who work for the Union and who often, as exceptions to what was just said, deeply believe in its mission have seen its vocation as the defense of West European distinctiveness, the preservation of those features of West European societies which, despite "Americanization" (industrialization in a capitalist framework) still distinguished them from America's society and polity. Union officials (especially if they are French) have often stressed the rural component of West European "civilization" as essential and specific: the relation to the land in countries with peasants in different from what it is in a nation of migrants with an agro-business of capitalist farmers. But that rural component is becoming a myth and a memory. The old-style peasants are vanishing, and it is the urban bourgeois and American-style farmers who have replaced them. The West Europeans have also been proud of pointing out that their cities had better management, better urban planning, and greater social co-hesion than American ones. While much of this remains true, urban planning did not prevent, indeed is often promoted, the ugliness and aridity of sprawling and artificial suburbs. Social cohesion has been undermined by the combination of immigration (and fierce resistance to it), drugs, crime, and unemployment. The West Europeans now speak of urban "ghettoes," even when explosions there result from the hostile coexistence of different ethnic groups rather than from the misery and sense of injustice of a locally predominant one. The once tight weave of the West European nations' social cloth has stretched and loosened; each one now has to cope with the "exclusion" of large numbers of national and (often il-legal) foreign misfits.

The West Europeans also liked to distinguish their welfare states, based on a mix of Socialist and Christian Democratic convictions, from America's laissez-faire society, especially in the matters of health care, labor practices, and unem-ployment benefits. Here too a rapprochement has occurred. In France after 1983 and in England after 1979 the role of the state in economic management was sharply reduced, and while not even Mrs. Thatcher dared to dismantle Britain's welfare legislation, everywhere the rising costs of social services, the economic cost of the laws that aimed at protecting labor from low salaries, exploitation, and arbitrary firings, and the successful competition in domestic and world markets of goods produced by countries with cheap labor are putting pressure on the governments to restore what is euphemistically called "flexibility" in the labor market and to trim the services provided by the state. This is made politically easier by another change that brings the European reality closer to America than to the supposedly distinctive "European model": for a variety of reasons, among which the recession is the major one, labor unions have either lost members mas-sively, or lost combativeness.

In education the West European *projet* had been democratization, but without sacrificing quality in the training of future elites, without endangering what the *lycée*, the *Gymnasium,* and the British public school had provided, and without reducing primary education to the level to which American public schools had allegedly sunk. This does not appear, on the whole, to have been achieved, and while standards fell in primary and in much of secondary education, higher edu-cation, a major political battlefield, has been transformed by mass access, but in ways that keep it inferior to the American system of colleges and universities. As for the distinctiveness of West European culture, it has pretty much vanished in all the realms of popular culture. These many changes explain why there often is so much determination to defend what is left today of European specificity. French and Spanish peasants and French, Spanish, and Italian movie and tele-vision producers and directors take out their anger on the United States because the government and the business interests in the United States seek to hasten trends that are unfolding anyhow. The Union is too weak and divided to protect adequately what is left. But this leads some Europeans to wonder what the higher purpose of West European integration is if their societies do not have anything specific to protect and to promote.

The sense of a loss or lack of *projet* is reinforced by developments in domestic politics. Here some features that were visible thirty years ago that distinguished Western Europe from the United States are still present, but they too contribute to paralysis. During the past thirty years, the decline of parliaments has continued and bureaucracy, even when its economic interventionism has been toned down, remains the ordering power in the nations (in Italy and France the growth of regional governments has simply added new bureaucratic layers). Threatened groups such as British and French miners or French peasants have continued to display a capacity for anger, vitality, and a disdain for compromise unknown in the United States.

Three new political characteristics interfere with the unification of Europe. The first is, to coin a phrase, the end of ideology. In 1964 communism, Social Democracy, and Christian Democracy were alive, if not well. We all know what has happened to communism, and the Christian Democrats and the Socialists have suffered heavily from the eroding and corrosive effects of power. Economic integration and the attempt to make the EMS function have put serious limits on the leeway of policymakers in the economic and financial arenas. With politics shifting from the enforcement of distinctive programs to the management of constraints, parties that began as programmatic movements lost their programs and their politicians sometimes lost their souls.

The margin of choice among competing partners appears paradoxically narrower than in the United States, whose two parties many Europeans had tended to deride as barely distinguishable. In countries where the state, even when weak, was seen as properly the guide of society, a notion that is far more controversial on this side of the Atlantic, the shift from creative leadership to prudent management was often seen as a fall. The original theory of West European integration had seen the decline of ideology and the prevalence of economic management as a boon for supranational unity: it would be based on a dynamic of interests because interests compromise, ideological passions divide. But managers are not innovators, and if there had not been the ideological drive that animated the Monnet group, or Jacques Delors, little would have been accomplished. Above all, leaders who are primarily managers find it hard to mobilize their publics.

Second, the failure of managerial politics to cope with unemployment and the host of social issues that accompany the recession, or with the relative decline of European industry which aggravates it, and the many scandals that the collusion between the management of state power and the business world has generated have driven many citizens into contempt for politics and politicians (a feature that is most prominent in Italy, but visible also in France, Spain, England, and Germany). It results in political fragmentation, votes for small parties, and above all a great deal of lassitude and skepticism toward the designs of politicians—such as Maastricht. Publics which had often seemed to ask and expect less from politicians than the "revolutions" promised by the latter (remember the French Socialists' slogan of 1981: *changer la vie*) nevertheless expected more and better than what their leaders delivered after they discovered that their promises could not be kept.

Third, new divisions complicate the task of politicians eager to proceed with European unification. In England the gap between the modern industrial and financial sector, boosted by Thatcherism, and the declining parts of the country, the gap between the affluent and the underprivileged, are dangerous for Tories addicted to trickle-down theories and puzzling for Socialists deprived of their old articles of faith. In Germany the many gaps and misunderstandings between the old FRG and the former German Democratic Republic (GDR) will take years to disappear.[8] In Italy we find not only the last supporters of the collapsing old system pitted against a (dis)array of reformers but a division between North and South. Comparable splits exist, of course, in Eastern and Central Europe between those who want their nations to embark on a "normal" course of capitalist free market development with liberal institutions and those who are buffeted by the storms of change, baffled by the new insecurities of employment and social services, and nostalgic about the protection that the state, however authoritarian, had provided for forty years. All these divisions oblige leaders to pay attention to the nation's social fabric first.

IV

What are the effects of these disruptive developments within the Union and in its external relations? It shows today a face that is both unfinished and unattractive; here we must again distinguish the inside from the external side of the faltering enterprise.

I do not mean to minimize what has been accomplished. For all its current tensions, Franco-German relations have been revolutionized, turned from hatred and war to reconciliation and friendship. Britain is a reluctant and ambivalent partner, but it is "in." Membership in the Union has been essential for the democratic progress of Spain and Greece. The "founding fathers" who saw the Union as indispensable for the peace and prosperity of its members have been vindicated. Brussels, for all the flaws of the institutional setup, is one of the last refuges of idealism on the continent. And yet, the glass remains half empty, or, to change the metaphor a bit, vinegar has been added to the wine. The Union's contribution to peace is being taken for granted almost half a century after the end of World War II, and what shocks its citizens is that such peace does not seem to be contagious. The Berlin Wall fell (certainly not thanks to the Community) but in a crucial respect Europe remains divided: ethnic conflicts among Europeans have been dampened in the West but they have exploded in the East after the removal of the Communist lid. And in the former Soviet Union the future is sufficiently ominous to put both internal and external peace in doubt. As for prosperity, the

Europeans have learned that however much they integrate their economies, it ultimately depends on events beyond their borders and control: on the soundness of the American economy, on how tough competition with the Japanese juggernaut turns out to be, on how quickly the "relocation" of business from Europe to the Far East and Southeast Asia disrupts or demolishes traditional West European industries, on the whims of often anonymous "speculators." Maintaining prosperity is a Sisyphean task. Herein lies the drama: the original impulses to rule out new fratricidal wars, to offer new horizons during the painful days of decolonization, to provide an escape from excessive dependence on the "big brother" across the Atlantic, and to turn recovery into prosperity through cooperation have faded and have not been adequately replaced. There is a vast difference between Western Europe as a zone of peace and economic integration (this has been achieved) and Western Europe as a common enterprise with a bold program at home and abroad.

At home the failure is visible in two areas: institutions and policies. Institutionally the somewhat Byzantine setup of the Union is a compromise between the inadequate and the impossible. The inadequate is the notion of a strictly intergovernmental operation. To be sure, without the governments' consent, the 1992 program of economic unification could not have been launched, but without the supranational Commission's work and the switch to qualified majority vote in the council, this program could not have been carried out.[9] The impossible remains the leap to a federal system: none of the West European Great Powers (excluding Italy) is ready for it, and two of them, France and the United Kingdom, remain predominantly hostile. The rather empty debate about "subsidiarity" is a symptom of the reluctance to transfer power decisively from the states to the central institutions of the Union. The advantage of the compromise is that it allows these to have effective authority in some important areas: agriculture, foreign trade, opening markets, and promoting competition. The disadvantage is the famous "democratic deficit." The most dynamic of the "federating" institutions is the Commission, which is also the most bureaucratic and technocratic. The most democratic (because it is elected by the people) is a parliament with scant powers and a mode of election that is, in fact, national rather than European so that the most ambitious representatives prefer to sit in the national assemblies and complain about having too little to say about what happens in the Union.[10]

The German government has made it clear that in exchange for letting its partners share with the Bundesbank (the de facto ruler of the EMS) control of the future monetary union it would like the powers of the European Parliament to be increased. But the Fifth Republic (which has, so to speak, swallowed or converted its erstwhile foe François Mitterrand) does not want to recreate the Third or Fourth Republics in Strasbourg. And the British government, used to dominating a theoretically sovereign British Parliament thanks to the logic of a two-party system (or to an electoral law that crushes third parties), is just as unenthusiastic about transferring power to a splintered multinational parliament. The result of all this is a setup of limited efficiency and even more restricted legitimacy. There still is no European political process, if one means thereby a transnational set of parties and elections of European rather than of national delegates to a common assembly.

As for the policies ground out by these clumsy institutions, they suffer not only from the fact that the Monnet wager on European integration consisted in focusing energies on a utilitarian calculus of material rewards and on "a logic that places material gain at the apex of social values,"[11] but also from the priority given in recent years to a particular kind of economic approach. The only common programs are found in areas of redistribution (i.e., areas where difficult compromises must be recurrently negotiated between the rich and the poor members) and in agriculture, where the inevitable retreat from the wasteful excesses of the Common Agricultural Policy guarantees fights and unpopularity. In every other respect the activities center on *deregulation,* within a very loose framework (the mutual recognition of national standards): a process that ultimately empowers businesses but does little to build a European state.[12] As a paradoxical consequence, the Commission's regulations of deregulation are often denounced by the members as trivial, fussy, and intrusive, but its authority in important matters of economic, fiscal, and social policy, science, technology, and education remains minimal. Those who, like Monnet and Ernst Haas, believed in the expanding logic of functional integration, in the dynamic that would force the states to grant ever more powers to the central institutions in order to remedy such deficiencies and imbalances, underestimated the resistance of national bureaucracies, executives, and parliaments to such transfers. If Mrs. Thatcher was sufficiently enthusiastic about deregulation to accept (imprudently) that it proceed by majority rule it was because she understood that the task would keep Brussels busy without making it strong.

Thus, the face the Union shows to its members is unfinished. The face it presents to the outside is often unpleasant. Two issues matter here: immigration and the problem of Eastern Europe. Concerning the former there is indeed remarkable European distinctiveness if one compares the Union to the United States, a distinctiveness that is fiercely and systematically buttressed but is anything but admirable. It is as if, having gradually become used to seeing in the citizens of other EU nations persons who, while different from true nationals, are nevertheless not aliens, the inhabitants of each of the EU countries had decided to treat those from outside the magic circle with extra suspicion and severity—a tendency mightily reinforced but not created by the recession. The combination of the Schengen agreements on open borders and new national legislation, especially in Germany and France, is an ugly attempt by each member to push on others the burden of screening asylum seekers and a common policy of the lowest common denominator. Blocking immigration except in the rarest of cases (when asylum cannot be refused under international law), persecuting illegal immigrants with venomous vigor, and, in the French case, making the integration of legal ones more difficult, shows how governments have tried to defuse the arguments and to deflate the growth of xenophobic movements by adopting some of their recommendations and thus by legitimizing their existence—as long, of course, as they do not turn murderous. This is the politics of meanness (it is especially bizarre in Italy, where the Lombard League looks at non-Northern Italians as unworthy foreigners). The opening of borders to foreign goods and services is accompanied by a closing of gates to people.

The prevalence of the politics of fear is evident not only in attitudes toward "invaders" from the poor countries of the Middle East or of North Africa or in fantasies about Islamic or Black hordes besieging a prosperous Europe (which reacts by arguing that the best way to prevent such onslaughts is to help the countries of the Third World keep their peoples at home through a policy of aid to development, an argument that happens to be accompanied by little aid). It is also visible in the timidity with which the Union and most of its members have faced the opportunity provided by the collapse of communism east of the old Iron Curtain. There are, of course, good reasons why Prague, Warsaw, and Budapest could not join the EU at once or quickly. But the Union has behaved as if it was more anxious to protect the fortress of Western Europe from the economic and ethnic turmoil of the East than it was to provide, through close association leading to guaranteed membership if stipulated conditions are met, a safety net for these countries. It is as if the peace and relative prosperity achieved in the West were too precious to be exposed to the turbulence in the East: self-protection is more important than propagation, quarantine than help.[13] The argument that the Union had to choose between "deepening" and "expanding" is specious: so far there has been neither, and a bold expansion might have obliged the members to face sooner the reform of the institutional setup (already too cumbersome for twelve) which Maastricht postponed to 1996, just as the expansions of the 1970s and early 1980s (from the Six to the Twelve) led to the shift to majority vote in the Single Act.

Especially at a time of domestic unhappiness and strife there is no hope for a popular push toward greater unity, for a move from below toward a Union both deeper and wider. As in other historical cases it is from the top that the initiatives will have to come. If there ever should be a European "nation of nations" and a Federal European state above the states that have already lost many of their powers, either through formal transfer to Brussels or through devolutions to "the market" or through simple impotence, it is the elites and the governments that will have to take the decisive steps: exactly what happened in the 1950s and in the mid-1980s. But what is lacking currently is elites and leaders with a daring vision. The convergence of Monnet, Schuman, Adenauer, and de Gasperi was exceptional. What obstructed progress in the 1960s was not the absence of a vision; it was the reluctance of other leaders to accept de Gaulle's vision. A less grandiose but uplifting convergence around the vision of "1992" brought together Delors, Thatcher, Kohl, and Mitterrand. Today, the French President merely survives,

Kohl has his hands full with the unexpected or perverse effects of his own vision for Germany in 1989, Britain acts as a brake, and Delors by himself can do little. Precisely because of the negative trends and factors on which this essay has dwelled, it would take the convergence of exceptionally bold leaders to transcend the current malaise, timidity, divisions, and retreats. But these same trends and factors make it difficult to see where such leaders would come from and who they would be.

Meanwhile, Western Europe suffers, paradoxically, both from the legacy of the postwar habit of dependence on American leadership in geopolitical affairs and from the decline of an American predominance which had assuredly been a factor of division (between Gaullists and Atlanticists) but also a goad toward a European entity capable of talking back to the United States. And it remains torn by disjunctions it cannot overcome: between politics, which is still national, and economics, national no longer; between economics, which is becoming common, and diplomacy and defense, where the Union still falters; between a settled West and an unsettled East. In 1964 I wondered about Western Europe's spiritual vitality. I still do.

Notes

1. Stanley Hoffmann, "Europe's Identity Crisis," *Dædalus* 93 (4) (Fall 1964): 1244.

2. On US official skepticism toward European Monetary Union, see Mark N. Nelson, "Transatlantic Travails," *Foreign Policy* (92) (Fall 1993): 75–91.

3. See Michael Brenner, "EC: Confidence Lost," *Foreign Policy* (91) (Summer 1993): 24–43, and Pierre Hassner, "Beyond Nationalism and Internationalism," *Survival* 35 (2) (Summer 1993): 49–65.

4. Indeed, such participation then became a major argument for *not* intervening as peace *enforcers* against any party or as champions of collective self-defense against an aggressor.

5. No French leader over the last ten years has succeeded in articulating a convincing conception of it.

6. Hoffmann, "Europe's Identity Crisis," 1267.

7. Ibid., 1260.

8. See Fritz Stern, "Freedom and Its Discontents," *Foreign Affairs* 72 (4) (September–October 1993): 108–125.

9. Cf. Robert Keohane and Stanley Hoffmann, eds., *The New European Community* (Boulder, Colo.: Westview Press, 1991).

10. Cf. Stanley Hoffmann, "Goodbye to a United Europe?," *New York Review of Books* XLI (10) (27 May 1993): 27–31.

11. Brenner, "EC: Confidence Lost," 26.

12. One could argue that it takes away regulatory powers from the member states, without any real transfer to Brussels.

13. A comparable timidity is being shown in dealing with the internal and interstate turmoil of the former Soviet Union, except for Germany's economic help to Russia. Cf. Robert Legvold's thoughtful and alarming paper, "Western Europe and the Post-Soviet Challenge" (unpublished).

Part Two

European Unity in the Cold War

3

Obstinate or Obsolete? France, European Integration, and the Fate of the Nation-State

I

The critical issue for every student of world order is the fate of the nation-state. In the nuclear age, the fragmentation of the world into countless units, each of which has a claim to independence, is obviously dangerous for peace and illogical for welfare. The dynamism that animates these units—when they are not merely city-states of limited expanse or dynastic states manipulated by the Prince's calculations, but nation-states that pour into their foreign policy the collective pride, ambitions, fears, prejudices, and images of large masses of people—is particularly formidable.[1] An abstract theorist could argue that any system of autonomous units follows the same basic rules, whatever the nature of the units. But in practice, i.e., in history, their substance matters as much as their form; the story of world affairs since the French Revolution is not simply one more sequence in the ballet of sovereign states; it is a story of fires and upheavals propagated by nationalism. A claim to sovereignty based on historical tradition and dynastic legitimacy alone has never had the fervor, the self-righteous assertiveness which a similar claim based on the idea and feelings of nationhood presents: in world politics, the dynamic function of nationalism is to constitute nation-states by amalgamation or by splintering, and its emotional function is to supply a good conscience to leaders who see their task as the achievement of nationhood, the defense of the nation, or the expansion of a national mission.[2]

This is where the drama lies. The nation-state is at the same time a form of social organization and—in practice if not in every theory—a factor of international nonintegration. But those who argue in favor of a world under more centralized power or integrated in networks of regional or functional agencies, tend to forget Comte's old maxim that *on ne détruit que ce qu'on remplace.* Any new "formula" would have to provide world order, of course, but also the kind of social organization in which leaders, elites, and citizens feel at home. There is currently no agreement on what such a formula is;[3] as a result, nation-states— often inchoate, economically absurd, administratively ramshackle, and impotent yet dangerous in international politics—remain the basic units despite the remonstrations and exhortations. They go on *faute de mieux* despite their alleged obsolescence. Indeed, they profit from man's incapacity to bring about a better world order, and their very existence stands as an obstacle to their replacement.

If there was one part of the world in which men of good will thought that nation-states could be superseded, it was Western Europe. Pierre Hassner, one of France's most subtle commentators on international politics, has reminded us of E. H. Carr's bold prediction of 1945: "We shall not see again a Europe of twenty, and a world of more than sixty independent states."[4] Statesmen have invented original schemes for moving Western Europe "beyond the nation-state,"[5] and political scientists have studied their efforts with a care from which emotional involvement was not absent. The conditions seemed ideal. After World War II, nationalism seemed at a low ebb, and an adequate formula and method for building a substitute had apparently been devised. Thirty years after the end of the war—a period longer than the interwar era—observers have had to revise their judgments. The most optimistic put their hope in the chances which the future may still harbor, rather than in the propelling power of the present. Less optimistic ones, like myself, try simply to understand what went wrong.

My own conclusion is sad and simple. The nations in Western Europe have not been able to stop time and fragment space. The political unification of Europe might have succeeded if, on one hand, its nations had not been caught in the whirlpool of different concerns, arising from profoundly different internal circumstances and outside legacies, and if, on the other hand, they had been able or obliged to concentrate on "community-building" to the exclusion of other external and domestic problems. The involvement of policy-makers in issues among which community-building is merely one has meant that the divergences among foreign policies have increased, not decreased.

Every international system owes its inner logic and its unfolding to a diversity of domestic determinants, geohistorical situations, and outside aims among its units. Every international system based on fragmentation tends to reproduce diversity through the dynamics of unevenness (so well understood by Lenin, albeit applied only in the economic realm by him). But there is no inherent reason why a fragmented international system need rule out certain developments in which critics of the nation-state have put their bets or their hopes. Why must the system be built of a diversity of *nations*? Could it not be a diversity of regions, of "federating" blocs superseding the nation-state, just as the dynastic state replaced the feudal puzzle? Or else, could not the logic of conflagration-fed-by-hostility lead to unification, the kind of catastrophic unification among exhausted yet interdependent nations which Kant sketched? Let us remember that the unity movement in Europe was an attempt to create a regional entity, and that its origins and dynamics resembled, on the reduced scale of a half-continent, the process Kant dreamed up in his *Idea of Universal History.*[6]

The answers are not entirely provided either by the legitimacy of national self-determination, the only principle which transcends all blocs and ideologies, since everyone pays lip service to it, or by the newness of many nation-states, which wrested their independence from another power in a nationalist upsurge and are unlikely to give up what they obtained so recently. But conversely, the legitimacy of the nation-state does not by itself guarantee the nation-state's survival in the international state of nature, and the appeal of nationalism as an emancipating passion does not assure that the nation-state must everywhere remain the basic form of social organization in a world where many nations are old and settled and where the shortcomings of the nation-state are obvious.

No, the real answers are provided by two unique features in the present international system. First of all, it is the first truly *global* international system. Regional subsystems have only a reduced autonomy; the "relationships of major tension" blanket the whole planet; interdependencies in the world economy affect all the non-Communist nations and begin to affect the Soviet group of nations. Domestic polities are dominated not so much by a region's problems as by purely local or purely global ones; these join to divert a region's members from the affairs of their area, and indeed make isolated treatment of those affairs impossible. As a result, each nation, new or old, is placed in an orbit of its own from which it is quite difficult to move away: the attraction of regional forces is offset by the pull of all the other forces. Or, to change the metaphor, the nations that coexist in the same apparently separate "home" of a geographical region cannot escape the smells and noises that come from outside through all the windows and doors, or the view of outlying houses from which the interference issues. With diverse pasts, moved by diverse tempers, living in different parts of the house, inescapably yet differently subjected and attracted to the outside world, the residents react unevenly to their exposure and calculate conflictingly how they could either reduce the disturbance or affect in turn the people in the other houses. Adjusting their own relations within the house is subordinated to their divergences about the outside world; the "regional subsystem" becomes a stake in the rivalry of its members about the system as a whole.

The common home could still prevail if the residents were forced to come to terms, either by one of them, or by the fear of a threatening neighbor. This is where the second unique feature of the present situation intervenes. What tends to perpetuate the nation-states decisively in the present system is the new set of conditions that govern and restrict the rule of force: Damocles' sword has become a boomerang, and the ideological legitimacy of the nation-state is protected by the tameness of the world jungle. Force in the nuclear age is still the "midwife of societies," insofar as revolutionary war begets new nations or new regimes in existing nations; but the use of force along traditional lines for conquest and expansion—a use that made "permeable" feudal units obsolete and replaced them with modern states built on "blood and iron"—has become too dangerous. The legitimacy of the feudal unit could be undermined by the rule of force—the big fish swallowing small fish by national might; or subtly and legitimately, so to speak, through dynastic weddings or acquisitions that consolidated larger units. But a system based on national self-determination rules out the latter, and a system in which force is a blunted weapon rules out the former. The new restrictions on violence even tend to pay to national borders the tribute of vice to virtue: violence that dons the cloak of revolution, or that persists in the form of interstate wars only when these accompany revolutions and conflicts in divided countries, perversely respects borders—it infiltrates them rather than crossing them overtly. Thus, all that is left for unification is what one might call "national self-abdication" or self-abnegation, the eventual willingness of nations to try something else. But global involvement hinders rather than helps here, and the atrophy of war removes the most pressing incentive. What a nation-state cannot provide alone—in economics or defense—it can still provide through means far less drastic than hara-kiri. For while it is true that economic interdependence in all its forms—trade, investments, travel, the management of monetary institutions—has weakened the autonomy of the nation-state, eroded its monetary, business, or tax policies, submitted its government to a host of transnational pressures,[7] it is not clear that a merger of nations would plug the sieve's holes rather than make the sieve bigger.

These two features bestow solidity to the principle of national self-determination, and resilience to the U.N. They also give shape to the "relationship of major tension": the conflict between the United States and the Soviet Union. As the superpowers find that what makes their power overwhelming also makes it less usable (or usable only to deter one another and to deny each other gains), lesser states discover that under the umbrella of the nuclear stalemate they are not condemned to death, and that they indeed have an impressive nuisance power. Thus, as the superpowers compete in a muted form all over the globe, the nation-state becomes the universal point of salience, to use the language of strategy—the lowest common denominator in the competition.

Other international systems merely conserved diversity; the present system profoundly conserves the diversity of nation-states despite all its revolutionary features. Rousseau's dream, concerned both with the prevalence of the general will (i.e., the nation-state) and with peace, was to create communities insulated from one another. In history, where "the essence and drama of nationalism is not to be alone in the world,"[8] the clash of noninsulated states has tended to create more nation-states and more wars. Today, Rousseau's ideals come closer to reality, but in a most un-Rousseauian way. The nation-states prevail in peace, they are not superseded because a fragile peace keeps the Kantian doctor away, they are not replaced because their very involvement in the world preserves their separateness. The "new Europe" dreamed of by the Europeans could not be established by force. Left to the wills and calculations of its members, the new formula did not jell because Europeans could not agree on their role in the world. The failure of an experiment made under apparently ideal conditions tells us a great deal, for it shows that a unification movement can fail not only when a surge of nationalism occurs in one important part but also when differences in how the national interest is assessed rule out agreement on the shape and purpose of the new, supranational whole.

The word nationalism is notoriously slippery. What I suggest is the following threefold distinction, which may be helpful in analyzing the interaction between the nation-state and the international system:

1. There is *national consciousness* (What the French call *sentiment national*)— a sense of "cohesion and distinctiveness,"[9] which sets one group off from other groups. My point is that this sense, which has important effects on international relations when it is shared by people who have not achieved statehood, is rather "neutral" once the nation and the state coincide. That is, the existence of national consciousness does not dictate foreign policy, does not indicate whether a people's "image" of foreigners is friendly or unfriendly, and does not indicate whether or not the nation's leaders will be willing to accept sacrifices of sovereignty. One cannot even posit that a strong national consciousness will be an obstacle to supranational unification, for it is perfectly conceivable that a nation might convince itself that its "cohesion and distinctiveness" will be best preserved in a larger entity.

2. For lack of a better phrase, I shall call it the *national situation*. Any nation-state—indeed, any state—is, to borrow Sartre's language, thrown into the world. Its situation is made up of internal features (these, in an individual, would be called heredity and character) and its position in the world. The state of national consciousness in the nation is only one element in the situation. It is a composite of objective data (social structure and political system, geography, formal commitments to other nations) and subjective factors (values, prejudices, opinions, reflexes, traditions toward and assessments of others, and others' attitudes and approaches). Some of its components are intractable, others flexible and changeable. Any statesman, whether a fervent patriot or not, must define the nation's foreign policy by taking this situation into account; even if he is convinced of the obsolescence of the nation-state (or of *his* nation-state), the steps he can and will take to overcome it will be affected by the fact that he speaks—to borrow de Gaulle's language this time—for the nation as it is in the world as it is. He cannot act as if his nation-state did not exist, or as if the world were other than it is. The national situation may facilitate unification moves, even when national consciousness is strong. It may be an obstacle, even when national consciousness is weak. The point is that even when the policy-maker tries to move "beyond the nation-state" he can do so only by taking the nation along, with its baggage of

memories and problems—with its situation. I do not want to suggest that the situation is a "given" that dictates policy; but it sets up complicated limits that affect freedom of choice.[10]

3. I will reserve the term *"nationalism"* for a specific meaning: it is one of the numerous ways in which political leaders and elites may interpret the dictates, or suggestions, of the national situation. It is one of the ways of using the margin the national situation leaves. Whereas national consciousness is a feeling, and the national situation a condition, nationalism is a doctrine or an ideology—the doctrine or ideology that gives absolute value and top priority to the nation in world affairs. The consequences of this may vary immensely. Nationalism may imply expansion (i.e., the attempt to establish the supremacy of one's nation over others) or merely defense; it may entail the notion of a universal mission or, on the contrary, insulation. It may be peaceful or pugnacious.[11] It is less a determinant than a criterion of choice, an attitude that shapes the choices made. But whatever its manifestations or content, it always follows the rule common to all manifestations of nationalism: it always pours the content into one mold, the preservation of the nation as the highest good. Nationalism thus affects, *at least* negatively, the way in which the freedom of choice left by the national situation will be used; indeed, it may collide with, and try to disregard or overcome, the limits which the situation sets.

The relation between these three factors is complicated. Nationalism (in the sense of the will to establish a nation-state) can be triggered by, and in turn activate, national consciousness in oppressed nationalities; but in colonial areas as well as in mature nation-states, nationalism can also be a substitute for a weak or fading national consciousness. In nation-states that are going concerns, national consciousness encourages nationalism only in certain kinds of national situations. A nationalist leader may assess the national situation in exactly the same way a nonnationalist one does, but the former may promote policies the latter would have rejected and oppose moves the latter would have undertaken. That bane of international relations theory, the national interest, could be defined as follows: N.I. = National situation × outlook of the foreign-policy-makers.

It is obvious that a similar national situation can result in differing foreign policies, depending in particular on whether or not there is a nationalist policymaker. It is obvious also that the national interests in different nations cannot be defined in easily compatible terms if the respective outlooks are nationalist, even when the situations are not so different. But the same incompatibility may obtain, even if the outlooks are not nationalistic, when the situations are indeed very different.

II

Let us now look at the fate of the six nation-states in continental Western Europe, first by examining the basic features of their national situations, then by commenting upon the process of European unification, later by discussing its results, and finally by drawing some lessons.

Western Europe in the postwar years has been characterized by features that have affected all of its nations. But each of these features has affected each of the six nations in a different way.

The first feature—the most hopeful one from the viewpoint of the unifiers— was a temporary demise of nationalism. In the defeated countries—Germany and Italy—nationalism was associated with the regimes that had led the nations into war, defeat, and destruction. The collapse of two national ideologies that had been bellicose, aggressive, and imperialistic brought about an almost total discredit for nationalism in every guise. Among the nations of Western Europe on the Allied side, the most remarkable thing was that the terrible years of occupation and Resistance did not result in a resurgence of chauvinism. Amusingly enough, it was the French Communist Party that displayed the most nationalistic tone; on the whole, the Resistance movements showed an acute awareness of the dangers of nationalist celebrations and national fragmentation in Western Europe. The Resistance itself had a kind of supranational dimension; none of the national Resistance movements could have survived without outside support, and the nations whose honor they saved were liberated rather than victorious. All this militated against any upsurge of the kind of cramped chauvinism that had followed the victory of World War I, just as in Germany the completeness of the disaster and the impossibility of blaming traitors crushed any potential revival of the smoldering nationalism-of-resentment that had undermined the Weimar Republic. There was, in other words, above and beyond the differences in national situations between indubitable losers and dubious winners, the general feeling of a common defeat and the hope of a common future: Resistance platforms often emphasized the need for a union, or federation, of Western Europe.

The demise of nationalism affected the various nations of the half-continent differently. There were significant differences in national consciousness, for one thing. In liberated France, nationalism was low, but patriotic sentiment was extremely high. The circumstances in which the hated Nazis were expelled and the domestic collaborators purged amounted to a rediscovery by the French of their own political community: the nation seemed to have redeemed its "cohesion and distinctiveness." On the contrary, in Germany especially, the destruction of nationalism seemed to have been accompanied by a lowered national consciousness as well: what was distinctive was guilt and shame, and the all too cohesive nation-state was torn apart by partition, occupation zones, regional parochialisms blessed by the victors. Italy was in slightly better shape than Germany, in part because of its Resistance movements.

The defeated nations—Germany in particular—were in the position of patients on whom drastic surgery has been performed and who lie prostrate, dependent for their every movement on surgeons and nurses. Even if one had wanted to restore the nation to the pinnacle of values and objectives, one could not have done so except with the help and consent of one's guardians—and they were unlikely to support such a drive. In other words, the situation set strict limits on the possibility of any kind of nationalism, expansive or insulating. The lost territories were beyond recuperation; a healing period of *repli*, comparable to that which had marked the early foreign policy of the Third Republic, was not conceivable either.

On the other hand, France and, to a lesser extent Belgium and Holland, were not so well protected. For, although the prevalence of the nation meant little in the immediate European context, it meant a great deal in the imperial one: if the circumstances of the Liberation kept national consciousness from veering into nationalism in one realm, the same circumstances tended to encourage such a turn with respect to the colonies. Cut down to size in Europe, these nations were bound to act as if they could call upon their overseas possessions to redress the balance; accustomed, through their association of nationalism with Nazi and Fascist imperialism, to equate chauvinism only with expansion, they would not be so easily discouraged from a nationalism of defense, aimed at preserving the "national mission" overseas. The Dutch lost most of their empire early, and found themselves in no so different a situation from the German and Italian amputees. The Belgians remained serene long enough not to have nationalistic fevers about the huge colony that seemed to give them no trouble until the day when it broke off—brutally, painfully, but irremediably. The French, however, suffered almost at once from dis-imperial dyspepsia, and the long, losing battle they fought gave continual rise to nationalist tantrums. The French inclination to nationalism was higher anyway, because there was one political force that was clearly nationalist. It had presided over the Liberation, given what unity it had to the Resistance, and achieved a highly original convergence of Jacobin universalism and "traditionalist," right-wing, defensive nationalism. This was the force of General de Gaulle. His resignation in 1946 meant, as Alfred Grosser suggests,[12] the defeat of a doctrine that put priority not only on foreign affairs but also on *Notre Dame la France*. The incident that led to his departure—a conflict over the military budget—was symbolic enough of the demise of nationalism. But his durability, first as a political leader, later as a "capital that belongs to all and to none," reflected a lasting French nostalgia for nationalism; and it was equally symbolic that the crisis which returned him to power was a crisis over Algeria.

The second feature common to all the West European national situations, yet affecting them differently, was the "political collapse of Europe." Europe did not merely lose power and wealth: such losses can be repaired, as the aftermath of World War I had shown. Europe, previously the heart of the international system, the locus of the world organization, the found of international law, fell under what de Gaulle has called "the two hegemonies." The phrase is, obviously, inaccurate and insulting. One of those hegemonies took a highly imperial form, and thus discouraged and prevented the creation in Eastern Europe of any regional entity capable of overcoming the prewar national rivalries. But the American hegemony in Western Europe, different as it is, has been a basic fact of life, even though it was more "situational" than deliberate. Its effects were better than usual, insofar as the hegemony was restricted to areas where the European nations had become either impotent or incapable of recovery on their own. The dominated had considerable freedom of maneuver, and indeed the American presence prodded them into recovery, power recuperation, and regional unity; it favored both individual and collective emancipation. But the effects were in a way worse, because the laxity meant that each party could react to this feature of all the national situations—i.e., American hegemony—according to the distinctive *other* features of the national situation. American domination was only one part of the picture. Hence the following paradox: American prodding and the individual and collective impotence of West European nations ought logically to have pushed the latter toward unity-for-emancipation. But the autonomy that each West European nation retained gave it an array of choices: between accepting and rejecting dependence on the United States, between unity as a weapon for emancipation and unity as a way to make dependence more comfortable. It would have been a miracle if all the nations had made the same choice. To define one's position toward the United States was the common imperative, but each one has defined it in his own way.

At first, this diversity did not appear to be an obstacle to the unification movement. As Ernst Haas has shown,[13] the movement grew on ambiguity. Those who accepted American hegemony as a lasting fact of European life as well as those who did not could submerge their disagreement while building a regional entity: for the former, it was the most effective way to continue to receive American protection and contribute to America's mission and, for the latter, it was the most effective way to challenge American predominance. But there are limits to the credit of ambiguity. The split could not be concealed once the new Europe was asked to tackle matters of "high politics"—i.e., go beyond the purely internal economic problems of little impact or dependence on relations with America.[14] It is therefore no surprise that this split should have disrupted unification in 1953–54, when the problem of German rearmament was raised, and in 1962–68, when de Gaulle challenged the United States across the globe.[15]

This is how the diversity of national situations operated. First, it produced (and produces) a basic division between nations I would call resigned, and nations I would call resisters. The resigned ones included the smaller countries, aware of their weakness, realizing that the Soviet threat could not be met by Europeans alone, accustomed to dependence on external protectors, grateful to America for the unique features of its protection, and looking forward to an important role for Europe but not in the realm of high politics. In the past, Italy had tried to act as a great power without protectors, but those days were over, and acceptance of American hegemony gave the creaky Italian political system a kind of double cushion—against the threat of communism, and also against the need to spend too much energy and money on rearmament. For the smaller states as well as for Italy, acceptance of U.S. hegemony was like an insurance policy which protected them against having to give priority to foreign affairs. Germany, on the other hand, accepted dependence on the United States not merely as a comfort, but as a necessity as vital as breathing. West Germany's geographical position put it on the front line, its partition contributed to making security a supreme goal, the stanch anticommunism of its leadership ruled out any search for security along the lines of neutrality. There followed not only acceptance of American leadership but also a wish to do everything possible to tie the United States to Western Europe. Gaining equality with other nations was another vital goal for Germany, and it could be reached only through cooperation with the most powerful of the occupying forces. Defeat, division, and danger conspired to make West Germany switch from its imperialistic nationalism of the Nazi era to a dependence which was apparently submissive, yet also productive (of security and status gains) under Adenauer.

As for the resisters, they, like the West Germans, gave priority to foreign affairs—but not in the same perspective. The French reading of geography and history was different.[16] To be sure, the French saw the need for security against the Soviet Union, but the "tyranny of the cold war" operated differently in France. French feelings of hostility toward Russia were much more moderate than in Germany, and, although it may be too strong to speak of a nostalgia for the wartime Grand Alliance, it is not false to say that hope of an ultimate détente allowing for European reunification, a return of the Russians to moderation, and an emancipation of the continent from its "two hegemonies" never died. The French time perspective has consistently differed from, say, the German: the urgency of the Soviet threat never overshadowed the desire for, and belief in, a less tense international system. Whereas West Germany's continuity with its past was wrecked and repudiated, France (like Britain) looked back to the days when Europe held the center of the stage and forward to a time when Europe might again be an actor, not a stake: the anomaly was the present, not the past. Also, on colonial matters, France (more than Britain) often found little to distinguish America's reprobation from Soviet hostility. And France worried not only about possible Soviet thrusts but also about Germany's potential threats: the fearful anticipation of a reborn German national consciousness and nationalism has marked all French leaders. An additional reason for dreading the perpetuation of American hegemony and the freezing of the cold war was the fear that such a course would make Germany the main beneficiary of America's favors. Germany looked East with some terror, but there was only one foe there; when the French looked East, they saw two nations to fear; each could be used as an ally against the other—but for the time being the Soviet danger was the greater, and if Germany was built up too much against Russia, the security gained in one respect would be compromised in another.[17]

The diversity of national situations also operated in another way. As I have suggested, situations limit and affect but do not command choices. A general desire for overcoming the cold war and American hegemony did not make for a general agreement on how to do so. What I have called the resisters were divided, and this division became decisive. If all the resisters had calculated that the best way to reach France's objectives was the construction of a powerful West European entity which could rival U.S. might, turn the bipolar contest into a triangle, and wrest advantages from both Russia and America, the "ambiguity" of the movement (between resigned *and* resisting forces) might not have damaged the enterprise until much later. But those who reasoned along the lines just described— like Jean Monnet—were sharply divided from those who feared that a sacrifice of national sovereignty to supranational institutions might entail loss of control over the direction of the European undertaking. Two kinds of people took this second line: the nationalists who were still eager to preserve all the resources of French diplomacy and strategy, in order, in the present, to concentrate on overseas fronts and, later, to promote whatever policies would be required, rather than let a foreign body decide; and, on the other hand, men like Mendès-France, who were not nationalists in the sense I use the term in this chapter, but who thought that the continental European construction was not France's best way of coping with her situation, who thought priority should be given to the search for a détente, the liberalization of the empire, the reform of the economy.[18]

The success of the European movement required, first, that those suspicious of European integration remain a minority—not only throughout the six nations but in their leadership, not only in the parliaments but above all in the executive branches. This requirement was met in 1950–53 and in 1955–58, but not in the crucial months for EDC in 1953–54, and no longer after 1958. The movement proceeded after 1958 in a dialectic of ambiguity. However, there was a second requirement for success: that the "minute of truth"—when the European elites would have to ask about the ultimate political direction of their community—be postponed as long as possible; i.e., that the cold war remain sufficiently intense to impose even on the "resisters" priority for the kind of security that presupposed U.S. protection—priority for the *urgent* over the *long-term important.* But this requirement was shaken during the brief period of nervous demobilization that followed Stalin's death in 1953–54, and then was gradually undermined by a third basic feature in Europe's postwar situation. Before we turn to it, one remark must be made: in French foreign policy, "resistance by European integration" prevailed over "resistance by self-reliance" only so long as France was bogged down in colonial wars; it was this important and purely French element in France's national situation whose ups and downs affected quite decisively the method of "resistance."[19]

The divisions and contradictions described above were sharpened by a third common feature which emerged in the mid-1950s and whose effects developed progressively: the nuclear stalemate between the United States and the Soviet Union. The effect of the "balance of terror" on the Western Alliance has been analyzed so often and well[20] that nothing needs to be added here; still, we might usefully inquire how Europe's gradual discovery of the uncertainties of America's nuclear protection affected the other factors we have discussed above.

The first thing we can say is that the nuclear balance of terror worsened the split between French "resistance" and West German "resignation." The dominant political elites in West Germany thought it merely added urgency to their previous calculation of interest. From the West German position, the nuclear stalemate was thought to increase the danger for the West: the United States was relatively weaker, the Soviet Union stronger and more of a threat. Indeed, the Social Democrats switched from their increasingly furtive thoughts of neutrality to outright endorsement of the Christian Democratic support of NATO. If America's nuclear monopoly was broken, if America's guarantee was weakened, West Germany needed a policy that was respectful enough of the United States' main concerns, so that the United States would feel obligated to keep its mantle of protection over West Germany and not be tempted into negotiating a détente at its expense. West German docility would be the condition for, and counterpart of, American entanglement in Europe. The West German reaction to a development that (if General Gallois' logic were followed) might lead to the prevalence of "polycentrism" over bipolarity was to search for ways of exorcising the former and preserving the latter. On the whole, the smaller nations and Italy, while not at all fearful about the consequences of polycentrism (quite the contrary), were nevertheless not shaken out of their "resignation." The mere appearance of parity of nuclear peril was not enough to make them eager or able to give priority to an activist foreign policy.

In France, the balance of terror reinforced the attitude of resistance. The goal of emancipation now became a real possibility. A superpower stalemate meant increased security for the lesser powers: however much they might complain about the decrease of American protection, there was a heightened feeling of protection against war in general. What the West Germans saw as a liability, the French considered an opportunity. West Germany's situation, and its low national consciousness, induced most German leaders to choose what might be called a "minimizing" interpretation of the new situation. France's situation—its high national consciousness and, after 1958, Gaullist doctrine—induced French political elites to choose a "maximizing" interpretation. They believed that the increasing costs of the use of nuclear force made actual use less likely, U.S. protection less certain but also less essential Europe's recovery of not merely wealth but power more desirable and possible. This recovery of power would help bring about the much desired prevalence of polycentrism over bipolarity.[21]

As this feud shows, the balance of terror heightened the division over method among the "resisters." On one hand, it provided new arguments for those who thought that emancipation could be achieved only by uniting Western Europe; that individual national efforts would be too ridiculously weak to amount to anything but a waste in resources; but that a collective effort could exploit the new situation and make Western Europe a true partner of the United States. On the other hand, those who feared that the "united way" could become a frustrating deviation reasoned that the theory of graduated deterrence justified the acquisition of nuclear weapons by a middle-size power with limited resources and that this acquisition would considerably increase the political influence and prestige of the nation. The increased costs of force ruled out, in any case, what in the past had been the most disastrous effect of the mushrooming of sovereign states—a warlike, expansionist nationalism—but they simultaneously made the value of small- or middle-size nations good again. According to this argument, the "united way" would be a dead end, since some, and not exactly the least significant, of the associates had no desire for collective European power at the possible expense of American protection.

Until the nuclear stalemate became a fact of European life, opposition to a supranational West European entity had come only from a fraction of the "resisters." In the early 1950s the United States had strongly—too strongly—urged the establishment of a European defense system, for it had not been considered likely to challenge America's own military predominance. In the 1960s the United States no longer urged the West Europeans to build such a system. American leadership developed a deep concern for maintaining centralized control over NATO forces, i.e., for preserving bipolarity, and a growing realization that Europe's appetite would not stop short of nuclear weapons. As a result, some of the "resigned ones," instead of endorsing European integration unreservedly, for the first time now showed themselves of two minds: they were willing to pursue integration in economic and social fields, but less so in matters of defense, lest NATO be weakened. It is significant that the Dutch resisted de Gaulle's efforts in 1960–62 to include defense in a confederal scheme, and that West German leaders put some hopes in the MLF—a scheme that would have tied European nations one by one to the United States—rather than in a revised and revived EDC. Inevitably, such mental reservations of those who had been among the champions of supranationality could only confirm the suspicions of "resisters" who had distrusted the "Monnet method" from the beginning. Thus, the national situation of West Germany in particular—a situation in which the U.S. policy of reliance on West Germany as an anchor for U.S. influence on the continent played an important part—damaged the European movement: West German leaders were largely successful in their drive to entangle the United States but found that the price they had to pay was a decreasing ability to push for European integration. European integration and dependence on the United States were no longer automatically compatible.

This long discussion of the different responses to common situations has been necessary as an antidote to the usual way of discussing European integration, which has focused on process. The self-propelling power of the unifying process is severely constrained by the associates' views on ends and means. In order to go "beyond the nation-state," one must do more than set up procedures in adequate "background" and "process conditions." A procedure is not a purpose, a process is not a policy.

III

Still, since the process of European integration is its most original feature, we must examine it, too.[22] We have been witnessing a kind of race between the logic of integration set up by Monnet (analyzed by Haas) and the logic of diversity (analyzed above). According to the former, the double pressure of necessity (the interdependence of the European social fabric, which will oblige statesmen to integrate even sectors originally left uncoordinated) and of men (the action of the supranational agents) will gradually restrict the national governments' freedom of movement. In such a milieu, nationalism will become a futile and anachronistic exercise, and the national consciousness itself will, so to speak, be impregnated with an awareness of the higher interest in union. The logic of diversity, by contrast, sets limits on the degree to which the "spill-over" process can curtail the governments' freedom of action; it restricts to the area of welfare the domain in which the logic of functional integration can operate; indeed, insofar as discrepancies in other areas prevail, even issues belonging in the area of welfare may become infected by the disharmony, because of the links that exist among all areas. The logic of integration is that of a blender which crunches up the most diverse products, replacing their different tastes and perfumes with one, presumably delicious juice. One expects a finer synthesis: ambiguity helps because each "ingredient" can hope that its taste will predominate at the end. The logic of diversity is the opposite: it suggests that, in areas of key importance to the national interest, nations prefer the self-controlled uncertainty of national self-reliance, to the uncontrolled uncertainty of the blending process; ambiguity carries one only part of the way. The logic of integration assumes that it is possible to fool each one of the associates some of the time because his over-all gain will still exceed his occasional losses, even if his calculations turn out wrong here or there. The logic of diversity implies that losses on one vital issue are not compensated for by gains on other issues (especially not on other less vital issues): nobody wants to be fooled. The logic of integration regards the uncertainties of the supranational function process as creative; the logic of diversity sees them as destructive past a certain threshold. Ambiguity lures and lulls the national consciousness into integration as long as the benefits are high, the costs low, the expectations considerable. Ambiguity may arouse and stiffen national consciousness into nationalism if the benefits are low, the losses high, the hopes dashed or deferred. Functional integration's gamble could be won only if the method had sufficient potency to promise a permanent excess of gains over losses, and of hopes over frustrations. Theoretically, this may be true of economic integration. It is not true of political integration (in the sense of "high politics").

The success of the approach symbolized by Monnet depended, and depends still, on his winning a triple gamble: on goals, on methods, on results. As for goals, it is a gamble on the possibility of substituting motion as an end in itself, for agreement on ends. It is a fact that Europe's transnational integrationist elites did not agree on whether the object of the community-building enterprise ought to be a new superstate—i.e., a federal potential nation, à la U.S.A.—or whether the object was to demonstrate that power politics could be overcome in cooperation and compromise, that one could build a radically new kind of unit, change the nature and not merely the scale of the game. Monnet himself was ambiguous on this score; Walter Hallstein leaned in the first direction, many of Monnet's public relations men in the second.[23] Nor did the integrationists agree on whether the main goal was to create a regional "security-community,"[24] i.e., to pacify a former hotbed of wars, or to create an entity whose position and strength could decisively affect the cold war in particular and international relations in general. Now, it is perfectly possible for a movement to use its continental nationalists as well as its antipower idealists, its inward-looking and outward-looking politicians—but only as long as there is no need to make a choice. Decisions on tariffs do not require such choices. Decisions on agriculture begin to raise basic problems of orientation. Decisions on foreign policy and membership and defense cannot be reached unless the goals are clarified, nor can decisions on monetary union (past the first stage of narrowing fluctuations between currencies). One cannot be all things to all people all of the time.

As for methods, there was a gamble that supranational functionalism would irresistibly rise. Monnet assumed, first, that national sovereignty, already devalued by events, could be chewed up leaf by leaf like an artichoke. He assumed, second, that the dilemma of the West European governments—having to choose between an integration that tied their hands and stopping a movement that benefited their people—could be exploited in favor of integration by men representing the common good, endowed with superior expertise, initiative, deadlines, and package deals. Finally, he assumed that this approach would take into account the interests of the greater powers and prevent the crushing of the smaller ones. The troubles with this gamble have been numerous. Even an artichoke has a heart, and it remains intact after the leaves have been eaten. It is of course true that successful economic and social integration in Western Europe would considerably limit the freedom governments continued to enjoy (in theory) in diplomacy and strategy, but why should one assume that they would not be aware of it? As the artichoke is slowly eaten, the governments become ever more vigilant. To be sure, their dilemma suggests that they might not do anything about it: they would be powerless to save the heart. But this would be true only if governments never put what they consider essential interests of the nation above the particular interest of certain categories of nationals, if superior expertise were always either a supranational monopoly or the solution of an issue at hand, if package deals were effective in every argument, and, above all, if the governments' representatives were always determined to behave in an EEC way, rather than as agents of states that are unwilling to accept a supranational community whatever the conditions. Functional integration may indeed give lasting satisfaction to the smaller powers precisely because it is for them that the ratio of "welfare politics" to high politics is highest, and that the chance of gaining benefits through intergovernmental methods that reflect rather than correct the power differential between the big and the small is poorest. But this is also why the method is not likely à la longue to satisfy the bigger powers as much: facing them, the supranational civil servants, for all their skill and legal powers, are a bit like Jonahs trying to turn whales into jellyfish. Of course, the idea is ultimately to move from an administrative procedure, in which supranational civil servants enter a dialogue with national ministers, to a truly federal procedure in which a federal cabinet is responsible to a federal parliament; but what is thus presented as linear progress may turn out to be a vicious circle, since the ministers hold the key to the transformation, and may refuse it unless the goals are defined and the results already achieved are satisfactory.

There was a gamble about results as well. The experience of European integration would mean net benefits for all and bring about progress toward community formation. Progress could be measured by the following yardsticks: in the realm of interstate relations, an increasing transfer of power to new common agencies, and the prevalence of solutions "upgrading the common interest" over other kinds of compromises; in the realm of transnational society, an increasing flow of communications; in the area of national consciousness (which is important both for interstate relations, since it may limit the statesmen's discretion, and for transnational society, because it affects the scope and meaning of the communications), an increasing compatibility of views about external issues. The results achieved in Western Europe so far are mixed: dubious on the last count, positive (but not unlimited) on the second, and marked on the first by unexpected features. There was some strengthening of the authority of the EEC Commission until 1965, and in various areas there was some "upgrading of common interests." On the other hand, the Commission's unfortunate attempt to consolidate those gains at de Gaulle's expense in the spring of 1965 brought about a startling setback for the whole enterprise; in their negotiations, the members have conspicuously failed to find a common interest in some vital areas (energy, transport, industrial and investment policies), and sometimes reached apparently "integrating" decisions only after the most ungainly, traditional kind of bargaining, in which such uncommunity-like methods as threats, ultimatums, and retaliatory moves were used. In other words, either the ideal was not reached, or it was reached in a way that was its opposite and its destroyer. If we look at the institutions of the Common Market as an incipient political system for Europe, we find that their authority is limited, their structure weak, their popular base restricted and distant.[25]

It is therefore not surprising if the uncertainty about results already achieved contributes to uncertainty about future prospects. The divisions among partisans of integration make it hard to predict where the "Monnet method" will lead if the process were to continue along the lines so fondly planned by the French *"in-spirateur."* Will the enterprise become an effective federation, or will it become a mere façade behind which all the divergences and rivalries continue to be played out? It was nonetheless remarkable that Guallist and American fears should converge in one respect: de Gaulle consistently warned that applying the supranational method to the area of high politics would dilute national responsibility in a way that would benefit only the United States; incapable of defining a coherent policy, the "technocrats" would leave vital decisions to the United States, at least by default. On the contrary, many Americans have come to believe on the basis of some of the EEC's actions in agriculture and trade that a united Europe would be able to challenge U.S. leadership much more effectively than the separate European states ever could. The truth of the matter is that nobody knows: a method is not a policy, a process is not a direction; the results achieved so far are too specialized and the way in which they have been reached is too bumpy to allow one to extrapolate and project safely. The face of a united Europe has not begun to emerge; there are just a few lines, but one does not know whether the supranational technique would finally give Western Europe the features of a going concern or those of a Fourth Republic writ large—the ambitions of a world power or the complacency of parochialism. The range of possibilities is so broad, the alternatives are so extreme, that the more the Six, and now the Nine, move into the stormy waters of high politics, the less they, and outside powers such as the United States that may be affected by their acts, are willing to extend the credit of hope and to make new wagers: neither Gaullist France nor America has been willing to risk a major loss of control. Contrary to the French proverb, in the process of functional integration, only the first steps do not cost much.

Two important general lessons can be drawn from a study of the process of integration. The first concerns the limits of the functional method: its relative success in the relatively painless area where it works relatively well lifts the participants of EEC to a new level of issues where the method does not work well any more—like swimmers whose skill at moving quickly away from the shore brings them to a point where the waters are stormy and deep, at a time when fatigue is setting in, and none of the questions about ultimate goal, direction, or endurance has been answered. The functional process was used in order to "make Europe"; once Europe began being made, the question had to be asked: "Making Europe, what for?" The process is like a grinder, a machine that works only when someone keeps giving it something to grind. When the members of EEC start quarreling and stop providing, the machine stops. For a while, the machine worked because the European governments poured into it a common determination to integrate their economies in order to maximize wealth. But with their wealth increasing, the question of what to do with it was bound to arise: a capability of supplying means does not *ipso facto* provide the ends, and it is about the ends that quarrels broke out. Each member state is willing to live with the others, but not on terms too different from his own; and the Nine are not in the position of the three miserable prisoners of *No Exit.* Transforming a dependent "subsystem" proved to be one thing; defining its relations to all other subsystems and to the international system in general has turned out to be quite another.

The model of functional integration—a substitute for the kind of instant federation that governments had not been prepared to accept—shows its origins in important respects. It is essentially an administrative model, which relies on bureaucratic expertise to promote a policy that political decision-makers are technically incapable of shaping (something like French planning under the Fourth Republic). The hope was that in the interstices of political bickering the administrators could build up a consensus, but it was a mistake to believe that a formula that works well within certain limits is a panacea—and that even within the limits of "welfare politics" administrative skill can always overcome the disastrous effects of political paralysis or mismanagement. Moreover, the model assumes that the basic political decisions, to be prepared and pursued by EEC civil servants but formally made by the governments, would be reached through a process of short-term bargaining, by politicians whose mode of operation is empirical muddling through of the kind that puts immediate advantages above long-term pursuits. This model corresponds well to the reality of parliamentary politics with a weak executive branch—for example, the politics of the Fourth Republic—but it was a mistake to believe that all political regimes would conform to this rather sorry image, and to ignore the disastrous results that the original example produced whenever conflicts over values and fundamental choices made mere empirical groping useless or worse than useless.[26]

The second lesson we should draw from the origin of the integration model is even more discouraging for advocates of functionalism. To revert to the analogy of the grinder, what happened in 1965 was that the machine, piqued by the slowing down of supply, suddenly suggested to its users that in the future the supplying of material to be ground be left to the machine. Bureaucratic institutions tend to become actors with a stake in their own survival and expansion. The same thing happens often enough within a state whose political system is ineffective. But here we are dealing not with one but with several political systems, and the reason for the relative ineffectiveness of the EEC's Council of Ministers may be the excessive toughness, not weakness, of the national political systems involved. In other words, by trying to be a force, the bureaucracy here, inevitably, turns into a factor that the nations try to control or at least affect. A new complication is thus added to all the substantive issues that divide the participants. Thus, the agricultural problem could have been solved "technically," since the governments had previously reached basic compromises, and had more or less agreed on the relations between Common Market and outside agriculture. But the way these accords were reached left scars, and the nature of the agreement meant a victory for one state (France) over another (West Germany). The whole issue was reopened, due not to the states' but to the Commission's initiative. In the crisis of 1965, the Commission's overly bold proposal for a common agricultural policy (along pro-French lines) *cum* supranationality (against French determination) did allow some of the Six, hostile in fact to the substantive proposals, to endorse the Commission's plan and stand up as champions of supranationality, while knowing that the French would block the scheme; the French, eager to get their partners committed to a protected agricultural market, preferred to postpone the realization of this goal rather than let the Commission's autonomy grow, and used the Commission's rashness as a pretext for trying to kill supranationality altogether; and the West German government, not too kindly disposed toward the Commission whose initiatives and economic inspiration were hardly in line with Erhard's views, found itself defending it (its head, now under French attack, was a German). To be sure, the Commission's dilemma had become acute: either its members resigned themselves to being merely patient brokers to their quarreling clients, and letting them set the pace; or else they tried to behave according to the ideal type of the Monnet method *and* as if a genuine community had already been established. But if prudence meant sluggishness, anticipation meant delay. Since 1965, all the important issues—including Britain's entry—have been hammered out between governments. The Commission has been discreet. This has not ended the arguments about the need for "stronger" institutions. Haggling about the kind of machinery one wants is a polite method for appearing to want to keep working together, while disagreeing completely on what one wants the machinery for.

IV

We must come now to the balance sheet of the "European experiment." The most visible result is the survival of Europe's nations. To be sure, they survive transformed: swept by the "age of mass consumption," caught in an apparently inexorable process of industrialization, urbanization, and democratization, they become more alike in social structure, in economic and social policies, even in physical appearance; there is a spectacular break between the past, which so many monuments bring to constant memory, and a rationalized future that puts them closer to American industrial society than to the issues of their own history. These similarities are promoted by the Common Market itself. It is of no mean consequence that the prospect of a collapse of the EEC should bring anguish to various interest groups, some of which fought its establishment: the transnational linkages of businessmen and farmers are part of the transformation. And no West European nation is a world power any longer in the traditional sense—i.e., in the sense either of having physical establishments backed by military might in various parts of the globe, or of possessing in Europe armed forces superior to those of any non-European power.

And yet they survive as nations. In foreign affairs and defense, not only has power not been transferred to European organs but France has actually taken power away from NATO. Differences in the calculations of national interest broadened with the advent of the balance of terror, as I have already argued. Even when, after 1968, these calculations came closer, they converged on avoiding rather than promoting foreign and defense policies: Brandt's Bonn has wanted to avoid upsetting Washington or Moscow; Pompidou had decided to lift the European car out of the bog by no longer raising the issues that had, with de Gaulle at the wheel, stuck it there. Paradoxically, the post-Czechoslovakia rapprochement in the *Ostpolitiken* of Paris, London, and Bonn has not brought about much of a "spill-over" into European political cooperation. Policies toward the United States have remained different, and even the *Ostpolitiken* are not identical. A common inability to affect the superpowers' détente or their rivalry in the Middle East has not been translated into a common stand either on force reductions (or build-up) or on oil-sharing. As for intra-European communications, the indubitably solid economic network of the EEC has not been complemented by a network of social and cultural communications; the links between some European societies and the United States are stronger than the links among them. Even in the realm of economic relations, the Common Market for goods has not been complemented by a system of pan-West European enterprises: firms that are unable to compete with rivals in the EEC often associate with American firms rather than merge with their European rivals; or else the mergers are between national firms and help to build up national monopolies. Finally, European statesmen express views about external issues that often appear to reflect and support their divergent definitions of the national interest; or, while superficially favorable to "Europe," they fail to show any active enthusiasm or great passion.[27] There is no common European outlook. Nor is there a common *projet*, a common conception of Europe's role in world affairs or Europe's possible contribution to the solution of problems characteristic of all industrial societies.

To some extent, the obstacles lie in the present condition of national consciousness. In two respects, similarities have emerged in recent years. There has been a rebirth of German national consciousness, largely because the bold attempt at fastening Germany's shattered consciousness directly to a new European one did not succeed: the existence of a West German national situation gradually reawakened a German national awareness, and reduced the gap between West Germany and France in this area. Moreover, the national consciences in Western Europe are alike in one sense: they are not like Rousseau's general will, a combination of mores and moves that define the purposes of the national community with intellectual clarity and emotional involvement. Today's national consciousness in Europe is negative rather than positive. There is still, in each nation, a *"vouloir-vivre collectif."* But it is not a "daily plebiscite" *for* something. It is, in some parts, a daily routine, a community based on habit rather than on common tasks, an identity that is received rather than shaped. Thus West Germany's sense of "cohesion and distinctiveness" is the result of the survival and recovery of a

West German state in a world of nations rather than a specific willed set of imperatives. In other parts, national consciousness is a daily refusal rather than a daily creation, a desire to preserve a certain heritage (however waning, and less because it is meaningful today than because it is one's own) rather than a determination to define a common destiny, an identity that is hollow rather than full, and marked more by bad humor toward foreign influences than by any positive contribution.

To be sure, negative or hollow national consciousness need not be a liability for the champions of integration: general wills à la Rousseau could function as obstacles to any fusion of sovereignty. But a patriotic consciousness that survives in a kind of nonpurposive complacency can be a drag on any policy: it does not carry statesmen forward in the way an intense and positive "general will" prods leaders who act on behalf of national goals, or in the way in which European federalists have sometimes hoped that enlightened national patriotisms would encourage Europe's leaders to build a new European community. The French may not have a sense of national purpose, but, precisely because their patriotism has been tested so often and so long, because pressures from the outside world have continued throughout the postwar era to batter their concerns and their conceits, and because modernization, now accepted and even desired, also undermines their cherished traditional values and their still enforced traditional authority patterns, French national consciousness resists any suggestion of abdication, resignation, *repli*. (So much so that the "Europeans" themselves have presented European integration as an opportunity for getting French views shared by others instead of stressing the "community" side of the enterprise.[28]) West Germany's national consciousness, on the other hand, is marked by a genuine distaste for or timidity toward what might be called the power activities of a national community on the world stage; hence the West Germans tend to shy away from the problems of "high politics" which a united Europe would have to face and avoidance of which only delays unity; a tendency, at first, to refuse to make policy choices and, later, to pretend (to oneself and to others) that no such choices are required, that there is no incompatibility between a "European Europe" and an Atlantic partnership and a reconciliation with the East. In one case, a defensive excess of self-confidence makes unity on terms other than one's own difficult; in the other case, an equally defensive lack of self-confidence projects into the foreign undertakings of the nation and weakens the foundations of the common European enterprise.

And yet, if the "national consciousness" of each European nation could be isolated from all other elements of the national situation, one would, I think, conclude that the main reasons for the endurance of the nation-state lie elsewhere.

They lie, first of all, in the differences in national situations, exacerbated by the interaction between each of the West European member states and the present international system. Earlier, we looked at specific instances of such differences; let us return to them in a more analytic way. One part of each national situation is the purely *domestic* component. In a modern nation-state, the importance of the political system—in the triple sense of functional scope, authority, and popular basis—is a formidable obstacle to integration. It is easier to overcome the parochialism of a political system with only a slender administrative structure, than it is to dismantle a political system which rests on "socially mobilized" and mobilizing parties and pressure groups, and which handles an enormous variety of social and economic services with a huge bureaucracy. To be sure, it was Monnet's hope and tactic to dismantle the fortress by redirecting the allegiance of parties and pressure groups toward the new central institutions of Europe, by endowing the latter with the ability to compete with the national governments in setting up social services. In other words, the authority of the new European political system would deepen as its scope broadened and its popular basis expanded. The success of this attempt to dry up the national ponds by diverting their waters into a new, supranational pool depended on three prerequisites which have not been met: with respect to popular basis, the prevalence of parties and pressure groups over executive branches; with respect to scope, the self-sustaining and expanding capacity of the new central bureaucracy; with respect to both scope and popular basis, the development of transnational political issues of interest to all political forces and peoples across boundary lines.

The executive establishment of the modern political state has one remarkable feature: it owes much of its legitimacy and power to the support of popularly based parties and pressure groups, but it also enjoys a degree of autonomy that allows it to resist pressures, manipulate opposition, manufacture support. Even the weak Fourth Republic evaded pressure toward "transnationalism" and diluted the dose of "bargaining politics" along supranational lines. Even the EEC civil servants' careers are made and unmade in national capitals. Above all, each nation's political life continues to be dominated by "parochial" issues: each political system is like a thermos bottle that keeps the liquid inside warm, or lukewarm. It is as if, for the mythical common man, the nation-state were still the most satisfying—indeed, the most rewarding—form of social organization in existence.[29] If we look at the states' behavior, we find that each reacted to the transnational forces that vitiated its autonomy by trying to tighten control on what was left. Multinational enterprises erase borders, but research, development, and technology, far from being "Europeanized," have been nationalized. The growing similarity and interdependence of West European industrial societies have not led to political integration. Indeed, insofar as all of them have become the scene of constant, often unruly group bargaining—what Raymond Aron has termed the politics of querulous satisfaction—their ability to divert attention to integration has been small. And, within the EEC's institutions, empirical muddling through—the political mode of operation of such societies—has been powerless to overcome paralysis whenever the members were divided (industrial and energy policy, social and regional policy, space, control of foreign investments) or to allow for the drastic revision of policies which incremental adjustments cannot save (agriculture).

The European political process has never come close to resembling that of any West European democracy because it has been starved of common and distinctive European issues. If we look at the issues that have dominated European politics, we find two distinct categories. One is that of problems peculiar to each nation—Italy's battle of Reds vs. Blacks, or its concern for the Mezzogiorno; Belgium's linguistic clashes; West Germany's "social economy" and liquidation of the past; France's postwar constitutional troubles and party splintering, later the nature and future of Gaullist presidentialism and the fall-out from May 1968. Here, whatever the transnational party and interest-group alignments in the EEC, the dominant motifs have been purely national. The other category of issues are international ones (including European unity). But here, the *external* components of each national situation have thwarted the emergence of a common European political system comparable to that of each nation. Here, the weight of geography and history—a history of nations—has kept the nation-states in their watertight compartments.

It is no accident if France, the initiator of the European-unity process, has also been its chief troublemaker; for by reason of history and geography France's position differed from everyone else's in the Community (and was actually closer to Britain's). For West Germany, integration meant a leap from opprobrium and impotence to respectability and equal rights; for the smaller powers, it meant exchanging a very modest dose of autonomy for participation in a potentially strong and rich grouping. France could not help being much more ambivalent, for integration meant on one hand an avenue for leadership and the shaping of a powerful bloc, but, on the other, the acceptance of permanent restrictions on French autonomy. A once-great power inherits from its past a whole set of habits and reflexes that make it conduct policy as if it were still or could become again a great power (unless those habits and reflexes have been smashed, as Germany's were). In other words, integration meant an almost certain improvement in the national situation of the other five nations; but for France it could be a deterioration or an adventure.[30] There is no better example here than the issue of nuclear weapons. Integration in nuclear matters meant, for France, giving up the possibility of having a nuclear force of her own, perhaps never being certain that a united Europe would create a common nuclear deterrent, at best contributing to a European nuclear force that would put West Germany in the same position as France. But the French decision to pursue the logic of diversity, while giving her her own nuclear force, also made a European nuclear solution more difficult and increased France's distance from West Germany. Moreover, a geographical difference corroborated the historical one: France had lasting colonial involvements. Not only did they intensify national consciousness; they also contributed to France's ambivalence toward European integration. The worse France's overseas plight became, the more European integration was preached as a kind of compensatory mechanism. But this meant that European integration had to be given a "national" rather than a "supranational" color; it meant that the French tried to tie their European partners to France's overseas concerns, much against these partners' better judgment; above all, it meant that there was a competition for public attention and for official energies between the European and overseas components of French foreign affairs. The great-power reflex and the colonial legacy combined in a policy of cooperation with France's former imperial possessions despite the cost; overseas cooperation is presented as a policy that has transfigured the colonial legacy and that manifests the great-power reflex.[31]

Thus, national situations multiplied the effects of differences among the various national consciences. But the endurance of the nation-state in France is due also to a revival of nationalism. Even without de Gaulle, the differences analyzed above would have slowed down European integration; but his personal contribution to the crisis of integration was enormous. Not only did he raise questions that were inescapable in the long run but he tried to impose his own answers. De Gaulle changed French policy from ambivalence toward supranational integration to outright hostility; from a reluctance to force the European states to dispel the ambiguities of "united Europe" to an almost gleeful determination to bring out differences into the open. De Gaulle also changed the national situations of the others, which sharpened antagonisms and led to a kind of cumulative retreat from integration.

It is true that the General was an empiricist, and that his analysis of the European situation was to a large extent irrefutable. What could be more sensible than staring from what exists (the nation-states), refusing to act as if what does not yet exist (a united Europe) were already established? But pragmatism is always at the service of ends, explicit or not. (The definition of a bad foreign policy could be: a foreign policy that uses rigid means at the service of explicit ends, or whose flexible means do not serve clearly-thought-out ends.) De Gaulle's empiricism was a superb display of skill, but on behalf of a thoroughly nonempirical doctrine. It is obvious that his distrust of supranational integration, perfectly comprehensible as a starting point, nevertheless resulted in a kind of freezing of integration and perpetuation of the nation-state. If his chief foreign-policy objective had been the creation of a European entity acting as a world power, his "empirical" *starting point* would have been a most unrealistic *method*. But it was not his supreme objective, and Europe not his supreme value.

De Gaulle's doctrine was a "universalist nationalism." That is, he saw France's mission as world-wide, not local and defensive; but this meant that Europe was just one corner of the tapestry; a means, not an end. "Things being what they are," it is better to have separate nation-states than it is to have a larger entity; while the latter could undoubtedly act better as a forceful competitor in the world's contests, it would have to be coherent to do so, and it was more likely to be incoherent, given the divisions of its members and the leverage interested outsiders possess over some of the insiders. The size of the unit was less important than its "cohesion and distinctiveness," for effectiveness is not merely a function of material resources: if the unit has no capacity to turn resources to action, the only beneficiaries are its rivals. In a contest with giants, a confident David is better than a disturbed Goliath. This is a choice that reflects a doctrine; de Gaulle's refusal to gamble on European unity went along with a willingness to gamble on the continuing potency of the French nation-state. Joseph Schumpeter defined imperialism as an objectless quest; de Gaulle's nationalism was a kind of permanent quest with varying content but never any other cause than itself.

Every great leader has his built-in flaw, since this is a world where roses have thorns. De Gaulle's was the self-fulfilling prophecy. Distrustful of any Europe but his own, his acts made Europe anything but his. Here we must turn to the effect of his policy on France's partners. First of all, there was a matter of style. Wanting European cooperation, not integration, de Gaulle refused to treat the Community organs as Community organs; but, wanting to force is views about cooperation on nations still attached to the goal of integration, he paradoxically had to try to achieve cooperation for a common policy in a way that smacked of conflict, not cooperation, of unilateralism, not compromise. Thus we witnessed not just a retreat from the Monnet method to, say, the kind of intergovernmental cooperation that marks the Organization for Economic Cooperation and Development (OECD), but to a kind of grand strategy of nonmilitary conflict, a kind of political cold war of maneuver and "chicken." With compromises wrested by ultimatums, concessions obtained not through package deals but under the threat of boycotts, it is not surprising if even the Commission ended by playing the General's game instead of turning whatever cheek was left. Its spring 1965 agricultural plan was as outright a challenge to de Gaulle as his veto of January 1963 had been an affront to the Community spirit. Just as de Gaulle had tried to force West Germany to sacrifice her farmers to the idea of a European entity, the Commission tried to call his bluff by forcing him to choose between French farmers' interests and the French national interest in a "European Europe" for agriculture, on one hand, and his own hostility to supranationality and the French national interest in the free use of French resources, on the other. Playing his game, the Commission also played into his hands, allowing him to apply the Schelling tactic of "if you do not do what I ask, I will blow my brains out on your new suit," and in the end buying his return at the price of a sacrifice of integration.[32] In other words, he forced each member state to treat the EEC no longer as an end in itself; and he drove even its constituted bodies to bringing grist to his mill.

But de Gaulle's effect on his partners was a matter of policy as well. Here we must examine Franco-German relations. Had West Germany been willing to follow France, he would have given priority to the construction of a "half-Europe" that would thereafter have been a magnet (as well as a guarantee of German harmlessness) to the East. West Germany's refusal led him to put a "Europe from the Atlantic to the Urals" on the same plane as a "European Europe" in the West; for the containment of West Germany, no longer assured in a disunited Western Europe of the Six, could still be gotten in a larger framework. The implications were important. First, there was a considerable change in West Germany's national situation. Whereas for more than fifteen years the United States and France tacitly carried out Robert Schuman's recommendation—"never leave Germany to herself"—the Franco-American competition for German support, the Gaullist refusal to tie West Germany to France in a federal Europe (so to speak, for the knot's sake), and America's disastrous emulation of the sorcerer's apprentice in titillating German interest in nuclear strategy or weapons-sharing, had all been factors that loosened the bonds between Germany and the West. Consequently, the domestic component of West Germany's national situation was also affected. Still concerned with security as well as with German reunification, but less and less able to believe that loyalty to their allies would deliver all the goods, the West German leaders and elites felt less dependent and constrained. Of course, objectively, the external constraints remain compelling. But de Gaulle's effect on Germany was, if not a rebirth of German nationalism, at least a change in the situation that gives national German action some chances. The temptation to use economic power to reach one's goals and the example of one's allies competing for accommodation with one's foe could not be resisted forever, especially when the past was full of precedents. To be sure, a nationalist Germany may well find itself as unable to shake the walls or to escape through the bars as Gaullist France was unable to forge the "European Europe." But the paradox of a revisionist France, trying to change the international system to her advantage despite her complete lack of "traditional" grievances (lost territories, military discrimination, and so forth), and a Germany with many grievances behaving in fact like a *status quo* power, could not last forever. The result, after 1969, was a West German *Ostpolitik* that followed France's example and solemnly acknowledged the inviolability of the *status quo*, yet in so doing asserted Bonn's right to an independent foreign policy. Of course, a less aggressively ambitious France might not have prevented West Germany from trying to follow its own path one day: the possibility of someone else's imitative *hubris* is no reason for *effacement;* but because the "essence and drama" of nationalism lie in the meeting with others, the risk of contagion—a risk that was part of de Gaulle's larger gamble—could not be disregarded.

Thus the nation-state survives, preserved by the resilience of national political systems, by the interaction between separate nations and a single international system, and by leaders who believe in the primacy of "high politics" over managerial politics and in the primacy of the nation.

V

This long balance sheet leaves us with many questions. What are the prospects in Western Europe? What generalizations can we draw from the whole experience? Is there no chance for the European Community? Is it condemned to be, at best, a success in economics and a fiasco in "high politics?"[33]

While nothing (not even the Common Market) is irreversible, no important event leaves the world unmarked, and after the event one can never pick up the pieces as if nothing had happened. This is true of the Common Market, and it is true also of General de Gaulle. It is not easy to sweep under the rug the curls of dust he willfully placed in the sunlight; it is not easy to ignore the questions he asked, even if his answers were rejected, since they are the questions any European enterprise would face sooner or later. Even the passing of his kind of nationalism has not transformed the national situations of the European states so deeply that all the cleavages discussed here have suddenly disappeared. To be sure, the failure of Britain's policy of maintaining close ties with the United States led to an "agonizing reappraisal" in London that in turn led to Britain's third, and successful, application to the EEC. In this respect, as well as in the rest of the Common Market, de Gaulle's disappearance eased the strains. France stopped trying to promote cooperation through cold war and lifted the veto on Britain. Yet Pompidou has combined a more conciliatory style with the Gaullist habit of raising questions about ends, at least in the economic part of the enterprise to which he has decided to devote his efforts. Even in this more moderate realm, the results have been mixed and do not disprove the previous analysis.

The diversity of national situations has been manifest again. The only part of Pompidou's grand design that his EEC partners have endorsed, a monetary union, has been badly battered. The common float of West European currencies, decided in March 1973, is limited (excluding the pound sterling and the lira) and fragile. West Germany's preference for economically liberal solutions, and the priority she gives to the fight against inflation, have made her suspicious of too strictly monetary a scheme, for she fears that would allow other nations to pursue both more statist and more lax economic policies while counting on help from the strong German mark to save them from trouble. But France's priorities—on full employment and peace and quiet on the labor front, even at the price of inflation, on modernizing without provoking widespread discontent, and on preserving the common agricultural policy (essential to protect her peasants from currency fluctuations)—and the French civil service's fondness for controls have led her to put monetary union ahead of economic harmonization. Moreover, the French have another target beyond EEC—the position of the dollar as a world currency—and they want to use monetary union as a lever to limit the influx of short-term capital from outside Europe. The West Germans (and, in all likelihood, the British) are opposed to controls on capital, out of a deeper attachment to and need for free trade, and out of a continuing desire not to antagonize the United States. But the economic union many Germans would prefer is considered by the French as something in which European distinctiveness would be diluted to America's advantage, and as a potential Deutschmark zone.[34] In order to prevent a new slowdown following the Community's enlargement, Pompidou tried to go beyond the economic realm by proposing a political secretariat, à la Fouchet, and to give his European policy the momentum of popular support, through a referendum. But the former proposal only underlined the old battle about institutions—which conceals, as before, a contest between French designs for Europe (hence her refusal to have that secretariat located in Brussels, along with NATO) and the others' desire to postpone the question of ends by escaping into supranationality. And the fiasco of the French referendum (which confirmed the relative indifference of French public opinion and proved that Pompidou's temporary return to the politics of ambiguity had not paid off[35]) forced him to dig in his heels in more orthodox Gaullist fashion. The road is rocky, and the car sputters, even after the smooth but modest European summit conference of October 1972. America's demands for EEC "concessions" on agriculture and external trade policy, and America's overt linkage of economics and security have once again divided the EEC between those who, for domestic or foreign-policy reasons, are eager to accommodate Washington, and France's desire to build a "European Europe"—at least in the economic realm, where Western Europe's collective power is greatest, and whose importance in world politics has grown apace with détente and the nuclear stalemate.

These setbacks do not mean that the European enterprise is doomed. One can conceive of a set of circumstances in which a speedy forward march could succeed: Western Europe could become West Germany's least frustrating framework at a moment when MBFR or U.S. unilateral cuts might oblige Bonn's leaders to envisage a spill-over of EEC into defense and diplomacy, Western Europe could be seen as Britain's best avenue of leadership in such circumstances, Western Europe could serve as the best compensation for a French political system that would again be beset by domestic troubles and in which "Europe" would be once more an alibi. Western Europe could become a full-fledged economic, military, and diplomatic entity through a major external shock inflicted by either superpower or by both, or through a deliberate, gradual transformation planned in concert with Washington and acceptable to Moscow. But such progress depends on the timely convergence of too many variables to be counted on—and now, in the external component of each West European state's national situation, not only American but Soviet moves and positions have a decisive (if divisive) effect. Within the Community's institutions, daily reality brings a permanent confrontation of national interests that may erode the nation-state's edges but perpetuates their will to exist.[36]

The European experience is of general significance. It tells us about the conditions which the national situations of the units engaged in an attempt to integrate must meet, lest the attempt be unsuccessful. Those situations ought to be similar, of course; but what matters is the nature of the similarity. Insofar as domestic circumstances are concerned, two conditions are essential. The units must be political communities, not in a substantive sense (common values, à la Rousseau) but in a formal one (many links of communications, and common habits and rules, across regional differences and across the borders of ethnic groups, tribes, or classes).[37] In other words, transnational integration presupposes integration within each unit.* These units need not be nation-states, in the sense of communities endowed with external sovereignty under international law; but if a newly independent state is a mere shell with no true community yet, the divisions within the population will badly hinder any trans-state integration: domestic integration is a prerequisite for it and will be a primary goal of any leader who tries to be more than the representative of a sect, class, tribe, or ethnic group. This explains why Latin American integration remains a chimera, and also why it has been so difficult in Africa and Asia to move beyond the nation-state. In many cases, the state is there, but not yet the nation.

Students of supranational integration have rightly stressed the importance of pluralistic social structures and elite groups in the units that try to integrate. But success here also requires that in each unit there be executive leaders who represent those sections of the elites which advocate union and whose power depends on the support of the integrationist elites and groups. Since many of the new states are single-party states with so-called charismatic (or should one say authoritarian?) leaders, this internal condition for unification is often missing.

As far as external conditions are concerned, what matters is not that the units be in "objectively" similar situations but that there be "subjective" similarity—a

---

*The distinctions I suggest are like marks on a continuum.

1. At one end, there are *cooperative arrangements* whose institutions have no autonomy from the various governments (OECD, the U.N. in most respects). These arrangements range from truly cooperative to hegemonial, i.e., from representing all the members to asserting the domination and extending the will of one of them.

2. Then there are *entities* with *central institutions* that have some authority, in the sense of legal autonomy from the components and legal power all over the territory. But these are *not* political communities in the formal sense, because there may be discontinuities in communications or transactions among the components, or because the cleavages within the entity deprive the central institutions of autonomy or effective power. (States such as the Congo or certain Latin American republics fall in this category, supranational entities like the EEC, and, within the limits of effective military integration, NATO.) These entities may be very resilient if they are states, endowed with international personality and institutions that have a formal monopoly or at least superiority of force over internal challenges; but if they are supranational (and especially if they are not simply an arrangement disguising the hegemony of one of the members), they are likely to be unstable, since the "central" institutions will be challenged by the central institutions of the component states. In other words, supranational entities will tend either to retrogress toward stage 1 or to progress toward stage 3.

3. Next come entities that are *political communities* in the *formal* but not the substantive sense. That is, their central institutions have autonomy and power, there are common habits, and the community's rules are enforced across internal barriers, but the central institutions do not have legitimacy all over the territory, and the habits and rules are not based on common values concerning the polity. This is the case with many nation-states which have "national consciousness" but are not political communities in the last sense.

4. Here I refer to nation-states whose central institutions are wholly autonomous, effectively powerful and legitimate, and whose society has shared values concerning the polity. These are political communities in the *substantive* sense. Needless to say, there are not many of them. The difference between stage 3 and 4 is largely a difference in the level and scope of consensus. I would reserve the term national to states in those two stages.

conviction on the part of the policy-makers that the similarity exists. The implication—and this is crucial—is that one must examine more than the relation of each unit to the international system at the moment. The similarity that matters is a similarity in the way different statesmen interpret historical and geographical experience and outline the future in the light of this experience. Integration means a common choice of a common future, but that requires certain attitudes about the past and the present.

As for the past, supranational integration is likely to be more successful when the voyager's baggage is light. If the state's past international experiences have been long or complex, if the state has enjoyed an autonomous existence on the world scene for a long time, integration will not be easy. Is it an accident that the only successful example of voluntary unification in the modern world is that of the United States (a fusion of units that had been colonies, not states, where neither the machinery of the state nor foreign-policy traditions had had time to develop)? In one sense, ridding a nation of overseas commitments (such as France and Britain have done) should make their luggage lighter. But, as we have seen in the case of France, old burdens tend to be replaced by new ties, the old *imperium* leaves lasting concerns, and the old responsibilities leave a continuing sense of responsibility.

The kind of similarity required in the present concerns the relation of the units to the international system. When a similarity in national situations is one of distance or insulation from the system, as was the case of the American states and to a large extent the case of Switzerland after the Reformation, concentration on the difficult job of unification becomes possible. A capital obstacle to integration anywhere in the world today is the loss of such distance, the impossibility of such insulation in the echo chamber of the present international system. But this obstacle can sometimes be removed.

For there is a second question: the degree of compulsion in the international system. When the national situations are similar because of an overwhelming external threat (as was originally the case with the Swiss cantons and the American ex-colonies), unification for survival or security may be imperative. A compelling threat can make up for different pasts and impose a common destination. One can argue that this was Western Europe's condition in the first ten years after the end of World War II, but a countervailing force could be seen in the different pulls of different pasts, with different kinds of involvements in the international system. The nations of Western Europe assessed differently the degree to which the threat from the East superseded other aspects of international politics. It was not an accident that the nation which considered the menace entirely compelling was Germany, divided and literally confronted with the threat, to the exclusion of almost everything else. It was not an accident that France and Britain never let the threat from the East dominate their entire foreign policy. In any case, Western Europe today is no longer dominated by the Soviet threat. Today's international system inflates each national situation, while it removes some of sovereignty's sting. In a way, the relative impotence of force, the postponement of the minute of truth, should reduce the significance of all differences in national situations. But since this is still a competitive system of fragmented states, Rousseau's iron logic applies: each state tries to exploit whatever margin of difference it has; and, since it ultimately matters much less than before, the incentive to unification in order to "pull more weight" is slim. The breakdown of the Soviet and American camps and the kind of weightlessness that nations have in the new international system because of the restrictions on force encourage different visions of the future, or a tendency to take the hazards and chances of a diverse present as they come, rather than planning too much for an inscrutable future. A rational observer, outside the contest, can argue that—precisely because the stakes in the international contest are more symbolic than real—nation-states ought to be willing to unite, for the outcome would be a new actor whose power could really be great enough to make a difference. But the logic of competition operates the other way. It conforms to the French proverb: one thing possessed is worth more than two things promised. In the immediate postwar system, it seemed that European nations were obliged to choose between insecurity apart or an Atlantic shelter together. The "halfway house" of Western Europe got started but did not progress far before the advent of an era in which separateness became attractive again.

The dialectic of fragmentation and unity gives the drama of Europe much of its pathos. In a "finished world," dominated by two giant powers, in a crowded world that resists the sweep of any one power's universal mission, there is something absurd and pathetic in the tenacious persistance of separate European national wills. Yet precisely because so many of the differences among them are expressed in the realm of foreign affairs, integration becomes difficult.

It has become possible for scholars to argue that integration is proceeding *and* that the nation-state is more than ever the basic unit without being contradictory, for recent definitions of integration "beyond the nation-state" point not toward a new kind of political community, but merely toward an "obscur[ing of] the boundaries between the system of international organizations and the environment provided by member states."[38]

There are important implications here. One is, not so paradoxically, that the nation-state is vindicated as the basic unit. So far, anything that is "beyond" is "less": cooperative arrangements with a varying degree of autonomy, power, and legitimacy exist, but there has been no transfer of allegiance to their institutions, and their authority is limited, conditional, dependent, and reversible. There is more than a kernel of truth in the federalist critique of functional integration. So far, the "transferring [of] exclusive expectations of benefits from the nation-state to some larger entity"[39] leaves the nation-state as the main focus of expectations, and as the initiator, pace-setter, supervisor, and often destroyer of the larger entity. In the international arena the state is still the highest possessor of power, and while not every state is a political community, there is as yet no political community more inclusive than the state. To be sure, the military function of the nation-state is in crisis, but since the whole world is "permeable" to nuclear weapons, any new type of unit would face the same horror, and since the prospect of that horror makes conquest less likely, the decline of the state's capacity to defend its citizens is not total, nor even so great as to force the nation-state itself into decline.

The endurance of the nation-state is demonstrated not only by the frustrations of functionalism but also by both the promise and the failure of federalism. On one hand, federalism offers a way of going "beyond the nation-state," but it con-sists in building a new and larger nation-state. The scale is new, not the story, the gauge, not the game. The federalist model applies the Rousseauistic scheme for the creation of a nation to the "making of Europe"; it aims at establishing a unit marked by central power and based on the general will of a European people. The federalists are right in insisting that Western Europe's best chance of being an effective entity would be not to go "beyond the nation-state," but to become a larger nation-state in the process of formation and in the business of world poli-tics: i.e., to become a sovereign political community in at least the formal sense. The success of federalism would be a tribute to the durability of the nation-state; its failure so far is due to the irrelevance of the model. Not only is there no gen-eral will of a European people because there is as of now no European people, but the institutions that could gradually (and theoretically) shape the separate na-tions into one people are not the ones that are most likely to do so. The internal problems of Europe involve matters that can be resolved by technical decisions by civil servants and ministers, rather than general wills and assemblies. (A gen-eral will to prosperity is not very operational.) The external problems of Europe are matters for executives and diplomats. And when the common organs set up by the national governments try to act as a European executive and parliament, they have to do so in a fog maintained around them by the governments, and are slapped down if they try to dispel the fog and reach the people themselves. In other words, Europe cannot be what some nations have been, a people that cre-ates its state. Nor can it be what some of the oldest states are and many of the new ones aspire to be: a people created by the state. It has to wait until the separate states decide that their peoples are close enough to justify setting up a European state that will weld the many into the one; and we have just examined why such a joint decision has been missing. The factors that make the federalist model irrele-vant to diverse and divided nations also make all forms of union short of federal-ism precarious. Functionalism is too unstable for complete political unification. It may integrate economies, but then either the nations will proceed to a full po-litical merger (which economic integration does not guarantee), in which case the federal model will be vindicated, or else the national situations will continue to diverge, and functionalism will be merely a way of tying together the pre-exist-ing nations in areas deemed of common interest. Between the cooperation of ex-isting nations and the breaking in of a new one there is no stable middle ground.

A federation that succeeds becomes a nation; one that fails leads to secession; halfway attempts like supranational functionalism must either snowball or roll back.

But the nation-state survives transformed. Among the men who see "national sovereignty" as the nemesis of mankind, those who put their hopes in regional superstates are illogical, those who put their hopes in a world state are utopian, those who put their hopes in functional political communities more inclusive than the nation-state are too optimistic. What has to be understood and studied now is, rather than the creation of rival communities, the transformation of "national sovereignty." The model of the nation-state derives from the international law and relations of the past, when there were only a few players on the stage and violence was less risky; it applies only fitfully to the situation today. The basic unit has become more heterogeneous as it has proliferated; the stage is occupied by players whose very numbers force each one to strut, but its combustibility nevertheless keeps them from pushing their luck. The nation-state today may be a new wine in old bottles, or in bottles that are sometimes only a mediocre imitation of the old; it is not the same old wine.[40] What must be examined is not just the legal capacity of the sovereign state but the *de facto* capacity at its disposal. Granted the scope of its authority, how much of it can be used and with what results? There are many ways of going "beyond the nation-state," and some modify the substance without altering the form of creating new forms. To be sure, as long as the old form is there, as long as the nation-state is the supreme authority, there is a danger for peace and for welfare. Gullivers tied by Lilliputians rather than crushed by Titans can wake up and break their ties. Men who slug it out with fists and knives, prisoners in a chain gang, are all men, yet their freedom of action is not the same. An examination of the international implications of "nation-statehood" today and yesterday is at least as important as the ritual attack on the nation-state.

Prospects of genuine European unification would improve if the international system created conditions and incentives for moving "beyond the nation-state." In a world where many more units succeeded in becoming genuine nations with pluralistic structures, and where, on the other hand, multipolarity led to greater autonomy for the subsystems and to new interstate wars, the conditions of unification would be met at least in some parts of the world: a less universal and intense involvement in global affairs, a more compelling threat of violence, greater internal harmony might allow the nation-state to supersede itself. But even so, the result might simply be an agglomeration of smaller nation-states into fewer, bigger ones. There are more things in the heaven and earth of the future than in any philosophy of international relations.

Notes

1. See Pierre Renouvin and Jean-Baptiste Duroselle, *Introduction to the History of International Relations* (New York, 1966).

2. In a way, the weaker the foundations on which the nation rests, the shriller the assertions become.

3. On this point, see Rupert Emerson, *From Empire to Nation* (Cambridge, Mass., 1962), Chapter 9; and Raymond Aron, *Peace and War Among Nations* (New York, 1964), Chapter 11.

4. E. H. Carr, *Nationalism and After* (London, 1965), p. 51, quoted in Pierre Hassner, "Nationalisme et relations internationales," *Revue française de science politique*, XV, No. 3 (June 1965), 499–528.

5. See Ernst B. Haas, *Beyond the Nation-State* (Stanford, Cal., 1964).

6. On this point, see my essay "Rousseau on War and Peace," in *The State of War* (New York, 1965).

7. See for instance Richard Cooper, "Economic Interdependence and Foreign Policy in the 70's," *World Politics*, January 1972; and Robert O. Keohane and Joseph S. Nye, Jr., eds., *Transnational Relations and World Politics* (Cambridge, Mass., 1972).

8. Hassner, *op. cit.*, p. 523.

9. Karl W. Deutsch, *Nationalism and Social Communication* (Cambridge, Mass., 1953), p. 147.

10. A more systematic and exhaustive analysis would have to discriminate rigorously among the various components of the national situation. If the purpose of the analysis is to help one understand the relations between the nation-state and the international system, it would be especially necessary to assess: 1) the degree to which each of these components is an unchangeable given (or a given unchangeable over a long period of time) or, on the contrary, an element that can be transformed by will and action; 2) the hierarchy of importance and the order of urgency that political elites and decision-makers establish among the components.

11. See Raoul Girardet, "Autour de l'idéologie nationaliste," *Revue française de science politique*, XV, No. 3 (June, 1965), 423–45; and Hassner, *op. cit.*, pp. 516–19.

12. Alfred Grosser, *French Foreign Policy under de Gaulle* (Boston, 1965).

13. Haas, *The Uniting of Europe* (Stanford, Cal., 1958).

14. See my discussion in "The European Process at Atlantic Cross-Purposes," *Journal of Common Market Studies*, February 1965, pp. 85–101. The success of internal economic integration raised these external issues far earlier than many expected.

15. The latter case is self-evident; the first, less so, since the crisis over EDC was primarily an "intra-European" split between the French and the Germans. But there was more to it than this. EDC was accepted mostly by nations who thought that Europe could not and should not refuse to do what thee United States had demanded—i.e., rearm in order to share the defense of the half-continent with the United States and incite the United States to remain its primary defender; EDC was rejected by nations who feared that it would freeze existing power relationships.

16. Although there was a minority of "resigned ones" in France, like Paul Reynaud.

17. An impressive continuity marks French efforts to preserve the difference between France's position and West Germany's: from the *préalables* and protocols to EDC, to Mendès-France's Brussels proposals, to de Gaulle's opposition to any nuclear role for Germany.

18. France's "integrationist resisters," like Monnet himself, often choose not to stress the "resistance" aspect of their long-term vision, but nevertheless aimed ultimately at establishing in Western Europe not a junior partner of the United States but a "second

force" in the West. Mendès-France's political vision never put the nation at the top of the hierarchy of values, but in 1954 (especially in his ill-fated demands for a revision of EDC at the Brussels meeting in August) and in 1957 (when he voted against the Common Market), his actual policies did put priority on national reform over external entanglements.

19. It is no coincidence that EDC was rejected six weeks after the end of the war in Indochina, that the Common Market treaty was signed by France while war raged in Algeria, that de Gaulle's sharpest attack on the "Monnet method" followed the Évian agreements that ended the Algerian war. The weight of the French national situation affected and inflected the course of even so nationalist a leader as de Gaulle. Even he went along with the "Monnet method" (however grudgingly) until the end of the Algerian war. It is not a coincidence either that the French leaders most suspicious of the imprisoning effects of the EEC were those who labored hardest at improving the national situation by removing colonial burdens (Mendès-France, de Gaulle), and that the French rulers who followed Monnet and tried to orient the pride of France toward leadership of a united Europe were those who failed to improve the national situation overseas (the MRP, Mollet). The one French politician who sought both European integration *and* imperial "disengagement" was Antoine Pinay.

20. Especially by Henry Kissinger in *The Troubled Partnership* (New York, 1965) and Raymond Aron in *The Great Debate* (New York, 1964).

21. One should not forget that the original decisions that led to the French nuclear *force de frappe* were made before de Gaulle, and opposition to the national deterrent came from men who did not at all object to de Gaulle's argument that Europe as a whole should stop being a client of the United States.

22. See my previous discussion in "Discord in Community," in F. Wilcox and H. F. Haviland, Jr., eds., *The Atlantic Community* (New York, 1963), pp. 3–31; and "Europe's Identity Crisis," *Daedalus*, Fall 1964, pp. 1244–97.

23. See, for instance, Max Kohnstamm, "The European Tide," in Stephen R. Graubard, ed., *A New Europe?* (Boston, 1964), pp. 140–73.

24. See Karl W. Deutsch, *et al., Political Community and the North Atlantic Area* (Princeton, N.J., 1957).

25. Under authority, I include three distinct notions: autonomy (the capacity to act independently of the governments, particularly financially), power (control over acts of others), and legitimacy (being accepted as the "rightful" center of action).

26. Compare decolonization. Along similar lines, see Francis Rosenstiel, *Le principe de "Supranationalité"* (Paris, 1962).

27. See the analysis of a recent French public-opinion poll by Raoul Girardet, "Du fait national aux necessités européennes," *Contrepoint*, Spring 1971.

28. On this point, see Raymond Aron and Daniel Lerner, eds., *France Defeats EDC* (New York, 1957).

29. See Emerson, *loc. cit.*

30. Britain's refusal to join EEC, before 1961, could not fail to increase French hesitations, for integration without Britain meant equality with Germany, and a clear-cut difference between France's position and Britain's, i.e., a reversal of French aspirations and traditions. Britain has on the whole rejected the "resignation-resistance" dilemma—and as a result, both the aspects of its foreign policy that appeared like resignation to U.S. predominance and the aspects that implied resistance to decline have contributed to the crisis of European integration: for France's vetoes in January 1963 and November 1967

meant a French refusal to let into Europe a power that had just confirmed its military ties to the United States, but Britain's previous desire to play a world role and aversion to "fading into Europe" encouraged France's own misgivings about integration.

31. See Grosser, *op. cit.*, Chapter 4.

32. See Thomas Schelling, *Strategy of Conflict* (Cambridge, Mass., 1960).

33. The best balance sheet (despite its jargon) is in Leon N. Lindberg and Stuart A. Scheingold, *Europe's Would-Be Polity* (Englewood Cliffs, N.J., 1970). For a more detailed assessment of current developments, see my contribution to Wolfram Hanrieder ed., *The United States and Western Europe in the 70s* (Cambridge, Mass.: Winthrop Publishers, 1974).

34. For a good discussion of the 1971 crisis, see Guy Berger, Edward L. Morse, and Michel Albert's articles in *Revue française de science politique*, April 1972.

35. The question asked of the voters—whether to approve Britain's entry into EEC, given "the new perspectives open to Europe" (undefined)—was too clever by half. Pompidou's speeches veered from "Europeanism" to "Gaullism," and a sizable part of the Gaullist electorate abstained or deserted.

36. See Maurice Couve de Murville, *Une Politique étrangère* (Paris, 1971), p. 382.

37. Haas's definition of a political community in his *The Uniting of Europe*, p. 5 ("a condition in which specific groups and individuals show more loyalty to their central political institutions than to any other political authority") is not very helpful in the case of states marked by severe domestic cleavages. There might be more loyalty to the center than to any other political authority merely because there is no other *political* authority, and yet one would still not be in the presence of anything like an integrated society.

38. Haas, *Beyond the Nation-State*, p. 29.

39. Haas and Philippe C. Schmitter, "Economics and Differential Patterns of Political Integration," *International Organization*, XVIII, No. 4 (Autumn 1964), 705–710.

40. Some assert that it is not even the old bottle, so great are the effects of transnational forces on the nation-states. See Keohane and Nye, *op. cit.*

4

No Trumps, No Luck, No Will: Gloomy Thoughts on Europe's Plight

The world spirit, as Hegel would have called it, or God, as others would say, decreed with a fine sense of irony that what should have been the Year of Europe would become the Year of World Crisis. With the fading away of the "Atlantic generation," with new leaders in several West European countries, with a new world agenda dominated by the "struggle for the world product," a massive transfer of wealth to the oil-producing countries, and the continuation of inflation and recession among the industrial nations, isn't a normative exercise indispensable? Isn't that great "act of creation" Henry Kissinger had demanded in his famous speech of April 1973 even more necessary now than when he asked for it?

Two caveats are in order. First, European-American relations have been the realm of prescriptive designs par excellence. We have had, over the years, the Atlantic design, first, with the Marshall Plan, NATO, and the early steps toward the integration of the West Europeans into an entity bound to the United States, later under the name of Atlantic partnership, used in order both to bless the development of that entity and to stress its true destination: playing its part in America's orchestra. We have had, on the European side, a variety of separatist designs à la de Gaulle, or in its Third Force or neutralist variants. We have had, on this side, either reactions against or amendments to the Atlantic design: schemes for sharing nuclear defense, such as the Multilateral Nuclear Force, schemes of disengagement (going back to Kennan's Reith lectures) or schemes of devolution to a uniting Europe, all opposed to U.S. overcommitment or to the overbearing character of Atlanticism; and the more recent trilateral scheme, a grandiose enlargement of Atlanticism aimed at incorporating a third "pillar," Japan, and at enlarging the common agenda. There are splendidly convincing, or at least eloquent, arguments for each of these normative constructs. Many are presented in this volume. Isn't there something disturbing about the abundance and persistence of these schemes—as if the stablest "structures of peace" were the grand designs, coexisting far above the realities?

This observation leads to a second question: if European-American relations have become a graveyard of grand designs, isn't it because all of these assume the existence or the growth of a European entity, either as a junior partner in the Atlantic or trilateral enterprise, or as a force with its own identity to which power can be "devolved," or which would be left standing should the United States "disengage"? Isn't the flabby nature of the European entity what makes most of the normative designs really academic? What if American hegemony were clearly both the cause and the effect of this flabbiness—and thus required no normative dressing up, being a massive, brute fact of life anyhow?

Thus the *préalable* to any prescriptive and forward-looking exercise ought to be a backward glance. And it should focus on the Europeans. In any of the designs, they are the missing link or the fatal flaw. Moreover, among the Europeans, the French will receive special attention, because they have played a decisive role both as initiators and as obstacles, as European idealists and as nationalists. The purpose of this retrospective is to assess the significance of the present apparent return to harmony: how much does the new state of European–American relations differ from the past? What is its import for the European entity? Only after one has reached some conclusions on these points can one suggest some directions for U.S. policy.[1]

The advent of Helmut Schmidt and Valéry Giscard d'Estaing led many commentators to talk about a new chance for West European unity *and* for friendly European–American relations. The signing in Brussels, in June 1974, of a new Atlantic declaration meant that the bickering which had marked those relations, especially between France and the United States, was now behind us. The first meetings between the new German Chancellor and the new French President suggested that the threat of a disintegration of the European Economic Community was being overcome and that a new *relance* could be expected. The European summits of December 1974 and 1975 vindicated these hopes, at least in part, thanks to a series of compromises on institutions, regional policy, and British demands. There also was a Franco–American compromise on energy policy, which reconciled the French approach with that which had been chosen by Washington and by France's eight partners.

A little history would do no harm. If European unity were in search of a myth, I would suggest Sisyphus, the unhappy symbol of all international organizations. European unification has been a succession of initiatives, followed by fiascos, followed by *relances*, followed by new crises. The European Sisyphus got to work in 1950. After the disasters of German rearmament he tried again. After the fall of the Fourth Republic, de Gaulle undertook a new *relance*, which ended with the failure of the Fouchet Plan in 1962. Then Pompidou tried anew until the intra-European and Franco-American rift at the beginning of 1974.

Thus we are at the *fifth* new dawn. Two recurrent crises have kept the West European Sisyphus at work. One has been crisis in France herself: the politico-financial crisis of 1958, the unexpected balance of payments reversal that followed the oil crisis and forced France's *de facto* devaluation of January 1974. The other has been a recurrent crisis in Franco–American relations. This does not mean that there couldn't be other causes of breakdown in the future (for instance, a major British economic and financial crisis). But it suggests that for the rock to move upward again, and stay at its new plateau, there would have to be at least, on the one hand, greater harmony of economic and financial policy among the EEC members and, on the other, a *lasting* rapprochement between France and the United States, i.e., a *major* change of policy either in Paris or in Washington: either the Americans must accept the French thesis of a distinctive West European identity (in association with, but without subordination to, American global designs); or else the French must endorse an "Atlantic" Europe taking its place in what Jobert has called Washington's cosmogony—a vision which France's European partners more or less explicitly prefer. In order to understand why none of these conditions have been met before, the trends of the past decade need to be re-examined.

Bad Trends, Old and New

Ten years ago, at a time when many social scientists on both sides of the Atlantic were predicting an "end of ideology" and a gradual alignment of European political and social systems on the American model, I tried to argue that this was a far too simplified and deterministic view. Differences between European institutions, legacies, and attitudes and American ones in political matters—the word political being used in its broadest sense, i.e., "concerning the polity"—were too deep to be erased quite so easily. I mentioned in particular the weight of a troubled past in each European polity, and contrasted it with American faith in political harmony and in the institutions that had survived so well since 1776. Obviously, much has happened since to puncture *that* analysis. First Vietnam, and later Watergate, have provided millions of Americans with the unsavory spectacle that seems so normal for Europeans, yet so scandalous here: deception and self-deception in the government, massive abuses of power and criminal acts in high places, the revelation of official cynicism mixed with incompetence—hence a serious crisis of public confidence in *both* political parties and in *all* branches of the government (save, perhaps, the judiciary), especially among the young, and the spread of cynicism in the electorate as well. There is a second way in which the American scene has come to look more "European": the mid and late 1960s have been marked by the prevalence of conflict between blacks (or other racial minorities) and whites, the young and their elders, the poor and (especially) those who had finally acceded to some ease, if not affluence. At the same time, and despite such upheavals as May 1968 in France, the political systems of Western Europe were gaining in legitimacy, and in a multitude of ways the weight of historical memories was lightening on a generation that was raised in the new conditions of mass education and economic growth. And yet these changes—which played havoc both with the original thesis of inevitable "Americanization" and with my refutation of it—did not mean that the two sides were meeting halfway. For the main trends of 1964–74 can be divided into two categories, both of which explain what I will call, in shorthand, the European semi-fiasco (semi, since there *is*, whatever its weaknesses, a Community of the Nine): those trends which continued from before 1964, and the new ones that have contributed to the difficulties or made them even worse.

A first persistent trend has been the tendency of each West European polity to remain locked in its own priorities and problems. Both European integration and the involvement of the EEC countries in the world economy have fostered interdependence, in the sense of increased sensitivity *and* vulnerability of each of the nations' economies to fluctuations and decisions outside.[2] But the nations of Western Europe have maintained the autonomy of their reactions and of their outlooks. Also, their situations have continued to be uneven, both with respect to domestic performance (cf. the British rate of growth vs. that of Italy, Germany, or France; the rigidities, habits, and demand pressures making for inflation in France, vs. the greater capacity for restraint and efficiency in Germany) and with respect to their dependence on the outside world (cf. the huge size, composition, and stability of German exports, as compared with the French, but also the far greater German dependence on the U.S. market; the lesser German dependence on outside energy sources, etc.). The combination of *unevenness* and *autonomy* has made further progress toward economic and monetary union an ordeal, as the sad story of the European currencies' "snake" between 1971 and the present has proved. The arcane debate between "economists" and "monetarists," about the proper method of economic unification, reflected largely the difference between the position and interests of Germany (fearful of having to subsidize, in effect, the inflationary economies of its partners) and the policies and concerns of France (eager to preserve her domestic priority to growth and full employment, and to create a European monetary bloc capable of challenging eventually American practices and privileges under the dollar exchange standard). The theoretical debate ended with the victory of the "economists," but the political debacle of the European Monetary Union in 1974 meant the practical frustration of both schools. For unevenness to lead to harmony (or harmonization), one would have needed either a quiet international environment in which an attempt to reach economic union through monetary coordination alone would have had a chance of success, or else the capacity of the political systems to reverse rather than accentuate the effects of unevenness. Actually, even the monetary road supposed a far greater pooling of reserves, a shared attitude toward the value and role of gold, and a determination to prevent, through credit, tax, and social policies, the national rates of inflation from becoming too different: none of this was forthcoming, for reasons having to do both with the U.S. obstacle *and,* above all, with the desire for domestic autonomy.

Domestic autonomy refers, not simply to the obvious fact that the "member states" are still pursuing their own separate courses in all areas which the EEC has not succeeded in regulating, but to the fact that each government remains responsible and responsive to *its* electorate, guided by its own electoral necessities and priorities, and inspired more by the need to devise a strategy that will support *its* presence in power, than by the need for compatibility with its foreign partners. Thus the economic policy followed by the team of Pompidou and Giscard d'Estaing between 1969 and 1973—full employment and laxity toward inflation—made sense given the domestic design and political strategy of Pompidou—until the oil crisis derailed it altogether. But it did not help the economic union, with a German partner whose priorities were exactly the reverse, and it had put a heavy strain on the common float even before the oil disaster. Ironically enough, in the period 1964–74, the only government that shaped its domestic policies according to an external design rather than to internal calculations was that of General de Gaulle until May 1968. But *his* external design happened not to be that of his partners, and his efforts were geared to maximizing French, not European, influence in the world. Moreover, the explosion of May 1968, although not a revolt against the gist of his foreign policy, was a rebellion against its domestic costs; de Gaulle's successor learned his lesson, and shifted priorities.

Thus even when a government is strong—in the sense that it has a safe and coherent majority—its framework of calculation may be narrow: cf. all the British governments' inability to regulate industrial relations or, in France, the problem of the shrinking base of the majority's electorate. When the governing majority is not homogeneous (cf. the German coalition), or perpetually in danger of fragmentation (Italy), autonomy may well mean even greater difficulty in escaping from the domestic inhibitions or imperatives, i.e., *less* freedom to "harmonize."

For autonomy means, not freedom of independent action, but distinctive ways of acting, or of not being able to act. The same economic problem—inflation, the rise in energy costs, or labor troubles, for instance—will be handled in different ways, depending on such factors as the importance, efficiency, structure, and habits of the bureaucracy; the degree of politicization and militancy of the unions and of other interest groups; the presence and strength of extremist ideologies; and of course the constitutional authority of the Executive. Contrary to earlier hopes, the combination of bureaucratic politics on top and "querulous satisfaction," or piecemeal dissatisfaction, below, the prevalence of bargaining about bread-and-butter issues, the process of incrementalism, even the interpenetration of elites, have not made integration easier. For each political system bargains in its own style, must be on guard against its own brand of divisive or ideological politics, and has to worry about its own set of parochialisms.

A second element of continuity has been American foreign policy, in a double sense: actual *moves* and actual *weight.* To be sure, there appeared two factors that seemed, for a while, to mark a drastic change, favorable to greater European unity. Henry Kissinger had been an eloquent critic of the tendency of past administrations to want a united Europe only if it does not "challenge American hegemony in Atlantic policy," and to speak to the Europeans with omnipotent paternalism and complacent arrogance. In 1969–70, preoccupied above all with Vietnam and preparing for its "breakthrough" with the two main Communist powers—SALT and the opening to China—the Administration seemed to be following Kissinger's academic recommendations: far greater friendliness toward France, no commitment to any preferred form of European unity, indeed, no grand designs. The scene changed after August 15, 1971, but the American economic offensive, in the eyes of many experts, seemed to be both a sign of and a reaction to something that Kissinger had forecast in his writings: the loss of U.S. hegemony, at least in the economic realm, due to a combination of events—the crisis of the "dollar exchange standard" collapsing under the weight of U.S. balance of payments deficits, superior productivity in Western Europe and Japan, and the slowdown in the U.S. rate of growth, et al. Insofar as American imperiousness on the one hand, American de facto predominance on the other had, in the past, made European unity more difficult by dividing Europeans into the meek and the unruly, wouldn't those two new factors, and even the American economic challenge, actually prove helpful?

Neither ultimately did, because neither meant what it seemed to mean. As some writers, like Raymond Vernon, had cautioned, the U.S. economy was still the "rogue elephant in the forest."[3] The United States, in its days of trouble, still had one possibility open to no one else—that of changing unilaterally the rules of the game and of obliging everybody else to pay a price for the creation of new rules acceptable to Washington. The measures of August 15, 1971, the two devaluations of 1971 and 1973, the *de facto* establishment of a floating rate system, amounted to just that. They resulted in a spectacular turning around of the U.S. balance of payments (and thus considerably lessened American interest in a formal new international monetary system). Then came the completely unexpected and paradoxical help of the Middle Eastern oil-producing powers to the United States. Far less dependent on Middle Eastern oil than its economic rivals, less troubled than they by the quadrupling of the price of oil, more capable of providing opportunities for investment as well as technological aid to the "new rich" developing countries, the United States has reasserted both its economic and its monetary predominance. At the same time, it was becoming clear that the "new" foreign policy of Dr. Kissinger, so different from the old in its tactics, in its overall design and flexibility, in its tone and its process of decision, was remarkably *like* the old one insofar as Europe was concerned. Two key notions of the April 23, 1973, address—Europe's merely regional interests, and European unity having to be subordinated to broader goals: those of the Atlantic alliance (enlarged to Japan) so as to be properly "outward-looking"—were weapons borrowed from the old Atlanticist arsenal, ideas still couched in George Ball language. They meant, as before, that the United States, the only power in the non-Communist world with global responsibilities, would set the directions and the framework in which the Europeans could move. Just as, before 1964, the Atlantic bond had never prevented the United States from dealing directly with Moscow over nuclear arms, or from adopting its own policy toward the underdeveloped countries, the neo-Atlantic commitment requested by Dr. Kissinger was not designed to limit U.S. freedom of action, but aimed at circumscribing the Europeans' sphere. The Europeans could unite "as long as, insofar as," etc. The speech gave a long list of "common" objectives; but the American approach to Moscow, from 1971 on, was made without any prior reorganization of intra-Atlantic relations. The fact that NATO remains organized exactly as before (except for the existence of the Eurogroup); that the United States still dominates the weapons procurements of its allies (despite, and indeed partly through, the Eurogroup); that the year 1973 also marked the adoption of one more American strategic doctrine, unilaterally and peremptorily proclaimed by Secretary Schlesinger, and not too clear in its implications; that the U.S. notion of consultation oscillates from mere information to total eclipse—all this also demonstrates continuity in practices which are precisely those that, in the past, had produced discord not only in the Atlantic pseudo-community but also in the European quasi-community.

In the past, the great objector had been France. Here we find the third element of continuity in 1964–74. Partly, this could be attributed to Gaullism: our ten-year period, after all, divides into two halves, with the General in power five years, Pompidou five more, the Gaullist party dominating the majority coalition and in control of both the presidency and the premiership throughout. But is it just Gaullism which explains why France has been the champion of resistance to the United States even when she has, for a while, tried (in Giscard's new Foreign Minister's words) to "dedramatize" her relations with Washington in order to make a European consensus easier? If this were the case, how would we explain the battle over the European Defense Community, or Suez? That France's stance is sharper and makes compromises that paper over basic antagonisms more difficult when "orthodox Gaullism" reigns is sure. But a "more courteous" stance—to use a Giscard term—and an aptitude for paper compromises are not necessarily the same as a substantive shift (recent European summits have been rich in such paper agreements). To explain France's disposition, we must turn to a multiplicity of factors:

1. A general approach to foreign policy, molded by the style of French education, by French analytical and conceptual reasoning, by the "lessons of history" as learned in school: international relations is a battlefield of national designs, where the stakes are survival, domination, power and wealth. Thus policies are seen as deliberate, calculations of national advantage as permanent, compromises as temporary, alliances and enmities as changing.

2. The legacy, among the elites—especially those over forty-five—of the hu-

miliations of dependence on another power in the interwar period, in the days of the Nazi occupation and even in the Fourth Republic (many of the centrists and rightists in power today were colonial "hawks").

3. A strong, if somewhat contentless, patriotism and desire for "cutting a grand figure on the stage," in the public at large. I have tried to analyze this rather elusive force elsewhere,[4] and to show that, at present, it provides little policy guidance. But it is there. It did contribute to Mitterrand's defeat in 1974, for the voters sensed the incoherence of the Communist–Socialist alliance in foreign policy. And it *limits* even if it does not *inspire;* i.e., it precludes abrupt reversals of foreign policy and makes of the "European idea" a welcome concept rather than a driving emotion.

4. What could be called the external configuration or situation of postwar France. France was not, like Italy, a nation that had tried a policy of aggressive grandeur and had had to pay dearly for it (if anything, France had had to pay for timidity, appeasement, and internal divisiveness). She was not, like Germany, a pariah and a divided country, condemned to pursue a chimera (reunification) and to live a nightmare (security). Like England, France was an impoverished ex-great power in full external retreat. But unlike England, she had no "American connection" or "English-speaking peoples" illusion; and unlike England, she showed extraordinary economic dynamism and imagination, despite the poor performance of the Fourth Republic's political institutions. All the other factors listed dictated a search for an active foreign policy (i.e., the opposite from Italy's search). Now, French foreign policy could not be active *and* entirely pro-American: not only because, after the experiences of 1918–45, few wanted really to play *brilliant second* to another power anymore, but also because the United States had already two such *seconds*, in London and in Bonn. Hence a field of forces limiting French choices exactly to two: either a *deliberate* challenge of the United States (but she could not go too far, for security reasons above all, and because of the abyss that such a policy would dig between France and all her neighbors) or a *deliberate* " construction of Europe" concentrating on common interests. (But sooner or later Sisyphus reaches the Sphinx's riddle, if I may scramble my Greek myths: does "common" mean common to the Europeans *and* the Americans, in which case what is Europe's distinctiveness; or does it mean those interests which distinguish Europe from America, and in this case what happens to European unity?)

5. An internal configuration that corresponds to, and fits into the external one. There are two main elements here. One is the constellation of political and social forces. As in Italy, there exists a French bourgeoisie—in industry, in the professions, in the armed forces—which sees in the United States a *feste Burg* against communism, not only abroad but at home. But this has never been either the *dominant* view of French bourgeois (anymore than the "rather Hitler than Blum" view had been, earlier), or the *only* view of those bourgeois who held it (they often criticized the United States for its anti-colonialism, for instance). The de-

sire to use foreign policy as an instrument of domestic protection against the far left, so overwhelming in the Italian case, was far more spotty in France, whose *grande bourgeoisie*, even in the late 1940s, felt far less unsure of itself than its Italian counterpart.[5]

On foreign affairs, the French political scene shows two different and partly overlapping alignments: a pro-European one, which includes most of (not all) the Socialists, the centrists, the right, and some of the Gaullists, leaving out other Gaullists (unless Europe had become France writ large) and the Communists; and one that should be called not anti-American but "anti-American hegemony," which includes the Communists, most of the Socialists and the Gaullists, and leaves out centrists and rightists. Thus an "anti-American hegemony" policy could not be openly disdainful of European unity, since the coalition behind it could not rule together on domestic affairs, and a "pro-European" policy cannot be too meek and mild about the United States, for the very same reason. Should the left finally come to power (in legislative elections followed by a new presidential one), the common denominator of its two fractions would have to be a policy not unlike that of the past. Should the present coalition break up, one could imagine two scenarios: a majority composed of rightists, centrists, and Socialists, or one composed of the left plus the Gaullists. In both cases, one remains within the same foreign policy perimeter, *à des nuances près;* and at present, both scenarios are unlikely.

6. The other internal element brings us back to the first of the three factors of continuity: national autonomy. What is distinctive about the French nation-state is *le phénomène bureaucratique.* This means, first, that France, like Britain and no other major state in Western Europe, has a bureaucracy with a long, strong, and self-perpetuating tradition of activity in foreign affairs; second, that French bureaucracy is also the matrix and the motor of French economic and social development, to a degree that is unique among liberal societies. Hence both a formidable resistance to its dismantlement, and a propensity to define Europe in "French" terms, i.e., to want it to be a network of rules and programs (and where should these come from, if not from the one civil service with the richest experience in that proliferating field?).

The Past Decade

Let us turn now to the *new* trends of the period 1964–74, and to the reasons why they have worsened the European predicament. The first one is the displacement of the center of gravity of world politics, from the diplomatic-strategic field to the chessboards of economic and monetary relations; or if one prefers, the grand entry of economics into the realm of high politics. In the previous period, as Richard Cooper has shown, economic and monetary relations within the developed members of the world economy had been largely separated from political and military relations, and ran on a distinct, largely depoliticized track. (As Robert Gilpin, in turn, has shown, this in itself resulted from a political decision or deal—a U.S. decision, a U.S.–Western Europe–Japan deal—and was therefore reversible.)[6] This separation had served as a shield behind which European integration was able to progress. In early 1968, the failure of General de Gaulle to rally the Six behind a common stand opposing the American-sponsored Special Drawing Rights (SDR) and demanding a reform of the Bretton Woods system was a forerunner of things to come. After 1971, the European Community was buffeted by two major storms, both of which are too familiar to be recounted in any detail. The first was the American offensive against the Common Agricultural Policy (CAP), the preferential agreements, the burden which the cost of American troops in Europe added to the U.S. balance of payments deficit, the "trade diversion" resulting from Britain's entry, and the American moves toward a new monetary system. This was of tremendous significance, not because such policies expressed an American "decline," but because they meant that the one area of autonomy granted by the United States to the Europeans in the past was now being revoked. In the early 1960s, the Europeans had divided over the issue of whether to *extend* the realm of cooperation from economics to diplomacy and defense, to which the United States clearly objected. This time, the United States was making rather self-righteous demands in the economic area, and promoting monetary policies that were bound to play havoc with the CAP (each change in rates resulting in a new painful round) and with the financial surpluses of creditor countries. In effect, Washington was, first, demanding that the Europeans help the United States reverse its global trade and payments deficits, and indeed help the United States return to a surplus position that would finance continuing American investments in Europe; second, the United States was resorting to monetary practices that were bound to complicate the life of the fragile European monetary union. Under these circumstances, the Europeans had only two possibilities. One was to resist, at the cost of straining their relations with the United States, and without being able thereby to impose their views about a stable monetary system to which the key remained the United States. But, as usual, resisting beyond a certain point meant splitting: there was a common will to protect the CAP, at France's intransigent insistence, but not to say no on all other points. The other possibility was to yield, as was done on several such issues.

At least this did not affect Europe's relations to the developing countries. European cooperation, and the expansion of the European economies, had taken place in a world of low energy costs and low raw materials prices. The sudden reversal, at the end of 1973, in addition to raising the specter of possible worldwide recession, to wrecking the balance of payments of all West European nations save West Germany, and to destroying the six-nation joint monetary float, once again posed in the sharpest terms the oldest dilemma: whether to seek redress in the shadow of the United States, or whether to argue that there was enough of a difference in position and interests between the United States and Western Europe to justify a separate European policy and a separate approach to

OPEC. As is well known, at first the French said no to the first alternative, and the other Europeans said yes to both. By the end of 1974, everything was declared compatible with everything else, but as we shall see below, European unity was not the winner. To conclude: above all an "economic animal," the European Economic Community could not fail to be the victim of the sudden appearance of high waves on the previously quiet international economic ocean.

A second new and damaging trend has been conspicuous in both of the episodes in which the first one had unfolded. The consistency of U.S. policy toward Europe, noted earlier, nevertheless takes on a completely different meaning when the *context* is no longer that of the 1950s and early 1960s. I do not believe that Dr. Kissinger, by contrast with his predecessors, decided that European unity was no longer in the U.S. interest. I think that, unlike his predecessors, he was always skeptical of its chances; more than they had been, he was impatient with the slow and rigid procedures of decision-making in Brussels, and prone to see in them a pretext for European provincialism and pusillanimity. Like his predecessors, he does not want European unity *at the expense of* U.S. interests; but unlike theirs, his conception of the U.S. interests that should be protected is huge. This sounds paradoxical, since he had denounced earlier policies as overextended and as straining U.S. psychological and physical resources. And yet, there has been a triple change.

1. A change in substance: the United States is no longer primarily the leader of a grand alliance (which also has a vested interest in preventing a large-scale war); it is the builder of a "structure of peace" which entails a transformation in the nature of all major relationships, alliances as well as antagonistic bonds, and the creation of a complicated system of worldwide balance and regional balances. This means a high *priority* to dealing with Moscow and Peking, a considerable amount of attention spent on defusing powder kegs in Southeast Asia or the Middle East, and, more recently, a heroic effort at coping with the problem of economic interdependence: energy, recycling, food, etc.: in other words, global *movement* rather than worldwide *containment*. But with the emphasis shifting from manning the barricades, especially in Europe, to building a planetary framework, U.S. policy becomes much more *confining* for the Europeans: the same old tendency to circumscribe their moves now shrinks their compound into a cage.

2. A change in style: in its switch from stolidity to maneuver, the United States has shifted from its "free world partnership," "common interest of the West" style, not to one but to two others: a pure "national interest" style, manifest not only in brutal Connally-isms but also in subtler Kissinger "linkages"; and a neo-idealistic style, but on a *global* scale, and so far largely reserved for speeches. The latter does not overtly conflict with a European entity; yet it stresses the latter's confinement by fitting the entity into the global "structures."[7] The *Realpolitik* style actually hits at the European entity, for it is both more *blunt* and more *divisive* than the earlier style: it both invites a test of strength with the less than cohesive European Com-

munity over every contentious issue, *and* suggests bilateralism as a perfectly conceivable, even desirable, alternative, should the confrontation yield no sufficient concessions. For it makes it quite clear that politics aims at rewarding the good and punishing the rambunctious.

3. A change in tactics. In order to achieve the necessary breakthroughs (toward the "stable structures" as well as the consolidation of U.S. interests) Kissinger has carefully chosen pivots on which to lean in order to turn stalled situations around. Thus he has leaned on China in order to change relations with *both* major Communist powers; on Moscow in order to break the long deadlock with Hanoi; on Egypt in order to break the Arab-Israeli impasse; on Saudi Arabia— less successfully—to regain leverage on OPEC. This virtuosity has been triply damaging to the Europeans. First, it reinforces their confinement: for it is not, for Kissinger, merely a matter of setting a global framework, it is a question of doing it oneself, *first* and in one's own way. This means in effect telling Brandt that he can have his *Ostpolitik,* but only after Washington has pushed its own; or telling the EEC it can have its dialogue with the Arabs, but only after the United States has made its own deals; or showing the Europeans that for the time being the Middle East is a *chasse gardée* of the superpowers (indeed of the United States); or demonstrating that Mutual Force Reductions (MFR) is above all a Soviet-American appendage to the great powers' détente. Second, it exacerbates the tensions between Washington and the Europeans, as long as Kissinger finds no pivot in Western Europe: France is too hostile or concerned with her own game, West Germany has been too reluctant to appear as having a privileged position, Britain remains too troubled and marginal, and Brussels seems devised to make the quest for a pivot fruitless. Without a pivot, yet with the need to keep the monopoly of initiative, Kissinger has been led to demand a say in the process of intra-European consultation. Third, should Bonn (which under Helmut Schmidt has played a highly visible role of go-between trying to harmonize domestic economic policies and energy policies both between the United States and the Europeans and within the EEC) become actually Kissinger's pivot, what happens either to European unity, should the others (and especially the French) balk, or to European distinctiveness if they don't?

Now whereas the change in the scenery of high politics is obviously here to stay, the triple shift in U.S. policy may not survive the eventual departure of the new Bismarck. But while he may not have made his actions durable, he may well have transformed the stage enough to make any alternative more favorable to European unity harder to achieve after him. This is so especially because of the third new trend.

It could be called a subtle regression of the European enterprise. I call it a subtle regression because—after the blockage of the years 1965–69—there was, after all, some motion: three new members, four summits, the Werner plan, the joint float, an embryonic regional fund, the common stands of the Nine on the European Security Conference, in November 1973, on the Arab–Israeli dispute, later on Cyprus, the beginning of serious talk on how to reconcile France and the Eurogroup countries over defense. And yet, against all this, there were three disturbing factors.

One was the fact that Britain's entry, and the negotiations that brought it about, in a way diverted the members—precisely in the years of the exceptional combination of Pompidou, Brandt, and Heath—from other tasks; and once Britain joined, it became clear that, far from bringing the grand new impetus which many had expected, she introduced into the EEC a new source of heterogeneity, due to her economic performance and the mood of her public opinion. Thus there was *more* acrimony.

Second, a new and dangerous phenomenon developed: the long lists of common endeavors adopted at summit meetings were not followed by any corresponding advances (with the partial exception of the monetary attempt). There was therefore a remarkable failure to progress *enough*, at a time when the centrifugal forces, described above, were exerting sharp pulls on the Community. To meet and defeat them, *more* progress would have been necessary, in matters such as economic and tax policies (so as to keep the rates of inflation and growth within common limits), social and regional policies, foreign investments, transportation, and of course energy. Only through such cooperation could the disruptive effects of short-term capital fluctuations and speculations against the weaker currencies have been dampened. But it was precisely the old prevalence of domestic priorities and habits that prevented such advances, then led to increasing discrepancies between national performance and policies, now that international economic issues were at the heart of world politics. Previously, in quieter days, it had merely led to a certain complacent failure to move beyond the free trade and CAP achievements. This time, the leaders knew they could hardly afford such complacency, and they solemnly adopted their lists and their calendars—yet nothing positive happened.

This also pointed to a third disturbing factor: despite the fresh blood provided by the new members, the Brussels institutions operated in a vacuum. Without a genuine impulse from the national governments and bureaucracies, the EEC Commission could only contribute to the impression of a car stuck in the sand with wheels turning in vain and merely throwing dust around: it too could, slowly, grind out its lists of suggestions and draft fine plans—but nothing would happen, or, as in the case of the monetary union, much less than the commissioners had hoped. This was a far cry from the days when the Commission had played a major role in shaping the CAP and the original association agreements. These symptoms of decline may have been overlooked, because of the relative solidarity of the Nine in the face of various U.S. demands, and because of the progress of the Davignon procedure. But a common stand on the European Security Conference meant little, given the limited significance and opportunities provided by that interminable charade, and the common stand on the Middle East was no more than a joint deploration—except that it determined Dr.

Kissinger to excommunicate any further such statements of European autonomy, however ineffectual. And during the crisis provoked by the Arab embargo, the members of the EEC were unwilling or unable to express publicly their solidarity with Holland: it was the multinational companies which practiced what the Community failed to preach.

One could, again, argue that there is no need for this new trend to last. Haven't the dangers of regression, indeed the destructive moves made by several members since January 1974, instilled in all a desire to pull away from the brink? Such a desire exists, as the Paris summit of December 1974 and subsequent ones showed. But there are powerful reasons that make it difficult to be too optimistic.

The Present Predicament

It could be presented in the form of a paradox: we are witnessing the end of the "Atlantic system," and yet this marks the demise of the "European Europe."

By Atlantic system I mean the postwar, interstate, and transnational system of economic and monetary relations, "Atlantic-centered, United States-protected, and New York-financed"; a system whose agenda consisted above all of issues *among* the non-Communist industrial states, whose transactions were taking place in the framework of a "liberal and self-adjusting free trade system" (for industrial goods) "based on stable and fixed monetary rates," and on the assumption of "steady access to relatively inexpensive raw materials."[8] As long as this system worked, the debate between partisans of a "European Europe" and champions of an "Atlantic Europe"—on both sides of the Atlantic—was largely a debate on issues of interest only, or primarily, to the two sides of the Atlantic: how much autonomy for European defense, given the inevitable reliance on U.S. strategic nuclear forces, the recognized need for U.S. troops in Europe? How much agricultural protectionism for the EEC? Should the allies of the United States be obliged to absorb unlimited quantities of dollars? Also, even though the Europeans were divided over the *goals* for which European economic resurgence and cooperation should be used, there was no doubt about such resurgence and the need for such cooperation. The grand designs evoked in the beginning of this essay all address themselves to these kinds of issues and all assume Europe's resurgence and internal cooperation.

Now the system has indeed broken down, but *not through Western Europe's doing, and indeed at the expense of Europe.* Despite the similarity between the current and past "new dawns," Sisyphus is facing something radically new. This is not the place to analyze that breakdown in detail, but in short it can be attributed to two principal forces. One is the United States' playing sorcerer's apprentice, first in provoking the collapse of the international monetary system, and in exporting inflation through its deficits of the 1960s and early 1970s, but also through its post-1968 diplomacy aimed at creating a new international order. The other is the OPEC group's raising the price of oil and imposing, so to speak, a huge tax on the citizens of the consuming countries. There are, to be sure, other factors, especially the increasing demands made by developing countries for a greater say in world affairs, either in the form of massive armaments or in conferences such as the one on food and those on the law of the sea. As a result, the new agenda which faces Americans and Europeans concerns not issues *between* them but *global* issues. The *contentieux* of American economic grievances that occupied commentators and conferences from 1971 to mid-1973 is gone. This, in turn, doubly increases the discrepancy between the two sides. For the United States is used to operating in a global system even if the new turbulent world in which it finds itself differs both from the "Atlantic system" of the recent past and from the rather classical scheme of world order Kissinger had originally envisaged. But for the Europeans, the end of the Atlantic cocoon exposes their inability to face global issues, after almost thirty years of concentration on either domestic affairs, or decolonization, or "community-building," or defining relations with the United States. This discrepancy in outlooks is bolstered by a discrepancy in usable power. I have already referred to it, in connection with the impact of the oil crisis. Whether we think of American opportunities for investments in OPEC countries or for OPEC investments in the United States, or of America's military trump cards, either in the form of arms sales to OPEC countries or as residual threats; or of America's capacity to "recycle" money—on its own conditions—to needy industrial or developing victims of the new cost of imported oil; or of America's technological and industrial advantages in the scramble for substitutes for oil; or of America's "bargaining chips" in dealing with the Soviets over military issues in Europe; or of America's possible uses of food and—we find that its assets are everywhere formidable. This does not mean that the old belief among the Europeans in the necessity of their cooperation is gone, but that their common faith in Europe's resurgence has been badly hurt.

Moreover, another consequence is the increasing discrepancy within Western Europe. Between West Germany and all the others, the gap is growing, insofar as the balances of payments, success in the battle against inflation, and the strength of the currency are concerned. The division of the EEC into essentially three classes of states—Bonn, with its huge export potential, its strong Deutsche mark, its trade and payments surpluses; Italy and (at least until the North Sea oil comes to the rescue) Britain, at the low end; France and the Benelux countries in between—makes cooperation and internal cohesion far more difficult. It puts Bonn in the unhappy position of having to act either as the constant rescuer of partners in trouble or as a kind of Shylock. It puts several other European nations before the choice of having to be in debt to the OPEC countries—through borrowing or by allowing massive foreign investments—or to be in debt to Bonn or, indirectly, to Washington.

In other words, now that the agenda is filled with global issues, the West Europeans face it with a house that is not only not in order, but increasingly heterogeneous. In theory, precedence should be given to putting that house in order so as to be able to face those issues coherently. Before the EEC can move forward again and adopt all the joint policies it has avoided for so long (including a less flimsy monetary unification), it must take two series of painful measures. First, there must be greater harmony among the internal economic policies of the members. Without aggravating a recession that could become cumulative and politically unbearable, they must bring the national rates of inflation down to a comparable, reasonably low level; otherwise, there will be no possibility of monetary coordination, and a further degradation of the commercial position of the states most exposed to inflation, with dangerous consequences for the CAP *and* the free trade policy. Second, there must be a coordination of the measures that the members have to take in order to cope with the enormous rise in the price of imported oil and other raw materials. Not all of them can simultaneously overcome this ordeal by increasing their exports massively, and by attracting Middle Eastern investments or providing technology or weapons to OPEC countries. Should they try, cooperation would be replaced by cutthroat trade competition, by a race for bilateral, barterlike deals with the oil or raw material producing countries, and probably by measures aimed at forcibly reducing imports, thus violating GATT and the Treaty of Rome.

In other words, the first priority is to arrest disintegration—with measures which the persistence of national autonomy will make difficult to streamline, with publics which, everywhere except in Britain, had come to expect a continuing high rate of growth as a natural right, and at a time when all the governments, for different reasons, are in a somewhat precarious condition. Again, this does not mean that disintegration *won't* be reversed by emergency measures of cooperation. But it means that the progression toward a full panoply of common policies will once again have to wait—and that the will to stay out of the abyss is not the same as the will to unity: once inflation and recession are tamed, or the balance of payments problems are eased, will the impulse to unite be overpowering enough, or won't the habit of national muddling-through prevail again? Recent compromises leave a strange taste: some, like the agreement on regional policy, or France's return to the joint float, are small steps forward; others appear more symbolic than substantive; others read like agreements to reweave Penelope's tapestry.

Another major factor intervenes. The *relance* of 1969 was made easier by the relative indifference of the United States to most of the issues that were then being discussed among the Europeans, by American sympathy for British entry, and by the Europeans' careful avoidance of the one subject that would have proved divisive because of the "American connection": the problem of military security. But today, most of the subjects that a *relance* would have to cover— further coordination of foreign policies, defense and armaments, monetary cooperation, a common energy program (whether it deals with oil or with enriched uranium), recycling, the regulation of foreign investments, a revision of the CAP, a common space program—are subjects in which the United States is not only interested but involved, and about which it tends to make its position brutally clear. Thus the road to unity goes through U.S. consent, as was demonstrated by the difficult bargaining that led to a re-evaluation of the price of gold—on terms drafted by Washington—as well as by the episode of the EEC–Arab conference plan. Theoretically, of course, there is another course: collective defiance. But here, indeed, there is nothing new under the sun—on the contrary. After more than twenty-five years, the habit of dependence has become second nature: it leads most Europeans to insist on their own identity, to support French attempts to have it defined or acknowledged, to criticize U.S. high-handedness—and yet to be satisfied with soothing words of respect, with the token of consultation, with the shadow of identity, and to leave the ultimate worries and decisions and the substance of power to Washington. Dependence breeds abdication and irresponsibility on one side, arrogance and exasperation on the other: Kissinger had warned about it most eloquently—ten years ago.

The course of events at the end of 1975 shows this: now that the Atlantic system is collapsing, it is Atlanticism that prevails in Europe, because the only choices open to the Europeans seem to be two: either, through division, they fall into the kind of paralysis and bickering that would compromise whatever has been achieved within the EEC in the past. Or else they cooperate for the solution of the global issues, but under American leadership, with the EEC playing the role of a subcontractor. It is the United States, today like yesterday, which controls the escalatory process in European deterrence, and whose decisions on its troops and weapons in Europe determine the security of Western Europe. It is the United States and the U.S.S.R. which decide how much leeway West European diplomacy can have in world affairs. It is on the U.S. economy that the future of the West European economies ultimately depends, for a large and lasting recession here would push them even farther down. It is the United States which has the decisive voice in any recycling scheme of adequate proportions. Hence the extraordinary reversal between the beginning and the end of 1974. At the beginning, when American pressure for a common approach to the oil crisis began, Jobert first sought an agreement among the Nine, and only then consented to go to Washington—where that agreement to rule out any new agency promptly exploded. At the end, eight of the Nine had joined the International Energy Agency, endowed it with a majority-vote procedure far more compelling than anything in EEC, and adopted sweeping plans proposed by Washington; and the French, without joining it, had agreed to cooperate with it. As a result, the common energy policy of EEC is likely to be little more than the execution, by the European members of IEA, of the policies adopted, not by the EEC, but by the IEA, and the locus of coordination with France.

In other words, having had to choose between disintegration and "Atlantic" integration, the Europeans have chosen the latter. In the days of the Atlantic system, they had already made the same choice in the realm of security. On the defensive against the OPEC revolution, just as against the massive Soviet presence in the heart of Europe, the Europeans have had to adopt the United States as their protector and, to a large although not exclusive extent, as their intermediary.* But whereas the EEC had never tried to extend to the military realm, energy is within its domain, and is not exactly unconnected with issues such as trade, or money, in which it has in the past attempted to make its distinctive mark. Thus, by a cunning twist of history, the rather petty issues that had crowded the inter-Atlantic agenda in the early 1970s have indeed been transcended by a new Atlanticism, due not to that lofty act of creation that Kissinger could not quite conjure up, but to the world-shaking consequences of the energy crisis, which Kissinger has masterfully exploited.

It is hard to escape the conclusion that the long-term trend in Western Europe has been a kind of renunciation, both of fuller, distinctive unity and of a world role. The reversal of Europe's economic fortunes, the revolt against the costs of defense or against conscription, the centrifugal pulls of domestic politics, all these factors rule out a sudden mutation. Europe today deserves Acheson's old judgment of England: it has lost an empire, but not found a role.

Twelve Propositions for One Predicament

I have no intention of doing a pastiche of Ronald Laing's *Knots* (although the study of schizophrenia and of double binds is an excellent introduction to that of Western Europe since World War II). And yet, the twelve propositions that follow all tend quite naturally to read like dilemmas, paradoxes, and vicious circles. They try to condense past experiences—and to explain why the future will be tough.

1. France wants to assert her independence. But France by herself has not got the weight. Therefore she needs Europe as a supplement to her power and as the true focus of independence. And yet a "European Europe" capable of action, i.e., not paralyzable by vetoes, and functioning with some form of majority rule, might not assert *its* independence, since most of the members either give priority to their ties with Washington, or want to make sure that the common policies are compatible with and satisfactory to Washington.

Thus there is some truth in Karl Kaiser's assertion that "substantial progress on the internal development of the Community and its assertion to speak with one voice in international affairs are not possible without a change in French policy."[9]

---

*In both cases, France is more resigned than convinced, and can be said to accept, *faute de mieux*, the overall situation, if not the specific institutions. France can have her own defense scheme and nuclear force, and her own energy policy and bilateral oil deals; but she has to cooperate with NATO and with the IEA (or U.S.-led recycling schemes) because she cannot ensure either her military or her economic security by herself: détente with the U.S.S.R., cooperation with OPEC, two major French objectives, require the shields provided by NATO and by oil-consumer agencies, given both the dependence of Western Europe on the United States, and the other Europeans' preference for "Atlantic" schemes.

What he means by that is a willingness of France to "submit to the Community as a group"; which, to the French, means giving up the goal of independence, or defining European commonness in "Atlantic" terms and accepting, in effect, the priorities set, and the confinement decided, by Washington. That particular knot may, at times, *appear* untied: when Washington stops pressing, or when the issue is too minor to affect American interests, or on the contrary when U.S. demands seem to go beyond what even the more pro-American Europeans are willing to grant, i.e., to hit at the very foundations of the EEC. But on the whole, Washington has been clever enough not to go too far, and imperious enough not to let Europe go too far. Behind the smooth communiqués and soothing comments of past months, one can find this knot drawn more tightly than ever. Giscard's reasoning after the Jobert phase and fiasco is exactly the same as Pompidou's after the end of de Gaulle's drama. As a French official cleverly puts it, France must use cunning with the superpowers as Prussia did with Napoleon between 1807 and 1813: "By accepting lesser ambitions for the external policy of the Europe of the Nine, and at the cost of a modicum of benign Atlanticism, France would above all seek, discreetly but firmly, the internal reinforcement of the Community from the triple viewpoint of economics, politics, and military affairs."[10] But what made sense, first in the days of America's own benign neglect, then at the moment when U.S. pressures on the EEC's cement and European fears of a superpower condominium seemed to provoke the birth of a "European identity," makes very little sense today. For the "triple reinforcement" is now either emptied of substance by, or subordinated to, the priority France's partners chose to give to their Atlantic connections, once the energy crisis appeared to jeopardize their interests far more dramatically than America's pressures and methods had done before. Today, "reinforcement" dwindles into the seasonable striking of compromises between "petty, rapacious national demands, and the Community becomes a transmission belt which allows Washington to jerk Paris back closer to Atlantic orthodoxy thanks to the friendly persuasion of France's eight partners and the mediating skills of Schmidt. Between the IEA and other grand Kissingerian schemes on the one hand, the understandings that link Bonn and Washington on the other, Europe, the last field of maneuver for French diplomacy, becomes both a shrinking vest and a straitjacket.

2. The recent shift to economic and monetary issues has resulted in a displacement of power within the EEC, toward Bonn, the one remaining surplus country, with the best record on inflation, exports that have survived four re-evaluations of the DM, and the most solid currency. And yet, despite Schmidt's assertiveness, Bonn continues to be the most inhibited of the West European "Big Three" (Italy—the fourth—isn't inhibited: it has opted out).

Thus (and this is one of the factors of the worsening European crisis) there is a discrepancy between economic might and political power. Because of "knot" No. 1, the French would-be motor often tends to behave as a brake. But the German dynamo is no motor. Some years ago, certain writers believed that once the Federal Republic accepted the division of Germany, it would be freed of the inhibitions Bonn had observed as long as restraints on national autonomy could be rationalized as prerequisites to reunification. But the forces that inhibit Bonn go deeper. There is the continuing concern with improving relations with Moscow and Pankow, so as to "humanize" the condition of the East German people; the continuing desire for West European cooperation, despite its financial cost to the "main provider of finance for the Community";[11] the continuing reliance on the United States for military and economic security; the new determination not to be financially drained by partners and clients—so that "national autonomy" for West Germany means little more than the obligation to juggle all four balls, and not to let any one fall to the ground. This explains why the advocacy of a Bonn-Washington axis, i.e., the overt choice of Bonn as Washington's European pivot,[12] is pointless: as Kaiser, again, puts it, "the choice would be deeply regretted, if not resented" in Bonn.[13] Paradoxically, it is only if Bonn serves as a go-between or buffer that it can play the pivot's role: a naked attempt to lead the Community—even if it is toward Washington—would be rejected by Bonn's partners. Bonn can, at best, serve as Washington's transmission belt to Paris and to that other, larger belt, the EEC. This means, in effect, that Bonn's economic might, which increasingly constrains its European partners' choices, ultimately serves Washington's political power far more than its own. Once more, the potential leader appears as a brake.

3. Each of the major actors on the American–West European stage wants something, and wants the opposite also—or, if you prefer, puts impossible conditions on getting what he wants.

Thus the United States has often complained that the main obstacle to true partnership is the absence of a European partner: nine middle and small nations do not one partner make. And yet, it does not want them to "gang up on the United States," as Mr. Nixon delicately put it, i.e., to join except on U.S. terms. And when they get together, Washington complains about the rigidities of the intra-European process of decision, insists on taking part in it, denounces its outcome when it differs from American preferences, tries to split up the collective "partner" when he does not behave, or else makes what could be called ransom demands in the name of the U.S. global responsibilities and under the heading of linkage.

Thus it is not too surprising if the result in Western Europe is a babble of voices, not the one voice allegedly preferred by Washington. Similarly, France wants a world role for Europe, but only on condition that Brussels follow the French line, and Paris refuses—even if it does so less abruptly and absolutely than from 1958 to 1973—either to grant to the EEC's central institutions powers that could be used in directions not previously agreed to by France, or to endorse (for instance in Euratom, or by joining the Eurogroup) common policies that could curtail French freedom of maneuver: all of which limits the effectiveness and the scope of the European entity in world affairs. West Germany wants to be anchored in Western Europe, and tied to France, but on conditions that deprive the former of any specificity (e.g., in defense and diplomacy), and that recurrently antagonize the latter. And Britain, clearly, has not resolved her own ambivalence: the Tory government used to behave in a way remarkably similar to France's; the Laborites seem to want commitments from their partners but nothing much in reverse.

4. An unorganized and splintered Europe is unfit for the "global partnership" offered by the United States. But American insistence on subordinating European unity to global concerns keeps Europe from organizing except within American-designed frameworks.

This goes back to the argument I presented years ago about the centrifugal effects of the involvement of each European nation in the international system: the more turbulent the latter, the more disruptive its effects on the European enterprise, which needs a kind of protective barrier of calm to allow it to concentrate on its own development. First the strains of decolonization, later the global designs of de Gaulle, now the global acrobatics of Dr. Kissinger accompanying the world economic storms, have interfered with "community-building." One reason why the Year of Europe (seen by Dr. Kissinger as a kind of gift to the Europeans, a generous reply to their call for attention) did evoke more resentment than gratitude among them is that, at a time when they were trying both to "absorb" their new members and to withstand the gusts of monetary fluctuations and speculations, they did not want to be distracted by having to cope with the planetary agenda of Dr. Kissinger. And precisely because there are always enough such storms and stresses occurring at any time, America's adding to them under the pretext of helping forge an "outward-looking" Europe can hardly be deemed anything but disruptive. In this instance, the last months of the constellation of Pompidou, Brandt, and Heath had to be spent largely meeting, resisting, or arguing with American demands, protests, and excommunications.

5. An unorganized and splintered Europe is not the mistress of its fate. But one reason, perhaps, why its efforts at uniting have been so halting may well be a gnawing awareness of the fact that a united Europe would not make that much of a difference.

This has to do with a variety of factors. Even a united Europe would be at a disadvantage, by comparison with the United States, in the economic dimension of its security (i.e., the high level of dependence on outside sources of energy and raw materials and on outside markets—even with the prospects of the North Sea oil reserves). Western Europe will, whatever its own efforts, continue to depend on the United States for the military dimension of European security. It faces multiple obstacles should it want to regain influence in parts of the world now dominated by one or the other or both of the superpowers. Moreover, the solution of many problems that afflict Europe cannot be found in Europe, and has to be sought at a higher level (so that it becomes a choice between a "neo-Atlantic" framework and a "North–South" one, as in the oil imbroglio, or else there is no choice at all). To be sure, a "Europe speaking with one voice" might speak more firmly at those higher levels, or to its tutors—but those tutors would still keep the gates, Europe would still be squeezed between other powers and blocs, and the "single voice" might anyhow not be very clear.

A reflection on what could be called the scope and consequences of genuine European "autonomy" is urgently needed. There was such autonomy in the realms of internal trade and agricultural policy. There could be also in areas such as social or regional policy. But over energy, foreign investments, the world monetary system, defense, i.e., global, or inter-Atlantic, or East–West issues, a "West European focus" can be at most an *element* in a solution or a *complement* to a solution. A European monetary union may strengthen the hands of the Europeans in future bargains with the powerful dollar; it cannot impose a new world scheme. Now, attempts at devising common European policies and positions may theoretically be the best way of affecting the solution of the problems that exceed Europe's own grasp. But it is not clear that the European *framework* always makes most sense for the Europeans' own interest (in the case of oil, they are a group of states highly dependent on OPEC's goodwill, for instance), nor is it always obvious to each member of the Community that a joint position that will be no more than a contribution to a distant outcome is worth paying the price of decreasing national freedom of action. For the tighter the geographical focus, the heavier the constraint: to search for a solution in a larger framework—NATO rather than EDC, a "new Bretton Woods" rather than EMU—may actually allow a good deal more freedom of action, especially the freedom to pursue one's own domestic priorities.[*]

6. Western Europe has an obvious interest in preventing a Soviet–American "duopoly" that would keep it (and Eastern Europe) a stake, not an actor, in political and military affairs, or in thwarting a *de facto* alliance between the United States and the richer developing countries (eager for industrial and military equipment), which would squeeze it out of economic influence and even perhaps welfare and wealth. Yet the actual dependence of Western Europe on the superpowers for security, on the "new rich" for energy and raw materials (and markets to earn the money for buying these), makes it extremely difficult, even futile, for the Europeans to assert their "independence." They could not, at the European Security Conference, obtain more than paper concessions from the Soviets, given Moscow's obduracy and Washington's reluctance to press too hard on this point. With respect to the developing countries, nobody wants to brandish too big a stick, and the French are those who advocate the softest speech. With respect to the U.S.S.R., first the Germans, later the British talked tough, and the French, the Italians, later the Germans tried to charm the minotaur. Being treated

---

[*]One reason why the "spillover" theory of functional integration proved far too optimistic was its failure to distinguish between issues over which autonomy existed, so that common mastery seemed to justify paying such a price, and issues over which it didn't.

as a "nonperson," to use Jobert's expression, is a humiliating experience, and in 1973—the Year of Europe—Europe was so treated, first (at the summit in the Middle East) by the Big Two, later—and how contemptuously—by OPEC. But when one depends on the humiliators, one rarely dares behave like a real person, for one might get not merely humiliated but trampled.

Which brings us to a corollary: it is obviously in the interest of a dependent Europe to consult broadly with the United States, or with the U.S.S.R. or with the oil-producing countries, since it is when the outside world is least stormy that internal progress is most likely. But the more one consults with the mighty, the easier it becomes for the consulted ones to hint that such and such a move by their consulters would be deemed unfriendly. (Do not undermine my peace efforts in Egypt! Do not plan a West European defense system, for it would be a new military bloc and might oblige me to tighten the screws in Eastern Europe! Do not gang up with the United States and other oil consumers, for we might have to raise our prices and cut production!) And the more paralyzing such friendly advice becomes.

7. Europe is the victim of everybody else's linkage. But it cannot play "linkage" in return, for it has precious little to link.

Kissinger and Nixon can state that the American military shield, and American economic grievances, are not unrelated. Moscow can link détente and economic cooperation. Middle Eastern nations can promise oil against nuclear reactors or Mirages. What can Europe do? I do not mean to suggest that it has no assets. France, Britain, Italy have weapons to export. Most of the European nations have industrial know-how to sell to countries that do not want to be locked into monogamous embraces with Washington or Moscow. The poorer developing countries need foreign aid from Europe. But Europe suffers from two terrible deficiencies: no monopoly of anything (by contrast with the OPEC stranglehold), and not enough of what it has. Ultimately, in military as well as in economic terms, nobody's security is dependent on Europe: the ultimate guarantee is either in oneself, or in one or the other superpower.

8. There can be no coherent Europe without effective (i.e., both legitimate and "performing") central institutions. Yet their effectiveness presupposes an agreement on purposes.

This is the old "Monnet dilemma." He and his supporters hoped that once the general goal of a united Europe was set, and common institutions were established, they would then gradually decide on the directions and move toward the goals. But there have been two catches. One is that *none* of the members has been willing to let the institutions proceed toward objectives that he did not approve. It is a grave mistake to believe that France has been the only obstructor. Holland has consistently objected to a common energy policy (which would have regulated the multinationals). Germany has blocked a regional policy within EEC, and been most reluctant to envisage a European defense system outside NATO. Nobody except Mr. Spinelli has seemed to want much of an industrial policy.

Without a clear agreement on purposes, the existing institutions can grind out proposals, not policies. The second catch has been that recurrent temptation, the fling into wishful thinking: if Europe doesn't progress, it must be because its institutions are too weak; let us therefore strengthen its institutions, have its parliament elected by universal suffrage, extend the scope for majority rule in the Council of Ministers, multiply the meetings of heads of governments, increase the powers of decision of the Commission, and so on. Institutions are indispensable to prevent a consensus on goals from disintegrating, and to give it precision and follow-up. But they are no substitute for that consensus.

9. Even for merely preserving and protecting the past accomplishments of the Community, the present institutions of Brussels are inadequate. But merely to "reinforce" them would not be the answer.

Their real deficiencies do not reside in the weakness of their *powers*, but in two other sources. First, with the exception of the CAP (a painful exception that confirms the rule), the EEC is based much more on an economic liberal model than on a planning one: there is an internal free trade and free capital movements area, but no common industrial or investment policies. Even the Werner plan led, not to economic coordination or even to a joint monetary policy, but merely to a joint float, unaccompanied by measures that could have saved it from the storms that blew in from the outside. This means that the institutions of Brussels have found themselves floating above those formidable regulatory machines, the national bureaucracies. Insofar as the nation-state is still in control, Brussels has the crippling disadvantage of either leaving to the members whole areas connected with, and partly decisive for, the internal free trade area, the CAP, and the monetary union; or else producing its own proposals which end up in dusty folders; or else carefully bargaining with the separate bureaucracies in order to reach compromises that might have a chance of success, yet not so paradoxically turn out to be both too little and too much (cf. the experience of industrial and of scientific policy). Second, insofar as *each* nation-state actually experiences a loss of control, for all of the reasons which have put economic sovereignty at bay—the role of the multinationals, the way in which the international economy carries inflation or recession, the divagations of capital movements—the problem is the same in Brussels as, say, in Paris or Bonn: reactive regulation in self-defense means essentially cutting oneself off from the world economy, with serious political and economic penalties. Moreover, whereas one or the other country, pressed by its own momentary priorities, can face such penalties for a while and take its own measures, an agreement by all of them to adopt common measures to regain control has never been possible, if only—once again—because of the "American connection," as well as because of differences in economic philosophies between planning countries (like France even under a right-wing coalition) and more liberal ones (like Germany even under Socialist rule). Thus in neither set of cases is institutional reform the solution: we are back at knot 8.

10. Should there be an agreement on new goals and policies, stronger central institutions would be necessary. But they would not suffice.

I have insisted throughout this essay on the resilience of those politico-administrative containers, the nation-states, even when they have similar economies and comparable social systems. We are not dealing here with relatively flimsy or lightweight political systems such as those of the states of the American union, at the time when federalism became a reality. This suggests that it will not be enough to cap those tight national networks with a supernetwork in Brussels, or (depending on the subject matter) with several "central" networks, such as the one in Brussels for the economic realm, and another one for defense and diplomacy. For to have two levels of strong institutions is to plan either conflict or paralysis. At best, there will be the introduction of one new and formidable layer of delay, more bargaining, more splitting of responsibility (cf. the addition of a "regional" level to the communes, cantons, and *départements* in France). Any devolution must entail a dismantling, any addition must be a replacement. In institutional matters, one can say both: *on ne détruit que ce qu'on remplace* (A. Comte), i.e., the states will last as long as there is no substitute for them, and *on ne remplace que ce qu'on détruit*, i.e., the new central institutions will remain ineffective unless the national bureaucracies are deprived of powers and lines and programs and personnel, the old networks are disrupted or bypassed, and new ones are built around the central institutions. This is both different from, and even more difficult than, a transfer of allegiance. Hence one more cause for pessimism.

11. There has always been most progress when the Europeans were able to preserve a penumbra of ambiguity around their enterprise, so as to keep each one hoping that the final shape would be closest to his own ideal, and to permit broad coalitions to support the next moves. And yet there always comes a moment when a terrible clarifier calls for a lifting of ambiguities, at which point deadlock is more likely than resolution.

The clarifier may be a statesman. First it was de Gaulle, in his questions to the other Five and to Britain, summoning them to accept his view of a "European Europe" and dismissing as nefarious the ambiguities of Monnet's conception. Then came another demand for clarification, in the shape of Henry Kissinger, who requested an "Atlantic," or neo-Atlantic, commitment from the Europeans. The clarifier may also be an event, a challenge that forces a clear choice. The oil crisis (exploited by Kissinger) has been such an event. A Soviet–American deal, for instance at MFR talks, or even a unilateral American withdrawal of tactical nuclear weapons, that would tend toward a partial denuclearization of Central Europe, might be another. Most of the Europeans have always resisted demands for clarification, not out of cowardice, but out of an instinct for survival: to clarify, to choose, means to cut some possibility off. Yet not to clarify, when one is summoned to, means both, in effect, to accept internal division, and to prefer the hedgehog's tactic to any bold advance.

12. It is unlikely that the European enterprise will make rapid progress, reach

full federation, or even lead to a full economic monetary, diplomatic, and military confederation. But it is equally unlikely that it will unravel.

Americans have always tended either to salute European unity too soon, or to bemoan European disintegration too fast. There are huge material and psychological reasons why some modicum of unification is in everyone's interest. The scope of economic interdependence between the members of the EEC is such that they have no other choice. The absence of a purely national alternative, or its costs, or its insufficiency, in diplomatic and military affairs, make it advantageous for each of the members to present himself as both a free agent and as part of even an embryonic and faltering Community. None of this may be sufficient to reverse the trends gloomily described above, and to make of a European entity the fifth side of the pentagonal "structure of peace." Nor does it mean that some unexpected great shock inflicted by Washington, Moscow, or some OPEC, may not once and for all sweep away all the doubts, obstacles, and factors of inertia (although it would have to be a delicately calibrated shock: large enough to threaten the survival, not merely the security or well-being, of Western Europe, but not large enough to kill). Yet if one had to hazard a prediction, it would be that the "European idea" will stay alive, that the European enterprise will continue, gropingly and painfully, and that thanks to it the nations of Western Europe will play in world affairs a role slightly less modest than that which they could otherwise perform.

What Is There to Do?

Normative exercises of this sort have a certain built-in hubris, in that they tend to exaggerate the extent to which American policy can determine European behavior. I have myself indicated how much importance Washington's moves have had, both as an integrating and as a disintegrating factor in Western Europe. But even if ultimately the fate of Western Europe is in the hands of others, the Europeans' capacity to affect that fate, and to set limits to the capacity of others to shape it, remains. The United States cannot "build" a West European entity: neither exhortations to unity nor pressures on the EEC have resulted in sufficient coalescence among the Europeans. "What is there to do?" is therefore first of all a question to be asked *of the West Europeans*. Even in a world of global issues which somehow devalues the autonomy of Western Europe; even with the power disadvantages mentioned throughout this essay; even with the formidable obstacles of bureaucratic inertia, pressure group politics, self-perpetuating domestic parochialisms, and weak governments, do the West Europeans want to try to overcome or at least minimize their handicaps, and play a common and distinctive role? Even if they cannot, by themselves, solve their own problems, and make more than a modest contribution to the solution of the common problems of an interdependent world, do they have the will and ability to devise their own contributions and partial solutions? Or will they use the new globalism as one more alibi:

will what Giscard has called the shift from a civilization of groups to a worldwide civilization become an excuse for not behaving as a group? There is one more paradox here: those Europeans who turn to "outward-looking" solutions, and to vast frameworks in which Europe's distinctive voice cannot emerge, are often in reality the truly inward-looking ones, for they leave the answers to others.

Narcissism,[14] abdication, and a retreat from a concern for power on the world stage (often disguised as a concern for residual power to maneuver at home) are symbiotic here. To be sure, the United States cannot be ignored by the West Europeans—especially when the skill of its Secretary of State and the recent trends of history have put so many threads into one weaver's hands. But America's might and weight have become a justification for European faintness. De Gaulle's analysis remains valid, whatever one may think of his policy: without a federator within, Western Europe is either incapable of adequate progress toward unity, or prone to let the United States be the federator. My own analysis leads me to the conclusion that this will not change, unless highly dramatic circumstances—a new and far more explosive war in the Middle East, an American attempt to resolve the energy-and-payments problem by force—literally oblige the West Europeans to dissociate themselves from the United States without, however, falling into that other form of sloth or cowardice, "Finlandization." One can build scenarios of that kind. At present, they seem unlikely. One can neither rule them out—nor hope that they would come true.

We are thus left with, so to speak, the American side of the "dumbbell." A full discussion of what Washington ought to do will be undertaken elsewhere. A few suggestions are, however, in order. First, the old "solutions" proposed for European-American relations are inadequate, both because they assume a European entity that simply isn't there and because they do not fit the new global issues. Even when they were offered in reaction against the "Atlantic system," they envisaged a very different end to it from the one that brought it down. Thus disengagement—essentially a military formula—fails to take into account both the obstacles to the emergence of a West European military organization in the aftermath of American withdrawal and the unraveling effects a military disengagement might have on the rest of the network of American interests in Europe. Similarly, devolution was not devised primarily for economic issues. Should one try to expand its meaning, and for instance advocate a "neo-mercantilist" solution—a world of regional economic and monetary blocs replacing the broken-down Atlantic system—one would still have to prove that one would really stabilize economic relations in the world by restoring national economic autonomy, and that there would be self-restraint among the blocks; and one would have to show that Western Europe is able and willing to be such a bloc. As for trilateralism, it is inadequate to cope with the problems of the Third and Fourth Worlds and—in contrast with the other two schemes—pays scant attention to the issue of military security.

Are we thus left with nothing better than the present policy, a perpetuation of the grandiose American attempt to preserve what I have called indirect primacy, and to shape the solutions of all the issues? The present reassertion of American preponderance over Western Europe, the fact that *at present* the United States has become more important than ever to the West Europeans both for their military and for their economic and financial security, should, however, not create illusions. In the long run, the "globalization" of issues will tend to make the United States less decisive and relevant to Western Europe, because of a gradual, uneven, but unmistakable shift of wealth from the industrial world to large parts of the developing world, and because of the increase in military power of the Communist nations as well as many of the developing countries. The Atlantic reflex of the dependent consumer nations of Western Europe should not make one forget that for several years already they have been defining their positions—or refrained from defining positions—with an eye on Moscow as well as one on Washington. And the rush to the International Energy Agency is due in large part to a desire for being in a better position to negotiate with the "new rich," and to convince the United States that—to use the clichés of the day—conciliation, not confrontation, must be the objectives in "North–South" affairs.

If this is so, then the question for the United States is double. Should—miraculously enough—the West Europeans resume the quest for their own "personality" and take initiatives which, given the issues, cannot fail to concern the United States, what should Washington do? Should America encourage or discourage that quest? The reason I have given in the days of the Atlantic system for American encouragement remain valid: I continue to believe that in the long run a policy of primacy is doomed, that given the similarity of values and the broad range of common interests between the Europeans and the Americans, the risks involved in such a policy are outweighed by its advantages, and that in those areas where the interests and assessments differ, greater European assertiveness would actually be helpful. Should Washington opt for encouraging the European quest, it could begin by not objecting to West European initiatives even if they seem, in the short run, to run against or to delay more global or "Atlantic" approaches; and it could, in military affairs, prod the West Europeans toward "devolution," at least in the conventional realm. Should the United States, however, prefer to discourage European distinctiveness, all that would be needed would be a continuation of its policy of 1973–74.

Notes

1. For earlier assessments, see the author's "Europe's Identity Crisis," *Dædalus,* Fall 1964; "Obstinate or Obsolete," *Dædalus,* Summer 1966 (new version in the author's *Decline or Renewal?* [New York, 1974], Chapter 12).

2. On these dimensions of interdependence, see Robert O. Keohane and Joseph S. Nye, "World Politics and the International Economic System," in C. Fred Bergsten, ed., *The Future of the International Economic Order: An Agenda for Research* (New York, 1973), pp. 115 ff.

3. Raymond Vernon, "Rogue Elephant in the Forest: An Appraisal of Transatlantic Relations," *Foreign Affairs*, April 1973.

4. *Decline or Renewal?*, Chapter 13.

5. Cf. my essay on Italian foreign policy in S. Graubard and F. Cavazza, eds., *Il caso italiano* (Milan, 1974), pp. 379 ff.

6. Cf. Richard Cooper, "Economic Interdependence and Foreign Policy in the 70s," *World Politics*, January 1972, and Robert Gilpin, "The Politics of Transnational Economic Relations," in Robert O. Keohane and J. S. Nye, eds., *Transnational Relations and World Politics* (Cambridge, Mass., 1972).

7. Cf. Kissinger's interview to James Reston, *State Department Bulletin*, November 11, 1974, p. 634.

8. Zbigniew Brzezinski, "Recognizing the Crisis," *Foreign Policy*, Winter 1974, p. 63.

9. K. Kaiser, "Europe and America: A Critical Phase," *Foreign Affairs*, July 1974, p. 730.

10. J.-G. Leroy (pseudonym), "Le petit homme, la France et l'Europe," *Contrepoint*, No. 15, 1974, p. 83. We may note that the "Prussian analogy" was a favorite of the Vichy politicians trying to justify their *Collaboration d'Etat* with Germany.

11. Helmut Schmidt, "The Struggle for the World Product," *Foreign Affairs*, April 1974, p. 451.

12. For a rather brash argument in favor of such an axis, see C. Fred Bergsten's testimony, *American Interest in the European Community*, Joint Hearings before the Subcommittee on Europe and the Subcommittee on Foreign Economic Policy of the Committee on Foreign Affairs, House of Representatives, 93rd Congress, November 8, 1973, pp. 89 ff.

13. Kaiser, "Europe and America," p. 739.

14. Cf. Jacques Freymond, "Europe Atlantique—Europe européenne" (mimeo), pp. 17–18.

5

Uneven Allies: An Overview

This essay tries to examine the broad choices open to American foreign policy toward Western Europe in the near future—roughly the next ten years; this is about as far as any political scientist's horizon can be stretched. In order to do so, I shall first make some analytic remarks about the past, showing the elements of continuity in the U.S.–West European relations; and I shall assess the significance of the present moment, whose importance and novelty are well worth stressing. Only then will I discuss America's future choices. The story of U.S.–West European relations is so complex that a fair treatment would require a comprehensive essay dealing both with American and with West European achievements, fiascos, policies, and aspirations. This essay may appear unfair to the reader because it covers primarily the American side and addresses itself critically to American choices, past and coming. Let me reassure him, or cool his indignation: I have been at least as severe for the West Europeans in several essays, including one that I see as a kind of companion piece to this one—the other side of the coin.[1]

Past

My purpose in this first section is not to provide a sketchy history (although a book devoted to it is sorely needed). It is to point out the threads that run through the whole story, and the innovations introduced in the early 70s by the diplomacy of President Nixon and Henry Kissinger.

A. There are three common threads that run through the story, from the late 1940s to the early 70s.

1. The first, and most obvious, is the broad range of common interests acknowledged, publicly or privately, in words or in actions, by Western statesmen on both sides of the ocean. These have, of course, provided the basis for the association since the beginning of the cold war. To the United States, Western Europe has been a major concern in all three ways.

a. The physical security of Western Europe has been a priority in U.S. strategic policy. The United States has seen world affairs as a huge contest for power and influence between Washington and Moscow and Western Europe as a decisive stake in the balance of power. The deterrence of a Soviet attack that could either have led to the conquest of Western Europe by the USSR, or—if limited but successful—exposed the inability of the United States to protect a vital interest abroad, has been an objective less important only than the deterrence of an attack on the United States. Washington therefore gave its nuclear guarantee to Western Europe, while deploying American forces and tactical nuclear weapons there to serve as links to America's strategic nuclear forces and as security for the guarantee. These moves have also had another aim: to deter our allies from the temptation of the kind of neutralism that (given the inevitable disproportion between Soviet and indigenous West European forces) might have amounted to "Finlandization," i.e., a neutrality "tilting" in Russia's direction.

b. The economic well-being of Western Europe has been a major objective of U.S. policy since the Marshall Plan. This was partly a reaction to the "economic consequences of Versailles," to the spectacle of Europe in the 30s; partly a result of the conviction that an economically weak Europe would be a breeding ground for communism, especially in light of the existence of strong Communist parties in Italy and France; partly a policy aimed at facilitating the reintegration of West Germany into a self-confidence and productive "neighborhood"; partly a foresighted calculation about the opportunities a prosperous Western Europe would provide for American trade and investment.

c. The close association of Western Europe with U.S. foreign policy in general was also deemed essential. In other words, the desired partnership was not limited to an American guarantee of Western Europe's safety and an American preoccupation with Western Europe's prosperity. Washington wanted, on the one hand, to be able to count on the support of its European allies, if not for military operations in the rest of the world (we realized Western Europe's fears of involvement and the risk of further depleting their meager forces), at least for America's major diplomatic moves, especially toward the USSR: the existence of a regular, two-way alliance strengthened America's hand in dealings with Moscow. On the other hand, Washington also hoped to be able to count on the cooperation of these allies (and of Japan) in the functioning of the international monetary system and in the various international institutions—the UN itself, or GATT, or the ILO, etc.—that provide the framework of global economic activities.

This third concern—for diplomatic support—is more than a logical extension of the first two; it transcends them, and deserves special mention because of its significance for our allies. Whereas the first two (physical security and economic well-being) were clearly in their interests (whatever difficulties might arise over a specific strategic doctrine or the terms of economic aid, for instance), the third one put a kind of unwritten obligation on them and could at times be a cause of diffuse distaste.

Nevertheless, Western European leaders have spoken and acted as if they too had no doubts about a broad range of common concerns. Without any way of influencing U.S. strategic policy directly, they have shown their interest in a strong American nuclear force (indeed de Gaulle's repeated questioning of the plausibility of America's guarantee was derived from his analysis of the effects of America's *loss* of its overwhelming superiority over the Soviet Union). They have, without exception, shown no desire to "appease" the USSR, and, when pursuing their own policy of détente, it was always from the base of a military situation of strength. Despite divergences among themselves on matters of degree, they have been favorable to a reasonably open trading system for industrial goods and have refrained from crippling regulations on capital movements and foreign investments, in conformity with American preferences and with the rules of international conventions and institutions predominantly based on American concepts. De Gaulle, the only West European statesman who seemed, after 1962, to launch a global challenge against the United States, did not remove France from the North Atlantic alliance, though he did pull it out of NATO; and his attack on the "dollar exchange standard," while stressing its drawbacks for France and Europe, was based on his conviction that this system would ultimately prove untenable for the United States as well—which it did.

2. A second thread might be called circumscribed support to West European unification.

a. On the one hand, American policy from the late 40s to the early 60s strongly encouraged the West Europeans to go "beyond the nation-state." There was, here, a remarkable blend of "ideals and self-interest," to use the title of Robert Osgood's fine study.[2] Self-interest suggested not a divide-and-rule policy, but American support for a European entity capable of overcoming the traditional enmities between Western Europe's nations (particularly between Germany and her neighbors) and of "speaking with one voice." The more united the partner, the more effective and reliable he would be. The disproportion between the United States and the several middle-size or small nation-states in Western Europe was seen as a source of trouble in the association, rather than a condition for American predominance. This was the case, not because altruism and self-abnegation had grabbed the minds and hearts of American policymakers, but because what they wanted from their associates—military cohesion, economic prosperity *and* liberalism, overall support—seemed to be more achievable through unity than through fragmentation. It was also an enlightened form of self-interest that dictated Washington's acceptance of the "non-liberal" or "inward-looking" features of the European enterprise, especially the Common Agricultural Policy and the overseas association agreements. For these concessions to regionalism and regional protectionism, limiting American access to several markets, were seen as the price to be paid for obtaining a more cohesive and united partner. Moreover—a point rarely stressed here—the establishment of a vast open market for industrial goods and capital in Western Europe allowed a prodigious expansion of U.S. investments there—so much so that Servan-Schreiber described American industries in Europe as the second largest industrial force in the world, second only to America's own.[3]

But there was also a strong streak of idealism, a conviction that what had proved so good for America's political development and economic growth federal institutions and a vast, open market would be beneficial for the Europeans as well. The support so markedly shown by American statesmen for so long for the "Monnet method" of European unification was based on a fascinating blend of calculation (the more "supranational" the institutions, the weaker the influence of those European nation-states that were still concerned with making *their* distinctive mark on world affairs) and ideological preference (the latter being at times expressed so vigorously as to delay or complicate further West European unification). That Americans should be the "best Europeans" was often a hindrance and an irritant.

b. On the other hand (and this may explain why there was, after all, no contradiction between the ideology and the calculation), there always was a hidden (and at times not so hidden) condition to American enthusiasm for European integration: it had to be, so to speak, fitted into the overall design of U.S. diplomacy and strategy. The United States did not support *just any* kind of West European entity. Insofar as it expressed a preference for a certain kind of institutional formula, it was because Washington hoped that the "right" institutions would produce the "right" outcome. What American policy demanded, in effect, was that the West European "partner" observe one restraint and two imperatives. The restraint was in the military realm: especially after the procedural rejection of the European Defense Community (EDC) by the French National Assembly, defense was considered in Washington to be a *NATO* domain. This meant a jealous concern for keeping in American hands the power to decide on the right strategy, for preserving the structure of military integration that put West European conventional forces under an American commander-in-chief, and above all for keeping the monopoly of decisions regarding escalation. Hence Washington's opposition, strongly expressed by the Kennedy Administration, to "independent" nuclear forces. Hence the tortuous episode of the Multilateral Nuclear Force (MLF), invented to keep France's neighbors from being tempted to imitate her independent course and to join her in military "separatism." Hence also the strong pressure put on our allies to equip their forces with American weapons. There could be a "European voice," a "Eurogroup" within NATO, and there could be a nuclear committee for consultations, but there was not going to be a *separate* West European defense entity, however much we were in favor of a West European economic and even political community.

As for the imperatives: one was specific; one was broad. Specifically, we wanted an "outward-looking Europe" in economic matters, i.e., a Europe that would lower its external tariff, organize its agriculture in a way that did not shut out American goods, and refrain from turning association agreements with developing nations into *chasses gardées*. Broadly, we wanted what the French called an "Atlantic Europe," i.e., a Europe giving priority to the American connection, and we disliked the Gaullist concept of an *Europe européenne* concerned above all with defining a separate identity. For such a quest could not help magnifying differences with the United States and would result in Europe's taking global policy stands of and on its own. Here we come back to the third American concern I had mentioned above: we desired European support in global policy, but it was to be *our* global policy. Indeed, we took—in the UN or at Suez—our own approach to colonial matters and did not hesitate to dissociate ourselves from the policies of some of our European allies. We never considered that our alliance should keep us from engaging in "summitry" with the Soviet Union, particularly over arms control. In other words, the imperative of an Atlantic Europe turned out to be a second restraint on Western Europe, having to do with the higher reaches of foreign policy. And if we opposed the "Fouchet plan" approach to European institutions, while supporting Britain's application for admission to the Common Market (even though Britain was most unlikely to accept any federal scheme for Europe, indeed anything much beyond the Fouchet plan), it was because we thought that an international scheme would give too much influence to French views and vetoes, unless Britain became a member and helped isolate and neutralize France.

3. This brings us to the third thread: uneasiness and division among the West Europeans. I have analyzed elsewhere the reasons that come out of the separate histories, political and social systems, and national perceptions of the leaders and elites in Europe's nation-states.[4] Here, I want to stress only the reasons that are related to American policy and to European–American relations, my point being that ever since the beginning, the United States has been as much a factor of division as of integration.

a. Uneasiness was bred by what could be called a genteel, often unconscious paternalism in American attitudes. We are here in the treacherous realm of psychology more than in that of politics, but that does not make it any less important. To be sure, as Dean Acheson once blurted out in reply to a question, alliance politics isn't pathology or therapy. Yet the United States, having emerged from the Second World War as the most powerful nation on earth, was confronted with allies who had all experienced, or were in the process of experiencing, a clamitous decline in prestige, power, and influence, along with huge internal problems of material reconstruction, moral rehabilitation, or "identity." What America displayed was an extraordinary release of energy and a joyous, meddling, and universal exercise of leadership. To European statesmen, inevitably preoccupied by domestic priorities and, in many cases, colonial turmoil, America's "can-doism" became something of an alibi for dependence, an excuse for leaving global problems to the Protector—and this could always be rationalized as the safest way of keeping him involved in Europe's fate. Thus, insensibly, inevitable dependence (on America's military might, on American economic aid, and later on American capital, technology, and internal welfare) became a rationale for what could be called external subordination (by contrast with the satellites of the Soviet Union, subjected to internal as well as external *Gleichschaltung* [homogenization]).

Moreover, America's hearty encouragement for federal formulas had a way of overshooting the mark: such schemes as the draft for a European Political Community (1953), prepared with the help of distinguished American scholars and officials, or the European Defense Community, being premature, not only failed but backfired, for every setback dampened the enthusiasms and lowered the sights of the "Europeans" themselves. Indeed, their own tendency to concentrate on the institutional issues (supranationality, majority vote, the role of the European parliament, etc.) both reflected and reenforced a tendency to leave shrouded in ambiguity the external purpose of the "European enterprise." Should it be a Third Force, a "second pillar in the West" (probably Monnet's notion), a separate entity à la de Gaulle, or an "Atlantic Europe" as described above? Should it turn its back on power altogether and merely provide the world with a model of "depoliticized" community relations, to be imitated by other regional groups in search of peace and welfare? For a while, the Chinese and the Russians, rather than attack each other, talked about Albania. The various schools of thought about Europe could avoid facing both the depth of their disagreements on goals and the constraints on their opportunities by focusing on the juicy legal issues.

b. Uneasiness developed also because American policy toward Western Europe was based not merely on the accurate assumption of common interests, but on the broadest possible reading of the range of community, and on the subtle postulate that in realms where there could be some doubt or debate about Europe's interest, the United States knew best and had the best interests of Europe in mind. This was manifest on the colonial issue. To be sure, Washington correctly identified the long-term trend (and indeed made a terrible mistake when cold war considerations led it to endorse a colonial power, as in Indochina after January 1950). But being right and making it clear nevertheless breeds resentments when one is the dominant power.

At least the colonial issue was liquidated. But the same problem arose in connection with all three of the areas of common interest described above. In the realm of strategy, there was the subtle difference due to geography, between a Protector who, rationally, could afford to choose between a strategy of deterrence and a strategy of defense for Western Europe, and protégés for whom defense, i.e., war, whether conventional or nuclear, meant death. The Protector could envisage a "graduated" strategy of intermediate solutions between a "classical" conventional fight and the suicidal resort to strategic nuclear weapons, with the conviction that the very existence of such intermediate solutions would in fact reenforce deterrence, since an "all or nothing" strategy would appear quite hollow to the enemy. But the protégés would fear that any strategy which seemed to reassure the foe that he did not risk immediate incineration if he moved, would be only too plausible and encourage him to take risks. So that even on the subject of deterrence (the only one the Europeans wanted to hear), there was an uneasy tension between America's search for a strategy of "rational" deterrence and the Europeans' preference for the "rationality of irrationality"; between America's fascination with "flexible response" and limited nuclear counterforce, and the Europeans' obstinate embrace of strategies creating the maximum of uncertainty, the better to maintain the enemy's fear of escalation. Their distaste for devising "rational use" strategies against a failure of deterrence has persisted. Hence also the paradox of more than 7,000 tactical nuclear weapons placed by the United States into Western Europe, but no NATO agreement on their proper role. The West Europeans have never entirely lost their fear that the United States, with its monopoly of nuclear decision, might be just a bit too prudent and too slow for Europe's good. Hence the reluctance of the European members of NATO to endorse the MLF, which would in no way have ended that monopoly.

In the realm of economic and monetary affairs, uneasiness was concentrated in two areas. There was some resentment at American efforts to get the European Economic Community (EEC) to lower its external tariff at once—one of the few cements of a community initially rather poor in common policies—and at American protests against the Common Agricultural Policy (CAP). More seriously, in the 60s, there were rising misgivings against the cavalier way in which the United States, rather than take potentially painful domestic measures to reduce its balance-of-payments deficits, counted on its allies' willingness to absorb huge quantities of dollars without demanding their conversion into gold and used its commercial surplus to invest heavily in Europe.

Finally, the American desire to have general diplomatic support never went over well. There was a fear of being dragged into American anti-Communist adventures overseas; and the Europeans either tended to believe that Washington exaggerated the worldwide aggressiveness and cohesion of communism, or else thought that they were too weak and too exposed to share the front lines with Washington everywhere. Fearful of total destruction, they never saw any contradiction between their demand for a total American commitment to the deterrence of Moscow's threat to Western Europe, and their determination not to be dragged into a confrontation between Washington and Moscow or Peking in Asia, Africa, or the Middle East—between their desire for total solidarity where they were (i.e., in Europe and in their own colonies) and their preference for dissociation elsewhere. The Europeans rather felt that the Americans were the ones who contradicted themselves, insofar as they seemed to expect global support while keeping their own hands free, for instance, in arms negotiations with the USSR. Moreover, once they had gotten over their fear of American rashness in the days of the "rollback" rhetoric, many West Europeans believed that the United States could much more easily live with the Continental status quo—i.e., the division of Europe—than they. Whether they dreamed of a grand reunion of the two halves, or believed that the best that could be obtained was a lowering of barriers and a multiplication of contacts between these halves, they felt that this was a specifically West European interest—indeed, perhaps a specifically European interest—which collided both with obvious Soviet resistance or hostility and with U.S. complacency.

c. Uneasiness, however, led to division, not to rebellion. For reasons that lie outside the scope of this essay, the West Europeans split between "orthodox Atlanticists," ambivalent Atlanticists, and Gaullists. It was not, or only in appearance, a split between France and all the others, even though Washington sometimes read it that way. There were various politicians and interests in France who disapproved of de Gaulle's tactics and objectives. But there also were, among France's neighbors, many political figures who sympathized, if not with de Gaulle's style, and certainly not with his nationalist emphasis, but with his critique of America and his ambitions for Europe. Thus—especially in West Germany—there were leaders who could be called *pro forma* Atlanticists yet hidden Gaullists. Given West Germany's particular geographical position along the Iron Curtain, precedence had to be given to the security relation with the United States; but they were not unhappy to hear the French statesman draw global perspectives different from Washington's and raise sharp questions about American practices, for this was a way of having Washington's complacency shaken without having to pay any price.

Yet the practical result of this division (and of the purely intra-European factors of discord) was that the Community remained a rump. Politically, there was neither supranational federation (de Gaulle dealt it one last killing blow in 1965) nor Fouchet-plan intergovernmental leadership: the combined opposition of Holland, within, and of the United Kingdom and the United States outside, had killed *that* in 1962. After EDC, there was no attempt at a common defense, since the United States did not favor it, and France's secession from NATO in 1966 made such prospects even more remote. There was no coordination of foreign policy. There was merely a free market for goods, capital, and labor, a complicated agricultural policy, a foreign economic policy essentially limited to trade negotiations with associates and with the United States. From 1963 to the fall of de Gaulle from power in 1969, the EEC was deadlocked. This deadlock in effect kept the Community alive, a truncated testimony to the high hopes of the 50s, but it also preserved American predominance and prevented the birth of any "European nationalism" that might have challenged Washington. Western Europe's impotence was demonstrated at the time of the Soviet invasion of Czechoslovakia; the West Europeans deplored the casualness of America's reaction—the United States had its eyes on Vietnam and on Chicago—yet they themselves said little, did nothing at all, and were rather relieved to see the crisis stay local.[5]

B. To what extent have these general trends been transformed by the new leaders and events of the period 1969–73? Again, having dealt with this period in more detail elsewhere,[6] I will limit myself to what is most essential for an understanding of the present and of the future.

1. With the benefit of some hindsight, one can now see that, from the viewpoint of West European unification, this period constituted a remarkable—and lost—opportunity.

a. At its most superficial level (but is it?), this period saw the coming to power in Paris, Bonn, and London of three men—Pompidou, Brandt, Heath—whose feelings and calculations toward Washington were not identical, but for whom the creation of an effective West European identity was a common priority. Brandt was less "Atlantic" by far than Erhard or Schroeder had been, partly for *Ostpolitik* reasons; Heath wanted to prove that England in the EEC would not be Washington's Trojan horse; Pompidou, for all his Gaullism, accepted as a fact the death of de Gaulle's dream of a "Europe from the Atlantic to the Urals," as a reality the dangers and limitations of a French solo performance, and as a necessity the resulting priority for what Gaullism had sometimes derisively called "la petite Europe."

b. Moreover, some of the intra-European factors of discord had been fading away. The gap between pseudovictors (France and Britain) and losers of World War II (Germany and Italy) had vanished. Colonial distractions were over. Bonn was less unsure of itself; Paris (after May '68 and the financial crisis of November '68) and London (facing economic sluggishness, social strains, and payments problems) were less sure of themselves. The three countries' *Ostpolitiken* were finally on the same wave length; all three were seeking a détente, yet with the hope that recognizing the status quo would help soften it up.

c. Finally, there was a new French strategy. It aimed at a revival of the EEC after the years of deadlock. It lifted the veto on Britain as a precondition to that revival; and it set aside the issues of ultimates de Gaulle had raised, for they had provoked American opposition and intra-EEC paralysis. Thus, on the one hand, precedence would be given to what might be called a "safe," internal issue, monetary unification, as a way of linking the West European economies more tightly. On the other hand, the West Europeans would refrain from deliberately challenging American preferences or policies: a common European foreign policy, a separate defense were not on the agenda. (Indeed Pompidou proclaimed the necessity of American forces in Europe.) Since the new American president and his chief adviser had, on their first trip abroad, come to Paris to bury the hatchet, and in particular to indicate both continuing support for the idea of a European entity and indifference to its institutional make-up, this prudent French policy of reenforcement without collision seemed to have a good chance of success. But its success depended on one prerequisite: a calm external environment, so that the entry of Britain *and* the "deepening" of EEC could take place and be digested without outside interference. In other words, the new strategy rested on the hope that with the removal of two major irritants—de Gaulle's grand challenge and the Johnson policy in Vietnam—there would be no reasons for new friction between a prudent, if "inward-looking" Europe, and Nixon's United States. But things did not turn out that way.

2. American policy toward Western Europe underwent several important changes. To be sure, the conviction that there were crucial common interests persisted. So did the specifications about the limits and the content of West European unity: given the West Europeans' own avoidance of the issue of defense au-

tonomy, the Nixon–Kissinger team did little to encourage any alternative to or reform of NATO in defense matters (even if overt hostility to the French nuclear force disappeared). Nor did the United States move away from the preference for an economically "outward-looking" Europe. But there were two major innovations.

a. The first was the new priority to transforming relations with the two major Communist powers. To be sure, the West Europeans had preceded the United States on the road to Moscow (Kissinger had initially been critical of Brandt's approach). They had regretted America's refusal to deal with "Red China." Washington had been more skeptical than its allies about the Soviet-sponsored Conference on Security and Co-operation. But this was not really the point. The new political strategy of the United States seemed to imply a subtle demotion of Western Europe's importance. Western Europe had to remain an ally because its safety and prosperity provided the United States with essential trump cards in dealing with the USSR, but even this suggested than an end-in-itself had become a tool. Only yesterday, the global policies of the United States, which the Europeans were either told to support or were kept away from, had seemed less central than the U.S.–West European relationship; and whenever the latter appeared to lose its relative dominance—as during the Vietnam years—many Europeans and Americans screamed bloody murder. Now these global policies were taking clear precedence. Indeed, the rise within the U.S. Congress of a strong pressure for the reduction of American conventional forces in Western Europe, while resisted by the administration, seemed both to underline this fall from grace and to be its perhaps unintended yet plausible consequence. In other words, in the grand attempt to turn relations of enmity into merely adversary, indeed partially cooperative, relations, it seemed that Western Europe mattered less. But was this not something that would actually serve the designs of Pompidou?

b. It might have, except for a second innovation. The first left Western Europe aside; the second quite literally attacked it. I refer to a double change. It was a switch in style: the return to a "national interest" approach, after years in which the dominant mode of U.S. policy had been the "interest of the free world" style. If the new compass was to be the *national* interest (in part because, on such a basis, a new approach to Moscow and Peking was much easier), then the old American sense of urgency about West European unification, the preference for dealing with one composite partner instead of nine national ones was gone, and in fact notice was being served that the new criterion would be applied to past policies, for instance, in the realm of economics. Indeed, there also came to be a switch in substance after August 1971: the import surcharge, the suspension of convertibility, the devaluation aimed at recreating a trade surplus, the proposals for world monetary reform aimed at eliminating payments surpluses abroad, the offensive against the CAP, the protest against trade diversion resulting from Britain's entry, the drive against reverse preferences and the "Mediterranean policy" of the EEC, the pressure toward a new round of trade negotiations pointing to a zero tariff on industrial goods (and also, in NATO, the demand for "fairer" burden-sharing and new offset agreements)—all of these amounted to a revocation of past "concessions" consented in exchange for the hoped-for political advantages of a united Europe. The latter was obviously felt to be either unlikely or less necessary; while America, in its own time of economic and monetary difficulties, would not refrain from putting pressure on, and trying to dissolve, the glue of the EEC.*

c. The two separate innovations came together in Kissinger's "Year of Europe" speech of April 1973. On the one hand, the old notion of an Atlantic Europe was reasserted: i.e., Europe's unity was not an end in itself; it had to be subordinated to a higher goal, which transcended Europe and included not only the United States but Japan. On the other hand, this diminution of Western Europe was taking on an entirely new dimension for two reasons. First, Kissinger was demanding in effect that the Europeans join the United States in a whole (if vague) series of worldwide undertakings. Second, he was obliquely asking for concessions in trade matters, because of the interrelatedness of security and economic issues ("linkage"), while raising once again the security issue in terms that could not help but revive European fears, since he stressed the impact of "nuclear parity" on deterrence and the need to define the "requirements of flexibility" anew. Later, in the lengthy discussions on a joint Atlantic declaration, he raised the issue of consultation in a way that suggested that despite his repeated assurance that Washington still favored European unity, the United States wanted not only to make sure that its *outcome,* in policy terms, be right (i.e., "we will expect to be met in a spirit of reciprocity") but also to take a more active part in the *process* so as to have more of a say in the outcome. Thus subordinated to a far more ambitious and global American policy, told to make adequate economic and monetary concessions, and asked to consult more intimately with the United States, the European entity, whose unity Washington said it was still supporting, was not left with a great deal of autonomy. In exchange, it was told merely that "the United States will never knowingly sacrifice the interests of others . . . consciously injure the interests of our friends": obviously, defining these interests for them was not felt to be injurious.

d. This far more heavily conditional and confining approach to Western Europe corresponded to two changes in U.S. policy-making: one, so to speak, at the top, the other in depth. At the top, I refer to the mode of operation of Kissinger. Convinced that creativity and bureaucracy are enemies, that leadership is personal, that flexibility and maneuver and secrecy are the highest attributes of a creative diplomacy, that control is the precondition to success (all very Gaullist attitudes), Kissinger proved far better at dealing with responsible statesmen in

---

*This was the time when members of the administration were complaining that it was often easier to deal with Moscow or Peking than with the allies.

command of their own policies than with collective structures, whether coalition governments or international organizations. Hence his preference for man-to-man rather than institutionalized diplomacy, for dealing with French, German, or British leaders rather than with the heavy Brussels machinery. In the latter, he could not fail to see either a rigid complication, or a smokescreen that European statesmen could hide behind in order to resist American pressures or delay response to American demands. (Tolerance, if not enthusiasm, for the rather clumsy and inefficient bureaucracy of Brussels, requires considerable faith in Europe's capacity to overcome national habits and institutions, and nothing allows one to believe that Kissinger ever had such faith. So as usual his behavior turned into a self-fulfilling prophecy.) Further, in order to unfreeze situations that had been marked by sclerosis or inertia, he would lean on a "pivot": Chou En-lai, to unblock the relations with both Communist powers; Brezhnev, to get SALT and détente going; both these men, to act on Hanoi; Sadat, to launch the post-Yom Kippur piecemeal settlement policy; Faisal (without result) to have some leverage on OPEC. But in the Pompidou–Brandt–Heath period he found no comparable pivot on the European scene.

At the deeper level, his policy unfolded at a time when the attitude of the relevant American publics was changing both toward Western Europe and toward the outside world in general. Congress was growing more restive about U.S. military engagement abroad, and more critical of Western Europe's trade policies and alleged failure to "neutralize" (i.e., pay for) the balance-of-payments losses incurred by the United States because of its forces in Europe. The foreign policy establishment that had guided diplomacy and strategy in the cold war days and nurtured the belief in Western Europe's importance and unity was now partly depleted by age, partly demoralized and splintered by Vietnam, partly disconnected from the new administration. Nixon, always suspicious of the "Eastern establishment," and Kissinger, its product and protégé but reluctant to take advice and intent on protecting his initiatives and calculations, were keeping it in the dark. The priorities and attention of the public-at-large were turning inward (as any teacher of international relations or reader of newspapers has observed). And yet the public was satisfied with the maintenance—at lower cost in blood and crises—of U.S. predominance. And it was pleased both by the prospect of a détente with enemies and by the new toughness toward increasingly competitive allies (suspected of wanting to take advantage of their access to the American market after having fattened on American investments, which, some said, meant fewer jobs in the United States). The public thus left Nixon and Kissinger free to pursue their global acrobatics. Complacency instead of the old consensus, voyeurism (or mere appreciation of the fine spectacle provided by the two men) rather than the participation that had verged on hysteria in the days of Joe McCarthy—this was the new public mood, and it was not very friendly to Europe.

3. The effect of the new policy and mood on Western Europe was complex. At the cost of "roughing up" chronology, I would stress the following aspects.

a. Superficially, the new American approach seemed, unwittingly, to goad

Western Europe to greater unity. While de Gaulle had been the aggressor, so to speak, the partners of France refused to follow him. Now that Nixon and Kissinger were firing the shots, there was a tendency to close ranks. The new American policy toward the USSR was applauded as long as it merely tended to slow down the strategic arms race (the acceptance of approximate equality with Moscow did not provoke in Western Europe the same anxieties as in Senator Jackson's mind). But there was a fear of direct U.S.–Soviet talks and deals that could create an imbalance dangerous for Western Europe's security (and, even more, self-confidence), even while preserving the global balance; hence considerable anxiety regarding Mutual and Balanced Force Reductions (MBFR), even among those Europeans who endorsed the idea. There was a fear that—at the Conference on Security and Cooperation in Europe (CSCE) or at the summits—the Big Two might be putting the development of their own mutual relationship ahead of West European concerns. The statement on the prevention of nuclear war at the 1973 summit seemed to indicate that the superpower dialogue had been given public precedence over NATO obligations, and Kissinger's perfectly justified denials about the letter did not quite dispel doubts about the spirit. All of this made it possible for the West Europeans to begin—at last—foreign policy coordination with the preparation of a common stand for the CSCE; and it led Pompidou to allow Jobert, in 1973, to raise for the first time since the early 60s the issue of a separate European defense.

As for the "direct attack" on the EEC, it ended up (also on the surface) reenforcing the Community. The common float of six of the nine currencies in 1972 was an attempt to create an "island of stability" in a chaotic world, pending an agreement on a new global system. The CAP was preserved, and American demands for other concessions warded off. Kissinger's request for "a new Atlantic Charter" allowed Jobert to rally his colleagues behind the idea of a separate document stressing Western Europe's own identity. Thus America's new, more stringent attempt to define the limits and nature of European unity, which previously had contributed to arresting it, now seemed to help it move along—in a direction that was not what Washington had wanted.

b. At a deeper level, however, centrifugal forces were at work, precisely because a *solid* reenforcement would have required a quiet world. On the one hand, the reaction of many West Europeans to the first aspect of Kissinger's diplomacy had been symptomatic of the craving for dependence I have mentioned. They complained of being neglected; they kept pulling Kissinger's sleeves (which explains in part why he thought that his "Year of Europe" speech was meeting their demand for attention). To be sure, when he did pay attention again, they did not like what he requested, but at least it seemed to suggest, however contentiously, that the old relationship still mattered. It was bad to be so publicly demoted to a lower place in what Jobert called America's cosmogony,[7] but it was good to be shown that one fitted in it. Thus, even in the summer of 1973, behind the façade of European solidarity that so irritated Kissinger (obliged to receive a Danish EEC spokesman with no powers of negotiation), there were subtle differences between French activism—which rejoiced at Kissinger's *gaffes* and the attitudes of several other countries, which deplored them and had no desire for a break.

On the other hand, the attempt to strengthen European unity found its most serious limit in the uneven impact of outside winds on a heterogeneous group. The "monetarist" approach to economic unification was a short cut that required intense internal cooperation (a pooling of reserves, a reevaluation of gold, comparable credit policies) as well as a stable environment. But periodic reshufflings of currency rates among the major powers, huge speculative movements of private capital, and different domestic priorities at a time of rising inflation exposed the monetary "serpent" to recurrent distortions between its component parts, and neither the lira nor the pound was even able to join it. External storms meant that energy had to be spent on simply keeping whatever had been accomplished from being blown away. Different internal economic priorities doomed attempts at finding new areas for common policies: there was not sufficient will; attention was mobilized by domestic tasks. Hence the futility of the Paris summit of 1972. And Britain, far from bringing a new dynamism into the EEC, turned out to be a headache even under Mr. Heath. Britain's economic weakness and the persistence of political opposition to the EEC in Britain obliged him too to beg out of some of the common enterprises (thus, the float) while demanding specific aid in other respects (regional policy).

This explains the kind of West European *Götterdämmerung* of October '73– Spring '74. At first, the fear of the consequences on Western Europe of the Arab oil embargo and restrictions, the unwillingness to be drawn, if not into the conflict, at least into a de facto alliance with the United States by America's use of European bases for its airlift to Israel, indignation at being left out of the resolution of the crisis by the superpowers produced apparent unity—a unity of lamentation, in the form of a common statement on the Arab-Israeli dispute. But soon all appearances exploded: internal solidarity was not strong enough to produce a statement of support to Holland; the Copenhagen summit ended in deadlock on regional and energy policies; each member looked after its own bilateral deals; the common float disintegrated when France, faced with a run on the franc and the impact of the quadrupled price of imported oil, jumped out in January '74; and Secretary of State Kissinger, in proposing a consumers' front under American leadership, provoked an open break between Jobert and his partners. This time, France was isolated, not merely—as so often in the past within EEC, but far more seriously, by the fact that her eight associates chose to join a new agency outside EEC. In a grand symbolic finale, the three leaders of the phase that was coming to such a crashing end—Heath, Brandt, and Pompidou—all disappeared, while Kissinger remained.

Present

What is the significance of the present moment—the situation which has prevailed since the Organization of Petroleum Exporting Countries (OPEC) decisions on the price of oil and the general derangement of the "American world economic system" of the postwar period? This is the system characterized by the supremacy of the dollar, low industrial tariffs among the developed non-Communist powers (free trade playing the same ideological role of bulwark and ram for the most advanced power, as in the British system of the nineteenth century), a high rate of economic growth, the spectacular rise of largely American multinational corporations, and cheap access to the energy and raw materials of the Third World. We are at a turning point.

A. The objective conditions have been deeply transformed.

1. For all the industrial powers this is a period of intense crisis.

a. Cheap access to oil abroad is over, and there is a risk of "more OPECs" covering other raw materials. Moreover, economic nationalism in the developing countries is liable to lead them to nationalize basic resources and industries producing them, to restrict the multinationals to a commercial role, and to try to limit their profits. Even if no cartels comparable to OPEC emerge, the developing nations are unlikely to give up their current offensive against the postwar world economic order, their demands for a redistribution of the world's wealth, and their determination to exploit whatever assets they possess, whether these consist in products needed by the industrial powers, or in masses of votes in international bodies, or in sympathy for their cause among fractions of the ruling elites or intelligentsia of the advanced nations.

b. Unevenly (see below) but quite generally, the increase in the cost of oil has created balance-of-payments problems for most of the industrial countries, and there is a danger that each one will try to seek remedies in bilateral deals with oil-producing countries, in export subsidies aimed at making the execution of these deals possible, or in import restrictions and exchange controls, in sum, in the destruction of the "open" economy. Moreover, the accumulation of huge reserves by the OPEC countries, far in excess of what several of them can use productively for their development, or even for shiny weapons, creates new risks of financial strain on the banking system of the industrial nations, especially if much of the revenue acquired by OPEC is used for short-term, easily maneuverable deposits.

c. In addition, and quite apart from the oil drama, the "open" world economy is suffering from a combination of inflation and recession. The inflation has, undoubtedly, many causes, and experts disagree about the fundamental ones. Some point to the decreasing productivity of capital, others to the pull of demand and the push of pressure groups, others to the inflationary effect of American monetary practices both at home and until the switch to floating rates in March 1973 abroad. The result has been a depreciation of the currencies of those countries most affected by inflation (and this has undoubtedly been one incentive for OPEC's action).

Measures taken, in the United States and elsewhere, to fight inflation by restricting credit and curbing the resources of enterprises have provoked a decline in investments, a fall in industrial activity, and a rise in unemployment. Where the government has decided to combat recession with budget deficits (through tax cuts), there is a new danger of inflation, unless the capital market can be tapped without competing with private enterprises eager for funds. This means that, in order to absorb the inflationary impact of such deficits while paying for imported oil, such governments may need the help of OPEC. That is, the creditors may be asked to keep the debtors afloat! Meanwhile both the inflation and the recession are fed by the oil crisis. Imported oil costs much more, and the hike in prices constitutes a tax on the industrial powers. Some of the measures they will have to take in order to cope with it—a reduction in imports, domestic conservation programs—may contribute to the recession; others—a shift from production for the domestic market to exports, the development of substitutes for imported oil—may contribute to inflation, as well as to economic dislocation and domestic shortages. Further inflation in turn might provoke further OPEC price rises. A spreading recession in the industrial world would make paying for OPEC oil more difficult; while a quick recovery would increase the level and the load of oil imports.

d. There is, at present, nothing more than a stopgap, de facto international monetary system. The "dollar exchange standard" collapsed in part because Japan and Western Europe could no longer absorb gigantic amounts of dollars, in part because fixed rates could be maintained only by painful and politically unacceptable domestic monetary and credit constraints so as to eliminate imbalances. Short-term capital flows made possible by the "open" economy were putting intense, speculative pressure on the weaker currencies, and domestic priorities (inevitably the first concern of governments) made the external goal of exchange stability seem arbitrary or perverse. But the successor system of "dirty floats," whether or not it is inflationary (as is argued by those who point to all the structural factors that prevent a decline of prices in interdependent industrial economies), is no more than a *pis aller.* If "a major drawback of a system of freely fluctuating rates is that it substitutes market reconciliation of inconsistent payment objectives for the reconciliation of objectives through international cooperation and agreement,"[8] managed floating rates add to this drawback the risks of constant maneuver. The establishment of an international monetary system capable of imposing effective constraints on international liquidity and of inciting governments to create the internal conditions for the stability of their currencies has been postponed because of present uncertainties—which this postponement feeds.

2. But there is a second objective change—*among* the industrial powers.

a. On the one hand, the United States has emerged as a relative winner: OPEC did for Henry Kissinger what he had not been able to achieve by himself. OPEC's coup may have been a disaster, or at least a major headache, for the industrial world as a whole, but it had windfall aspects for the United States. Far less dependent on imported oil than Europe or Japan, the United States faced a less stringent payments problem. It is in the United States, the most advanced industrial power, with a stable political system and a currency that, for all its recent weakness, remains the world's most demanded reserve, that OPEC funds are most likely to be invested. It is from the United States that OPEC countries can best buy the technology, industries, and brains they need for their development and the weapons they covet for their ambitions. It is the United States which, as a major oil producer and a leader in technology, has the greatest opportunities to develop substitutes for imported oil and for oil generally—and to sell them to its allies. It is the United States which is most able to be the "lender of last resort" in secondary recycling, i.e., to raise the money needed by countries with balance-of-payments crises and insufficient OPEC investments, loans, or orders. In other words, whereas a drastic reduction in the price of oil would be a blessing for its allies and save them from having to slave for OPEC, Washington could live well with a merely moderate reduction—just enough to keep the development of oil production and new sources of energy at home profitable. Of course, the United States has suffered some very hard knocks: the recession, the crisis of political authority at home, the debacle of Indochina abroad. But on the subject of the so-called "ungovernability" of Western democracies, it is hard to say whether Western Europe is better or worse off than the United States; the recession has not been limited to the United States, and the lamentable end in Indochina was but the inevitable outcome of a long course of error.

   b. On the other hand, the crisis has demoted a Europe that had become used to seeing itself, along with Japan, as a major "civilian power," more important to world trade and more productive than the United States. It has also aggravated Europe's internal heterogeneity. As we have seen, France in 1974 had to leave the joint float so as not to become a dependent of the strong Deutsche Mark, and if it decided to rejoin it by mid-1975, it was largely in order to prevent the revaluation of the franc against the falling dollar from continuing and thus undermining a French export drive that, for all its successes, was still far more fragile than Germany's. Bonn, with a low rate of inflation, a somewhat smaller dependence on imported oil than its neighbors, a very strong currency, exports that had triumphed over four revaluations, and huge payments surpluses, is in a much more enviable position than its partners (even though this strength has its own drawbacks, while recession has hit Germany too). Britain, for deep structural reasons, and Italy, for primarily political ones—but is it easier to change a stalemated political system than a sluggish economy?—are in very serious trouble: their currencies are under constant pressure and their reserves are running out. France is in temporary trouble—temporary insofar as the restoration of its payments equilibrium without continuing recession depends partly on the smoothness of domestic events, partly on the prosperity of its biggest client, West Germany, whose own prosperity depends on the United States. This vulnerability of the West European economies to America's is another factor that, in the present phase, casts a pall over Western Europe; but unlike the oil problem, this one can hardly be said to give a relative advantage to the United States.

3. The consequence of these events and problems is a sudden change in the context of U.S.–European relations. Yesterday's issues either related to the "Soviet problem" (i.e., the complex of problems concerning the physical and political security of Western Europe), or else they were "bilateral" U.S.–European issues concerning trade, agriculture, offset agreements, the negotiation of mutually acceptable exchange rates, etc. Today, in addition to the Soviet-related issues, whose very persistence underlines Western Europe's dependence on America's might, the new problems on the agenda are global. The bilateral issues are either gone or look trivial. They have been blown away by the storms and made irrelevant by the removal of the taproot of discontent: America's sense of relative decline, compared to her allies, in the period 1969–73. Instead, we are faced with issues such as a new monetary system, the price of oil and the payments difficulties resulting from it, the link between raw materials or energy prices and the prices of industrial goods, food and famine, the disposition of the oceans, new technologies to replace or complement oil, the plight of the oil-poor countries of the Third World, the hideous question of nuclear proliferation, the stuffing of conventional weapons into powder kegs, and of course the perils of a spreading recession and the Arab–Israeli dispute. The ugly word "globalization" reflects both the shift and the headaches.

B. The subjective conditions have of course also been transformed.

1. This is a period of reexamination on both sides of the Atlantic. But here again there are deep differences.

a. The United States, ever since 1941, has been used to "living globally." Coping with world-wide issues is not exactly new: indeed, both George Ball and Henry Kissinger have remarked that the United States is the only non-Communist power with global responsibilities. Kissinger's activism has aimed at replacing one set of global issues (those of the cold war confrontation) with another; his "state of the world messages" bear testimony to this. He has succeeded beyond expectation. But the "shock of recognition" for the United States consists in discovering (rather angrily and partially) that the kinds of global issues that crowd today's agenda are not those which the neoclassical or neo-Bismarckian design and diplomacy of the Nixon–Kissinger era had hoped to bring to the fore. They centered on the relations between the superpowers; insofar as they paid attention to economic issues, it was either in order to use them as baits (with respect to the Soviets) or in order to redress imbalances with the allies—i.e., as a kind of political warfare, at our initiative. Instead of this we now find ourselves faced with a host of issues involving above all the Third and Fourth worlds, and these issues, largely economic, are raised by others in such a way that they actually endanger our long-range "situation of strength" vis-à-vis the Communist powers—either because our challengers, while active in the open international capitalist economy, attack the rules of the game as drafted by the industrial powers, or else because our critics actually reject the capitalist model both for their economies and for the world economy. It is therefore not always clear whether

Kissinger is the sorcerer, or the sorcerer's apprentice. Moreover he has discovered that, in the realm of Soviet-related issues, NATO's military strength cannot prevent a possible weakening of Western Europe through domestic developments, especially in Mediterranean countries; while détente, at Helsinki or in arms talks, did nothing to curtail the long shadow of Soviet might on Europe's façade; indeed that it perhaps made these domestic changes behind it easier.

b. Reexamination is even more painful on the other side of the ocean. However damaging to some Europeans' pride the "fall from grace" in America's eyes and moves may have been in 1969–73, it corresponded to a period of high hopes for Europe's development and world influence. Now there is a genuine fall; gone is the faith in constant growth, which had accompanied the whole European enterprise. Instead, there is awareness of economic insecurity, added to the never-departed sense of military insecurity. Strategically, Western Europe knows that it can less than ever match the Soviet Union. Economically, it has been made rudely aware of its dependence both on the United States (inflation, recession, etc.) and on the OPEC countries (and the other raw materials producers). The latter dependence was always there, but it had remained hidden, unlike the Red Army—one more proof of the importance of perceptions and of the "necessity" of crises. Meanwhile domestic shifts in southern Europe have added a sense of political insecurity.

This overall European fall does not affect the perceptions of all countries in the same way. Bonn, used to dependence in the fields that have been central to its diplomatic strategy and foreign policy, aware of economic fragility because of historical memories in part, and yet least affected by the change in Europe's fortunes, can afford to see in its relative eminence not only a reward for sound management but an opportunity for external assertion. The shift from Brandt to Schmidt both expresses and symbolizes this new perception. Britain, under Labour party management, can see in the change a new reason for skepticism regarding the higher ambitions of the European enterprise and in the North Sea oil a saving card, to be kept strictly national. But France, which had been the most ambitious for Europe—while the most niggardly on common institutions, lest too big a dose of supranationality divert Western Europe from those far-reaching distinctive goals—is the most seriously hit, both because (by contrast with Britain and Italy) it has been hurt while operating at a (relative) peak at least in terms of growth and foreign trade—and because the new global issues have provoked one more European identity crisis. The fact that Jobert, a convinced and committed "European," turned intensely nationalist in his last weeks in office, while Giscard, another "good European," seems to turn *mondialiste* ("the world has moved from a civilization of groups to a global civilization") indicates both disarray and distress.

2. From the changes in perceptions, let us proceed to changes in policies, which set the stage for our consideration of future options.

a. American policy toward Europe has changed in tone, pace, and substance, but only partly in significance. The "Year of Europe" speech had called for a joint declaration of intent to transcend petty issues and turn toward new common problems. It was friendly, indeed pleasing, in tone; it suggested no pressing deadline; and while calling for collaboration on energy, it remained vague. By the time the declaration was signed in June 1974, it had been overtaken by events. Kissinger, irritated by the troubles he had encountered in the process of getting it, by Western Europe's attitude toward the Yom Kippur War, by the reluctance he felt among his allies toward his rather militant (although not military) approach to OPEC, switched from a tone of patient sympathy to one of increasing and public contempt. He pressed the allies very hard for a rapid alignment of the consumer countries: the International Energy Agency (IEA) was set up fast and given vast amounts of work, and the same happened a little later with the recycling facility he proposed. As for substance, instead of a mere commitment to face new problems and to solve existing ones, the new policy entails the eclipse of the old ones and action—not mere talk—on the oil crisis in its various political and economic dimensions.

And yet, if the "attack" on the EEC has therefore apparently stopped, it may well be only because the two main implications of the Nixon–Kissinger approach to Europe have been not only confirmed but triumphantly reasserted. The limited role of Europe in America's global policy, indeed the merely instrumental or supplemental role of Europe, is more evident than ever. First there is now the grand strategy toward OPEC: here Europe's role merely consists in joining the common consumer front, so that OPEC countries may not play divide-and-rule, while the United States tries to regain the initiative which OPEC moves have taken away. Second, there is the new general approach to the developing nations; here, switching (once the IEA was in place) from "confrontation" to "conciliation," Kissinger let the preparatory conference requested by the French fail, and immediately after that failure (which had exposed once more the Europeans' own divisions), he made the concessions that would have ensured its success— thus proving that only the United States, not Europe, retains the key to a bargain with the nations of the Third and Fourth worlds. Third, there is America's mediation of the Arab–Israeli dispute (not exactly unconnected with the oil problem), but since Kissinger here cannot count on Europe's support, he shuts the allies out (and tells them to shut up), putting on his door the sign: Do not disturb. In this way (and by changing America's objectives in that part of the world), he has so far retained the initiative. Finally, there is détente, in which Europe's role is minimal so far as he is concerned.

Kissinger is trying to keep his tracks separate—in good divide-and-rule fashion. The USSR is relegated to the fourth track; Europe to the first two; the Arab countries are functionally split between the first three. But Kissinger maneuvers all four. This shows that the other implication of his earlier policy toward Europe—the desire to control its development and policies—is still of capital importance. Only it is done now, not through demands for consultations and concessions, but through demands for alignment; not by insisting that the EEC open itself up, so to speak, to American goods and preferences, but by requesting that it close ranks and be tugged behind the American vessel. The questions this policy raises are obvious: is this "demotion" of Europe wise, and insofar as Kissinger has reestablished control, what will he do with it? Where is the vessel going?

b. If America's policy has the same meaning in a new context, Western Europe's represents a major shift, all of whose implications are not yet clear. It can be summed up as follows. For years the EEC had hesitated between an "Atlantic" and a "European" Europe. It had dodged a clear-cut choice and usually been divided whenever pressed to make one. (The one exception was the year 1973 before the oil price hike, as we have stated before; but even then the "tilt" toward the French conception, in reaction against U.S. postures and pressures, was not strong enough to overcome internal sluggishness and discord.) In 1974, eight of the Nine chose an "Atlantic" Europe, by accepting the IEA and Kissinger's strategy. The ninth—France—with no other effective avenue of activity but Europe, resigned itself to "alignment," with the hope that this conciliatory attitude would allow the Nine to resume their Sisyphean march toward a "European Europe," now that a major factor of paralysis, the Franco–American discord, was removed from the EEC and that France had made some institutional concessions to its associates. We have seen that Pompidou, in his friendliness to the United States in 1969–72, had made the same calculation. But a policy that seemed justified in the years of "benign neglect" by the United States and had to be dropped when the United States itself began showing unfriendliness makes much less sense today when the United States, both in its calls for allied solidarity and its own initiatives toward OPEC and the other developing nations, seems determined not to leave much breathing space for a distinctive West European voice. There is a false symmetry between France's nonparticipation in, yet cooperation with, NATO and her nonmembership in, yet cooperation with, the IEA. Defense was never an EEC function, whereas energy was always supposed to be within its orbit and has clear connections with issues that go to the heart of the EEC: industrial policy, trade, monetary cooperation.

In other words, the Europeans, having discovered that their economic security is endangered by OPEC, have turned *to the United States,* just as they turned to the United States when they realized that their military safety was threatened by the USSR. It was obvious, in the latter case, that liberal democracies would choose America's protection rather than appease an overpowering totalitarian Empire. But it was not obvious that Western Europe would also turn to the United States in the energy crisis. Indeed, Jobert—speaking for Pompidou—had pushed for an alternative solution: a collective European approach to OPEC, based on the idea that Europe had a great deal to offer, that its interests were not identical with America's (given the different dependence on imported oil), that the OPEC countries themselves might prefer to deal with Europe separately, and that a common consumer front might put the Western Europeans under America's political, economic, and financial dependence without necessarily saving them from OPEC. His partners and Pompidou's successor have in effect preferred a choice dictated this time, not by a felt community of political values with Washington, but by a felt community of economic systems: rather a "common front of industrial powers" than a "North–South alliance." If the threat of exploitation and blackmail comes from OPEC, a consumers' front led by the United States—whatever disadvantages *might* result for the neediest consumer nations—would at least be able to meet strength with strength. West Germany, from its own more enviable position, had made this calculation from the start.

Now this choice, in turn, raises two major questions. First, what is the domain of action left to the EEC in and of itself? What is going to be "European" that is not either being kept jealously national (such as labor relations, incomes policies, taxation) or bilateral (such as deals with separate Arab countries, or each member's *Ostpolitik*), or "neo-Atlantic" (such as energy and the payments problems connected with it or the issues of raw materials, development, and food to be discussed in "global" conferences or agencies)? In these last the industrial powers tend to from one component, with Western Europe either dividing or else following the lead of the more powerful United States. Are not the new issues in the economic realm of such global magnitude (by contrast with the old intra-European issues or the purely "bilateral" U.S.–European ones) that the geographical framework of the Nine is irrelevant to their solution, which exceeds both the limits and the capacity of Western Europe—a sad reality that has always prevailed in the realm of military security, but now extends to so much more? Now that the EEC has a new motor (the Council of Presidents, no longer tied to the notion of unanimity) and the promise of a better transmission (an Assembly to be elected by universal suffrage), will it—if one may use this metaphor—still have any fuel to go anywhere? Will it not become a mere subcontractor of America's global schemes? At best, will it not just be the forum in which joint positions will be prepared for presentation to other, broader bodies which will actually be in charge of dealing with the issues—a forum for proposition but not for decision? Has not OPEC brought about de Gaulle's oldest nightmare—*l'Europe américaine*?

This brings me to the second question, for France: France's grudging, partly concealed, but undeniable alignment (in the realm of energy and of arms production) is undoubtedly more tactical than real; it is being rationalized as a necessary precondition for any future distinctively European policy, rather than as a change of heart. But will it allow France to prod a "de-dramatized" European Community toward genuine achievements of its own (and not merely toward recurrent promises of future achievements)? Will France's good will toward Washington allow it to put the whole Kissinger train on the rails of the kind of "North–South" policy the French seem to be aiming for, but for which some of its European partners (such as Bonn) show little enthusiasm, and which Kissinger himself seems quite determined to "preempt"? Or will the European institutions not become rather the transmission belt for Kissinger's signals and commands and a straitjacket for France? Will France not find itself a prisoner on the train it has joined? Who is hijacking whom?

Future

A. Any discussion of alternatives must either take the form of a series of scenarios covering a wide range of possibilities (cf. the Kahn–Wiener book on the year 2000)[9] or else be based on definite assumptions that limit that range by ruling out either "far out" hypotheses or (alas) more likely ones, but of a kind that make forecasting too difficult. I will adopt the second method. (The first would require a volume and still be of dubious usefulness.)

1. My first assumption is the continuing importance of Western Europe to the United States. It is sufficiently great to justify that much overworked expression, a "special relationship." The three ranges of common interests postulated by the United States since the late 40s are still present.

a. In the realm of military security, I would argue that the interest of the United States remains in the existence of a Western Europe that is both safe from military attack or nibbling from the East, and sufficiently confident in its capacity to deter such encroachment not to be tempted to glide into "Finlandization," i.e., into a policy of accommodation to Soviet demands (for instance, a veto of any extension of EEC activities in diplomacy or defense, always opposed by Moscow). It has been argued that the physical safety of the United States would not be threatened by the "loss" of Western Europe. But clearly the complex balance of world power, which does not consist of the nuclear strategic stalemate alone, would be imperiled (far more than it was by the Soviet move in Cuba in 1962). Besides, the main concern of a great power, after physical security, is influence. Surely this is what the massive build-up of Soviet might is aiming at: the expansion of Soviet influence and the eventual neutralization of Western Europe as an actor in world affairs. The very reason why Western Europe remains a major, if currently inaccessible, prize for Moscow explains why it remains a crucial stake for the United States.

b. What is more, military safety and the political self-confidence it breeds are closely connected with economic orientation. A "Finlandized" Western Europe could be prosperous (Finland is). But would it remain part of the "open" international economy, would it accord shelters, springboards, and good treatment to United States investments, dollars, goods, and services? America's original interest in Western Europe's recovery has been transformed into an interest in Western Europe's prosperity and financial solvency, because of the very strength of the links of trade and financial involvement that make of the North Atlantic (if you'll pardon the expression) a coprosperity sphere. The political base of this "community" of advanced capitalism *is* the security link established in the late 40s. Quasi-instinctively, this is what NATO's European members understood when they decided to follow Kissinger's oil strategy.

c. On the new global issues that have, along with oil, come to the fore, as well as on what might be called the "old" global issues (such as East–West relations or the Arab–Israeli dispute, which is far more than a regional powder keg), it remains important for the United States to be able to count either on Western Europe's support and cooperation, or on its benevolent self-restraint. The United States would be weakened if some of its allies, owing to domestic shifts, switched to neutrality; or if the Europeans appeared as rivals on the road to Moscow (for the USSR could then prove more demanding in its dealings with Washington); or if they behaved as the last cold warriors at a time when the American strategy is to entangle the imperial bear in a fine net. In the complex relationships that will have to be established with the developing nations, even an American administration intent on "conciliation, not confrontation," to use the French cliché, has an interest in obtaining *good* terms from conciliation and therefore in presenting to these nations a reasonably coherent front. The aim would be to limit, for instance, the danger of competing bilateral deals between separate consumers and producers of oil, or the danger of financial collapses among the advanced countries due to payments crises. Nor can a new international monetary system be established without the support of the West Europeans. Nor can the world's food problems be tackled without their cooperation, given the importance of Western Europe's agriculture.

d. To conclude: America's interest is both positive (enlist support) and negative (prevent the unraveling of a network that is one of its main assets in the world struggle for influence). But this does not imply either of the two following propositions. First, it does not mean that these American interests can only be covered by the perpetuation of present policies and institutions (such as NATO). If the end is clear, the means allow for choices—and disagreements. (To take an example from the first range: if "Finlandization" is bad, would "Swedenization" threaten the American interest?) In particular, the necessity for and advantages of a *united* Western Europe—as a means to these ends—remain a subject of intense discussion.

Second, U.S.–European agreement on common interests does not mean that *all* West Europeans agree on the range and character of these common interests. There are huge variations here. If I may hazard a vast oversimplification, I would say that the consensus is greatest on security (leaving out only Western Europe's Communists), far more limited in economic matters. Thus there are many non-Communists who believe that either domestic national priorities or West European priorities, which require planning, should be given precedence over the maintenance of the "open" capitalist Atlantic economy; indeed that they entail the regulation of foreign investments, or the control of capital movements, or the building of a separate monetary bloc. Consensus is probably even more restricted regarding relations with the world outside of Europe. There support for the notion of *separate* West European interests remains strong. The questions raised above about the importance of recent developments was whether the "Atlantic" road selected by the EEC would really allow for these separate interests to be heard and heeded, but not even the most enthusiastic supporter of IEA believes that American and West European interests in the energy crisis, or indeed in the world of the developing nations, are identical.

2. My second assumption concerns precisely the West Europeans.

a. I will assume that what I have just said about the present consensus will continue, even if there are major internal political changes. In Britain (especially after the referendum on Europe), in West Germany, the Benelux countries, Denmark and Ireland, the range of foreign policy alternatives offered by competing political forces continues to be extremely narrow. There may be shifts in tone and style: a Strauss regime in Bonn would not behave like Brandt's—but neither does Schmidt's! I see no reason to expect, however, or fear more than that. This leaves us with France and Italy. Concerning the first, my own shorthand prediction is that the advent of a left-wing government would probably usher in a period of domestic turmoil, but that the tensions in Franco–American relations would not exceed those we have known in the Gaullist era. Communists and Socialists would find a common denominator in resisting American pressures and demands in the second and third realms, but the Socialists—intent on demonstrating their independence from the Communist party—would cling to "Europe" as their raft, and this would in itself limit their inclination to loosen the ties between France and the international capitalist economy, given the strength of the EEC's ties to it. In other words, the old tug-of-war between France and her partners about control of the direction of the EEC would resume, but the very need of the Socialists for an external anchor would, paradoxically, make them less likely to accept isolation and an EEC paralysis as cold-bloodedly as did de Gaulle throughout and Pompidou in his last weeks. As for military security, the Socialists keep toning down their criticism of the *force de frappe*, they stress the need for armed forces, and they show little inclination to "appease" Moscow. Indeed, here too their anti-Atlanticism and their objections to French military nationalism might find as a common denominator the idea of a West European defense system, which is anathema to both the French Communist party and to Moscow. The easiest way to resolve *that* Communist–Socialist tension would be to stick to the status quo.

On Italy, there are two answers, one serious, one flippant. The flippant one is that—short of having a government determined to expel the United States from its bases—it does not really matter: Italy has largely opted out of active politics in the world arena. The serious one is that a Left-Center coalition (the "historical compromise") would need EEC support on payments issues at least as much as the current coalition; that the Italian Communists have gone very far toward endorsing the EEC not merely as a fact of life but as a good thing; that they have shown an interest in reassuring the United States so far as NATO and "the present equilibrium of forces in Europe" are concerned; that their relations with Moscow are poor and have worsened over events in Portugal; and indeed that a coalition capable of putting order and honesty into Italy's corrupt bureaucratic–financial chaos should be welcomed by all her partners, so long as it does not rock the military boat—which the Communist party says it has no intention of rocking.

b. I will also assume that the West Europeans will keep the EEC on its present course (the question about the *substance* left to EEC remains, however). They will try to save the CAP (perhaps by revising it), to keep Britain in the Market as a full participant, to develop a regional policy, to harmonize their economic courses (which does not necessarily mean detailed coordination), to preserve the internal open market for industrial goods, capital, and labor, and to define common stands (diplomatic, economic, financial) on global problems as often as possible.

Whether this will amount to much is another matter. Everything depends on world events, on the West Europeans' own will to overcome factors of division and inertia, and on the United States. But the West European nations will keep going through the motions, even if these do not take them very far. Each one of them derives benefits, tangible or intangible but real, from the Community's existence; indeed one could almost argue that the Community is less a prelude to an entity "beyond the nation-state" than a means of reinforcing the nation-state. Each one of them needs the façade, or figleaf, of EEC too much to drop it. Naked without it, most of them need the semblance of collective power it provides, for want of the real thing. To put it differently, as long as the clothes are there, they may believe, or believe others will believe, that there is an emperor. Or else, as in Bonn's case, they need the EEC, not as a protection from the cold, but as a pole to which it is good to be tied, for this attachment preserves one, at least a bit, from the conflicting pushes and pulls of the superpowers.

In the second place, I assume that the old obstacles to the emergence of a strong entity will continue: that is, there will still be divergent domestic priorities, and vast bureaucratic and parochial systems will still resist breaking the heavy crust of their intricate patterns and busy self-involvement. Differences in resources, in national policies, and institutions will continue to make joint programs difficult and compromises laborious. Different assessments of Western Europe's ultimate interests in world affairs will also persist. Concerning these, there may (as at present) occur a temporary bowing to necessity, a muting of divergences on distant ends, while one concentrates on surviving in the near future. But I would predict that the very difficulty of defining a separate or specifically "European" interest on many of the new global issues will tend to perpetuate a subtle, or at times open, tension. On the one hand there will be statesmen concerned above all with the *issue* and intent on finding a globally acceptable outcome even if it has no specific European mark, dimension, or function; on the other, statesmen more concerned with Europe's *identity*, intent on making a distinctively European contribution to the solution. I would also predict that, for complex reasons, the former will be German and English, while the latter will be French. In any case, this will mean that the EEC, both for internal and for external reasons, remains a perpetual adolescent staggering through an identity crisis.

3. My third assumption—or rather assumptions—concern the United States.

a. I begin with a negative and very shaky one: there will be no cataclysm. By this I mean two things. No depression *à la* 1929, for should the predictions of recovery prove false and the recession deepen and drive the United States and its European clients to despair at a time when they are all pressed by OPEC and other developing countries and when the vindication of earlier predictions about the decline of capitalism could lead to a toughening of the USSR, then the United States might well find no other way out than some grand military adventure in the Middle East, undertaken on behalf (even if not with the consent) of the so-called West. I also mean no Arab–Israeli war leading to a Soviet–American military confrontation; or to a new embargo on oil or price hike that would meet Kissinger's conditions for a military intervention (it is difficult to imagine OPEC's thus triggering it without such a war, or the United States' feeling strangled otherwise, except if the recession spreads). A fifth Arab–Israeli war that did not produce a new "oil war" in its wake and was stopped by the superpowers in circumstances close to those of October 1973 would not be "cataclysmic" in this sense (although it could be for the populations and armies involved). The reason I make this assumption is not that I think such calamities impossible, alas. But these would transform the international landscape in a way that cannot be adequately forecast. (Robert W. Tucker's recent neat and reassuring sketches are no more convincing than his earlier pretty and heart-warming picture of neo-isolationism.)[10] Also, in the aftermath of such cataclysms, U.S.–European relations would not be the most interesting or important issue.

b. A positive assumption is that whatever happens in 1976, the broad outlines of American foreign policy will not disappear. To be sure, it matters enormously whether Henry Kissinger will remain the captain of the battleship or not, for many features of current U.S. policy are his own (just as many traits of French foreign policy in 1958–1969 were de Gaulle's). If Kissinger stays in charge, an exercise like this one is purely academic both because he is not the most influenceable of men, and because his strategy is a peculiar mix of permanent thirst for uninhibited control with what the French call *disponibilité*, that is, the determination to keep all directions open, to be flexible and free to maneuver from that pinnacle of control into whatever field of action may appear promising or inescapable at a given moment. In other words, the current exercise becomes an attempt to say what should be done, but either will be done anyhow if he thinks it is the right thing at the right time, or else will be ruled out by his very personality and style of action. My main point, however, is that even if he should leave office, some important features are likely to persist, just as he has preserved some essential traits of his predecessors' policy. To be sure, both the style of the policy and the style of policy-making are too intimately tied to him to be transmissible. But a great deal is.

Concerning what might be called "posture," I would rule out any "neo-isolationism," any *drastic* voluntary curtailment of American military and economic positions abroad (this does not rule out, for instance, a reduction of the number of bases in Japan or the Philippines or of the size of our force in South Korea). That there should be some battle fatigue in the public at large with a world that we do not seem able to "manage" easily, is perfectly normal; that Congress should try to reassert its authority in foreign affairs after twenty years of docility is unsurprising. Neither phenomenon amounts to a repudiation of America's postwar stance.

On the other hand, I would "rule in" as likely, even after Kissinger, what I have called elsewhere a policy of "indirect primacy," an attempt to preserve America's eminent role by getting others to adopt favorable policies, or by creating frameworks or constraints limiting the capacity of others to adopt hostile policies and imposing high risks and penalties and frustrations if they try.[11]

Concerning not posture but policy, I will make a hedged assumption about détente. I believe work on arms control will continue between the superpowers, and I do not believe in a return to the tone of Soviet–American confrontation in the 50s. But between deep hostility and "entente and cooperation," there is a huge zone which the word détente does not help delimit. As the second half of 1975 has shown, a new chill, new tensions are perfectly possible, if only because Soviet détente policies abroad entail ideological tightening at home—hence the will to protect the regime in Moscow and in the satellite nations from the very "infiltrations" that détente breeds; and also because détente does not prevent the superpowers from backing rival factions in helpless third countries. Much will depend on America's own economic and military strength and on leadership changes in the USSR. Further collaboration—over forces in Europe, or scientific projects, or joint economic ventures—is not ruled out. But *at best*, I do not see the rivalry ending or any "convergence" of regimes.

My other assumption about policy is that "global" issues will continue to dominate the agenda—that is, all the issues that concern the foundations of economic interdependence and have, in recent years, become "high politics." These include the establishment of a new world monetary system, a new division of industrial labor in the world, the impact and control of multinational corporations, the pricing and supply of raw materials and sources of energy, tariff and nontariff barriers to trade, the problems of food and foreign aid, the management and conservation of natural resources on earth and in the oceans, etc. This means, inevitably, that the relative "demotion" of Western Europe, or of purely bilateral U.S.–European issues, in America's agenda of priorities will not be reversed: policy toward Europe will tend to be part of, dependent on, or subordinated to the global policy of the United States on a given issue.

Hence a paradox: despite the very broad assumptions of common interests by the United States, Washington's attention to Western Europe is likely to remain both less high and more instrumental than in the days of the cold war. Conversely, a Western Europe that is much *less* convinced either of the vast scope of common interests or of the identity of views on ends across the Atlantic may well be the loser in this change of American attitudes and priorities. A more "global" outlook in Washington does not ensure that Washington will always have the specific West European interest in mind. In the very long run, "globalization" may well make the United States less vital and important to the Europeans should the relative power and wealth of "non-Atlantic" nations increase without a corresponding increase in the "Soviet threat" or Soviet political influence in Western Europe. But in the foreseeable future, the dependence of Western Europe on the health of the American economy (a fact of life), on American military protection (both a fact and a choice), and on America's leadership to minimize economic insecurity vis-à-vis the developing nations (partly a fact and certainly a choice) means that "globalization" only makes the tie more important to the Europeans—at a time when Washington finds it less crucial and when many Europeans find the price to be paid for it less acceptable. Or to put it a bit differently: the absence of a world role may have bothered Europeans little in a less *mondialiste* world, to use Giscard's formula. In the new world, that absence is more likely to be felt, or rather the price of "being-in-the-world" without being able to affect it is likely to be far more painful—just when the capacity to affect it declines even further.

B. This suggests that the most critical choices are actually Western Europe's.

1. That statement may appear in flat contradiction with two points made above.

a. I have argued that there is a serious risk of evaporation of EEC's substance, a narrowing of the agenda; that the Market may be crowded out by new global institutions (IEA) or by revitalized old ones (the Organization for Economic Cooperation and Development [OECD] or the International Monetary Fund [IMF]) and enfeebled anyhow by internal failure to develop common "intra-European" policies. But a risk does not mean a necessity: this *is* a area of choice. Evaporation, which statesmen might *present* as a necessity, would be the result of a drift, that is, a lack of will, a policy by default—which is a form, indeed a very frequent form, of choice.

b. I have assumed that Western Europe is likely to "behave as it has customarily behaved" (the old Kelsen *Grundnorm*). But this was a way of ruling out either a collapse and dissolution of EEC or a leap into some harmonious millennium: between that floor and that ceiling, I am assuming struggle, a contest around options.

c. My thesis throughout this and other essays has been that the United States, out of sheer might as well as deliberate policy, can have a powerful impact on Western Europe and help it unite, or else provoke discord or "evaporation." But the United States by itself cannot "build" a West European entity any more than a South Vietnamese nation: neither exhortations to unity in the 50s and early 60s nor the less friendly pressures of the early 70s have succeeded in co-alescing a European will. Could the United States actually destroy the EEC? Perhaps, and we shall have to see whether this would be in our interest; though united Europeans could make such deliberate destruction difficult or costly for us. On the other hand, if we aim, not at preserving what has been achieved, but either at strengthening and extending it or at fitting it into the new world, only the West Europeans themselves can ultimately do so.

2. Thus a normative discussion really ought to begin with Europe's own choices and most desirable course. This lies entirely outside the scope of this es-say. Yet a few indications, however sketchy, are necessary to define the range.

a. At one extreme, there is still *l'Europe européenne.* To be blunt (and even though I am myself a nostalgic supporter of that chimera), it is made unlikely both by the circumstances and by its own ambiguities. The circumstances in-clude, first, the old pattern of domestic divergences among EEC's members, plus different attitudes toward the United States which make a consensus on a "dis-tinctive" Europe improbable. Second, there are the new realities evoked above: what is Europe's distinctiveness on the new range of issues? Or rather, is Europe-by-itself not just a community of weakness in this realm, exactly as it has been in the realm of military security? Third, the hypothesis behind de Gaulle's "Euro-pean Europe" (and its various avatars) was a decline of the United States, a strengthening of Western Europe, *and* a receding or retrenching of the Soviet Union. This would allow the two halves of Europe to grow closer together, with the Western half playing the role of a magnet thanks to its rising power, pros-perity, and autonomy. But Czechoslovakia in 1968 and Soviet policy since then have shown that Moscow is interested in détente as a way of consolidating, not overcoming, the European status quo. This has taken much of the dynamism and purpose out of the idea of a "European Europe." For the root of the resistance of France's partners, and even of several French politicians, to that idea has always been the conviction that Europe-by-itself would still need the American nuclear umbrella, plus some American troops, forward-based systems, and theater nu-clear weapons, to make the umbrella plausible both to Moscow and to Washing-ton; and the conviction that this dependence must inevitably restrict the mean-ing of Europe-by-itself and force it to pay a price. The same reasoning also applies in the matters of energy, payments for oil, and the world monetary system, as Raymond Aron points out in his essay.

As for the ambiguities, there are several "European Europes." Here we can play a game of models. In the realm of defense schemes, there is the Western Euro-pean Union (WEU) model: a separate European defense scheme allied to the United States (with formidable question marks about tactical and strategic nu-clear weapons and, as Aron argues, the nature of French defense policy, whose ambiguity presumes both France's perhaps illusory freedom of action and the possibility of à la carte cooperation between Paris and NATO, but postpones any genuine effort at European defense). Then there is the "Swedish model": a West European "nonaligned" defense scheme that is based on "the calculation that, sooner than see Europe overrun by the Soviet Union, NATO forces would intervene." (But how is this American interest made evident to Moscow without "a military presence substantial enough to make American intervention prompt and effective,"[12] and how can this be achieved without a formal alliance?) There is finally the idea of a West European component in a pan-European collective security scheme, with sharp arms reductions and the end of military blocs; but would not this be a big step toward collective Finlandization?

In the realm of money, a "European Europe" would mean a return to a policy of monetary unification. Quite apart, however, from the obstacles on which the previous attempt foundered and which the new discrepancies within EEC have worsened, divergences about the shape of the ideal *world* monetary system would be reflected in different attitudes and schemes for intra-European monetary unity.

In the realm of energy, does a "European Europe" mean one that defines its own energy policy (import or consumption cuts, new technologies for substitutes, etc.) in order to bring about a common consumers' front or in order to negotiate directly with the OPEC cartels? Does it mean one that works out its own recycling facility—without either the United States or OPEC?

In the general realm of relations with the developing nations, is a "European Europe" one that defines itself as a coalition of advanced countries whose wealth, employment opportunities, and trade are threatened by the demands for a new world economic order, or one that sees its mission as that of accommodating these demands in a gradual but systematic way? None of these question marks means that some distinctiveness is out; only that its limits are sharp, its purposes uncertain, and therefore its chances of rallying all the participants minimal.

b. At the other extreme, there is, behind a façade of EEC business-as-usual, a drift into fragmentation, competition, and what might be called piecemeal or selective neutralism: unilateral cuts in the defense budget or (in the British and French cases) the abandonment of efforts to modernize nuclear forces; mutually harmful import restrictions, export subsidies, and exchange controls to deal with payments crises and recession; unwillingness of the relatively wealthy (Bonn) to pay for what they deem wasteful or nonessential common programs, or to foot the bill for the needy; refusal of the latter to cooperate in any serious way unless their demands for help are met first. The risk of dissolution exists. But I would deem this "choice" unlikely for the reason indicated above—each of the partners, for different motives, needs the EEC. Britain has no other "live option," nor does France. Bonn does not want to rely on Washington alone and needs the EEC as a kind of buffer against both Washington and Moscow. And so on. Keeping the EEC afloat means playing the perilous game of compromises and small package deals. The important thing is not to fall into the abyss after pushing to the brink.

c. In between, there is a choice that could be called "more of the same": an effort to develop simultaneously the internal cohesion of the EEC (by extending the range of common policies or at least perpetuating the existing ones, despite heterogeneities and strains) and cooperation with the United States in old institutions (NATO, IMF, OECD) and new ones (IEA, etc.); cooperation with the USSR in order to increase military safety by lowering the threat (if not by improving the defenses) and to create a safety valve in the economic realm (including energy: uranium imports); and cooperation with the Third World in order to avoid the dreaded confrontation that would expose Western Europe's fragility. Such a policy would obviously receive Japan's support. It has two great advantages. One is external. It juggles enough balls to soften somewhat the drawbacks of dependence: greater internal cohesion may, for instance, help the European arms industries survive the current onslaught of more advanced American technologies and weaponry; good relations with the developing nations and Moscow help keep Washington a bit more at arm's length; good relations with Washington save one from being embraced too tightly by the bear or squeezed dry by OPEC; while dealing with all of these makes the failure to "deepen" European integration less conspicuous and the need to keep trying less harrowing. The other advantage is internal. By eschewing definitions of ultimate purposes, this policy *avoids* the divisive issue of choosing among "missions for Europe," which would otherwise be forced by *l'Europe européenne*'s own ambiguities. The policy of "more of the same" depends on not clarifying these.

But this points to a drawback: there always comes an event, or a man, that obliges such deliberate mists to dissolve. At this moment there has to be a choice among internal cohesion, cooperation with the United States, cooperation with the East, cooperation with the South: "instead of" replaces "and"—and choices are sources of trauma. Moreover, this policy of pleasing everyone allows the Europeans to give themselves the illusion of progress by concentrating on a favorite pastime—the institutional reenforcement of the EEC—thus mistaking better (or merely bigger) machinery for an improved output. And yet, for reasons having to do both with the world scene and with the delicate balances of domestic politics in the EEC countries, it is this ambiguous middle range which strikes me as most likely: like the Republic according to Adolphe Thiers, it is the regime that would divide the Europeans, and each polity, least.

C. America's choices will be discussed now. I have expressed earlier my belief in an important degree of continuity, should a "post-Kissinger era" begin soon. But there is room for change and there are ranges of alternatives, both because Kissinger's audacious enterprises have recently become more like astute improvisations than like a systematic creation, and because many of his policies (for instance, those concerning OPEC and the developing nations) are under sharp attack, and not only from the political opposition.

1. It follows from what was written above that the most fundamental American choices concern America's *global* policy, for these will determine to a large extent the nature of American policy toward Western Europe. This, needless to say, is

not the place to unveil a Grand Global Design. But there is a point in describing ranges of alternatives. The question is not whether the United States should "exert leadership"; it will and can hardly escape from it. The question is *how* and *what for?* And this in turn can be divided into three related issues.

a. What should be the proper *framework* of American action? The politics of interdependence can always degenerate into sheer chaos because of the number of actors, all eager both to maximize their leaky power and to interfere with one another; because of the number of partly separate yet partly connected functional issues; because the name of the game is the manipulation of interdependence, that is, my exploitation of your own interest in helping me lest you be hurt, or of your interest in not hurting me too much lest you be hurt. One can distinguish analytically the politics of *interdependence,* that is, of (usually) non-zero-sum games or, at least, restrained games (resulting from economic solidarity or from nuclear solidarity) from the politics of *interaction,* of (usually) zero-sum games in situations of mutual hostility capable of destroying all restraints.[13] The latter have traditionally been structured, that is, given some semblance of logic and order, through alliances and guarantees. The new politics of interdependence desperately need structure in the form of bargaining coalitions and institutions for joint management[14]—whose durability and reliability in a system of competing sovereigns is, of course, dubious, as Hobbes well knew.

Here, the range of choices for the United States is as follows. First, will we encourage the development of reasonably stable structures of bargaining and institutions of collective management, even though they may seriously hamper freedom of maneuver either for us as a state, or for American multinational enterprises? Or will we give priority to maximizing this freedom and prefer unilateral action, bilateral deals, and *ad hoc* institutions or coalitions? Past behavior, especially in the Kissinger era, suggests a fundamental preference for the latter. Second, insofar as we acknowledge the need for "ordering structures" and institutionalized diplomacy, will we accept more broadly participatory or egalitarian ones, even though they may boost the role and magnify the scanty or limited assets of the weaker states or of states whose whole power derives from one simple component of power? Or will we prefer those coalitions and institutions that we tend naturally to dominate, partly in order to preserve the full margin of our overall superiority, partly in order to safeguard a traditional kind of international hierarchy—one in which the top countries are those with the biggest military arsenal, the highest degree of economic development, and the greatest stake, if not in the whole status quo, at least in keeping what they have achieved?

b. What should be the *style* of American action? At present, it oscillates in *tone* between an intensely pugnacious one, whether it is for the defense of a purely national interest (cf. the recent drive to sell American fighter planes to our NATO allies, or our reluctance, in recent years, to link Special Drawing Rights (SDRs) and foreign aid, or our preferential use of aid and food for the benefit of selected clients) or of that of the "community" of industrial nations, and an intensely idealistic one that stresses constructive interdependence and common tasks beyond politics. Unfortunately, the latter tone has often seemed reserved for homilies, the former for policies. But there is a range of choices here—it being understood, of course, that constructive idealism will rarely extend to self-abnegation.

Next to tone, there is *mode of operation*. Here the range goes from what Thomas L. Hughes has called "personalism"[15] to what its chief practitioner himself calls (in the domestic context) "institutionalization." At one end of the spectrum lies the solo performance, with its great assets of flexibility, flamboyance, and confidentiality, but its drawback: fragility. For it depends too much on the relations between personalities abroad and neglects the vital domestic "turf" needed for roots to grow: congressional support and the involvement of a broad public. As a result, its chief advantage, creativity on the world scene, can easily wilt into sterility. At the other end of the spectrum lies what Kissinger used to criticize as the bureaucratic style: weighed down by problems of coordination, by the harrowing task of permanently coaxing influentials and reassuring interests; threatened by the risk of perversion inherent in the priority of domestic consensus-building, that is, the gradual shift of emphasis from the foreign policy need to the domestic politics of the issue. And yet this is a style that may have its advantages so long as it avoids this risk; for it gives to partners and opponents a sense of solidity that may help make the politics of interdependence more predictable.

c. What should U.S. policies aim for, in *substantive terms?* Here, of course, one would have to deal with a huge number of issues. But a few stand out. Insofar as interdependence based on the common interest in "nuclear survival" is concerned (an interest that implies that the logic of interaction, that is, of unrestrained or zero-sum games, be either contained or removed in those areas where it still prevails, as it does in the Arab–Israeli dispute), there is a question of scope and speed. How far do we want to go in involving the USSR in such an effort? How far do we want to go in trying to arrive at implicit or explicit agreements with Moscow and with our allies to limit the export of arms to third parties, especially in dangerous regions, and to delay and prevent the proliferation of nuclear weapons? How far do we want to go, beyond arms control, toward strategic arms reductions?

Insofar as interdependence based on economic solidarity is concerned, do we want a monetary system that will preserve, this time through greater flexibility than in the postwar era, the privileged position of the dollar, or will we accept a system that puts pressure even on the United States for the elimination of payments imbalances through domestic measures? Will we continue to try to solve the food problem of the developing nations by exporting food surpluses from the United States and other advanced countries, or will we help the former increase drastically their own food production and cut down on unstable export crops toward the industrial world, even though this change will entail large-scale social reform by regimes likely to be unfriendly to foreign enterprises? Do we want an international network of agreements on raw materials, energy sources, natural resources, trade *and* investment that aims at a gradual, unbrutal transfer of wealth, not only from the old to the new rich but from the rich to the poor, at the possible cost of a new world distribution of employment and industries, various temporary measures of industrial and trade protectionism for the developing countries, and a far greater say for them in the management of world monetary and trade institutions? Or shall we try to resist on a global scale the kind of democratization that has occurred, often brutally, and yet in far less unmanageable conditions (owing to the authority of the central government, national consensus, factor mobility, etc.) in domestic political and social systems over the past two centuries?

These are the overarching choices. If one relates them, one sees that the United States has, broadly speaking, a range of alternatives that extends from a policy of traditional hegemony—for the preservation of its own preeminence and of the present type of international capitalist economy—to a policy of initiatives toward common, "reformist" actions aimed at making the world both safer and more egalitarian. Let me make my own preference clear (if it is not already): I would like the United States to move in the latter direction, because I fear that otherwise the old model of the "state-of-war," temporarily and partly pushed aside by the new model of interdependence, would prevail again. For one can expect both chain reactions resulting from old-fashioned hostilities, and economic chaos as well as military contests resulting from the mismanagement of economic solidarity, that is, from aggressive, unguided, and unchanneled attempts at egalitarianism revolutions from below instead of reforms planned from above.

2. Let us move back to Western Europe and discuss desirable American objectives, again in terms of alternatives.

a. A first question is a kind of preconsideration. Ought the United States define these objectives in foreign policy terms (what would we like the West Europeans to do, or what should we do together on the coming issues?), or should we try to influence their *domestic* political scene in order to have West European governments that are likely to recognize and conform to the range of common interests? To be sure, what kinds of governments would be "desirable" depends in part on our choice of foreign policy goals. My reason for putting this problem first, however, is double. In every region, both the balance of military power and what could be called the balance of influence between forces hostile to the United States and forces friendly or at least not antagonistic to us can be upset not merely by changes in military might—the loss of a battle or of a base, a drastic cut in our armed presence—but also by the effects of economic policies or trends and—above all—by changes in regimes, governments, and ruling elites. NATO, in fact, can far more easily be weakened by political developments, say, in the countries of its "southern flank," than by very unlikely military disasters. To use martial language, the home front, not the front line, is the weakest spot.

Second, for prudential and normative reasons, I believe that we should refrain from the manipulation of domestic politics and should realize that it is through our *foreign* policy behavior that we are most likely to affect our partners' (and even opponents') internal equilibrium. In prudential terms, we must by now understand that the days when American diplomats, CIA agents, labor leaders, or intellectuals could affect favorably the outcome of elections, the balance of party leaderships, the splitting or merging of unions, the tendencies of magazines are over. Indeed, any American public statement is likely to backfire: a few more declarations about Communism in Italy, and the "historical compromise" might finally have its day! Of course, some European politicians may tell us that our support would help them, or they may keep their rivals from power by telling them that, alas, *we* would not tolerate deals with them. But in most instances, this is a meaningless game in which we, not they, are the pawns. "The United States" is being used as a club by Italian Christian-Democrats determined anyhow not to let Communists embrace them, just as we are being taken for a ride by French "friends" who tell us how much they would like to be more cooperative, but cannot disregard such dire domestic constraints as the Gaullists or the Communists.

Normatively, I find many of the practices of domestic manipulation by outsiders disgraceful and disastrous, insofar as no stable world order will ever exist unless it is made of authentic (I did not say: necessarily democratic) national regimes, not puppets. A temporary gain obtained by "destabilizing" an Allende (already undermined by his economic errors) or by propping up a Thieu is, in the not-so-long run, likely to be offset by the price one has to pay later. That is also the lesson of the Greek experience. Moreover—here, too, the prudential and the normative converge—those who begin as "our boys" may end up proving to be rather tough nationalists, precisely because they have to establish their authenticity. After all, it was the CIA that put the Shah of Iran back in power in 1953.[*]

Of course, some European governments will be easier to deal with than others; some are more likely to share our view of our common interests than others. A Giscard is more pleasing than a de Gaulle. A leftist government in France or Spain, a Communist-Christian Democrat one in Italy would create problems. On the other hand, I see no way for us to prevent their coming to power if domestic developments make it inevitable, and no alternative to our trying to work with them if they do—unless we were to foment coups, a course I would condemn as repugnant. And I can imagine American statements and gestures that could make matters worse and earn us the animosity of the new rulers whom we were trying to thwart or to keep from power. There are enough links among Eu-

---

[*]Aron both misunderstands my position and, in practice, agrees with my recommendations. I do not believe that diplomacy can "confine itself to interstate relations" in a world in which foreign policy becomes the external projection of domestic needs and drives. But diplomacy has other ways of affecting societies than those whose moral *and* practical bankruptcy has been exposed by recent investigations.

ropean officials, parties, and interests across national borders for us to let the West Europeans influence one another's domestic trends—as in Portugal. We are, basically, outsiders—concerned outsiders, to be sure, but fortunate enough to be able to count on our allies' sense of self-interest when it comes to trying to affect events in, say, Spain or Italy or Greece. On the other hand, the question we ought to ask is not: how can we best intervene in order to prevent or arrest such complications, but what foreign policy should we pursue in order to minimize the difficulties which such domestic "setbacks" would raise? And so, we come back to essentials.

b. One foreign policy alternative would consist in downgrading the EEC and dealing with Western Europe in ways that dilute or deny its specificity: that is, either bilaterally, à la carte, with those governments that prove most amenable; or through multilateral agencies (such as the IEA or "recycling" facilities) in which we take the lead and try to prevent the "ganging up" of the Europeans. Insofar as bilateralism is concerned, C. Fred Bergsten has advocated that the United States establish a Washington–Bonn rather than a Washington–Brussels link, given the convergence or identity of interests on the monetary system, trade, agriculture, investments, and now, I suppose, recycling.[16]

Obviously, such a policy would be based on the calculation that European "togetherness" is at best an illusion or an unnecessary complication, and at worst a *point d'appui* for opposition to American views, a bunker for resistance. If European unity is a "poor show," if Europe's dependence is the reality, why support the appearance? And if it is a reality, but always potentially hostile, why not undermine it? Several European commentators have attributed such Machiavellianism to Kissinger, who has acted and talked at times as if he wanted to vindicate their suspicions. Whether these are fair or not, impatience with the "myth of Europe" is often expressed by young United States officials, who do not partake of the "Monnet mystique" of the 50s and cast a very cold eye on the limited achievements and unlimited rhetoric of the West Europeans.

However justified such irritation may be, this is not a good policy choice. First, it is not desirable, because it is not at all clear that if we divide, we rule. The original blend of self-interest and idealism is still valid: an at least *somewhat* united Western Europe (I did not say *any* united Western Europe) serves our interests; a fragmented one might not. For we must count with the power of contagion. If we play favorites, or even if we merely deal with different countries over different issues, we will encourage the centrifugal trends that threaten to disrupt the tenuous network woven by the EEC, as well as by NATO, and to promote an unraveling that could lead to selective neutralism or disastrous beggar-my-neighbor policies. In particular, Mr. Bergsten's solution would incite the French to harden their opposition on monetary and economic issues, to diminish their rather wide (and widening) cooperation with NATO, to "look South"—and East—for support and deals. Moreover, it would make Bonn itself uncomfortable. For Bonn can only act as "Washington's assistant" *within* EEC or NATO. An overt "axis" would in fact isolate Bonn and make it less useful a relay for Washington than it is in the present context. Also, the "disaggregation" of Western Europe through separate deals and the "drowning" of Western Europe in large pools would risk encouraging both the development and the disruptiveness of anti-American political forces, for these would resist and resent the pressures from those pools and feel freed of any intra-European restraints by such deals. We would have bred in Europe what has been so often disastrous for us elsewhere: the fusion of nationalism and anti-Americanism.

Second, such a policy is not really feasible, even if one deems it partly desirable. There is no way in which the United States can prevent the EEC from having its own role in matters of trade negotiations (although the United States can, of course, restrict the EEC's range of policy choices). Nor can Washington prevent the Nine from trying to have something common to say in the "group of ten," or the IMF, or in tripartite conference with the "richer" and "poorer" developing nations; or eight of the Nine from consulting with France about what to do at the IEA, or even from joining France in carving out, if they so desire, a specific energy policy for the EEC; or eight of the Nine from thinking about ways to keep the United States deeply involved in NATO, while also trying to find ways to overcome France's "separatism." Bonn itself will tend to resist American blandishments, out of fear that a tendency that exists already within the EEC, that of making Germany an all-purpose cashier, would be magnified in the global schemes of Mr. Kissinger; for it is easier to resist weaker partners than Big Brother. Meanwhile the economic strength of West Germany has if anything sharpened commercial rivalry between Washington and Bonn (cf. Bonn's nuclear deal with Brazil).

c. A second policy alternative could be called more-of-the-same. We would not discourage greater European unification, and we would (as does Kissinger) point out that it is in our allies' own interest to unite in order to reach "a degree of financial solidarity, a degree of equalizing burdens, and a degree of ability to set common goals that cannot be done on a purely national basis.[17] But we would continue to give effective precedence to broader frameworks, such as NATO, or the IEA, and recycling schemes within or outside the IMF; and we would make it clear that it is through these schemes and in these frameworks that our contribution to Europe's physical and economic security will be given. This means, in effect, that we would continue to extract a double price in exchange: a price in terms of control of the substance or direction of the Europeans' own schemes and frameworks (EEC, "Eurogroup"); and a price in terms of such conditions for our support as their buying American armaments, importing American technologies for oil substitutes, accepting American requirements about the financial policies to be pursued by beneficiaries of "secondary recycling," or signing trade concessions and offset agreements, etc. If this has worked so far, why should it not work just as well tomorrow? It both preserves a useful shell, or residual basis, of European unity and allows global strategies and bargains to receive precedence. It both protects America's primacy and gives the West Europeans the satisfaction of playing at their own game, of working on their own enterprise. It has helped contain the nationalist ambitions or excesses of de Gaulle, it has groomed the new Germany, minimized the effects of Italy's drift, and given a semblance of a role to Britain without detaching it from the American leash. And yet, there are some serious drawbacks.

The biggest is psychological. It is a perfect formula for perpetuating the sense of dependence, the resignation to pettiness, the abdication from world influence of the Europeans, the very flaws Kissinger never fails to flail. For it creates among European leaders and elites the lulling conviction that Uncle Sam will "do what is right," while encouraging them to show their own distinctiveness in a string of joint regrets, warnings, laments, and whines blaming Washington alternatively for being too soft or too tough. It undermines their self-confidence by parking them in confined reserves, where their inefficacy or sluggishness is a cause for reproach. It feeds a certain self-contempt, for they are not stupid enough not to notice who commands, or to know that if *they* also benefit, it is because he who commands has an interest in *their* benefiting. And such self-contempt—in fine Sartrean fashion—feeds in turn an impotent rage against Washington.

The purely political drawback is that this indeed is a formula for permanent mutual resentment. Already one sees a tug-of-war within the IEA and the "recycling" schemes between the consumer-front approach of Kissinger and the Europeans' desire to involve the OPEC countries, partly in order not to be left alone with Washington. But one can also forecast, within whatever international bodies will deal, or be set up to deal, with the issues raised by the developing nations, European sullenness should the United States seize the initiative in and reap the advantages of bargaining with them, and American contempt for the Europeans' oscillation from *mondialiste* lingo to economic and financial jingo.

The area in which the American attempt to preserve control and predominance has already led to considerable friction is of course NATO. To summarize arguments I have developed in testimony to senatorial subcommittees:[18] the present structure of NATO, the presence of a high number of American troops and tactical nuclear weapons under that structure, is an irritant in U.S.–West European relations, directly and indirectly. Directly: because the Europeans' dependence on these forces and weapons as well as America's latest conventional armaments provides us with strong temptations of blackmail, while making them aware of their humiliating tie to the uncertainties of our domestic political process and to the self-assurance of our more advanced technology. Indirectly: U.S.–Soviet negotiations constantly provoke jitters among West Europeans, for they fear agreements that could partly "uncouple" America's strategic forces from Europe's defense or open the door to a "denuclearization" of Central Europe under superpower control. Also, they keep having misgivings about our strategic doctrine, which determines the way in which our, *and their* forces will be used. We in turn are irritated by their suspicions and recurrent demands for reassurance. And yet, one of the ways in which this sense of collective impotence, of being at the mercy of the Protector or of the "condominium," could be at least partly over-come—the gradual establishment of a West European Defense entity—remains outside the pale, so long as our allies fear that it might serve as an excuse for American withdrawal or estrangement and we confirm these fears by our own failure to encourage any change in the institutional status quo.

To sum up: *they* feel that a paternalistic protection may always end in the Protector's taking, or agreeing to, measures that *he* does not deem contrary to Western Europe's interests (in matters of oil substitutes, or of limits on separate oil deals, or on payments solidarity, or on arms, or on strategy, or on arms control), yet which may not be the best from the specific viewpoint of *Western Europe*. Yet *he* resents their misgivings because of his own conviction that he has not "knowingly" sacrificed their interests: are American planes not cheaper and better than French planes, is the Schlesinger doctrine not a rational deduction from nuclear parity, are not American-guaranteed loans more likely than intra-European mechanisms, etc.?

d. Thus we come to a third course, which is a policy encouraging (and not just in words) Western Europe to unite and devise its own policies on as broad a range of issues as the Europeans themselves are capable of tackling. This is not properly a policy of "devolution," for I have no illusions (see above) about the possibility of a real European separatism in an age of global problems that severely constrain a half-continent squeezed between the superpowers, as well as between America and the developing world. Moreover, one "devolves" power to an existing entity capable of receiving it, and this simply does not exist. The EEC is currently too weak, and there is no defense system. What I suggest is a policy *aimed at making devolution possible.* It would encourage the emergence, not of an *independent* Western Europe (military and economic realities spell more dependence than independence), but of an autonomous entity, capable of devising, in cooperation with outsiders, measures that would be the Europeans' *own* contribution to problems that they cannot solve alone (instead of measures taken in the presence, under the leadership, or in reaction to the direct pressure of others), or their answer to problems which are clearly in their domain, or an attempt to diminish their dependence. This policy would see to it, on the one hand, that in the areas covered by the EEC (roughly speaking, economic and monetary issues), the Community is not asphyxiated by, drowned in, or subordinated to the wider agencies whose creation is indeed necessary; on the other hand, that in the area in which there is at present either no EEC, or barely a beginning—defense and diplomacy—a "European entity" or perhaps (this is a problem for the Europeans) distinct but overlapping European entities are made possible.

I find this alternative (to be spelled out below) desirable for negative and positive reasons. In the first place, the risks are limited. There is an "objective" *and* subjective solidarity of interests in the realm of security. The real danger of "Finlandization" would be far more effectively contained by this policy choice than by the first alternative, while the second—the status quo—always threatens to lead to it, should irritation prevail over co-operation. For the status quo by nourishing the Europeans' sense of almost irremediable inferiority, tempts them into both letting their own defense efforts slacken (as has been happening in several European members of NATO) and courting the USSR as a reassurance policy. This temptation might grow if the preponderance of the United States in NATO should lead Washington either to unilateral cutbacks or to extensive arms control deals with Moscow without sufficient European participation. On the other hand, a European defense entity, however limited or fragile, would have, so to speak, a vested interest in not letting itself be intimidated or seduced by the USSR.

In the economic realm, the mutual dependence of the European and American economies is such that a revitalized EEC would be unlikely to break it, unless anti-capitalist and anti-American majorities take over in *most* of its members— an unlikely prospect. Few politicians within the EEC would deny that there *are* common interests of oil consumers, that financial solidarity is needed to prevent selective blackmail by OPEC. Similarly, all would agree on the need for a new international monetary system.

Of course, on all these issues, there could be clashes between assertive Europeans and the United States; but these would be severe *only* if the United States had opted for what I have called a policy of global hegemony, in which case it would not have embraced this third course of devolution. There might be broad policy differences over the way in which Third World problems and demands should be met, or the Arab–Israeli conflict solved. But there are differences among the Europeans as well, and we have no reason to expect that the conception most opposed to that of Washington would always prevail. Kissinger seems to assume that on such issues the Europeans would, against their own self-interest, choose "appeasement" out of a mix of guilt feelings for past colonialism and dependence on imported oil and raw materials. But the measures he himself has proposed (the floor price for oil, the procedural concessions to the developing nations' demands) have exposed *him* to charges of appeasement by American businessmen, economists, Treasury officials, journalists, et al. And this derogatory attitude toward the Europeans, which may not be unfounded in the *present* context, becomes a self-fulfilling prophecy: the third course would help the West Europeans to overcome such inhibitions, lose the habit of counting on Washington to bail them out, and develop institutions and policies in which they simply could not afford to sacrifice Western Europe's interests.

Moreover, a certain amount of pluralism, the existence of alternative courses offered on the public stage, is a good thing: should *one* such course lead to a dead end, the others would become available. This is one of the positive advantages. The major one is partly psychological, partly political. Kissinger himself used to complain about the strain on America's mental and material resources imposed by American preponderance in the postwar world.[19] There is an art of letting go in order to be better able to influence events, orient trends, channel initiatives, dampen conflicts, disconnect dominoes, divide and distinguish among challenges. The attempt at global control is heroic but doomed—too much for one man, too much for one nation, however brilliant the man and powerful the nation. Having allies whom one has to scold periodically for their irresponsibility ought to make one find ways of making them behave responsibly—and this means letting them carry out responsibilities—or else demonstrate once and for all that they cannot blame their futility on anyone but themselves. If we are going to have any "stable structure of peace," it will have to be, not just multipolar, but multifunctional, with different (yet overlapping) hierarchies corresponding to each function or type of power. The United States, through its resources, positions, interests, and dynamism, will be present at or near the top of all; it does not have to try to be in control of each.

By substituting global mobility for the stolid immobilism of cold war policy, Kissinger has astutely preserved the American hegemony which World War II had largely created. But his own critique of it remains valid. In the specific case of Western Europe, the more the West Europeans are left, if not to themselves (the world will not leave them), at least with a domain of their own, the more likely they are to recognize a broad range of common interests with us—far more than if we always insist on defining it for them. Moreover, where they differ with us, it may often be in *our* interest to follow their advice; thus with respect to the "North–South" problem, if we leave aside Kissinger's astute but domestically still unsupported switch to "conciliation," the relationship of the allies may well be the reverse today of what it was in the days of dying colonialism. Popular-front governments, which might exploit the tensions inherent in the other two courses, would find in the European institutions that the third one favors both an effective harness on their "separatist" tendencies and a buffer absorbing whatever anti-American inclinations they might have.

However, there *are* obstacles and drawbacks. Just because the other alternatives entail tensions and costs does not mean that this one would be frictionless and cost-free. The frictions are built-in. Since there is military and economic dependence of western Europe on the United States, the kind of policy I suggest might well transfer some power to the former only at the price of transferring anxiety to the latter, for *we* will be left with ultimate responsibility, and *they* will have a greater opportunity to force the outcome they want. The old cry of no taxation without representation might be picked up by us. Meanwhile, given our ultimate responsibility, nothing we can do can entirely eliminate European anxiety about our performance. Also, in specific areas (see below) our self-restraint could result in sizable losses of the benefits currently linked to preponderance, or in sizable opportunity costs.

All of this may make the devolution policy look far less desirable. Nor is it clear that it is feasible. After years of dependence, and after being battered by the reversals of 1973–74, can the Europeans overcome their Oblomovian tendencies?

Can they turn away from the subtle comforts of relying on an ally who allows you the luxury of criticism and encourages your drift away from world responsibilities? Despite China's exhortations, are they not being pushed farther away from these anyhow, not merely by recent United States activism, but by such convergent phenomena as the harsh will of the Soviets, the superpower cooperation, the onslaught of OPEC, the claims of the Third World, the inadequacy of Western Europe as a framework for the solution of almost anything? It would be foolish not to raise these questions, after having criticized all other courses. I would only conclude, first, that the undesirable aspects strike me as less dreadful than those of the first two courses; second, that if indeed the devolution policy is unfeasible, if the wager on Europe is lost, then there will always remain—for all its failings— the second, that is, the present course. The risk of failure should merely incite both us and the Europeans not to dismantle anything that might have to be restored in the end. It should not deter us from trying to expand the specifically European institutions and policies that exist, or to create new ones.

Notes

1. Stanley Hoffmann, "No Trumps, No Luck, No Will," Chapter 4 of this book.

2. Robert E. Osgood, *Ideals & Self-interest in America's Foreign Relations; the Great Transformation of the Twentieth Century* (Chicago: University of Chicago Press, 1953).

3. Jean Jacques Servan-Schreiber, *The American Challenge,* first edition (New York: Atheneum, 1968) [*Le Défi américain* (Paris: Denoël, 1967)].

4. See Stanley Hoffmann, "Europe's Identity Crisis," Chapter 1 of this book.

5. On much of the above, see Pierre Hassner, *Europe in the Age of Negotiation* (The Washington Papers, Vol. I, No. 8) (Beverly Hills and London: Sage Publications, 1973).

6. Stanley Hoffmann, "Toward a Common European Foreign Policy?" in Wolfram Hanrieder (ed.), *The United States and Western Europe* (Cambridge, Mass.: Winthrop Publishers, 1974), pp. 79–105.

7. Cf. Michel Jobert, *Mémoires d'avenir* (Paris: Bernard Grasset, 1974).

8. David A. Walker, "Some Underlying Problems for International Monetary Reform," in Hanrieder (ed.), *The United States and Western Europe,* p. 185.

9. Herman Kahn and Anthony J. Wiener, *The Year 2000: A Framework for Speculation on the Next Thirty-Three Years* (New York: Macmillan, 1967).

10. Cf. Robert W. Tucker, "Oil: the Issues of American Intervention," *Commentary,* January 1975, pp. 21 ff.; "Israel and the United States: From Dependence to Nuclear Weapons," ibid., Nov. 1975, pp. 29 ff.; and his book, *A New Isolationism: Threat or Promise?* (New York: Universe, 1972).

11. Cf. Stanley Hoffmann, "Choices," *Foreign Policy,* no. 12 (Fall 1973): 3–42.

12. Michael Howard, "NATO and the Year of Europe," *Survival,* January-February 1974, pp. 23–24.

13. See my "Notes on the Elusiveness of Modern Power," *International Journal,* Spring 1975.

14. See Miriam Camps, *The Management of Interdependence* (New York: Council on Foreign Relations, 1974).

6

Fragments Floating in the Here and Now

Is there a Europe, was there a past, and will there be a future?
or
The lament of a transplanted European.

I

Let us take any Western European nation in the nineteenth century—say, France, the one I know best. At any given moment, a visitor could have heard vigorous discussions of its past: the nature, flaws, and benefits of the old regime, the causes of its fall, the respective virtues and crimes of the different phases of the Revolution, the reasons for the restless and unsuccessful quest for political stability that followed it, the effect on the nation of the dramatic fracture in its history brought about by the Revolution, the lasting impact of Bonapartism. All of these questions were constantly examined along clear-cut ideological lines and were reassessed by each generation of historians. History played a large part in the school curriculum, and the nation's past was imprinted thereby on the minds of its future citizens. "At age thirteen," says Jean-Marie Domenach—now in his mid-fifties—"my image of France was solidly formed. It linked the recent glory of the fatherland to Greek and Roman antiquity, with the help of classical humanities, which consisted in . . . an aesthetic and moral impregnation."[1] At the same time, intellectuals and politicians were offering various models of the future. Even a society as keen on tight self-protection against economic and social upheavals as that of nineteenth-century France never stopped arguing about what the future might bring and, above all, never stopped believing that it was ultimately up to its citizens to shape that future—whether by the restoration of a beneficial past or by the realization of one or another vision of progress. What struck observers most was the depth and multiplicity of disagreements. But the concern with the past and the future—the conviction that the latter would emerge from acts in-

181

spired by a proper reconsideration of the past; the belief that past and future were inextricably linked, less by historical determinism than through one's own consciousness of them; the idea that one was seeking one's future in one's stand toward the past; and that the future ought to be the enactment of the lessons learned from the past—all this seemed perfectly obvious and appropriate.

It may, therefore, appear obvious and equally appropriate to ask whether the same questions are raised in Western Europe today. But when its citizens consult the mirror on the wall to find reflections from the past or intimations of the future, they find a broken mirror and a blurred image. For Europe remains a virtuality, the past is mere spectacle, and the future is a riddle. Why this is so takes us into the story of postwar Europe's political, social, and cultural transformation, as well as of Europe's role in the world.

II

The reasons for Western Europe's failure to coalesce have been described so often—particularly by the author of this essay—that they do not have to be repeated here. The economic success story of postwar Europe, before and even in spite of the recession (success in terms of GNP, trade, per capita income, etc.); the cohesiveness of the EEC despite such serious challenges as Gaullism in the 1960s and the economic storms of the 1970s; the line of anxious applicants waiting to be admitted; the network of agreements that associate large numbers of non-European states with the Community; the coming election of its Parliament by universal suffrage—none of these facts invalidate my point. Western Europe remains a collection of largely self-encased nation-states. The various governments of Western Europe have found it useful to establish common institutions to deal with their common problems for the following reasons: most of them are advanced industrial societies and have open economies; they are all sandwiched, so to speak, between a potential foe endowed with massive military might and the only ally that can balance and deter Russia's might (yet the latter often exhibits an economic dynamism, and makes economic, monetary, or military demands that risk overwhelming its partners); and for the most part they have preserved the ties with their former colonies, whose development may now serve their own interests. But the basic unit of concern remains the nation-state, however inadequate.

There was, to be sure, a collective *projet* at the outset; its very ambiguity about ends—federalism or confederacy? a strong entity or a contribution to global solutions? free trade or common *dirigisme*? a new power bloc in the world or an exercise in transcending power politics?—helped it grow in the beginning. But later, when each new step seemed to require clarification of the final goals, its ambiguous nature began to plague it. The differential effects of outside pulls— from the US, the USSR, the so-called South, the monetary crises, the recession— have kept the Community members apart and forced the Commission and the

Council to spend most of their time in trying to keep them all in the same boat, rather than in charting a course for it. No sooner was the battle provoked by de Gaulle's insistence on defining their course his way ended by his retirement, than a new setback hit the champions of *relance:* Western Europe was buffeted by new, global problems—energy, currency, the quest for a new international economic order. Their solution not only was, as usual, envisaged in different terms by the Community's members, but also (as in the earlier and lasting case of defense) did not seem capable of being adequately provided by the existing institutions and within the framework of Western Europe. Broader institutions, often dominated by the US, or a global framework, as in the North-South talks, seem to make more sense. But these approaches are a kind of devaluation of the EEC and seem to provide new reasons for each member to play a separate game. As J.-F. Deniau, a seasoned practitioner and faithful advocate of European cooperation puts it,[2] Europe, when it speaks with one voice, has little to say and, anyhow, sounds *dépassée*. It is only when the foe or the dominant ally seems to push its advantages or privileges too hard—Stalin in the early 1950s, Kissinger in the summer of 1973, the Carter administration in recent months—that a reflex of self-defense throws the Western Europeans together. As soon as the pressure gets lighter, however, internal divergences and separate priorities regain the upper hand.

Es ist eine alte Geschichte. But it has gotten worse, not better. There are several reasons. Paradoxically, the greater the scope of the Community's activities, the more complicated the agreements become: each area is in the hands of technicians and specialists who excel in the display of obstacles. Progress requires cross-issue bargaining; but the latter, in turn, requires a common sense of direction. Summit meetings, on the other hand, merely record a desire to overcome obstacles and a decision to send each issue back to its experts—the vigilant guardians of national differences. Secondly, the oil crisis, the recession, and the expansion of the Community from six to nine have sharpened heterogeneity and deepened the gap between the most efficient and least unstable—Bonn—and the others, as well as among the others themselves. Thirdly, the generation of true believers—the founding fathers of European integration, many of whom were American—has no heirs. Its successors are pragmatic. They do not doubt the advantages that cooperation, overall, brings to their nations, or the augmented influence that "speaking as part of Europe" can give them. But they are determined to measure whether in each instance the benefits really exceed the costs; and precisely because they take the usefulness and existence of the Community for granted, they are not overly worried by temporary setbacks or general aimlessness. As one French writer put it in discussing the fate of syndicalism, one has moved from the age of apostles to that of administrators.

There is a difference between a corporation and a club, between a government and a committee. Europe may still be seen as a giant from afar, especially by those who, through some irony he would have bitterly enjoyed, mistake its function for de Gaulle's vision.[3] Looked at closely, however, Europe is a great idea that has been tamed, leashed, and co-opted. Just as, in French public affairs, every scheme for decentralization has ended up absorbed into the traditional administrative patterns, the revolutionary idea of a united Europe has ended up routinized. As Deniau, again, puts it, its Commission has not become a substitute for the governments but a supplementary one. The European movement grew out of a particular historical situation and represented a broad aspiration. But this longing, and the cunning procedures Monnet devised for its fulfillment, have not succeeded in creating a common will. Europe, today as in the 1950s, is a necessity and a possibility; but it is not a will, it is no longer much of an ideal and, as a result, it may end up being, like so many necessities, a missed opportunity. All too often, the Community forum has become a dumping ground for problems that are insoluble in the nation or the region or even within the narrow Western European framework. Periodically, the dwindling "Europeans," the worried Eurocrats, and national statesmen who measure the limits of the nation-state, seek an injection of fresh blood: the *relance* of Messina after the debacle of EDC, the *relance* of the Hague after de Gaulle, and now, after the buffeting of the past five years, renewed monetary cooperation and the popular election of the Parliament. But the danger this last move entails is not at all the realization of Michel Debré's nightmare: the sudden assertion of a supranational will in which a majority of Atlanticized Europeans override and overwhelm France's national interests (with the support of consenting and blinded French parliamentarians). Rather it is the opposite, a demonstration—either of the strength of the particular over the united (whether the particular takes the form of a transnational interest group or of sharp national differences tearing apart the fabric of transnational parties) or of the persistence of collective impotence (manifested through common stands that would either be resisted by the governments—as in the old Council of Europe—or, in matters of diplomacy and defense, would consist in mere deploration). In other words, the model may well be, not a States-General turning into a National Assembly at the initiative of the Third Estate in June, 1789, but the Parliament of the Fourth Republic.

There is no need to indulge once more in the *No Exit*-like attempt to apportion guilt and blame. Was it the fault of Western Europe's situation (another name for it, especially among French analysts, being the United States)? Or was it rather the failure of Europe's consciousness, its inability to shape a *projet* and to overcome the situation? It matters little, except insofar as each side's faults have become an alibi for the other. (Why should the US pay more attention to a bunch of nations that fails to get together to "share the burden" or to carry their own weight? How can the Europeans do great things when the US leaves them no breathing space, treats them as dependents, refuses to discipline its economy, or uses the pretext of free enterprise to crowd out European industries, etc.?) What does matter is the convergent effect of progressive disappointment and habituation to the EEC as it is: since there is neither ground for sudden worry nor reason for much hope, what has, throughout, been at the root of (partial) failure—that is, the resilience of the nation-state (whose failings explain the need for and partial success of cooperation)—is more prominent than ever. Wherever "Europe" was at first seen as almost a way to salvation, the loss of faith is most visible. In West Germany—because it has recovered status and influence so hugely—the European avenue, while economically advantageous, is by no means so essential as it once seemed. In Italy the domestic crisis leaves no room for the old myth of Europe as the undoer of national knots. In both cases, Europe remains necessary—as an outlet for German goods and a cloak for Germany's naked strength and as a source of material and moral help in Italy's lonely ordeal. But we are dealing with a utilitarian Europe. In France, the original faith has been eroded by years of "theological" disputes. If it sometimes seems as if it is most alive among British Europeanists, it is only because they are neophytes who have just entered the temple; their own representatives within behave far less like high priests than like bargainers closing deals in the City.

For the European enterprise to succeed, two closely connected things were necessary: (1) a kind of collective decision to repudiate or transcend the separate national pasts that had pitted the European nations against one another so often and (2) a collective determination to build a common future, a new European society and culture, and a new role in the world. The paradox, or the tragedy, of postwar Europe lies in this fact: if these common decisions are nowhere to be found, it is not because each nation-state has clung so fiercely to its separate vision of its past and its future, but because it has lost touch with the past and the future. To repudiate or transcend the past supposes that it is sufficiently alive to be resented or to inspire a will to break with it and to start afresh. Otherwise it is seen as so much dead weight, so irrelevant to the new situation that it has to be given up, traded in for a deliberately built new future. Shaping such a common future requires a kind of faith and political creativity—which is precisely what has been missing.

III

A superficial observer might marvel at the way in which the Europeans seem to have left behind the feuds and alienations of their past. Whatever happened to hereditary enmities? Spain, so marginal to European history for so long, except in the tragedy of its civil war, hurries to restore the old connection. If Northern Ireland fascinates, it is not only because of the Irish, it is also because there is something anachronistic about such hatreds and passions in Western Europe. And yet, if the hostilities entailed by separate pasts appear to have evaporated, the separate pasts have not; each European country is still concerned only with its own history, insofar as its people look back at all. Attempts at producing common history textbooks have succeeded only in smoothing the edges. To be sure, scientific history often deals with someone else's past—the best history of modern France in a long time is that of Theodore Zeldin—but in only a few countries is there a tradition of transnational investigation. The French have thrown little light on Germany's past, and Elie Halévy has had no successor. Popular history and the mass media deal almost exclusively with the national past. The media, of course, sometimes report on a neighbor's present—communism in Italy, for instance, is of concern to the French. But generally, television delves into a neighbor's past only when it is connected to its own national experience: German television showed *The Sorrow and the Pity* and a recent film on Pierre Laval because of Germany's involvement in wartime France.

The fundamental questions therefore are: How is the national past being examined? and What parts of it are considered important? The two queries are linked, for what is striking is a concentration on the recent past and a way of looking at it that I would call escapist. Here again, the media are informative. Television, the movies, and popular history have mass-produced stories about the troubled past of the 1930s and 1940s. What could be more normal, given its traumatic nature? The parades of the 1930s and the shadows of the war years fill French screens; Mussolini and Hitler obsess the Italians and the Germans; the British endlessly contemplate their finest hours; and Spanish novels and films, before Franco's death, posed poetic or picaresque riddles about and around the civil war. Does this reoccupation demonstrate a willingness to come to terms with a harrowing experience and to derive once again, for present and future behavior, painful lessons from it? I wish I could be sure. Instead I find in it something far softer and more superficial, perhaps because much of this quest is driven by little more than curiosity about the behavior of people who are still alive and present, or nostalgia about one's own earlier years. (Thus what seems like a turning to the past is really little more than an attempt to catch the beginnings of the present before they fade away.) Perhaps a deeper look, a confrontation with the tough moral questions raised by these grim years, is still too painful or (as the Occupation is for France) too divisive; nations, like individuals, repress the humiliating and the harrowing and would rather look at the picturesque than ponder shame or guilt. And so, what we get—in the case of Spain, for example—is a longing for humane normalcy, rather than a search for the reasons behind past inhumanity. Sometimes, as in Germany, there is a fascination with now-incomprehensible phenomena of mass hysteria and evil that has very little to do with soul searching. One looks at the spectacle as if what happened had been either a collective hypnosis perpetrated by one extraordinary man or a march behind the pied piper undertaken by only a part of the people, most of whom followed him into the abyss. Sometimes, as in France, we encounter an intellectual appetite for exercises in ambiguity; it is another way of putting distance between oneself and one's past. The German way tells us that what happened was exceptional, and from the exceptional there is little to learn. The French way tells us that each of us, like Lacombe Lucien, could have been a resister or a collaborationist or, like some of the characters in *The Sorrow and the Pity,* a hero, a criminal, or a coward; this is a subtle way of debunking the past, or reducing it to a moral shrug. Sometimes, as in England and in Italy, one reenacts the heroic hours—the Battle of Britain or the Italian Resistance—a melancholy yet exalting way of escaping from the sadness of the present and of reassuring ourselves about our highest potential. Thus one tries to bolster one's self-esteem: it has not been all bad, indeed some of it has been glorious. But when one finally realizes that one has been drugging oneself, what a sense of fall—witness *We All Loved Each Other So Much* or *The Glittering Prizes.*

For such concern with the recent past to transcend curiosity and spectacle, one needs elites—governments, intellectuals, educators—determined to connect the present and the whole of that recent past—not just its heroic or inspiring features, but also the ugly ones—in order that they may never be reproduced or that they may be finally erased. This is not what we find. Governments, politicians, those who are loosely called opinion leaders, have been willfully selective or evasive. They have either (like the British) diverted their people from looking at their present or (like Adenauer) protected them from their past by plunging them into the imperatives of the present. (Even scholars have occasionally behaved like hurt citizens when a foreigner has revealed an unwelcome truth: Robert Paxton's fine book on Vichy France[4] was not well received by an establishment that prefers to see in Vichy a set of grievous, often well meaning blunders rather than a deeply rooted logic of reactionary defeatism.) It is easier to tell oneself that moral choice is a matter of temper and circumstance, that one has been heroic, or that what made one evil is gone, than to tell people that their recent performance has often been shameful or that their recent valor has not prepared them at all for the very different challenges of the present (and indeed may have bled them white). To proclaim the former is easily dismissed as masochism or as an obstacle to getting people to improve their current lot, for one does not inspire others by rubbing their noses into past dirt. To proclaim the latter is equally discouraging—it rubs their noses into present dirt. *Lacombe Lucien,* with its romantic yet degrading love affair between the Jewish girl and the young collaborationist, was far more popular than the stark and unsparing *Black Thursday,* which showed the French police rounding up Jews for the Germans. As for the intellectuals, while some—a Böll, a Grass—have done what they could, many others, like Sartre, have used the terrible experiences of the recent past only as demonstrations of universal timeless paroxysmic dilemmas. Such a paradoxical, and in the end narcissistic, contemplation of one's finest or most villainous hours, such a variety of escapes, however useful in the present, have not only amounted to a refusal to draw any valid lessons; they have also often incited the next generation to rebel against their too easily satisfied parents, whether the rebellion takes the form of mere cynicism or of actual terrorism—the gentler or the stronger form of nihilism. But this connection has not been and still is not widely recognized.

At least the recent past is alive, if only as a horror show, a pageant, or a pep pill. What is striking is the growing disconnection from the more distant past. Of course, scholars continue to study it, often with great verve, new methods, and original interpretations. But their works rarely reach the general public, except when the authors have, thanks to television, become fashionable or objects of a cult (in which case their books are bought because of the author's fame rather than read because of their substance). One can sometimes hear learned writers arguing fiercely on the radio or the television about bygone events or personalities (one of the most heated debates I ever heard on France's famed *Dossiers de l'écran* concerned the fate of poor little Louis XVII). But these programs deal with the froth or the scum, not with the waves and their movements. The past is becoming an object of erudition or diversion, rather than a part of one's own being, through family or school transmission. What the French called *le passé vécu,* the experienced past, is displaced by the past as a product of specialists, a consumer product, a subject matter for scholars, or a spectacle.

One might be tempted to look for the explanation in the process of democratization. In traditional societies the elites derive their authority from the past and preserve it through the maintenance of customs and values (such as deference) whose very purpose is to delay change and to safeguard hierarchies. In democratic societies, preservation of the rites and habits of the past needs justification; the individual defines himself through his achievements and demands that authority be grounded either on his consent or on its own accomplishments; no democratic generation believes it has either much of a debt to its predecessors or much of a duty to do as they have done. If, as Tocqueville argued, the drive toward equality is the motor of modern society, the matrix of modern history, then the past always risks being rejected, both because it is a prehistory of inequality and because, if it were allowed to become a straitjacket slipped by each generation onto its successor, it would cripple that dogma of perfectibility, that belief in progress, which Tocqueville described as one of the biggest differences between democratic and aristocratic peoples.

But we must beware of such sweeping generalizations. For if we look around us, we find democratic societies in which *le passé vécu* has not receded. It may well be that the ideal type of democratization (the one Tocqueville tried to erect in the second volume of his great work) entails a destruction of ties, both to the past and between the members of that vast crowd of similar and equal men and women, restlessly left to their egoistic pursuits and panting to give themselves small, vulgar pleasures amidst the collapse of old beliefs and barriers.[5] But in order for this severing of ties to happen, democratization must be accompanied by a number of other quite separate and distinct destructions. This is precisely the situation we find in postwar Europe—but not everywhere. Let us admit that democratization may push away the past; still, we find by looking at some countries (say, Switzerland) that the distance between past and present can be either quite small or, when countervailing forces temper the innate "present-orientation" of democracy without preventing democratization itself, can even be nonexistent. In most of Western Europe, however, we find not counterweights, but reenforcements.

The most obvious of these is the speed of social change, the sweeping away of old customs and rites, the disappearance or transformation of old occupations, the reshaping of class distinctions, the revolutions in mores and morals, and the collapse of traditional modes of social control, all of which have been catalogued by sociologists (serious and pop). Yesterday, the past was all around us, and the relative stability of the social order preserved the relevance and meaning of old and durable controversies about the past. As long as traditional institutions, practices of social ascent, economic structures, religious dogmas, and personal values persisted, there were people who wanted to preserve them and others who argued for change; both groups had to evaluate the past for their enterprise. Today, so much of the past is dead that there is little left of it to preserve. The old solidarities and communities are gone; often even the old landscapes, along with the rituals, customs, and costumes, have disappeared. The advocates of change argue from the inequalities and perils of the present. Yesterday, there were conservatives and reactionaries; the former were rooted in the past (and tried to prevent rapid change, political or economic); the latter thought there was enough still left of the blessed past to make it possible to bring back what had, unfortunately, been toppled. Today, a conservative is someone who merely wants to slow down the pace of change or (like Pompidou) to make inevitable changes smooth for the individual. The reactionary is the real radical: he argues—as a particular New Right does in France—not for a return to the past, but on behalf of abstract principles—inequality between races and sexes, hierarchy and authority—which he is wise enough not to connect with any particular time or place.

The speed of change is one of the reasons the past seems so little relevant, but there is another related, but slightly different reason: a gradually growing sense of radical discontinuity. After the ordeals of the 1930s and the war years, the loss of the colonies, the seizure of political predominance by the superpowers, Western Europeans feel, more or less confusedly, that their normal historical development has been interrupted, that their past has been devalued, that their highest achievement—nationality—has plunged them into disaster followed by impotence, that they have moved from the age of self-determination to that in which the outside world determines their fate. The more distant past thus seems alien—not a prelude to the present; it is perhaps even a reproach.

This discontinuity is both expressed in and magnified by modern European historiography. Romantic history is gone, replaced by scientific history. Of course, romantic history was symbiotic with the nation-state; it was indeed a form and an agent of nationalism. It showed how the modern nation emerged from the tribes and the tribulations of the dark ages or triumphed over the machinations and oppression of foreigners. Present-day historians still operate, with a few grand exceptions like Braudel, within the limits of a nation; but the nation is no longer their object. The focus is often on culture and *mentalités*, but the approach is ethnographic, not political; it is the investigation of worlds we have lost, a sampling of vanished riches, not a celebration of how every stone fits into the national monument and every jewel into the nation's crown. Indeed, it often becomes an indictment of the nation, a kind of digging up of the bones of all those local cultures, cults, or customs that were killed by the national Molochs. It allows one to contrast the beautiful diversity of the past and the frantic ugliness of the present; but, unlike romantic history, it stresses both the discontinuity between past and present and the impossibility of reviving the dead. If, as one Frenchman put it, culture is what is left when everything else has been forgotten, the quest for bygone folkways is what is left when one wishes to forget everything else. Often, biography fills most of the gap opened by the demise of traditional history; it at least attracts many readers. But biography too is a kind of denationalization: in romantic history, the hero was the people, suitably idealized or idolized; today we indulge either in the nostalgia of past peoples or in curiosity about individuals.

A third accompaniment of democratization has contributed to the demise of the past: ideological disillusionment. We never used to see the past "objectively." We looked at it through the lenses of ideologies—liberalism, socialism, varieties of conservatism, Christian democracy. (I shall come back to this point in my discussion of the future.) None of these old prisms seems sufficiently helpful for examining the present stage, whether it is the social scene—with its (often immigrated) *Lumpenproletariat*, its stratified and not-at-all pauperized working class, and its proliferating and largely salaried middle classes—or the political scene—with its welfare states in precarious coexistence with a free, but by no means competitive market, and its formidably organized and encrusted interest groups. The situation of the individual—part-time member or free rider of one of these groups, part-time rebel against state and groups, integrated yet overadministered citizen, or "marginalized" and helpless victim—is unlike any that these earlier visions of the meaning and movement of history predicted. Thus, through speed and the savagery of history, we have not simply lost touch with the world that is behind us; it also appears that this world said many things that turned out to be false and thus has nothing more to say to the average European. There are three ingredients in this disaffection. First, the predictions turned out to be incorrect, and the past as the matrix of all good things to come stands discredited. Second, there were too many predictions: it is as if they had canceled each other out or annihilated one another, as religious dogmas do when too many sects argue about their meaning. There never was a single common faith in Western Europe. The closer a country comes to having one—for instance in England—the less disconnected it is from the past (although there is some disconnection precisely because past creeds and present realities seem unrelated). The differing views of the past that, only yesterday, made history seem present to the French or the Italians, have, by losing much of their meaning in the present, devalued the past for them. Finally, some of the predictions were not merely wrong, they were murderous; they turned Europe into a field of ruins: "the ideologies of nation, race and class have fed the fire. Everything, or almost, is burnt out now."[6] The fading away of the past is part of a general repudiation of totalitarian ideologies and of the totalitarian implications of ideologies.

Why does the same disconnection not exist to any comparable degree in the United States? Because, I believe, the three destructive forces I have listed have not operated here. In the first place, social changes have been vast and often disruptive, but they have come as organic changes within an established democratic society rather than as the searing agents of democratization—that is, as the gravediggers of values, hierarchies, social patterns, and constellations that were still predemocratic, a mixture of fading aristocratic and narrowly bourgeois societies. Paradoxically, because there has been, ever since the nation's birth, an expectation of quick mutations—the shedding of old skins and the growing of shinier ones that will, in their turn, be discarded when progress next requires it— change looks not like instability but almost like the condition of stability. The past can still be seen as the incubator of the present. This implies, of course, that such change must not be catastrophic. And indeed, in the second place, America has had no reason to experience radical discontinuity: this is the century of its emergence as the most powerful nation on the world stage, a rise for which its whole history has prepared it. In America we are still in the age of romantic history, in the midst of a love affair with the nation. Finally, and most important, we must go back to Tocqueville, or Louis Hartz, and the liberal consensus or common faith. The speed of social change may well be the same as it is in Europe (although one could argue that postwar Europe has been hastily catching up with America's brand of industrial society); but the irrelevance of past beliefs does not appear at all obvious to Americans. Whatever its transformations, their polity still seems in harmony with an unfolding of the "Lockean faith." Tocqueville would probably have some trouble recognizing his preindustrial small-town America; but the basic principles are still there, and the new institutions that have developed since his day are based on them.

The American creed has survived because the United States has been (or appears to the world and to its own people to be) a success story. Both this creed and other powerful bonds—ethnic loyalties, religious communities, class solidarities, or neighborhood associations—have mitigated the effects of social change and crises. In Europe, such ties have, on the contrary, been weakened or destroyed by a combination of factors: the speed and magnitude of change, a disastrous history, the corrosion of religion (and of such a quasireligious force as the early working-class movement) by secular ideological involvements and struggles, and the poverty of associational life in centralized nations. Therefore, contrary to what might have been expected, the democratic society par excellence, the United States, is closer to its past than the historical societies of Europe—a fact that confirms the impossibility of deriving any firm conclusion about politics or culture from a social ideal type such as democracy. The bones tell us nothing about the flesh or about the spirit.

A collective image of the past and the possibility of being inspired by this image thus depend on the preservation of collective ties, in the form of institutions or common values, among the citizens. Religion, the nation, and ideologies (which played so large an integrating role) partook of both forms. In Western Europe there used to be one group that defined its mission either as the defense of established institutions and values or as the mobilization of the people to create new ones: it was the intelligentsia, a kind of secular priesthood that owed its audience to the decline of organized religion and old regimes and to its frequent association with liberalism and nationalism (even though its prestige and authority were firmly rooted in persistent aristocratic values—which may help explain why it never played a comparable role in this country). Today, however, its attitude contributes to the erosion or erasure of the past. The relation of the intelligentsia to the past is, needless to say, far from simple. Let me take only the case of France. There we find every possible attitude, on the part of the intelligentsia, and yet somehow every one of them contributes to the break with the past. Malraux, in his quest for death-defying acts, became a celebrator of mankind's past artistic achievements and of France's national record. But his very style—his dazzling ellipses and his instinct for the difficult or the inaccessible, his heroic yet impractical hope of bringing the highest to the common man, his sumptuous threnodies, his fascination with exceptional men, and his part-whimsical, part-desperate doubts about humanity's future—somehow widened the distance between the past and us. Sartre, with his frenzied view of consciousness defining itself (and all of us) by throwing itself into and acting toward the future and his somewhat manichean view of the historical process as a discontinuous series of surges of spontaneity that fall back into the *pratico-inerte* as soon as organization and institutions take over, looks at the past both as a struggle of alienated beings driven by scarcity and as a record of failure. By contrast with Malraux, he was never concerned with its meaning for us (since we shall find meaning only through what we do next). Yet, in his long confrontation with Marxism, he at least proclaimed that whatever meaning history has lies in the acting out of human consciousness. Other intellectuals have rejected history altogether, or tried—to use the jargon of the time—to "evacuate the conscious subject": Lévi-Strauss asserts the importance of structures that owe nothing to man-made history and expresses his nostalgia for those societies that live outside history, "surrounded by (its) substance and . . . impervious to it";[7] Althusser reduces Marxism to a set of structural laws; Foucault discovers hidden structures of knowledge that dictate their rules to men; Deleuze and Guattari see man as a mere collection—not of feelings, desires, or ideas that can properly be called his own but of *machines désirantes* that drive, or rather push and pull him. It is not surprising that the confrontation with events has made it difficult for several of these writers to be consistent: events are clearly man-made, not just structural outputs; and in such confrontations, when writers had to decide—concretely—who was at fault, who caused the harm they deplored (and not simply what structure or what clash of machines resulted in what action, institution, or *dis-*

cours), they fell back not on history but on ideology. Foucault has shifted from the archaeology of knowledge to capitalist alienation, and the authors of *L'Anti-Oedipe* have denounced capitalism (and indeed, the whole modern system of production) as the root of poor Oedipus's schizophrenia.

Is there, then, nobody who wants to preserve the connection to the past? Surely many do, but for reasons that turn out to have rather little in common with the desire to nurture a sense of historical continuity or to use this sense as an enrichment of the present or an inspiration for the future. (De Gaulle was the last postwar statesman, along with the aging Churchill, to look at history in this way; and it is not merely a matter of age, since Adenauer, for many reasons, did not do so.) Ancient monuments are, of course, being piously restored; but is it because of what they mean today or because they are part of the "artistic patrimony" of the nation and, therefore, of its overall resources? Old buildings are being renovated and visited by eager groups, but is it a way of keeping the past in one's midst, or is it an alternative to a relief from the unmistakable horrors of much of modern European architecture? Old regional feasts and fairs are turned into festivals, but is this a means for reaching into the past or into the pocketbooks of tourists? National holidays are being celebrated, but is this done for the reasons a Robespierre once gave when he advocated such ceremonies or in order to provide governments with a moment of contrived harmony, and citizens with a day off?

The real reachers for the past fall into two groups. Paradoxically, the Marxist Left and its intellectuals—the heralds of change—have become the curators of the revolutionary museum. Radicalism has become a tradition. Since the present has a mixed record, the past can be used to show the depth—in time and scope—of the present evils. (For example, *Que la fête commence*, a quite wonderful film, uses the Regency of 1715 as a way of denouncing the social and political ills of today.) The past can also be used to assure the faithful that the day of reckoning will come, as well as to put them on guard against repeating the errors that have doomed revolutions in the past. But when turning to the past as a way of lecturing us about the present and expressing hope in the future becomes the last resort of revolutionaries, what appears at first as reconnection turns out to be one more escape. (I am thinking of the abundance of French literature about the Commune and of recent plays about the Revolution.) For such a turn is no longer a search and a scrutiny of the past. It is a consolation for the present—a series of parables that keeps us warm for a while in the middle of a very cold here-and-now. One leaves such books, plays, or movies feeling, contrary to the authors' wishes, that insofar as things were always so bad, there is little hope indeed; the past mainly serves as an explanation of and a diversion from present failure. Often today the best historians are either Marxists who are, personally, sufficiently unrevolutionary—that is, conservative—to use Marxist insights as a tool of historical research rather than using historical examples as an ersatz goad to Marxist revolution; or else they are ex-communists who have given up the promised land of utopia for the historian's territory. So we again find scientific history as a repudiation, overt or covert, of ideology, and as a way of looking at the past that disconnects it from the present.

The other group that goes after the past is made up of ethnic and regional minorities: as the majority grows distant from its past, these groups rediscover (or invent) theirs. The present is the age of *their* romantic history. This, too, is an old story—that of nationalism among peoples long deprived of sovereignty, for whom a digging up of alleged or real antiquity is a rebellion against the oppression of the recent past and the present. But just as there is something pathetic about the *passéisme* of Marxist revolutionaries, there is something ungainly about that of Corsican, Occitan, or even Scottish rebels. For here, the past is used not, as it was among the Germans, Italians, or Slavs of the last century, as a cultural basis for a modern creation—a nation—but as a protest against (largely) economic inequalities. Usually there is insufficient popular support (or often even desire) for establishing a separate nation in a Europe where the present nation-states suffer from multiple impotence (which new ones would only reproduce) and yet still have the capacity to defend themselves against secession.

In the educational system the teaching of history regresses. It used to be a major component of mass primary education and of the secondary education that a minority of privileged *and* gifted not-so-privileged youngsters received. Today, this preeminence is challenged by more practical or by more scientific disciplines. In a democracy, the authority of the teacher *qua* teacher is rather low. It rests on his expertise, not on his calling; and the prestige of his expertise depends on the usefulness of the knowledge he imparts. In France, the traditional supremacy of letters and history has ended; glamour glistens on mathematics. High school history is being diluted into social studies—the study of the contemporary. The hold of history in the school thus depends, above all, on the importance of the school as a seminary for teaching a civic faith that is rooted in history. In the United States, schools are often still such seminaries; on the other side of the Atlantic, they no longer are.

Those who find silver linings in every cloud might want to stress one advantage of this demise: will not young Europeans stop learning, internalizing, and reliving the ideological and national quarrels of the past? Maybe, and yet, such potential gains in tolerance and détente (the French word for which has become *décrispation*) are more than offset by important drawbacks; for the unexamined past lives on, and disconnection from it merely makes it more difficult to understand and cope with its formidable residues. It lives on, first of all, in the form of would-be but unfit masterkeys. Since the human mind craves comprehensive explanations for complex events and general causes for disparate effects—especially in countries such as those of Western Europe, where education used to be a missionary branch of the Enlightenment rather than a service for practical adaptation—what is more natural than trying to account for the bewildering array of contemporary changes in the sweeping terms of a seemingly "scientific" philosophy of history? Hence the persistence of Marxism, despite repeated, careful demonstrations of its inadequacy (a la Raymond Aron)[8] or periodic denunciations of its temporal incarnations (a la *nouveaux philosophes,* twenty-five years after Camus). A system of thought rooted in history has become an obstacle to understanding much of the present precisely because the growing evidence of its divorce from historical evolution is obscured by the decline of historical consciousness.

The past lives on, also, as a series of problems, tensions, atavisms—old institutions, modes of authority, or, to quote Michel Crozier,[9] models of rationality that no longer fit the advanced industrial societies of Western Europe, and constitute so many obstacles to individual desires, group aspirations, or collective efficiency. If the problems of class conflict are muddied rather than clarified by a clinging to old dogmatic formulas, the problems of persistent but counterproductive authoritarianism are made worse by the frequent failure to examine its historical roots, to understand why it has proven so resilient despite vast changes in social organization and in values, and despite the transformation or the weakening of many institutions (such as the family, the Church, and the school system) that used to be its props. The lack of historical reflection thus breeds the illusion of quick remedies or encourages the growth of antiauthoritarian utopias (like *autogestion*) that are too impractical, too naïve in their hope of doing away with power altogether, to do much harm to their foe; or, on the contrary, they foster the belief that new challenges to social order can best be met by "re-enforcing authority" (as in West Germany's reaction against terrorism). What a writer recently called postwar West Germany's confusion of democracy with anticommunism,[10] like Italy's confusion of democracy with a mix of parliamentarism and *clientelismo,* or France's confusion of democracy with bureaucracy legitimized by universal suffrage, is the joint result of an inadequate confrontation with the recent past and a growing estrangement from the more distant one.

It has been said that bad conscience—fed by the failures or crimes of the past—may at least have the virtue of instigating commitment. But when it is pure of historical understanding, it leads to blind nihilism. And when that same purity is not accompanied by any bad conscience, the failure of memory through disconnection from the past leads to a failure of imagination and will in connection with the future: the destruction—partly willed, but largely unwitting—of the past has not been the prelude to the construction of a new destiny.

IV

The future too, of course, is viewed in national terms because of the same idiosyncrasies that have kept the Western European nations from building a common state; they are partly deep residues of the past, partly distinctive features of their present political and social systems. Old blinders or worries, present crises, and opportunities loom large in such visions. The British, after years of vivisecting their malaise (the "British disease"), see a brighter future thanks to the combination of luck—the North Sea oil—and traditional virtues—rediscovered self-restraint and incomes discipline. The Germans, despite a party system that strikes foreign observers as more consensual than any outside the United States, worry about law and order and argue about the best way to protect a democratic system whose fresh roots are growing in a society where liberalism remains conditional—dependent on efficiency. Italians are entirely absorbed by the drama of the permanent crisis, and see as the only alternatives either a total breakdown—followed by some still unpredictable rule of violence and terror—or a coalition of the two huge secular churches—the Christian Democrats and the Communists. This coalition would feed the skepticism or anxieties of those who belong to neither party, those who trust one but not the other, and those who fear that the union of the two mastodons would give a colossal, final proof of impotence. The French oscillate between a new pragmatism that may turn out to be another word for complacency and immobility and an addiction to political divisions whose only merit is to keep alive the illusion of real choice. What is remarkable is how little each national vision is affected by the others. It is even more remarkable that none of them amounts to a national design.

They have one thing in common: a combination of two sets of experiences and expectations, which does not beget a vision of the future. For many years, Western Europeans have lived on the moving escalator of economic growth. The social dislocations and political changes it has brought about have, as I have already stated, riveted their minds on the present. At the same time, especially as governments for so long have suggested that (or acted as if) the solution to all tensions would be provided by further growth, the citizens were led to believe that the future could be summed up as a continuing and growing manna—the condition of the fulfillment of individual ambitions and desires, the prerequisite of greater social justice, and the way to equality of opportunity and results. In this sense, the imagined future was no more than a projection of what was most welcome in the present and the hope that what was currently unwelcome would be eliminated or tamed. The British, whose growth was smaller, told pollsters that they felt happy, happier than the continentals. But their own leaders worried about the effects of the lower rate, and the continentals showed a remarkable consensus in rejecting any thought that their tensions and frustrations might be relieved by a slowdown. If we mean by the word *political* a consideration of one's relation to others, to groups, to the community, and to the state in terms of values, beliefs, and power, the prevailing vision was singularly apolitical: its blandishments were bland, its appeal lay in its being so easy.

It was precisely because this vision of quantitative happiness, this somewhat mindless faith in a self-propelled expansion that apparently required no more from each citizen than his labor and a minimum of social integration, this failure to image another model of society, another kind of individual fate, another destiny for the nation seemed so tepid or boring to many of the young, that the "events" of May, 1968, occurred. But a rebellion is not a construction: no alternative vision came out of it. May, 1968, showed how the death of *le passé vécu* and the failure to bring a new design to life are linked. The young rebels may have thought they were reliving a revolutionary past, but they were only going through the motions: they acted, they did not reenact. A liquidation of what had become secondhand or bookish memories led nowhere—except to a deluge of books. Most of the young, whether they took part in this "happening" or not, seemed, in fact, to accept the common vision and to think of their own future in terms of individual security amidst general prosperity.[11] There seemed to be nothing between unlimited alienation and limited horizons, a rejection *intoto* of the prevailing values or a somewhat passive acceptance of them.

Then came the experience of the recession. It shattered the expectations of an ever-rising escalator. It revived old critiques of capitalism, old discussions about its final crisis. But no new alternative vision has emerged; it is as if people remained glued to the motionless escalator and waited for it to get well. The Europeans' own "revolution of rising expectations" made its sudden stop that much more jarring. But despite some talk about new models of growth or qualitative rather than quantitative growth, governments and citizens were joined in a desire to put the escalator back in motion; the only disagreements between or within nations have been over rates of recovery, fears of inflation and unemployment, and obligations of mutual solidarity. In other words, little has been learned from the troubles that have blurred the easy vision. No more-political action or proposal has appeared. This older and somewhat uninspiring vision—what French rebels had called *métro, boulot, dodo*—has simply been proven unreliable. The recession and its inequities confirmed the rebels in their rejection of the model (and probably helped turn some of them from spontaneous psychodrama to organized terror), while the passive acceptance of this model by the others lost some of its former complacency. And the millions, neither rebels nor conformists, who subscribe to the critique of capitalism offered by the Marxist Left, nevertheless live a double life or practice double-entry bookkeeping. They have seen their reasons for distrusting the model vindicated, yet they see no future other than one of economic growth. (They only wish the authorities in charge to be less distant, unreliable, greedy, or unfair than the profitmakers who have managed it so far.)

This brings us to a query about the institutions and forces that used to be, so to speak, the incubators of designs, the shapers of the collective will, or the sources of collective utopias. Among the most potent of these were the ideologies political forces offered to the citizens. What visions of the future do they now propose? Nothing much, really. One can divide these forces into several categories, which do not always correspond to distinctions between parties. First, there are the managers: the French *majorité*, the Italian Christian Democrats, the bulk of the three West German and the British parties, and the Spanish establishment that developed under Franco's shadow. They are the high priests of the prevailing model of growth, and all subscribe, with national or party nuances, both to Pompidou's conviction that the state's role is to straighten or smooth out (nothing more) the natural effects of continuing industrialization, and to Giscard's dictum that governing is just the art of *"gérer l'imprévisible."* There may be a vision here, but the least one can say is that it lacks inspiration. To quote the earlier French president —de Gaulle—"marrying one's century" may well be necessary, but does it prepare one for the next? De Gaulle, it is true, was not simply a manager; he had a vision, both of the past and of the future, and he still believed in national history and national will in the grand double drama of internal togetherness and external struggle. But his was, above all, a vision of rallying for and acting on the world stage. He talked of French and European might, not of French or European social and political organization (beyond the need for a strong state). When, at the end, he realized that this was the area in which a vision was most needed (given France's and Europe's limited range on the world scene) and when he came to see that without such a vision no dream of the world stage, however modest, could ever be realized, he fell—both because many of his own supporters showed no desire for imagination and because his own was ill at ease in this realm.

Next to the managers, there are the challengers: the Communists, the Labor and SPD Left, and the French Socialists. They too have had trouble with the future. Sometimes, as in England, their vision is so insular and goes so much against the common scriptures of growth as to appear almost perverse—thoroughly unappealing to the unconverted and singularly austere even to the faithful. Sometimes, their programs are not prophecies or calls to arms but mere critiques of present injustices and acute expressions of present discontents. Sometimes, as in the case of the French Socialists, they seem caught between residual (or is it revived?) utopianism—as in the drive for *autogestion*—against "professional politics" and against the centralized state that pretends to express the general will. The drive comes, if not like de Gaulle's view of France, *du fond des âges*, at least from the oldest Socialist and syndicalist fund[12]—as well as from rather routine sources of social democracy. Sometimes, as in the case of the Communists, the challengers are split between those who seek, at least temporarily, to collude diffidently with the managers—because of the scars left by past fascist experiences and, therefore, the need to give priority to the establishment or survival of democracy (however "formal")—and those who, like the French, cling to a Leninist model of revolutionary break with the established order while trying to de-Leninize the model just enough to capture voters whose ideal for the future is definitely not Leninist. In other words, they behave like a church that is afraid both of losing its distinctiveness by throwing out too much of a now-unappealing dogma and of losing its appeal by not throwing out enough (not an inaccurate description of the present Roman Catholic church). The compromise is neither stable or popular within, nor convincing outside.

Thus, the great ideological "spiritual families" of the past have either disappeared or propose no relevant future. What do Christian Democrats offer, except a plea for law and order, a spectacle of decay, or a touching faith in European integration as the *deus ex machina?* Has socialism succeeded in preserving its identity? Or has it not rather been endlessly torn between the managerial temptation, a stern egalitarianism, and a welfarism that accepts, in order to reform it, capitalist society; and when the costs of welfarism become unbearable as growth slows down (and welfarism tends indeed to slow growth by drying out investment), what more does socialism offer than a nostalgia for a new *projet de société* it cannot quite define? Has liberalism succeeded in moving beyond the reconciliation of political liberty with democracy, or the compromise between the market and some government control, which date from much earlier times? What can old conservatism offer when whatever it wanted to conserve is gone? What is the communist ideal, once you erase the Soviet Union from it—and even if you leave it in? The notion of the death of ideology has been accepted too easily and buried too soon. Its celebrators grandly overrated, in their Saint-Simonian faith in science and production, the degree to which the advent of postindustrial society would inject pragmatism, erase class differences, tame class conflicts, modernize party systems, and eliminate Luddite extremists. Ideologies are still there, though, especially on the Left—as is normal since the Left is the refuge and hope of those who dislike the established order. Traces of ideological thinking can be found all over the picture; but insofar as ideologies offered plausible visions of the future, the much-rejected notion was not so wrong. Either there are no such visions or else they are not plausible, like those spun out by hundreds of *groupuscules.* They describe the ideal future as what will miraculously arise when the present society has been entirely destroyed—a grand release of spontaneity, a fusion in fraternity, but no discernible social order. And the visions are based less on faith than on hate, as in the beautiful scene of destruction at the end of Antonioni's *Zabriskie Point.* Marxism is still present—often omnipresent—and diffuse. But it serves as a tool for analyzing the flaws of the status quo and as a goad for proposing the demise of the present—not as a blueprint for the future. Societies that depend on growth, and whose citizens expect it even when they criticize its present motors: societies, moreover, that have been bitten, or have barely escaped being bitten, by the "carnivorous idols" Bernanos talked about in the 1930s, ask formidable questions of each ideological vision of the future. The questions were often either not raised before or were deemed secondary—Will it work? At what costs? Societies that have suffered from the disease of unrestrained ideologies on a rampage, and have put their hopes in the benefits of economic growth, now impose a reality test on political visions, even if their own vision of the future is singularly unpolitical and unreal.

Those who announced the end of ideology believed that the advent of a pragmatic age would propel Western Europe toward a plannable future—postindustrial society. But such pragmatism presupposes either that political problems have been reduced to technical ones (to be solved by experts) or that the old ideologies are to be replaced by a new one—the ideology of advanced liberal capitalism—which would dampen and thus help resolve disputes. If both postulates are wrong and the old ideologies are dead or dying, one is left immersed in a dreary present, a jungle of group conflicts, with no standard for their solution. And the very intensity of the struggle for power and product, the very absence of any grand cause, the very myopia of each class, profession, and association concentrating on its claims makes it almost impossible for any vision of the future to emerge.

The other forces from which such visions used to emanate are in no better shape. I have already mentioned the Catholic church. Its image of the future used to be shaped by its conception of the past, by the accretion of values and dogmas transmitted from generation to generation. Inevitably, now that this heritage is being liquidated—partly because it is incompatible with the dynamics and mores of the modern world and partly because it has been compromised by past collusions between the Church and antidemocratic political ideologies and elites— the Church is left without a vision of the future and exposed to another kind of collusion—with the political and social activists of reform or even revolution. Yesterday's involvement with secularism condemned the Church to unpopularity; but the secularists on whom it used to lean had borrowed their own design and dogmas from the Church. Today, it is the Church that does the borrowing— from people caught in or drifting amidst the troubles of the present.

The army also used to offer a vision of the future. But it was one of a struggle against other European nations for revenge or supremacy, or against the barbarians for law and order and civilization. Of course, the willingness to resort to force, the usefulness of force, indeed the greatness of force, were essential to this vision: as de Gaulle wrote, "the sword is the axis of the world, and greatness cannot be divided."[13] Force today is doubly devalued: pragmatically because the risks are too great and the rewards too slim, and intellectually because its prestige in Europe has not survived the orgies of violence of two world wars. Armies reduced to deterrent and latent or oblique functions or to "punctual" rescue operations have trouble finding volunteers or keeping draftees from displaying their boredom. At any rate, they too are in a limbo, between a past they can only celebrate with ambivalence and a future they cannot like.

Again, the intelligentsia offers no more vision of the future than of the past. It may once have played a role as the purveyor of utopias, but there are not many utopias to be found today. Marxists abound—as critics of the present. But they are now bereft of a future. It was relatively easy to propose one—as there was no socialist society anywhere—before 1914. Now there are too many, and the most orthodox is the biggest disappointment of all. When reality begins to shackle the imagination and to betray hope, resentment alone remains—and sometimes indeed, as in France in the past months, the resentment turns away from the present toward a wholesale repudiation of Marxism altogether. To be sure, Italian and French syndicalists and their sympathizers have, as I said before, articulated the utopia of *autogestion;* but in their drive to appear responsible—that is, not utopian—the revolutionary force of the idea, which was still considerable after May, 1968, and the "hot Fall" of Italy, has been eroded. Pragmatic proposals have replaced the Sorelian myth. Intellectuals are still the experimenters, but their experiments have been, so to speak, privatized: they deal with the realms of aesthetics, linguistics, theater, and the movies, with psychoanalysis, and with poetry. Sometimes their experiments carry them into local social-welfare operations, like the French *Lacaniens* and antipsychiatrists after 1968; but this occurred precisely because the wider political scene had proven so disappointing.[14] As Crozier points out, the traditional role of the intellectual—to serve as a self-appointed conscience and guide of the nation, and thus to propose ideals and to speak out about its present and its future—has to a considerable extent disappeared. Sartre's last active years as a writer have been spent on his negative identity, called Flaubert.

For a while, in the 1960s, it seemed that the old intellectual would be replaced by the new problem-solving social scientist, who would lend his expertise to the managers and lead them to careful reforms. But on the one hand, the multiplication of "perverse" (or counterintuitive) effects, the latent dissatisfaction of many of the experts with a role that seemed to them like a fall from the pedestal of the past and like mere service of the prince, the impatience of the managers with experts more concerned with their own research priorities than with those of the state—all doomed or at least dwarfed that experiment. On the other hand, social science, especially when it divorces itself from public philosophy, rarely goes beyond what Max Weber called the disenchantment of reality—revealing, unveiling, and debunking. Now, any vision of the future must go beyond this point or, rather, stay on this side of total lucidity, if it is to be a call or guide to action. For one cannot act without somehow underestimating difficulties or overestimating those whom one wants to rally. Intellectuals *qua* prophets had idealized the People; the social scientists' job is to describe the real, not the imaginary people. Action simplifies, social science complicates.

Insofar as social engineering continues, with carefully reduced expectations, it reflects what I said about the citizenry as a whole: its practitioners have demonstrated little imagination about the future and have proven that even its limited promises may not be kept after all. Members of the intelligentsia who have turned away from that troubled partnership in social engineering have gone in one of two directions, and sometimes in both. One is specialized, scientific research or arcane experimentation. This choice preserves that distance between the intellectual and the average man, that equation between intellectual work and prowess that is a legacy from the aristocratic age—although it is now divorced from the nineteenth-century artist's desire to lead the masses into a promised land. Of course, among those who choose this direction, very little is being said about the problems of everyday life, ethics, institutions, work, and leisure. The second direction is a residue of this grand claim—a kind of debased nostalgia for it: it is the desire to be "popular," fashionable, a media *habitué* or a media event, a troubadour of spontaneity or a mod synthesizer of concepts that are in or on the air. (Witness the sudden discovery in France, in 1977, that power is everywhere. What would Molière have done with that?) But in this case, the once-prophet becomes a mere critic, who peremptorily denounces what the powermongers have done, but who refuses to say what they should have done, since all politics is contemptible. A narcissistic, self-appointed spokesman for the victims of the universal Gulag, he abdicates all responsibility for imagining a better world, merely calls for resistance whenever the powers-that-be step on the little man's toes, or sympathizes with the longings of adolescence. This has happened to the *nouveaux philosophes* (they were not reluctant), and it also characterizes much of the writing of Alain Touraine. Even a work as careful in its attempt to avoid both esoterism and grand rhetoric as the Crozier-Friedberg call for a new kind of social theory strikes one as singularly ahistorical and modest about the future:[15] change must come through experimentation *à la base*, through the gradual learning of new collective capabilities; there is no way to describe it in advance, nor should too much of it be attempted at any given moment, since people cannot stand a heavy dose of upheaval. It is as if much of the European intelligentsia, after witnessing the shambles and crimes perpetrated by the "isms" it used to embrace, had turned away in horror, not merely from such "isms" but also from the kind of *prospective* they provided and perverted. The welcome rediscovery of those virtues dear to Camus—modesty and limits—has led to a retreat from political thought altogether. Since the air was foul, those who helped make it so have decided to stop breathing.

The intellectuals, through their writings and through the role they played in and around political parties, used to peddle visions of the future. While their wares may have reached only a small portion of the public, their influence was much broader; their ideas became known not only through the parties, but also because of another transmission belt—the system of education. Nowhere was schooling merely a set of training techniques, a transmission of accumulated usable knowledge, or a machine for "social reproduction." Not only in the Gymnasium, lycée, or public school attended by the few, but in primary education for the many, the school system transmitted values, formed citizens (some as responsible participants, some as obedient subjects), and provided them, more or less overtly, with images of the future. The educational system of the Third Republic, whose textbooks were written by distinguished scholars and intellectual administrators, propagated a vision of the future that combined the preservation of traditional French bourgeois values and the progressive unfolding of the Enlightenment—science, rationality, material gains, and increasing possibilities of self-determination for individuals long oppressed by routines or dogmas, as well as for nations. It was a remarkable blend of the traditional and the revolutionary, well-fitted to a society that resisted rapid changes in behavior and habits yet was permanently in love with the idea of change, the ideal of emancipation, and a self-image as a beacon of light. It is not a coincidence that the most influential intellectual godfather of schoolteachers before the First World War was Jaurès, a visionary who was also the finest product of his nation's culture and the very symbol of nineteenth-century optimism.

As in the intellectual world, we are now witnessing an eclipse of the future in the school system. It has been replaced with "present shock": a proliferation of options and subjects, an often frantic or overstuffed attempt at putting into the hands of the young as many tools as possible to help them understand and navigate in the present (hence a high rate of obsolescence and a breathless, permanent revision of curricula). To be sure, there is much of this kind of scurrying in America as well; but there, the beliefs of the *angewandte Aufklärung*[16] surround and give meaning to the disconnected bits and pieces. This is not the case in Western Europe. The public cult of growth is not a substitute, for it is a cult of means, not ends; and if there is one group that is often sullen, bitter, and hostile toward the cult, it is the teachers. Not only is their prestige falling, as I have pointed out before. But, trained to transmit established knowledge to pupils whose function it is to receive it, they are confronted instead with the need for their own permanent reeducation, with the duty to transmit methods and data that in a short time may prove to be wrong and with young men and women who are increasingly impatient with the old-style pedagogy. Both in reference to what is to be taught and how best to teach it, the very speed of change, already found partly responsible for the receding of the past, also contributes to the blackout of the future. The school is caught between students concerned above all with their own opportunities in nations marked by disruptive changes—as well as by vast surges for collective social ascent—and teachers who do not always comprehend the changes, and who often feel that in growth-obsessed societies they have lost much of the high ground they held in the days when efficiency, consumption, and the production of goods were not the highest values. The only function of the school seems to be running after (or behind) adjustment: its fate parallels that of European societies, which used to see themselves on top of their own fate in a world shaped by them. Yesterday, the school was a force for social integration that taught values drawn from the past and expectations about the future. Today, if it is such a force at all, it is as a purely functional agent of preparation for the present.

If "no model of civilization emerges from the present-day drifting culture, no call for reform and pioneering,"[17] if radical criticism so often turns out to be no more than criticism without a vision for replacement of what is to be destroyed, there is still another reason: the displacement of the intelligentsia by the media, or perhaps the rush of the intellectuals themselves to become (pardon the expression) "communicators" rather than creators. This is often seen as a means of remaining "relevant" in nations where the public no longer turns to its great writers for guidance—unless they write for mass consumption or appear on the screen. Indeed, the media have become a screen between the intellectuals and the public. The former feel that their only alternatives are isolation (which they fear) and capitulation (which they often seem to crave). I call it capitulation—not merely joining what one cannot fight—because the media impose their own constraints. Whether—depending on the country and the medium—they revel in muckraking or in celebration, they too tend to emphasize the present, either to condone or to condemn it. The past is a source of entertainment, the future a dangerous bone of contention. A few moviemakers may invent futures, but it is rare, and usually only to warn us about present trends (for example, Truffaut's *Fahrenheit 451*, which is based on a story by American Ray Bradbury). Television, in Europe, shuns the controversial for political reasons (as in France), scrutinizes the present to heighten citizen awareness (as in England and West Germany), or endlessly serves up old movies and adaptations of novels. The press, with few exceptions, sees its role as purveyor of information and analyses of the present; the recently created "ideas" page of *Le Monde* almost seems designed to highlight the plight of the modern intellectual—he sounds esoteric when he talks of his own research, and puerile when he tries to walk in the steps of the older thinkers and muse about anything outside his own field.

If the media are the daily opium, the provider of food in the citizen's daily life is the bureaucracy. Just as the media have pushed aside or domesticated the intellectuals, who used to invent futures, the bureaucrats have taken over the state, which used to choose one and build it. Ruling has become managing, and the bureaucracy manages us all, or almost all of us. "Marginalized" people—immigrant workers, or workers and employees who live in the shadow economy on which the visible one often relies for survival (as Suzanne Berger has shown),[18] shopkeepers, artisans, and peasants on their way out, or students parked in university ghettos with no job possibilities when they come out, may fall outside the bureaucracy's net. They are either living in a hopeless present or "recuperated" by nihilists. The citizens who perform in the carnival of growth, those who are under the net—with their bargaining power, institutions, and associations that are the essence of modern corporatism—are, for all the weapons at their disposal, *administerés*. Pressuring the bureaucracy on whose benefits, directives, incentives, and guidelines they depend is their constant concern as producers or consumers. (This is one reason why the use of the word *corporatism* is misleading: in orthodox corporatist theory, the groups are autonomous and have taken power away from the state; today, they are tied to it in symbiotic alliance or contest.) The bureaucracy also contributes to the general immersion in the present. True, there is some official concern with planning the future, but it is less a matter of vision than a question of deterrence; without foresight, without an evaluation of trends, an extrapolation of curves, there will be disasters, and the bureaucracy's role is to insure smoothness. But, almost by definition, it cannot begin with a utopia and provide the means to bring it about. It must start with the present, with today's notions of what is desirable (full employment, no inflation, better housing, the stability of families, adequate health care and schooling, growing productivity, sufficient supplies of energy, better working conditions); it then tries to insure that tomorrow will meet the standards and demands of today. I do not mean to suggest, as Henry Kissinger did, that bureaucracy is the born enemy of creativity and imagination; I would only point out that this is not its domain or its duty. The vision must come from somewhere else; when there is none, when no people or leader give them directives about the kind of future that ought to be created, then the bureaucracy's essence—the middle range, coping with what exists, trouble-avoidance, and predictability—occupies the whole scene. Its own weight, its importance in the daily affairs of Western European societies, tends to be rather overwhelming anyhow (much more so than in the United States, even in a country such as Italy, where the state is weak and the bureaucracy is far from efficient). The reasons are many: parliaments cannot cope, or else they try to do little more than protect special interests; so many ministers are managerial types or are easily tamed by the bureaucrats; the margins of choice are so small; and, above all, the economic and social functions of the state are so large. This situation not only seriously limits the leaders' capacity to realize whatever vision they may have; it also inhibits their ability to shape any vision at all. Everywhere in the capitalist world, the state that wants to avoid recession and inflation finds that its margin of maneuver is severely constrained by the dynamics, domestic and international, of the capitalist economy; the more extensive the functions and bureaucracy of the state, the more visible these constraints and the more inhibited the state's capacity to imagine and prepare a different future. It was fascinating to watch, in the French Socialist party, the struggle between the utopians and the "realists" (and, sometimes, between utopian and "responsible" fragments of a same personality, such as Michel Rocard). Societies doomed to constant efficiency and success are deadly not only for ideologies but for all far-reaching visions of the future.

Thus, none of the forces or institutions that used to breed visions of the future, and that also served as instruments of social integration and control, perform as innovators anymore. Another factor obliterates visions of the future. There are no outside models to inspire one and to allow one to say: see, my future is no utopia, since it already works somewhere else. Neither superpower is an inspiration. There are many reasons why America is not—even though Europe's model of growth and the techniques for promoting growth are borrowed from the United States. To Europeans, America is a supermarket, not a religion; one turns to it for recipes and goods, not for its spirit or for its value as a model of society. There is also the simple fact of America's power and presence: can the heir to a long and glorious past, the dreamer of a united Europe (whatever the failure of will and the blurred image of the past) legitimately accept the master's way of life as an ideal? Indeed, the more they lift or imitate, the more Western Europe's societies begin resembling America, at least superficially, and the more they are bound to proclaim that the borrowing is a means to something original. The difference in world power strengthens and inflames an old European tendency to cultural snobbery—how can one take as an ideal a nation whose cultural achievements do not measure up to one's own? This pose remains important, even in places such as England and Germany, where the next reason is not so strong. Europe's traditional ideologies, however irrelevant or faded in their power to describe a future, remain, with the single exception of liberalism, distant enough from American experience to serve as screens between it and the Europeans. It is not surprising to find in France, side by side, a Marxist critique of American capitalism and imperialism and a right-wing onslaught on American egalitarianism, commercialism, homogenization of cultures, pernicious universalism, and lack of aesthetic sense. "A corpse in good health," a source of perversion, degradation, and infection, a country which "drops everywhere the eggs of its ugliness"—these themes are spun by some Gaullists and also some neo-Fascists.[19] (However, the critique of capitalism and imperialism sometimes comes from the Right, the aesthetic critique from the Left, as in Werner Herzog's unforgettable movie *Stroszek,* whose antihero finally kills himself in the wasteland of America, the country of the cold and of artificial hens gone mad in an amusement gallery.) Moreover, as Aron has pointed out, America is a country whose idea of the future is nothing but the fulfillment of its ideas at birth:[20] it is not a prophecy, but a vindication (so that any crisis of values or institutions breeds a kind of fundamentalist revival). The Western Europeans find no such decalogue at their origins: their revolutions are either unfinished or have failed. For all these reasons, there have been more piecemeal imitations than overall celebrations of the American model. Finally, America's own ideal (but do Americans understand it?) is highly nationalistic: it is the realization of America's mission, it is the triumph at home and abroad of a certain conception of man's relation to God and to government, which was born in rebellion against and developed in separation from Europe. And so we have come full circle.

If America never became the ideal even when it was the example, the Soviet Union has ceased being either. "Eurocommunism" is not a very helpful concept. But what the three Communist parties of France, Italy, and Spain have in common is a deliberate distance from the Soviet Union—whether in the form of an open attack on the essence of the Soviet system, as in Carrillo's case; as jerky repudiations of key elements of the Soviet state and ideology, as in Marchais's; or in polite and friendly estrangement, as in Berlinguer's. The French example shows that it is more difficult to jettison the Nessus's tunic of a Leninist organization and frame of mind, than to get rid of the concept of proletarian dictatorship and the single-party state. Yet the lesson is clear: no significant Western European Communist party, except Portugal's, proposes the Soviet Union as a model of socialism; each one explains that Western European circumstances make it irrelevant. Moreover, the new generation of Communist voters knows more about the crimes of Stalin, thanks to the media, than older party members were ever allowed to guess. As for the savage kinds of communism or extremist Marxism, they are orphans. Whether they were of Trotskyite origin or not, they had always looked askance at the Soviet Moloch. They used to believe that the sun would rise in the Far East, in Mao's China; but the end of the Cultural Revolution and the fall of the Gang of Four have made them aware of a bitter fact: the Chinese model may not be so different from the Soviet one after all, whatever the national enmities and differences in levels of development and policies between the two. (One such orphan, the *Tel Quel* group of French intellectuals, having moved beyond Red China, has now discovered the United States as a country where, given capitalism's constraints, little may be accomplished but a lot is permitted: artistic experiments, group rebellions, experimentations—who would have thought that the search for spontaneity would cross the Atlantic, or rather the Pacific?)[21] Yugoslav workers' control is a dubious case; Guevara is dead; Castro is a Soviet client; and Régis Debray is a prize-winning novelist.

V

We have once again come full circle. The fading of the national past could have meant the giving up of a narrow identity in preparation for and in favor of the adoption of a new broader European one. But this would have required an image of, a will for, a common future. *Tout se tient:* with no clear visions of the future, how can Frenchmen, Englishmen, etc., desire a *projet* for Europe? And if they are encased in their national present, how can they do anything but lose contact with a past that is both increasingly less vivid, less present, less relevant, and something of a reproach? How can they be more than conformists complying with a perplexing present, half-citizens, half-protestors, or pure rebels whose revolt, when it does not merely express itself in terror, takes, as in May, 1968, the form of a half-finished blend of disparate, uprooted old ideas thrown into a Cuisinart for quick concoction? For a vision of the future as pure release, à la *Zéro de Conduite,* what slogan is more telling than "under the pavement, the beach"?

The disappearance of the past is partly a disappointment with that past—with what history and human action have wrought—thus it is very different from that deliberate historical break that revolutionaries intent on building a new order and creating a new man provoked in 1792, or in 1917, or in 1949 in China. It means exhaustion, not energy; drainage, not arson. In turn, the lack of a sense of the future has further depressed, devalued, and discolored the past; when one does not know where one is going, when there seems to be nowhere to go and nothing new and better to accomplish, what is the point of retracing one's steps? It takes a combination of faith in, ideas about, and will to build one's future to keep an interest in the past from becoming mere scholarship or leisure. There has been enough democratization, in the sense of a liquidation of the residues from the nondemocratic past, enough denationalization—even in France—enough "disideologization" (pardon the word) to disenchant the past. But the result is a vacuum, not a will to build either a common European future, or a new national one. As we have seen, this is a story in which cultural, political, economic, and social factors all mix.

In the nineteenth century, the nations of Western Europe were marked by an original combination of lively, even heated ideological quarrels about different visions of the future, especially the political future; there was broad public consensus about the social order, the general direction, and the nation's role in the world. Those who felt left out had their own vision. Today, the quarrels are more about the present, and the public consensus, almost everywhere, is what I once called, for France, a consensus by default—the present is embraced less for its virtues than for its benefits (when they flow), less for its values than because any alternative is seen as either worse (whether it is the return of a frightening past experience or the imposition of the Soviet model) or more divisive. As a result, the continent that has always prided itself on its sense of roots and innovation appears more uprooted and less creative than the other model that makes Europeans so uncomfortable—the United States. Tocqueville's nightmare of disconnected individuals under a tutelary state is more present in Europe than in America. What he did not foresee was that individuals would also be disconnected from the past and the future, that voluntary associations (in which he saw a corrective to disconnection) would often only add group egoism to individual acquisitiveness, and that the state would be both bloated and trapped.

We are left then with two questions for morose or worried speculation. First, can one live forever in the economic present, comforting oneself with comparative statistics and a half-cozy, half-worried enjoyment of goods, freedom, and rights? Second, to what extent are the poverty of inspiration and imagination, the concentration on the here and now, related to the European nations' fall from international eminence? Are images of the past and visions of the future tied either to struggles for national identity or to the possibility of strutting on the world's stage, to fighting or speaking out for a great cause, national or not? France's intellectuals lost their voice, at the moment when France ceased to be a pacesetter for other nations and a leader in world affairs. Britain's inability to have a clearer vision of its future than its partners cannot easily be explained as a result of the cult of growth (although it results in part from the penalties that must be paid for forgetting the criterion of efficiency). It can be explained in part by the "end of ideology"; for even though the scope of ideological battles was not as wide there as on the Continent, Britain was once inspired by deep political and religious creeds. Still, this explanation does not go far enough. Was not Britain's image of its future always associated with a vision of a great role in the world—and was not de Gaulle's intuition about the necessity of such a role as a goad to internal creativity correct after all? If there is such a connection, the plight of Western Europe is not likely to end. For if the fall from the heights has broken that part of the *élan vital* that expresses itself, not in daily work and often-successful responses to the challenges of growth, but in the ability to find stimulation in the past and to will a future, then the very imprisonment in the present, the vital impulse's engulfment in the daily adjustments and crises, make the recovery of a sense of time (backward and forward) and the discovery of a common will unlikely. And so, each nation remains encased in its present self, giving an occasional backward glance at the recent past for remorse or consolation and a worried glance at the near future. Only a uniting Europe that could look at the whole of its fragmented past would be able to will a future. But how can it emerge, if its members have neither the drive nor the necessary incentives to transcend themselves into Europe?

Notes

I want to express my gratitude to my friend and colleague Judith Shklar, whose comments and suggestions have been invaluable—as usual.

1. *Ce que je crois* (Paris, 1978), p. 82.
2. *L'Europe interdite* (Paris, 1977), p. 150.
3. Cf. Fritz Stern, "The Giant from Afar," *Foreign Affairs* (October, 1977).
4. *Vichy France* (New York, 1972).
5. See *Democracy in America,* vol. 2, chap. 5 and 6 or Part Four.
6. Domenach, *Ce que je crois,* p. 201.
7. Quoted in Mark Poster, *Existential Marxism in Postwar France* (Princeton, 1975), p. 327.
8. See both *L'opium des intellectuels* (Paris, 1955) and *Plaidoyer pour l'Europe décadente* (Paris, 1977).
9. In *The Crisis of Democracy* (New York, 1975), p. 39ff.
10. Jane Kramer, "Hamburg," in *The New Yorker* (March 20, 1978).
11. Cf. Gérard Vincent, *Les Lycéens* (Paris, 1971).
12. See Jacques Julliard, *Contre la politique professionnelle* (Paris, 1978).
13. Last sentence of *Vers l'armée de métier* (Paris, 1934).
14. See Sherry Turkle, *Psychoanalytic Politics,* (New York, 1978).
15. *L'acteur et le système* (Paris, 1977).
16. See Ralf Dahrendorf's book by that name (Munich, 1963).
17. *The Crisis of Democracy,* p. 33.
18. See her essay, "The Survival of the Traditional Sectors in France and Italy," in: Suzanne Berger and Michael J. Piore, *Dualism and Discontinuity in Industrial Societies,* (Cambridge, 1980).
19. See *Nouvelle Ecole,* "L'Amérique," no. 27–8 (1975), esp. pp. 64, 93ff.
20. *Plaidoyer pour l'Europe décadente,* p. 136.
21. See *Tel Quel,* "Etats-Unis," no. 71–3 (Fall 1977).

7

Reflections on the Nation-State in Western Europe Today

Gone are the days when the champions and the theorists of European integration either called for or predicted the gradual transfer of powers from the nation-state to a new European entity, either through a voluntary abdication of sovereignty, or through the subtle interplay of functional processes and economic interdependence. Today's reality is complex and messy. The nation-state has survived as the centre of political power and the focus of the citizens' allegiance; nationality remains the basis of citizenship, the main countervailing force that resists all the dissolvents of community. However, the nation-state coexists with a European enterprise that has limited but real powers, and considerable resilience. Indeed, the relations between the Community and its members are not a zero sum game; the Community helps preserve the nation-states far more than it forces them to wither away, and in recent years both the Community and its members have been battered by the economic storms. The notes which follow are meant, on the one hand, to examine the developments of the 70s, and on the other to raise a few questions of political theory.

State and Society Revisited

Data

The most striking reality is not the frequent and well-noted impotence of the so-called sovereign state. It is its survival, despite the turmoil. In Western Europe, the nation-state has withstood the massive removal of political confidence, the challenge to the social order of "consumer capitalism" and the "desacralization" of the state, manifest in France in 1968, and to a lesser extent in Italy and in some sectors of West Germany. It has also withstood the economic troubles of the 1970s: inflation and recession; an increase in unemployment that exceeds by far what had been deemed politically tolerable; the plight of important traditional industries; the fragmentation of the labour markets and the development of dual economies; the advent of the era of "zero sum societies" marked by acute conflict among social groups for the distribution of a national product whose growth had slowed down or vanished; the dilemmas of governments caught between expansionist policies potentially disastrous for price stability and for the balance of payments, and restrictive policies with divisive internal effects; a general crisis of the welfare institutions caused by rising costs, and by the rigidifying effects of social protection and bureaucratic regulation on the national economy. The nation-state has also survived the insidious or perverse effects of economic interdependence, which entail a loss of control by the state over various essential instruments of policy—especially credit and monetary policy—because of the unintended consequences of attempts at using these instruments (i.e., attempts at raising interest rates in order to fight inflation, which attract vast amounts of foreign capital into the country; attempts at restricting access to foreign multinational enterprises, which incite them to settle in another member of the Community, etc. . . . .) and also because of the capricious role of uncontrolled forces—public or private external actors—on which no state has a grip.

   This does not mean that the nation-state has carried out its economic, social and cultural functions successfully. But what has occurred has been complex. A number of predicted disasters have failed to take place. The end of deference, caused by changes in values as well as in social organization, has not led to the collapse of the educational systems, of professorial as well as of professional authority, which François Bourricaud[1] seemed to expect: a legitimacy based on traditional obedience (or awe) has been replaced by a legitimacy based on functional competence. The Catholic Church has shown an extraordinary ability to adapt; here again traditional obedience based on dogma has faded, and been replaced by a new legitimacy made of "reasoned faith" and widely recognized services to the polity. The challenge of "new forces": regional separatisms, the ecologists, the women's movements, all of which questioned the established practices of the nation-states, has been contained. The collapse of what Claus Offe has called "competitive party democracy"[2] has been avoided. There have been vast shifts among parties, but no "decline of the party system as the dominant force of mass participation". Theories of ungovernability have come in many forms; some have focused on the governments' overload resulting from rising social demands, others have stressed the effects which collapsing social controls, proliferating social interactions, and the communications explosion have had on the political sphere. But in reality, there has been, instead, a fragmentation and even a lowering of public expectations and (as shown by the decline of the French Communist Party and of the CGT) a conspicuous absence of socio-political upheavals despite the frustrations of unions and other pressure groups.

   While no West European government has succeeded in overcoming what is quite clearly a major and protracted capitalist crisis, three features stand out. The first is the ability of governments with a narrow popular majority to impose extensive sacrifices even on that part of the electorate that voted for the opposition, without major political dramas. The second feature is a greater ability of all West European governments on the one hand to experiment and to muddle through than in the 1930s (the rates of popular participation have been high, the fate of extremist parties has been sad) and on the other hand to maintain a higher level of social protection than in the United States despite the crisis of the welfare state. Thirdly, and paradoxically, in most instances, the reaction of the public and of the political elites to the partial impotence of the governments, to the constraints of economic interdependence, or to those imposed by dependence on the health and moves of the dominant economy: that of the United States, has been to cling to and if possible to re-enforce the nation-state. Growing opposition to the Community in England, a certain revival of German national feelings (if only in the form of a desire not to be a pawn of the super-powers), the French turn to a quite distinctive neo-Keynesian approach that is highly voluntaristic (by contrast with the Giscard-Barre approach), Italy's own closing of ranks under the threat of terrorism, are all manifestations of a national "*sursaut*".

As before, each nation-state of Western Europe has reacted *in its own way*. Not only does each one have its own profile, consisting in a peculiar configuration of economic data (rates of inflation, unemployment and growth, balance of payments, etc . . .), but each one has faced the crisis according to its own political culture. For instance the contrast continues between a German approach marked by the memory of 1923 inflation (and what it did to Weimar) and a French collective phobia of unemployment and tolerance for inflation (Giscard lost largely because his priorities were the other way around). Each country has tried to fashion its own economic policies by combining and manipulating available instruments on behalf of national objectives (i.e., through national strategies involving the management of money and the rate of exchange, the budget, tax, social security, industrial and agricultural policies, energy policies etc . . .). And each one has displayed its own political constellations, rooted in national political factors.

Thus, one can, with equal justification, talk about a relative bankruptcy of the nation-state, in so far as efficiency is concerned: the economic data speak for themselves; and talk about a double resilience of the nation-state, in so far as each one has survived, and done so in its own distinctive way.

Theories

This resilience invites us to re-examine our theories, in two different realms: normative philosophical theories, and empirical sociological ones.

We still think in terms of the classical philosophical model of the liberal polity. As I have argued elsewhere,[3] it "was based on three assumptions which have turned out untenable": emancipation of the individual, transparence (i.e., the society as a sum of individuals), and a limited state, either presiding over or marginally contributing to social harmony.

Reality does not correspond to this model. Individual emancipation has been thwarted by the recurrent crises of capitalist economies as well as by the permanent huge concentration of private and public power in capitalist-cum-welfare societies, by the social limits to growth which block individual satisfactions (cf. Fred Hirsch's analysis of positional goods, and of the role of collective bargaining),[4] and by the effects of external events—the international state of war. Hence, in much of the modern literature—from the Marxists to Dahl and Lindblom—an indictment of the market, whose inequities stunt the development of the individual, and an analysis of the way in which both capitalism and the welfare institutions aimed at correcting it have given birth not to a fulfilled but to a fragmented person, not to a citizen but to a highly selfish and particularistic individual. Instead of transparence, we find the destruction of civility by the struggle for limited goods, and the opacity of groups which are frequently hierarchical and authoritarian (especially public bureaucracies), or oligarchic, conflictual and closed. As for the state, instead of reflecting society, it has become a separate social system, both victimized and bloated. It is victimized by the need to respect the laws of capital accumulation, the dynamics of capitalism, the constraints of international economic and strategic relations; by the logic of individual acquisitiveness, the drive of the "citizens" toward individualized calculations and benefits (which often undermines or thwarts policies of redistribution, and therefore social harmony); by the disproportion between costly attempts at correcting social inequities, and meagre public resources. And the state is bloated by the growth of a quasi-professional, representative elite for whom politics is a career rather than a service, by the growth of a bureaucracy often impervious to external control, and by the enormous extension of its own scope.

A reconstruction of the political theory of the modern polity is thus needed. It has barely begun, and it is difficult. Many of the alternatives to the (obsolete) liberal model are non-democratic. Attempts to conceptualize a democratic one have been plagued by three factors. First, there is excessive abstraction—a flaw that affects the most ambitious effort, John Rawls's Theory of Justice. Secondly, the very resilience of the contemporary nation-state, despite the obsolescence of the liberal model and the crisis of the welfare or social democratic one, creates a sense that the best one can do is describe, explain, rationalize and deplore that Strindbergian couple, the modern state and the truncated individual—a kind of normative abdication. Thirdly, attempts at offering a new normative theory at a tolerable level of abstraction often suffer from a kind of *passéisme*, a nostalgia for formulas rooted in the past.

This is the case of the neo-liberal (or neo-conservative) theory, which advocates reliance on the market yet somehow idealizes what Ronald Reagan calls its "magic" and conveniently forgets all the reasons that led to the attempts to correct its inequities—attempts whose own flaws or perverse effects are the only ills neo-conservatives observe. It is also the case of the *auto-gestion* utopia, which has the same aims (emancipation, transparence, harmony) as the liberal model, but fails to provide satisfactory answers to three important questions: how can what one French author has called an "auto-institutionalized society"[5] reconcile territorial and professional self-management with indispensable central guidance? How can the community as a whole be protected against group selfishness, i.e., preserve the interests of the nation (and of outsiders), and the needs or claims of the future? Can the citizen increase his participation in all the groups, functions and roles in which he is involved, and if not, what is the best form of delegation?

A precondition for the reconstruction of political philosophy may well be a better understanding of contemporary society, i.e., a more sophisticated empirical sociological theory.

In turn, such a better understanding requires, as a first step, the discarding of the models that have dominated empirical theory in the 70s—the various sociological models of industrial society. They have come in multiple forms. Suzanne Berger has distinguished its liberal from its marxist incarnations (they differ in their explanation of change and in their respective emphasis on cooperation vs. conflict)[6] Philippe Schmitter has listed three models of change (structural differentiation, historical materialism, political economy).[7] But all offer what Suzanne Berger has called a "unitary theory of industrial society". It presents social integration as the product of the market, of increasing social mobility and mobilization. It stresses the central role of technology and, in James Caporaso's terms, "the expansion and rationalization of economic structures, the decline of smaller, less efficient firms, the elimination of small agricultural holdings",[8] all leading to higher growth.

These theories are misleading, because they are reductionist in three ways. They reduce social phenomena to mere effects of economic factors; thus, they discount the autonomy of politics, they deny the specificity of other sources of cleavage (ideological, ethnic, religious, linguistic, etc . . .). They are based on a theory of change which (like many theories of political development) is quasi-teleological, leaving no room for either the undetermined dialectic of groups within society, or the unpredictable impact of external events; thus they discount both the irreducible heterogeneity within each society and the discontinuities across borders, in other words the multi-directional nature of history; they focus on "industrial society" instead of the nation, on "society" rather than on the complex and conflictual agglomerations that make it up. And they reduce, in fact, the state to an epiphenomenon, produced by economic and social relations. Its autonomy is either denied (the state thus becoming a mere receptacle and by-product), or limited to whatever is functionally necessary to defend the social order (the state as guardian of the higher or long-term interest of the dominant class); or else the state is being reduced to a set of institutions somewhat decoupled from the rest of society, yet still analyzed primarily as the target or victim of social forces (the besieged state).

Here, unlike what we found in the realm of political philosophy, a reconstruction has begun. In order to understand both the resilience and the relative impotence of the nation-state, as well as the sharp difference between state performances, we need what I would call a state-centered pluralistic and structured approach. It must be state-centered, because of the double autonomy of politics (the domain of social demands focused specifically on the state, thus becoming political issues) and of the state (constrained by these demands, dependent on support, yet endowed with a capacity to innovate and to act on its own). It must be pluralistic, because of the diversities within society and the state as well as among states and societies. It must be structured, because each nation has its own keys and dynamics, produced by history and by the configuration of economic interests, social forces and institutions. This approach would be less predictive and more analytic than the current prevailing one. It can be summarized in four propositions.

One: The famed distinction between state and society is a necessary point of departure because there is, in the modern nation, a functional differentiation between them which results from the monopoly of authoritative decisions and of public force enjoyed by the state. But it is a bad compass for analysis. For what is striking everywhere is the role of political parties as intermediaries between and agents of (both) the state and society; the increasing penetration of society by the state (as Philippe Schmitter has noted, "neo-corporatism" facilitates governability—at a cost); and the increasing public role played by large private organizations, whether or not they operate in a kind of symbiosis with the state bureaucracy or as partners in the majority coalition: witness the help the unions have often given to the state in the economic crisis of the recent past, either by presenting demands for a "structural" state policy that implicitly recognizes the necessity of industrial reconversion (as long as it is planned), or else by agreeing to limit wage demands in exchange for progress on other issues (for instance a reduction of the length of work or an improvement in working conditions) or in exchange for the maintenance of social benefits.

Two: The nation-state is a social system in which the state, positively or negatively, plays a decisive role. I would propose distinguishing three notions. One is the autonomy of the state, which concerns the influences and pressures of society on the state, and has three dimensions: the capacity to resist particular pressures (including those that emanate from the majority parties or from fragments of the bureaucracy), the resulting capacity of the state to produce its own ideas and goals, and the capacity to turn its preferences into decisions (cf. the remarkable study by Eric Nordlinger).[9] A second notion is the strength of the state, which consists both of its capacity to be autonomous and of its internal capacity to act; the latter, in turn, depends on two factors: the organization of the state and the balance between its scope and its resources. The third notion is the effectiveness of the state, i.e., the ability to achieve results by influencing society, which of course depends on its autonomy and strength, but can, even in the case of a strong and autonomous state, be crippled by internal obstacles (for instance, excessive centralization) or by external (i.e., social) resistances caused by a multiplicity of factors: technical or political mistakes made by the government, inequalities and extended privileges, opposition to change, etc. . . . We need to focus on the ways in which, more or less autonomously, more or less strongly, more or less efficiently, the state acts, not merely as a mediator between internal demands and external pressures, but as a *shaper* capable of moulding its own domestic support, of choosing among internal interests and external constraints, of playing some against others, of using the fragmentation of interests and classes in order to fashion—to preserve or to reform—the social order, of using the challenges of complexity, the expansion of its scope, and the imperatives and constraints of the international system in order to define the common interest. It is this ability to appear not as a receptacle, or a prisoner of its base, but as a creator, as a dampener or a solver of conflicts, which is the key to its effectiveness. Whatever the official ideology, in every post-war West European nation, the state has been granted an overall responsibility for and by society. Being the focus of expectations, it can easily be a source of disappointment; but it also has two paradoxical assets: it can attenuate (as Crozier has shown)[10] the crisis of social control that affects European societies, or deprive it of political expression; and it helps preserve the political parties as forces that resist the universal privatization of concerns and counteract group fragmentation. Thus—not in the old legalistic way, but in a more sociological perspective that looks at the constant interactions with society—we must again examine closely the state's own structures and institutions, which make it more or less capable of playing its creative role.

Three: Each nation-state proceeds in its own way. As Peter Katzenstein's work has shown,[11] the main variables are the following ones. Some are structure and process variables: the degree of centralization of the state, the configuration of central political power (the constitutional system—especially concerning the issue of Executive autonomy—and the party system), the degree of centralization of the main interest groups, the degree of state penetration into society (which entails an analysis of the main policy instruments), the nature of the relations between the state and the principal interests (who leads whom, who deals with whom?), the relationship to the outside world (degrees of openness, of sensitivity and of vulnerability). Also, there are ideological variables: the visions of the main actors, as well as their historical memories. And finally, their main policies must be examined.

Four: Despite the creative role of the state, all the nation-states of Western Europe have a narrow range of manoeuvre. Whatever the momentary national economic policy, all have a high vulnerability to inflation, largely because of external constraints (dependence on exports, energy imports, a common commitment to an open international economy). All have to be deeply concerned with industrial restructuring—an imperative for internal economic growth and external competitiveness. None can afford to compress wages and social benefits, *à l'américaine,* because of the risks of social explosions. On the one hand, the combination of a narrow margin of choice with the lynchpin role of the state, or of huge state scope and limited resources, or of strength and ineffectiveness, produces new lines of cleavage and tensions in society. On the other hand, paradoxically, the narrow margin of choice reenforces the system: the voters tend to behave pragmatically, with a firm grasp of the "reality principle", and extremist parties have only the choice between staying in a ghetto (cf. the French CP before 1981 and perhaps British Labour) and acting with moderation (cf. the Italian CP). This resilience is partly caused by the very factors which the sociological theories of industrial society overlook or deem dysfunctional: external ones, such as the European Community (see below), or the cushioning role of migrant workers, on whom the burden of adjustment can be pushed; internal ones, such as the reservoir provided, in periods of economic crisis, by the so-called declining classes, or the fragmentation of issues and groups, i.e., the social discontinuities and heterogeneity which make possible the kinds of bargains that either push economic difficulties away from the centre to the periphery (cf. the role of the regions in Italy) or divert public attention from economic difficulties (cf. the appeal of "law and order", used by conservative governments to keep the support of economically threatened groups).

The Nation-State Versus the Community

Theories

After the remarkable explosion of theories about integration in the 1950s and early 60s, we find a sudden drought.

The grand theory which had been, implicitly Jean Monnet's and, explicitly, Ernst Haas's, has performed much better as an initial goad than as a permanent explanation. Derived from the theories of industrial society, it suffered from the same weaknesses. It relied on technology as the fuel, and on the logic of the market as the motor of integration: the drive for economic modernization would lead to political unity. It was the old Saint-Simonian dream of depoliticized progress, accompanied by one idea that, at first sight, seemed on the contrary quite political: the idea that the gradual dispossession of the nation-state and the transfer of allegiance to the new Community would be hastened by the establishment of a central quasi-federal political system (however, it was conceived as largely bureaucratic in nature).

What this theory neglected was, in the first place, the difference between two kinds of politics. I have, in the past, called them "high" versus "low", but this can be misleading if it suggests that foreign policy and defence are always and exclusively "high", which is not the case, and economic and social policies are "low", which is certainly false, especially in periods of economic crisis. I would prefer to distinguish the politics which aims at or allows for the maximization of the common good, from the politics of either *do ut des* (strict reciprocity) or of the zero-sum game. Whether an issue falls into one or the other category depends on its momentary saliency—on how essential it appears to the government for the survival of the nation or for its own survival, as well as on the specific features of the issue (some do not lend themselves to "maximization of the common good" or to "upgrading the common interest"), and on the economic conjuncture. At any rate, the politics of reciprocity and of the zero-sum game reenforce the existing states.

The theory also overlooked the differential impact, on the various nations, of external countries (such as the two superpowers). Moreover it underestimated the ability of the actors, especially the major ones, to stop or to slow down the building of a central political system (the role of counter-ideas, if you like) and the ability of national bureaucracies to resist the transfer of power to the new central one (the power of inertia). It would be of little use to replace the Monnet-Haas theory with a "world systems" approach borrowed from Wallerstein. The world system may be a useful concept for economic theory. For a historian or political scientist, it is a majestic fiction.[12] The world economic system is not a prime mover, nor a God-like distributor of roles and divider of labour, but the outcome of discrete political decisions made by the separate units. These, as usual, are constrained by the effects of their own moves: they are submitted to common forces, often beyond their own control; but they are not governed by these forces; once more we find here the error of teleology, and the teleology of technology. Indeed, in the case of the West European entity, the whole question is whether Europe's place in the "world system", i.e. in the international division of labour, will be defined by the nation-states' separate decisions, or by the EEC.

The way of moving toward a new theory should be the following. We must begin with the units themselves; what are their domestic priorities and the foreign policy goals of the member states, to what extent are they compatible, and can they best be fostered by cooperation? Then we should examine the impact of the environment on the separate actors. Finally, we would study the institutional interplay between the states and the Community's organs.

Recent trends

The history of the EEC in the past ten years shows some persistent realities. At the level of the units, we find, first, that the political life of each has remained dominated by the specific national configuration of the variables listed above, not by the constellation in Brussels. Secondly, each national bureaucracy has preserved its peculiar features, thus making effective common policies more difficult, given the different patterns of strengths and weaknesses of each bureaucracy, and the bureaucracies' different attitudes toward public regulation and control (cf. the history of the steel crisis, or of energy policy). Thirdly, different traditions and outlooks in foreign policy have continued. All these factors explain Community failures or fiascoes in areas like transportation, industrial policy, fisheries, and employment.

At the level of the Community we find, on the one hand, common obstacles. In defence, there is both common dependence on the US and a lasting split between France and the states that remain in the military structure of NATO; also, much harm has been done to the Community by the "globalization" of issues within its jurisdiction—the fact that the half-continent is an inappropriate framework for dealing with energy, with North-South issues or with the Arab-Israeli conflict. On the other hand, the old institutional morass has persisted: the "federal" institutions have weak powers, and their main organs often paralyze one another; these troubles, in turn, have depressing effects on the other components of the emerging or expected "central" political system—community-wide interest groups or party alignments.

To these continuing elements, some new developments have been added. Several have been positive. If one compares the EEC today with the Community of 1974–1975,[13] one finds a number of innovations. One is a limited but, so far, tenuously successful attempt at monetary cooperation, the EMS, based on a common interest of Bonn and Paris—Bonn's interest in a zone of monetary stability and in a scheme that would protect the Deutschmark from becoming too strong, Paris's interest in an external constraint on domestic inflationary pushes.

Equally positive has been the definite evolution and rapprochement of foreign policy objectives. Each of the major West European actors has tried to get "the best of all possible worlds"—Bonn has moved from total reliance on the US in defence and diplomacy (and on European integration for rehabilitation), to a partial liquidation of the specific German problems (Berlin and the iron curtain), which has allowed West Germany to develop its relations with Moscow and with Eastern Europe. France has moved from a multifaceted, almost maniacal search for independence from the US (under the American umbrella), to a combination of military autonomy plus co-operation with NATO, détente plus activism (in Africa and the Middle East), a national energy policy plus oil deals. London has moved from the "special relationship" and the Commonwealth to entry into the Common Market. As a result, two of the three major actors—West Germany and France—have developed strong links with Moscow, and all three, for reasons that are partly similar and partly different, have somewhat detached themselves from Washington. Indeed, the US has often played an involuntarily integrative role: by inflicting recurrent shocks on Bonn (cf. Carter's non-proliferation, "locomotive" and human rights policies), through the divagations of American economic and monetary policies (which have fostered a European desire for protection against the fluctuations of the dollar, and now against America's high interest rates), because of the passivity of US policy in the Arab-Israeli conflict since Camp David, and because of Washington's insistence on the indivisibility—hence the death—of détente ever since the invasion of Afghanistan.[14]

Other developments have been negative. First, the institutional crisis has got worse. The EEC's institutions are weak, because they lack autonomy (from the member states) and because their capacity to act is small. The European Council, designed as a kind of supreme command, has been counter-productive: it has decapitated the Council and compounded the problems of congestion and enforcement. The Council has declined, partly because of overspecialization. The

Parliament, now elected by universal suffrage, has not vindicated either the nightmare of Michel Debré (who thought it would behave like the Third Estate's deputies in 1789) or the dream of the Federalists; it has simply and sumptuously displayed a rich array of cleavages (national, ideological, and along the lines of interests). Secondly, the enlargement of the Community has proven indigestible. It has worsened the language problem and weakened the cohesion of the Commission, hence adding to the institutional crisis. Britain has, almost every year, asked for special treatment and renegotiated its contribution to the budget. Greece is now acting in a similar way.

The Community's balance sheet is thus mixed. In internal (European) affairs, there has been more frequent resort to article 235 of the Treaty of Rome, which allows for an extension of scope, but there are—by comparison with the initial period of the 1950s—no more common goals, only common concerns. Franco-German reconciliation has been achieved; the strong earlier impulse for innovation—away from the dismal past—has been replaced by an equally strong desire—on the part of the members and of the central Brussels bureaucracy as well—to preserve the status quo. Partly as a result, common policies are rare (and the oldest, the Common Agricultural Policy whose establishment helped strengthen the Community, has now become a source of Community weakness; it is in deep trouble because of different national performances, different national policies in agriculture, different national attitudes toward inflation, and the effect of monetary manipulations). There is, as the Committee of Three remarked in its October 1979 report,[15] a disproportion between efforts and outcomes: a huge amount of political and administrative labour produces meagre results—recurrent deadlocks and minimal compromises. The original "project"—a gradual pooling of sovereignties—has in fact been sacrificed to the politics of enlargement: enlargement and what Maurice Schumann used to call "deepening" have turned out incompatible. And the economic crisis of recent years has affected the Community adversely in two ways: each government has sought, above all, national solutions—even when there was an *air de famille* among the economic policies of Schmidt, Thatcher and Barre, even more so after the election of Mitterrand; and Community efforts at devising common plans (for industrial reconversion, for instance) or at preserving common policies (agriculture) have been disrupted by protectionist moves and monetary manoeuvres.

In external affairs, however, the members have behaved increasingly as an entity. With the EEC, there has been a display of activism on North-South matters (Lomé II) and of solidarity with Britain in the Falkland Islands crisis (sanctions against Argentina); outside of the framework of the treaty of Rome, European political cooperation has progressed far beyond the first steps of the "Davignon procedure"; the Nine (or Ten) now define common stands without first consulting Washington. This has been partly caused by an institutional paradox (most of foreign policy coordination is not encumbered by the organs set up by the Treaty of Rome), partly the result of a *fruite en avant*—a compensation for internal paralysis, partly the product of estrangement from Washington. But the ratio of common acts versus common statements—deplorations and exhortations—remains low, and some of the common acts (such as Lomé II) have a limited scope.

The best way of analyzing the EEC is not in the traditional terms of integration theory, which assumes that the members are engaged in the formation of a new, supranational political entity superseding the old nations—an outcome that was originally possible but has become increasingly more unlikely—and that there is a zero-sum game between the nation-states on one hand, the EEC on the other—a very false notion. It is to look at the EEC as an international regime, as defined by Keohane and Nye:[16] a set of norms of behaviour and of rules and policies covering a broad range of issues, dealing both with procedures and with substance, and facilitating agreements among the members. From the viewpoint of the participants, such a regime provides both restraints and opportunities—it limits the state's freedom of unilateral action (for instance, here, in agriculture or in external trade) and it imposes financial loads (cf. Britain and West Germany), but it gets others to share one's burdens (cf. regional policy) or to accept restraints in one's favour (the CAP): i.e., it provides the participant with external support (hence the crucial importance of coalition-building, issue by issue, year after year).

The comparative study of international regimes shows that they are most likely to be established in areas where, and at moments when, "sovereign" national actions are likely to be insufficient or unproductive: when joint actions produce better results, for each member, than "uncoordinated individual calculations of self-interest",[17] in areas of high "issue density", marked by interdependence and linkages among the issues.[18] But the study also shows that regimes may be doomed to paralysis or failure when the balance of constraints and opportunities shifts in the direction of the former. The experience of the EEC confirms this. Its establishment resulted from the conviction of the members that purely national action in a variety of economic domains was no longer satisfactory, and that a number of major non-economic goals could best be achieved by setting up a collective regime. Its performance has conformed to the observation that regimes require a principle of long-term reciprocation (i.e., I refrain from maximizing my self-interest now in the hope and expectation that you will return the favour when I need it in the future),[19] and are able to survive changes in the original patterns of interests because of a shift in the criteria by which national decisions are made (i.e., from a more selfish to a more enlightened definition of the national interest) and because of the interest which the members develop in the institutions themselves.[20] But the difficulties encountered by the EEC in handling the economic crisis of the 70s and early 80s results from the inability of the members to agree on common constraints (i.e., from the persistent differences in priorities and in monetary and fiscal policies) and from the inability of the central institutions to devise common opportunities to overcome a crisis largely caused by extra-European forces. As Miles Kahler has written, "national elites have chosen certainty of declining effectiveness over the perils of coordination with the same risks".[21] It is not so much the distribution of power among the members which has changed, endangering the regime, as the relative attractiveness of individual versus common action at a time when the latter does not seem to promise better outcomes than the former.

However, for almost every one of the members, the overall balance of restraints and opportunities remains acceptable: hence the resilience of the Community. The balance is different for each state, and it has evolved. In the case of West Germany, legitimation has become less important, yet economic and political benefits continue to assure Bonn's loyalty to Brussels. In the case of France, containing West Germany is no longer a dominant concern, but foreign policy influence, and the contribution the Community makes to the modernization of French industry and agriculture remains essential. For Italy, membership of the EEC has been important both for domestic politics and as a key factor in what might be called deparochializing Italy. The only partial exception is Britain, because of the costs imposed on a member that remains economically more turned toward non-EEC countries than the other members of the Community, and whose agricultural policy rests on very different principles. These costs exacerbate the fundamental and unresolved British contradiction between external burdens and domestic imperatives, a contradiction de Gaulle largely eliminated in France's case.

Far from being static,[22] the notion of an international regime allows, indeed incites, the study of change: a regime can flourish or decay, it can degenerate into a mere façade behind which the rule of self-interest prevails, or tighten into a quasi-political community. Analyzing the EEC as an international regime allows one also to see better what, to "integrationists", is a paradox or a contradiction: such regimes, in exchange for curtailing the states' capacity for unilateral action, serve to preserve the nation-state as the basic unit in world affairs and actually help governments perform their domestic tasks. Although the traditional model of sovereignty is clearly obsolete, the nation-state today survives even though some of its powers have to be pooled with others, and even though many apparently sovereign decisions are seriously constrained, or made ineffective, by the decisions of others as well as by economic trends uncontrolled by anyone. International regimes help the state survive, by providing a modicum of predictability and a variety of rewards.

We must go farther: the EEC regime is unique (it has central institutions and a common market), and it has served not only to preserve the nation-states, but paradoxically to regenerate them and to adapt them to the world of today. Far from leading to a supranational, European nation-state, it has put pressure on the members to modernize their economies: cf. France and its agriculture, the UK and its industry, and the way in which the EEC's North-South policies and attempted opening to the imports from the New Industrial Countries (NIC) gradually incite the members to accept a new international division of labour. The EEC has also served as an alibi for governments too weak to take unpopular measures on their own, or strengthened their hand against protectionist or inflationary pressures (indeed, in the past, Britain and Italy have preferred to turn to the IMF for help, because the IMF's conditions were less constraining). And the Community has served as a playing field for "inter-issue bargaining", allowing for complex deals in which concessions in one realm were offset by gains in another. In all these ways, and despite its internal flaws, the EEC regime has strengthened the nation-state's capacity to act at home and abroad.

Problems for the future

One major problem for the future of the EEC results from the differences in economic performance among the member states. Different rates of inflation, in the long run, threaten the survival of the EMS, or expose it to recurrent shocks, and increase protectionist pressures in countries that cannot easily devalue in order to compensate for the decreasing competitiveness of their exports. The difference between countries that try to mitigate the current economic crisis with "orthodox" policies, and France, which has launched an experiment in national action against unemployment through the extension of the public sector, may also result in a kind of creeping protectionism in France. Some of the members are more threatened than others, by the common predicament of European industry—the squeeze between the US and Japan on one hand, the NIC's on the other. Economic divergences thus risk undermining or fragmenting the EEC regime. When the states have weak governments, and ineffective and divergent policies, negative solidarity between the nation-state and the EEC operates: both suffer. When the governments are strong, and their policies are effective and convergent, the impact on the EEC is ambiguous.

In the 1980s, the question mark of a common defence may become more salient, especially if tensions between the US and Western Europe increase. In defence, there is no European regime, but a multiplicity of regimes—NATO integration (Bonn), a mix of independence and cooperation (Paris), a combination of the two (London). Now, the future presents a paradox. The capacity of each state to assure an independent defence will keep declining. This means a major change in the traditional cement of nationhood: the state's ability to provide security had been a major ingredient. (There are other ingredients, precisely because of the increasing role of the state in supplying economic and social services. But these new cements are more ambiguous: they tend to make the state less autonomous, and to be sources of contention more often than factors of national solidarity). Nevertheless, a common West European Defence regime would probably be very difficult to establish. It would not eliminate (even if it would partly alleviate) the fundamental plight: the need to rely on America's nuclear guarantee (and on an American conventional and nuclear presence, which gives credibility to this guarantee); this is a fact that is likely to be used by European opponents of a new EDC, and especially by all those who want to keep West German fingers as far away as possible from nuclear triggers, or who fear Bonn's preponderance in a conventional defence regime. Should the Americans withdraw their nuclear guarantee (except in case of a Soviet nuclear attack),[23] the result is more likely to be increased fragmentation (i.e. French reliance on nuclear weapons, Bonn's on a mix of conventional defence and détente) than a common West European security regime, given the obstacles to a pooling of nuclear efforts and the unwillingness to prepare for a conventional war, i.e., to abandon deterrence for defence.

Moreover, a common defence regime would be much more damaging for the nation-state than the economic and monetary regimes achieved so far. These have strengthened the nation-state more than they have dispossessed it. A defence Community would require a leap toward more powerful central institutions: here, the relation between Community and states is a zero-sum game. This is another reason why so little has been undertaken. But this vacuum, or absence, is a major source of weakness, both for each West European nation, and for the "civilian" European entity as a whole.

Notes

1. François Bourricaud, "Individualistic mobilization and the crisis of professional authority", *Daedalus*, Spring 1979, pp. 1–20.

2. Claus Offe, "Competitive party democracy and the Keynesian welfare state", unpublished paper July 1981.

3. Stanley Hoffmann, "Some notes on democratic theory and practice", *Tocqueville Review*, Vol. II no. 1, Winter 1980, pp. 59–76.

4. Fred Hirsch, *The Social Limits to Growth,* Harvard University Press, 1976, pp. 170 ff.

5. Cornelius Castoriadis.

6. In: Suzanne Berger and Michael J. Piore, *Dualism and Discontinuity in Industrial Societies,* Cambridge University Press, 1980, pp. 132 ff.

7. Philippe Schmitter, "On organizing interests", unpublished paper, 1979.

8. James Caporaso, "The European Community in the world system", English version (May 1979) of paper published in the *Revue d'intégration européenne.*

9. Eric Nordlinger, *On the Autonomy of the Democratic State,* Harvard University Press, 1981.

10. In M. Crozier, Samuel P. Huntington and Joji Wanatuki, *The Crisis of Democracy,* New York University Press, 1975, pp. 39 ff.

11. See especially Peter Katzenstein, "Problem or model: West Germany in the 80's", *World Politics,* July 1980, pp. 577–598.

12. See the critique by Theda Skocpol, "Wallerstein's world capitalist system", *American Journal of Sociology,* March 1977, pp. 1075–90.

13. See my essay "No trumps, no luck, no will", Chapter 4 of this book.

14. See my essay "The Western Alliance: drift or harmony", *International Security,* Fall, 1981, pp. 105–125.

15. *Report on European Institutions,* Council of the European Communities, 1980.

16. R. O. Keohane and J. S. Nye, *Power and Interdependence,* Little Brown, 1977.

17. Stephen D. Krasner, "Structural causes and regime consequences", *International Organization,* Spring 1982, p. 191.

18. Robert O. Keohane, "The demand for international regimes", *Int. Org.,* Spring 1982, p. 339.

19. Keohane, ibid., p. 342, and Robert Jervis, "Security regimes", *Int. Org.,* Spring 1982, p. 364.

20. Arthur A. Stein, "Coordination and collaboration", *Int. Org.,* Spring 1982, pp. 322–3.

21. Miles Kahler, "The survival of the state in European international relations", unpublished paper, April 1981.

22. Susan Strange, "Cave! Hic dragones", *Int. Org.,* Spring 1982, pp. 488–91.

23. See the article by McGeorge Bundy, George Kennan, Robert McNamara and Gerald Smith, "Nuclear weapons and the Atlantic Alliance", *Foreign Affairs,* Spring 1982, pp. 753–768.

Part Three

From Community to Union, From Cold War to New World (Dis)order

8

The European Community and 1992

I

Not much attention was paid in March 1985, when the European Council, whose members include the chiefs of state and government of the 12 member states, decided that it should constitute a single market by 1992. After all, the European Community had been established in 1957 with the goal of a common market, and many people believed that the goal had been reached; tariffs within the Community had been abolished, a common external tariff put in place and a controversial common agricultural policy instituted.

Those who knew better realized that Europe remained a maze of border controls, government subsidies to national industries, closed national systems of procurement in military and other key public sectors, and national regulation of industrial standards, copyrights, transportation, banking, insurance and health requirements for the entry of goods. Thus, many were discouraged; after all, the goal of a full economic union had been proclaimed in the early 1970s but never met.

Americans in particular had been enthusiastic about European unity in the 1950s and 1960s—often more so than many Europeans—because they had a vision of a United States of Western Europe, symbolized by the name of Jean Monnet. They grew disheartened when Charles de Gaulle, in the 1960s, was able to destroy that dream and force his partners, in the so-called Luxembourg compromise of 1966, to stick in effect to the rule of unanimity. The Community settled down into one more international organization in which diplomats and bureaucrats haggled over technicalities. American curiosity moved to other parts of the world.

By 1988 it had become evident that this time, something new had indeed happened in Western Europe. Three months after the council's 1985 decision, the European Commission, which is the executive branch of the Community and consists of 17 officials selected by the national governments but independent of

229

them, published a White Paper that listed no less than 300 areas for action, with deadlines for proposals by the commission to deal with them. Ever since, the commission has been turning out directives, and the Council of Ministers, which takes most of the final decisions, has examined and usually adopted them. It was the White Paper that set the deadline of 1992 for the achievement of a truly common market. By the middle of 1989 about half of the obstacles had been removed—or at least ordered to be removed.

The task undertaken by the Commission of the European Community (EC) is both gigantic and intensely technical. Progress so far has consisted of such measures as the replacement of the hundred-odd forms required of the members' citizens at European borders by a single administrative document; the directive of June 1983 that provides for the mutual recognition of professional qualifications—a measure that should allow engineers and doctors (although not lawyers, who will need to take an exam in the country into which they move) to settle anywhere in the Community; another decision to eliminate the remaining controls on capital movements; a directive that allows a bank, licensed in its home country, to operate throughout the Community; a decision to remove restrictions on road transportation; various moves aimed at the deregulation of European civil aviation (whose fares are much higher than U.S. fares); a 60-page directive on the regulation of engineering machinery, and another one that liberalizes the terminal equipment market—a sector each country had heavily protected. Funds that support the poorer countries of the Community have been doubled, and represent the equivalent of the Marshall Plan. The commission is also playing a very active role in antitrust cases, a role which entails opposing mergers that have anti-competition purposes or ordering governments to stop subsidizing forms illegally.

The ultimate beneficiaries of all these measures are likely to be both the producers and the consumers. Border controls alone cost between three and four percent of total trade in 1983. A truck that could travel 750 miles in Britain in 36 hours needed 58 hours to cover the same distance form the Channel to Milan. Changing money into local currencies would cost a traveler going to 10 of the 12 member countries 47 percent of his money. The closed character of public procurement is another important cause of high prices, especially in computers and telecommunications. If the council and the commission continue their efforts, European industrialists will achieve economies of scale that will allow them to operate more efficiently than if they were confined to their domestic markets, and the consumers will gain from the commission's competition policy, which is strongly supported by the jurisprudence of the European Court of Justice.

II

What explains this sudden burst of activity? A few years ago, it was fashionable to lament about "Europessimism." Suddenly "1992" has become the symbol of a European renaissance. It can best be explained as the conjunction of a common experience and of key personalities.

The experience was that of the Community's dark age—roughly from 1973 to 1984. In 1972, three years after the resignation of General de Gaulle, who had opposed Britain's entry into the Community, Britain became a member. Many people had expected its very capable officials, many of whom were fervent "Europeans," to take the lead and inject new vigor into the Community. Instead, there followed more than ten years of quarreling about the amount of money Britain had to contribute to the EC's budget—Britain in essence asking for a renegotiation of the terms on which it had been allowed in.

Moreover, when the oil crisis of 1973 hit, the Community was incapable of agreeing on a common policy; most of its members followed America's leadership, with France dissenting. It suddenly appeared that many of the economic problems that plagued Western Europe could only be solved on a global level, and that the Community's regional framework was irrelevant. Finally, the economic slowdown of the 1970s, with the rise of massive unemployment, led the governments to ignore the Community and give priority to strictly national, and often divergent, attempts at coping with the crisis—through alternations of expansive and restrictive fiscal policies, and such measures as what the French called "the social treatment of unemployment": retraining, subsidies to firms willing to hire new workers, unemployment compensation and so forth.

The result was a sense of failure. The national policies had only limited success; there was little growth, excessive inflation and persistent unemployment. During these years Japan became a major economic actor, and the new industrial countries of Asia followed Japan. Europe witnessed the decline of many of its traditional industries, such as steel and shipbuilding, and discovered that in many areas of high technology it was being outpaced by Japan as well as by the United States. Attempts by governments (especially that of France) to promote mergers of firms so as to create "national champions" in such areas as telematics did not succeed in reversing the trend. Governments, after years of trying to improve their national economies through such attempts and through deals with unions and business organizations, became aware of the rigidities of the labor market as well as of the many other obstacles to industrial efficiency and technological progress. If national solutions did not work, there remained one way out: what the French often call a *fuite en avant*, an escape by a forward leap—into Europe. Competitiveness on the global market remained the main issue, but now it appeared that regional integration was, after all, the prerequisite.

Nevertheless, Europe would not now appear so promising if, during the "dark years," steps had not been taken to preserve the Community from decay and to strengthen it in some important areas. The most significant and successful effort was the establishment—afrter several false starts—of the European Monetary system (EMS) in 1978. It was the brainchild of West German Chancellor Helmut Schmidt and French President Valéry Giscard d'Estaing.

The abrupt American decision to scuttle the postwar system of fixed exchange rates and to replace it with floating rates had worried the Europeans, who were afraid of the effects of monetary instability on their trade and balance of payments. The EMS provided for a tighter system than the global one; fluctuations of exchange rates were to be contained within a narrow band (known as the "snake"). Even though Britain did not join, it cooperated with the EMS, which has tended to be a Deutschmark zone. The main merits of the EMS have been its contribution to the reduction of inflation and the pressure it puts on the governments if not to coordinate their fiscal and economic policies, at least to follow similar ones, under the surveillance exerted by various Community committees. Bonn's policy of monetary stability has become the continental norm. When the Socialist government of France in 1981–83 tried to pursue a Keynesian policy of public spending to counter the recession, French balance-of-payments difficulties and the run on the franc quickly forced it to choose between quitting the EMS and reversing its policies—and it did the latter.

Another measure of progress during those years was the Esprit program, a scheme of industrial cooperation in information technology promoted by the very able Belgian Commissioner Etienne Davignon with the collaboration of the 12 major electronic companies of the Community, and with Community subsidies. Still another prerequisite for the future leap was the settlement of time-consuming disputes over British money, over the budget, and over the Common Agricultural Policy, the reform of which was finally undertaken in 1984 to make it less expensive (at absorbs 70 percent of the Community's budget) and less wasteful (the reduction of butter stocks and of the production of wine being the priorities).

Thus, by 1984, the members had overcome many obstacles. Moreover, disenchantment with Keynesian policies, the wave of economic liberalism spreading from Reagan's America (particularly the appeal of deregulation), the recognition by French and Spanish Socialists of the superiority of the market over a command economy, of the futility of nationalizations and of the virtues of competition—all this created the right climate for the European revival. Just as in the 1950s when the Christian Democrats of France, Italy and West Germany turned to "Europe" partly as an escape from the limits or frustrations of their domestic policies, the Socialists of France, Italy and Spain—followed in 1989 by Britain's— found in "Europe" a substitute for their traditional public policies at home.

However, general conditions only lead to the right results if the right people are in the right place at the right moment. This is what happened in 1984–1985.

After the fiasco of his first economic and social policy, French President François Mitterrand, an old "European," was determined to use the six months of his presidency of the European Council in 1984 to make spectacular progress. The new German chancellor, Helmut Kohl, could only view with favor a plan that would, on the whole, benefit West Germany's strong industry. Prime Minister Margaret Thatcher, as an apostle of deregulation, had no reason to resist, and was also eager to prove that Britain was not the saboteur of the Community it had often seemed to be. The Single European Act—whose long-term effects, as the ratification debates showed, were probably underestimated by all the governments—was presented to the British Parliament as a treaty that would make it possible (by majority votes) to bring to Western Europe all the benefits of deregulation, while preserving (through the requirement of unanimity) national sovereignty in areas essential to Britain, such as taxation, the free circulation of individuals and the rights of workers.

Above all, the new president of the EC Commission—the person whose impetus can be decisive—was Mitterrand's former Minister of Finance Jacques Delors, who had been a key adviser to the reformist Gaullist Prime Minister Chaban-Delmas in 1969–1972 and later became a moderate Socialist. He had been very influential in turning around the economic policies of Mitterrand's government in 1983. A former official of the French labor union inspired by progressive Catholic thought, he exemplifies the synthesis of Christian democracy and socialism on which the Community was built. His commitment to a United Europe is as strong as his obstinacy and energy. Delors, who was reappointed for a second four-year term last year, is as important to the enterprise today as Jean Monnet was in the 1950s.

III

This new enterprise builds on the institutions and achievements of the earlier one, but it is not a mere continuation. A comparison of the two efforts is instructive.

The Common Market of 1957 was limited to six neighbors: France, West Germany, Italy, Holland, Belgium and Luxembourg. The first European experiment was a reaction to what academics sometimes call "high politics"—considerations of national security and power. The Coal and Steel Community of 1951 was launched as a way of promoting the reconciliation of France and Germany and of anchoring the one-year-old Federal Republic in the Western Alliance. The European Economic Community was established by the 1957 Treaty of Rome after the fiasco of the European Defense Community, which was scuttled by the French National Assembly in 1954, and after the humiliation of the British and French during the Suez crisis of 1956. In both instances, the six members chose economic means to reach political objectives—the ability to speak with one voice in world affairs—because these means prompted less internal resistance and because the whole realm of defense was dominated by the United States. Indeed, the main underlying issue—the one that de Gaulle, between 1958 and 1969, made brutally explicit—was the ability of the Six to stand up to, distinguish themselves from, and cooperate as an equal with the United States.

Throughout the 1950s and 1960s this issue became entangled with a quasi-theological debate about the Community's institutions. Jean Monnet, the "inspirer" (de Gaulle's rather hostile term) of the 1950 and 1957 enterprises, supported a sort of federal setup—limited to the economic sectors covered by the 1957 Treaty of Rome—with the independent EC Commission as its chief body. The Common Market of 1957 diluted Monnet's dream by making the council of state representatives the real decision-maker and by creating a parliament that was not elected by universal suffrage nor provided with any real powers (the switch to universal suffrage a few years later did little to enhance its authority). De Gaulle excommunicated federalism (called "supranationality" in Monnet's euphemistic jargon) by insisting on the primacy of the council and on the principle of unanimity for decisions. He saw in Monnet's design a danger that French sovereignty would be destroyed by irresponsible "European" bureaucrats, whom the United States could manipulate by exploiting the clashes of national interests among the six countries.

De Gaulle preferred a "Europe of states": a concert of governments that would build "Europe"—first in the West, ultimately in the East as well—on the basis of well-balanced bargains in areas of common or mutual interests. So did Britain, but de Gaulle kept it out of the Community on high politics grounds: Britain's closeness to Washington. Finally, the first European enterprise remained limited in scope (as well as geographically); agriculture and the removal of tariffs and quotas on trade were the only links forged among the Six.

The post-1984 undertaking is very different. Today the Community has 12 members and is far more heterogeneous. With Portugal, Greece, Spain and Ireland in the Community, 20 percent of the member countries have a per capital income inferior to 60 percent of the average; in other words, it has a "North'" and a "South" of its own. The EC Commission—de Gaulle's target after 1958—has been a major actor, as has been the new European business elite fostered by the Common Market's removal of some barriers. In the 1950s many businessmen, especially in France, were very hostile and fearful of the project. The main goal now is not "high politics" but the competitiveness of Europe in a world in which the number of industrial and commercial players has multiplied; the stake is what Helmut Schmidt once called the struggle for the world product, rather than for traditional power (although wealth and power have become ever more closely tied together).

While the United States remains a major trading partner of the Community, the new effort is aimed much less at establishing a "partner" of equal weight to cooperate with, and to resist domination by, the United States than at resisting the challenge from Japan, whose aggressive external economic expansion and fierce protection of its own market the Europeans resent. This shift in emphasis reflects the relative decline of American power.

The theological battle about the Community's institutions is not dead—Jacques Delors is the new Monnet and Margaret Thatcher the new de Gaulle in this connection—but it has been suspended and replaced by a remarkable pragmatism. In 1985 Europe's statesmen did not follow the federal path favored by

Alfiero Spinelli's draft treaty of European Union, which the European Parliament had endorsed in 1984. They preferred the goal of a single market to the straight path of political integration. To be sure, the Single European Act signed in 1986, which amends the Treaty of Rome and endorses the commitment to a unified market, allows for decisions in most areas to be taken by a qualified majority instead of unanimously, but the European Council remains the top decision-making body.

The earlier supranationalists often saw the states as the enemy; today's activists see them as indispensable partners, whose sovereignty is to be pooled rather than removed, and to whom enforcement of Community decisions is entrusted. There is also, now, an impressive network of national and transnational lobbies in Brussels and Strasbourg (where the European Parliament meets), of experts' and bureaucrats' committees advising the commission and the council, and of ties among cities, regions and enterprises. The scope of the Community is larger, thanks to the EMS and to the mass of joint ventures, cross-border mergers and direct investment abroad that now tie the members together.

Some things, however, have not changed. The political motor of the Community remains the Franco-German entente; when it sputters, progress stops; when it functions, advances are made (because Britain wants to avoid being isolated). As in the first effort, the members find it easier to agree on removing obstacles than on formulating common policies (which would require greater powers for the federal bodies—the commission and the parliament). The best example of this is the set of principles adopted for the unification of the market. One principle—stated by the Court of Justice in a 1978 case that pitted the French liqueur *cassis de Dijon* against West Germany—is that the members would grant each other "mutual recognition" of their regulations and standards, i.e., the conditions set in one country have to be accepted by the others. The other principle is home-country control: the right of a firm to operate throughout the Community if it is licensed in one of the member countries. These principles make it unnecessary for the commission and the council to spend too much energy on "harmonization"—the adoption of a single European set of standards—or on promoting "European" companies. There will be instead a kind of free market of competing national standards.

Another similarity between the earlier effort and the current one concerns the dynamics of unification. Neither effort has been accompanied by a popular, mass movement. In the first enterprise, there was often considerable domestic opposition (witness the fate of France's own brainchild, the European Defense Community, in France); the moves toward integration were the product of a small layer of key politicians and civil servants. Today, these actors and the business elite are driving the effort, and, as shown by the high rate of voter abstention (about 41 percent) in the June 1989 elections for the European Parliament, the general public is not very involved. This lack of interest may be because the European bureaucrats have been clever enough to bury the controversial issues under a mountain of 300 technical directives and because the parliament, despite its new powers (granted by the Single Act) of amending council decisions and approving agreements of association between the Community and other states, continues to appear remote and bogged down in technicalities. The election campaigns were much more about domestic politics than about Europe.

Furthermore, in neither effort has the nation-state necessarily "lost" whatever power was "gained" by Europe. The main winner has not been a supergovernment of Europe; the national governments and bureaucracies remain the chief players, for instance setting up and revising the Common Agricultural Policy and very actively taking part in the mergers and collaborative schemes devised (or merely executed) by firms.

A final similarity is that the European enterprise remains primarily economic. Efforts at coordinating foreign and defense policies—the former under the auspices of the European Council, the latter mainly through the West European Union, a sleepy organization set up in 1955 as a substitute for the Defense Community—have remained fitful and limited.

IV

To these limits must be added the other difficulties the new undertaking faces—difficulties which guarantee that the year 1992 will not see the full realization of a unified market. What has begun is a process that will go on for many years, and which is galvanized by but cannot be bound to the artificial deadline of 1992.

The method pursued in Brussels has the advantage of appealing to the desire of all groups for expanded production and trade at lower prices, and of leaving to the future the determination of the losers. Enormous interests are at stake, for this massive attempt at deregulation will provoke shifts in wealth and therefore power among nations, regions, classes and sectors that nobody can yet fully forecast, but that create anxieties and resistances galore. There is the fear that the results will amount to the victory of the richer countries over the poorer ones (hence the fierceness of the battles over the size and distribution of the funds granted to the poorer nations, such as Greece) and of the richer sectors over the poorer ones (hence the disgruntlement of farmers, whose income is falling despite the costly agricultural policy). There is also the fear that the new Europe will represent the triumph of the most efficient and powerful economies over the others.

The story of the EMS is one of West German preponderance; Bonn has preserved its trade surplus with its neighbors despite the upward movement of the Deutschmark because their currencies have moved up along with it. France and other members of the EMS often fear that having lost mastery over their monetary and foreign economic policy, they will have to take measures curtailing their economic growth (hence increasing unemployment) in order to remain within the EMS and preserve the equilibrium of their commercial balance. French industry, which has, on the whole, smaller firms and less available capital than West German industry, and which has begun playing the game of internationalizing itself rather late, worries that the removal of all barriers within Europe will flood the French market with foreign imports. On the other hand, the heavily protected and not very efficient West German transport and telecommunications industries may be the losers in the unified market. And Italy fears that Italian capital, when controls are lifted, will move to countries that provide higher returns on savings, and thus stop financing Italy's public debt.

Labor is afraid that the removal of barriers and increasing competition will lead to a large number of business failures and layoffs, and to business moving to countries with lower wages and social benefits such as Spain. The labor markets of Western Europe are far less integrated than the capital markets, and further integration would require a common social policy and collective bargaining on a Community-wide scale. But there is little governmental enthusiasm for such moves, which would disrupt delicate domestic balances and affect national competitiveness; policies for coping with this "social dimension" of Europe remain nebulous.

The attempt by the EC Commission to draft a statute for European companies has been plagued by disagreement over provisions for worker participation— West Germany objecting to anything less than the co-determination granted by its own law, and Prime Minister Thatcher rejecting any scheme that would boost the power of unions, which she fought so vigorously in Britain. Labor's sullenness contrasts with the frenzied activity of businessmen, who are engaged in formidable contests in the form of mergers, joint ventures, buyouts and takeover bids aimed at obtaining either the best position through transnational alliances in Europe or the best position in their country against the expected onslaught of competition from abroad.

These multiple fears and oppositions explain some of the setbacks and delays encountered by the pioneers of "1992." Attempts by the commission, prodded by Delors, to define a common social policy have not gone much beyond generalities and the recognition of diverse national practices, failing well short of the guaranteed minimum income that some labor organizations have called for. Plans for a Community-wide television broadcasting network have been stymied. Little progress has been made in matters of copyright and patents. Opening up procurement in the four traditionally protected "national" areas (energy, telecommunications, transportation and water supply) is only beginning.

The two most troublesome sectors among those covered by the White Paper have turned out to be border controls and indirect taxation (no attempt is being directed at unifying direct taxes).

The abolition of all border controls is fiercely resisted not only by customs employees but also by Prime Minister Thatcher, who believes these controls are indispensable in the fight against drugs and terrorism. Moreover, each country remains free to impose its own conditions on the admission of refugees and immigration—a very hot political issue, as the rise of Jean-Marie Le Pen in France has shown; the abolition of border controls would make the enforcement of such national policies far more difficult.

The unification of indirect taxes has hit a number of snags. One concerns the value-added tax; countries with low rates or very limited coverage for the tax (such as England) fear that raising the rate and increasing the coverage would be inflationary. On the other hand, France, which gets 40 percent of its public revenue from taxes on consumption, resists the loss of government income a lowering of its rates would entail. A compromise is now being negotiated; it would set only a common minimum rate, and Britain could retain its exemption of "social items" from the tax. Some members also oppose a reduction in the rates of "sin taxes" (on alcohol or tobacco). At the meeting of the European Council in December 1988 Mitterrand threatened to delay the lifting of controls on capital movements until a common scheme of taxation on interest and dividend payments was devised, so that French investors will not be tempted to send their money to countries where such taxes are low or applied only to residents. But after the Bonn government decided to scrap its domestically unpopular withholding tax on interest, the EC Commission's attempt to devise a common withholding tax collapsed.

In two important areas not covered by the White Paper, divisions persist, hindering progress. Many officials believe that the unified market will require a centralized monetary system, with a single currency (the European Currency Unit or EMS, which exists already but plays only a minor role in transactions) or at least fixed exchange rates between the national currencies, and a central bank. Otherwise, once capital movements are free, currency volatility might increase and put unbearable strains on the present European Monetary System. This drive is resisted both by Britain, eager to preserve some autonomy for the pound, and by the Bundesbank, which plays in fact the role of a central bank for the EMS and is, as a national bank, freer in its decisions than if it were transformed into the equivalent of the Federal Reserve for 12 countries. Moreover, the West Germans insist that any central bank would have to be independent of political authority—whereas the Bank of France is an instrument of government policy.

In April 1989 a committee headed by Delors proposed a three-stage plan toward full monetary union, but the European Council, meeting in Madrid in June, avoided a showdown with Prime Minister Thatcher by agreeing only to proceed with the first stage—reinforced cooperation in economic and monetary policy. It agreed to plan an intergovernmental conference to prepare the later stages (and to revise the Treaty of Rome to allow for the transfers of state power that monetary union would require). Such a conference would require unanimity to succeed. Ultimately, unless Britain's position changes, its partners will have to choose between a highly diluted version of the Delors plan and a union without Britain.

The other area in which sharp disagreements persist is "political cooperation," the code name for diplomatic coordination. At the council meeting in Rhodes in 1988 the 12 leaders were not able to agree on a common response to the new position of the PLO, even though, in the late 1970s, some progress had been made in establishing a common West European stand on the Arab-Israeli conflict. Nor has there been a unified response to Soviet leader Mikhail Gorbachev's initiatives and calls for a "common European house": French distrust, British caution and the West German wish for a new and generalized détente do not blend. Indeed, the desire of all three countries for some diplomatic autonomy will continue to set limits to diplomatic harmonization, and keep this area from being as successful as the path to the single market. But the increasing importance of economic issues in world affairs is likely to reduce the difference between the Community's well-established foreign economic policy and its shakier political coordination, as in the case of its relations with Eastern Europe.

V

These hesitations and divisions show not only that "1992" is going to be a long and difficult process, but also that the shape of the future European entity remains uncertain, dependent on the personalities of the main statesmen, on the economic situation of Europe and on the international political climate. The enterprise can proceed as long as there is, if not a common purpose, at least sufficient ambiguity to accommodate a variety of national purposes: Bonn's desire to find in the Community both a field of economic power and a legitimation of its links with the German Democratic Republic and of its Ostpolitik, France's intention of tying the Federal Republic solidly to Western Europe (in exchange for the reduction of French economic and monetary autonomy), Spain's will to become a major player in European affairs and to pressure its economy into efficient modernization, and Britain's enthusiasm for deregulation. But sooner or later these ambiguities will have to be clarified. At present there are two sets of uncertainties: internal and external.

The first internal one is the main object of debate between Thatcher and Delors. The British Conservative leader sees the new enterprise in the perspective of economic liberalism, as an exercise in removing obstacles to the free movement of people, goods, capital and services. Her Europe is a true common market, with as little governmental intervention as possible. In this respect, she is the heir of British policy in the 1950s, which aimed at the creation of a vast free trade area in Europe and established the European Free Trade Association (EFTA) with those continental West European states that had not joined the Six, precisely because the latter wanted to build a common entity.

Delors acknowledges that economic integration must precede social harmonization and that deregulation must come first. However, the French Socialist leader, who has devoted most of his public life to issues of social policy, emphasizes the need for joint actions, for a framework of European rules and institutions to guide and discipline the market and to prevent the social and regional injustices that unfettered competition—especially among gigantic firms and conglomerates—could produce. As he has often put it, "savage capitalism" is not his ideal; cooperation must temper competition and harmonization must complement the destruction of barriers. What is at stake is the extent to which the new Europe will be the preserve of businessmen and of the market-oriented conservatives, rather than a more social-democratic Europe in which public power will have a major role and workers will feel protected.

The second, and connected, internal issue concerns the institutions of the new entity. The deregulated market dear to Thatcher needs no other institutions than the present ones, and, indeed, requires that the central bureaucracy in Brussels remain weak. The trouble is that the main actors in this market, the business elites, may end up being accountable to no one, and in a position to manipulate both the national and the central bureaucracies that try, often competitively, to control them. Delors' vision is far more institutional; he wants if not greater powers for the European Parliament at least a more energetic supervision of Community decisions by the national parliaments, and above all more powers of enforcement for the EC Commission, so that its directives will not be disregarded by states with very strong bureaucracies (France) or states with very messy ones (Italy). He also wants increased independence for members of the commission; when a government doesn't like the activities of the commissioner it has designated, it can simply refuse to reappoint him, as Thatcher did in the case of Lord Cockfield, the author of the White Paper.

Against such a conception, Prime Minister Thatcher invokes the defense of British sovereignty, just as de Gaulle insisted on French sovereignty. (But he was more consistent: he believed in a highly interventionist state, whereas she believes both in the British state and in an open, unfettered market.)

What is at stake is the future of the nation-state in Western Europe. Delors' logic is ultimately that of the construction of a federal state, albeit one that would deal only with issues that the member states cannot resolve by themselves (this is the "principle of subsidiarity"). The transnational market would be accountable to the federal government. Member states would have extensive residual powers in areas such as education or justice, but the central institutions would regulate and supervise the common economy and ultimately the common defense and diplomacy. Legitimacy would be provided by universal suffrage, expressed in the election of the European Parliament.

Other "Europeans" who reject Thatcher's stand nevertheless hesitate to follow Delors. In truth, most governments find it easier to cede powers to the market than to a central government above them. If they prevail, the new entity will be a very original experiment indeed, a construction in which there will be extensive common functions, but functions carried out through bargains negotiated among and enforced by the member states, and where loyalty will remain centered in the nation, as it is today. (Open any European newspaper: national issues, and particularly the distinctive features of national politics, dominate the daily news.) As best loyalty will be split, unevenly, between the nation and a Europe with rather weak central institutions.

Whether such a confederal model could last is a fascinating question. Both the United States and the Swiss Confederation have moved from such a condition to a more federal, which means more centralized, state. But the differences among the 12 members go much deeper than those among the Swiss cantons and the states of the United States of America.

Some believe that the more the members are willing to pool and to share their theoretical sovereignty, the stronger will be the need to build up the central institutions, especially after Prime Minister Thatcher is gone. In this view, she represents, like de Gaulle, a transition between the imperial past and the European future, during which nationalism—combined with a pragmatic albeit distrustful view of European cooperation—serves to restore national self-esteem, a necessary prelude to any abandonment of sovereignty.

But others argue that the more the states' effective sovereignty shrinks, the stronger will be their determination to protect what is left of it, and to find ways of controlling the growth and direction of the institutions in Brussels. Some believe that the demands of the disadvantaged or victims of economic integration will lead to action at the Community level, others fear a strong national backlash—especially if redistributive efforts at the Community level are limited both by the size of its budget and by the constraints of the EMS.

The differences among the members will be even greater if the Community expands further and admits Turkey, the most recent candidate, and such possible new applicants as Norway and Austria. This raises the questions concerning the Community's relation to the outside world, the second set of uncertainties. Already, the Community has a wide and complex network of agreements with external associates in Europe, the Middle East, North Africa and a large number of former colonies in Africa, the Pacific and the Caribbean. The move toward a single market has placed on the agenda the problem of the Community's relations with the EFTA countries, with which it would like to make new arrangements, collectively rather than having to deal with the separate demands (or applications) of the six members. The Community's members are reluctant to admit Austria because Austria's neutrality is seen as a handicap for the common diplomatic and defense policy of the future. Also, the European Parliament is on record against the admission of Turkey, whose demographic growth is deemed unmanageable in a Europe whose people could circulate freely.

The issues that excite Americans most are those of the external economic orientation of the enterprise. Will it be "Fortress Europe," a protected market, or will it be an open Europe? Clearly, the purpose of the whole effort is not merely to increase wealth by removing obstacles to production and technological progress, but also to increase Europe's power in a world in which economic and financial clout is as important as military might. The current transformation is aimed at making the penetration of external markets, through trade and investment, easier for European countries, many of which depend on exports for their growth and have capital available for placement abroad. It is also aimed at minimizing the penetration of the Community by forces deemed unfriendly. American entrepreneurs or officials are not the main targets (although France wants to curb U.S. programs on European television), but it is difficult to devise external barriers against Japan or South Korea that do not affect U.S. investors and companies as well.

The main bones of contention (in addition to such hardy perennials as the Common Agricultural Policy, which favors European farmers at the expense of American farm exports) are found in two sectors—neither of which is covered by the rules of the General Agreement on Tariffs and Trade, that somewhat graying Bible of free commerce (from which recent U.S. trade legislation departs considerably).

One is the domain of financial services. Foreign banks and insurance companies will be allowed to set up branches in the EC if reciprocity is granted by their country to European banks and companies. Americans are not justified in believing that this means the exclusion of American establishments because the legislation of certain states of the United States is restrictive. The Community has moved toward a very lax definition of post-1992 reciprocity; banks and insurance companies already operating in EC countries before 1992 will be treated as European.

Access of foreign companies to key sectors of public procurement is likely to remain restricted, however, even though American companies established in Europe qualify as European companies.

A third area of possible contention is the automobile industry. The Europeans want to keep Japanese car imports down as long as the Japanese market is closed to their cars, and they might impose a quota on cars produced in the United States with predominantly Japanese capital or a high content of Japanese parts.

A protectionist Europe remains unlikely, however, not only because of international legal obligations, but above all because of West Germany's and Britain's opposition, the many alliances between EC and non-EC (American, Swiss and Swedish) enterprises and the high level of European investments abroad. (In 1987, European companies invested $37 billion in the United States, but American ones invested less than $2.5 billion in Europe.) However, much will ultimately depend on the state of the world economy and on the behavior of the United States and Japan. All one can see at present is a tendency both in the United States and in Europe to give a more restrictive interpretation to the notion of reciprocity—one that looks at outcomes in specific sectors rather than at the fairness of procedures and at overall bargains. Also likely is the continuation, in Japan, of a strategy aimed at maximizing the global power of the industries in which it has the lead. A world economic recession could not only turn the world economy into a contest of protected regional blocs, but could also slow down the dismantling of barriers and definition of joint policies within the Community.

VI

The external economic orientation of Europe will also depend on the international political context. Until now, the cold war and the importance of the Atlantic alliance to the United States and its European allies have had a dampening effect on trade quarrels. The United States has tolerated what it sees as European protectionist measures because the prosperity of Western Europe was an overriding American goal, and the need to preserve the American military protection of Europe has often caused the Europeans to react with moderation to American economic demands or restrictions.

If the Soviet-American contest should cease being the most important issue in world affairs, conflicts of economic interest among allies might well escalate, and both sides might behave more like blocs competing for economic and financial preponderance than like partners submitting to the same rules of fair competition, free trade and monetary cooperation. This would be the case especially if the Community progresses far beyond the present stage of the EMS and begins to pool its foreign exchange reserves, to oversee the creation of national money and to use the ECU more widely.

The other external uncertainty is precisely the one that concerns the role of Europe on the world's diplomatic and strategic stage. The cold war has dominated that stage and the United States has felt strong enough to maintain its forces in Europe, its nuclear guarantee and the structure of NATO. In this situation, the different strategic priorities of France and West Germany, the different weapon systems of the British and French nuclear forces, the different assessments of the Soviet threat and of the perils and benefits of arms control among European countries, the institutional split between those that are part of the military organization of NATO and France, which insists on its autonomy—all condemned the European undertaking to remaining what is sometimes called a mere civilian power, or a merchants' enterprise.

If the cold war continues to fade and the United States shifts its priorities to other issues and other continents, the West Europeans—still too close to the Red Army for comfort, but less dependent on American presence and protection against a clearly more defensive Soviet Union whose own priority had shifted to internal reform—would find it easier to build, over time, a common defense scheme with joint weapons procurement, a respectable conventional army (largely West German), a Franco-British nuclear shield and a predominantly deterrent strategy. We have not reached that stage yet; at present the negotiations on conventional force reductions are a NATO affair, and the West Germans are eager for military cuts, economic cooperation with the Warsaw Pact countries and political détente—rather than for a new West European security system. But the moment might arrive later, after conventional reductions have begun and the presence of both superpowers in Europe has shrunk.

In the more relaxed international climate of recent months, an economically powerful European Community has already begun to exert strong attraction on the countries of Eastern Europe, and to help the gradual transformation of two former Soviet satellites, Poland and Hungary, into states whose relation to Moscow would be comparable to Finland's. The new role of the Community in coordinating assistance—even from the United States—for Poland and Hungary was recognized by the leaders of the seven major industrialized nations in Paris on July 15. In the past, when the cold war heated up, the Federal Republic's allegiances to NATO and to Europe increasingly conflicted with the desire, not for German reunification, but for a rapprochement between the two Germanys, even though the Western orientation always prevailed. In a climate of détente, the two directions become far less divergent, and a strongly European Germany can have more influence on its neighbors to the East.

Thus, in the diplomatic and strategic realm, much depends on the fate of Gorbachev and on American policy toward him; here, unlike in the economic realm, Europe is not a full-fledged actor yet, and whether it becomes one will be settled by those very outside forces that have, since the Second World War, divided the old continent and dominated their respective halves.

The will to build a European entity, spurred by the ineffectiveness of purely national solutions, exists without a doubt in the economic domain, but the devaluation of the nation-state does not mean its demise, even in this area. In the traditional domain of power politics, paradoxically, the progress of European unity depends on the devaluation of power politics—something that has often been prophesied, but has never in the past lasted for very long. Will the logic of economic efficiency and the fear of modern war combine to make the future radically different from the past?

The answer will depend, in part, on the lifting of a last uncertainty, which is both internal and external, and which could affect the Community even—indeed especially—if the future is different and if the fears of military insecurity in Western Europe diminish. It concerns West Germany.

There can be no European Community without Bonn and Paris. In Paris a new generation of politicians and high civil servants appears to have come to the conclusion that France's national objectives—except, perhaps, in the realm of nuclear weapons—can only be reached through European means. But some Europeans fear that the Federal Republic, now the dominant economy in Western Europe and (largely thanks to this) the central player in East-West relations in Europe, might in coming years reach exactly the opposite conclusion. They fear that Bonn might find excessive the burdens imposed by the Community (for instance, German contributions to the costly Common Agricultural Policy and to the structural funds that subsidize the poorer members), that Bonn might decide that West German industry is sufficiently strong, and that West German interests in Eastern Europe are sufficiently distinctive and important to make further ties between Bonn and the other Community members unnecessary, rendering obsolete the function of legitimation that the Community provided when Bonn was weak and widely distrusted.

Until now, in truth, the balance of benefits and burdens imposed by the Community on West Germany has been very favorable (e.g., West German farmers are admirably protected by the Community). While the recent behavior of West German officials and businessmen (such as Foreign Minister Hans-Dietrich Genscher's enthusiasm for Gorbachev, Kohl's about-face on the taxation of interest, and West German refusal to buy the superior French technology for fast railways) and the prospect of a Socialist-Green coalition government in the future have awakened such fears in France, the nightmare of Bonn's emancipation from its Western orientation appears unwarranted. However, the need to provide West Germany with sufficient benefits to keep this orientation worthwhile may itself create tensions in other countries (for example France, whose population is growing faster than Germany's, may want greater possibilities of economic growth than the Deutschmark-dominated EMS allows). Will France and others be willing to tolerate West German hegemony in the Community under any circumstances or in every field?

Such a predicament might well never occur, however. Each of the major West European players might continue to display enough of a mix of strengths and weaknesses to rule out the preponderance of any one of them. In the near future the Community is likely to keep progressing, although more laboriously as the tougher issues, long postponed, have to be faced; it is also likely to serve at least as a common shelter against an eventual recession, unlike in the 1970s. Ultimately, as in the 1950s and 1960s, the European Community's capacity to unite and its limits will be shaped by the events in, and the moves of, the other major countries of the world at least as much as by the patchwork of ties established among the interest groups, the parties and the people and by the domestic politics and economic performances of its member nations.

9

A Plan for the New Europe

1

Only six months before the Berlin Wall collapsed, at an international gathering of scientists in May 1989, a distinguished West German editor gave a rosy speech describing Europe as he wished it to be in the year 2000—a Europe with relaxed and manifold contacts between its two halves. Someone pointed out to him that he had failed to mention the Berlin Wall. The reason for his omission, he replied, was that if East Germany destroyed it, West Germany might have to build a new one to keep the East Germans out.

The speed of events in the last months of 1989 has been such that the unexpected has become the norm. In a few weeks, Communist rule in the Soviet-controlled countries of Eastern Europe has collapsed peacefully, and German unity has suddenly become a central international issue. A race has started between the breathless escape of East Germans from their cage and the slow and complex process of West European integration—indeed between what De Gaulle used to call "Europe from the Atlantic to the Urals" and the smaller Western Europe of the Twelve. If a revolution is a historical earthquake whose occurrence comes as a surprise and whose upheavals and aftershocks cannot be forecast, it is a revolution that we are witnessing.

Why were officials and academics incapable of predicting it? Insofar as the revolution began with and could not have unfolded without Gorbachev, the culprit is the theory that dominated Western thinking about the Soviet Union: the theory of totalitarianism, which assumed that the state had succeeded in controlling or neutralizing civil society, and that in order to understand what has been happening in the USSR, "Kremlinology"—the study of who was who, where, up or down, in the Kremlin—would suffice. The main, and not very popular, competing theory described an authoritarian, bureaucratic system in which organized interests were well integrated.

What these notions missed, apart from the dynamism and political skill of Gorbachev himself, was the degree and variety of discontents in Soviet society, and above all what might be called the Gorbachev generation: the growing conviction among people in their forties and fifties, occupying important positions in the Soviet system, that the prevailing system was increasingly inefficient, dangerous for Soviet power, and contrary to the interests of the Soviet people. The ability to compare it to foreign systems, thanks to travel abroad and to the many contacts with foreigners, that the era of détente had made possible, has had a major part in shaping this consensus. It is always easier to notice a consensus, and to analyze the reason for its growth, after it has been created than during its incubation—as was the case, for example, with the consensus concerning containment that developed among the American elite between 1945 and 1947.

What made the new Soviet situation so easy to miss in this instance was the phenomenon of double bookkeeping characteristic of authoritarian regimes: the same people would be the loyal servants of Brezhnev's "stagnation" in their public lives and increasingly deviant in their private thoughts. Gorbachev made it possible for them to put their ideas and their conduct in harmony, and he gave both legitimacy and a sense of direction to their beliefs.

In the case of Eastern Europe, experts had few doubts about the lack of popular support for Communist rule. But they tended to assume that the Soviets would not loosen their grip, and they completely underestimated the fluidity of the limits that the Soviet government put to its toleration of change. Many thought that the USSR would not allow more than local versions of Communist perestroika. When it became clear that the pressures for radical change were growing, it was thought that the Soviets might give up ideological control but strictly and forcefully preserve their national security requirements. To be sure, they are still insisting on safeguarding the Warsaw Pact, but the definition of what Soviet national security actually requires in Eastern Europe appears to be in flux.

Western observers did not expect Moscow to be as reluctant to use force, and to allow its client regimes to use it, as Gorbachev turned out to be. Nor did they fully measure the scope of social emancipation from the grip of the Communist party and the amount of repressed anger and impatience waiting for an opportunity to explode, in countries such as East Germany, Czechoslovakia, and Bulgaria—even among Communist party members, or among the once docile crews of official television. Nor did they remember that at various moments in history— 1848, 1968—contagion becomes an autonomous force.

Social scientists are not good at dealing with revolutions while they happen (later, they explain why the upheavals had to take place). So far, because of the Soviets' new repudiation of force, we have lived a kind of 1848 in reverse, and there are many reasons to rejoice at the almost entirely nonviolent removal from power of longstanding tyrannies. But there are also reasons for anxiety because events may be running out of control.

2

Six sources of apprehension need to be examined. First, a happy outcome of the new revolution depends to a large extent on Gorbachev's success at home. His supporters tell us that the momentum of his policies is now irreversible, and that there is no way of turning the clock back. But clocks have been turned back—in recent Chinese history, and in past Russian history as well (remember the fates of the earlier parliaments there), Gorbachev has so far been most skillful at keeping many balls in the air, or at explaining that those that fell to the ground were meant to fall; but it is all too easy to imagine that the same momentum his friends invoke could produce political, ethnic, and social tensions which he would no longer be able to contain, and that once more a long night of repression might settle over the Soviet Union—to the relief of many bureaucrats and citizens fed up with disorder and shortages. This would not necessarily lead to an attempt at regaining control by force in Eastern Europe, but insofar as both democratic evolution there and a reunification of the continent depend on Soviet cooperation, regression in Moscow would seriously damage the process of change in Europe.

Second, this process depends not only on Soviet internal politics but also on the international economic environment—which means, to a large extent, the American economy. A severe recession would make it more difficult for the Western nations to provide the aid that the Eastern European nations need, and would slow down progress toward a single and relatively open market in the European Community.

Third, in the countries of Eastern Europe, and to a lesser extent in the Soviet Union itself (especially in its non-Russian parts), there is a serious gap between the demands and expectations of an increasingly mobilized and vocal population on the one hand, and the capacity of political institutions to respond and to channel its aspirations. To be sure, each country is different. But in all of the East European cases, and in some Soviet republics (such as the Baltic ones), the dominant institution—the Communist party—is in crisis, and, except perhaps in Poland (but even Solidarity is a coalition), the opposition is either fragmented (as in Hungary) or gathered in resistance movements created to challenge the status quo rather than around specific programs of reform. Free elections, to be fruitful, will require that coherent political parties emerge from such movements, as happened in Western Europe in 1945.

This, in turn, will take time, and a race is on between the time needed for political sorting out and the time available before political bickering and economic deterioration may result in widespread disenchantment and new authoritarian "solutions"—in countries that were not democracies before communism was imposed (with the exception of Czechoslovakia). To be sure, Western nations can provide expert assistance, and try to help the new political forces in the East create free parties, effective unions, etc. But this will not be easy. The Western nations would do well to try to coordinate such assistance (if only as insurance against too much self-interested help), and it must be both skillful and discreet, so as not to constitute interference in the affairs of others. Much has been written about the nationality problems that have emerged in the USSR and may reemerge in a Balkanized Eastern Europe, but there may also be serious ideological divisions, both among and within nations, and attempts by angry groups to settle scores.

Fourth: the world has rediscovered the German problem. A few months ago, German reunification seemed most unlikely; now it appears inevitable, and the real problem is when—early or late—and how. The situation is rich in paradoxes. West German leaders are ambivalent—afraid of an influx of people from East Germany, worried by the cost of raising the former GDR to the level of the Federal Republic in a reunified state, yet incapable of repudiating the old goal of unity, especially in an electoral period in which each party believes it has to appear more eager for national unity than its rivals. François Mitterrand, having proclaimed in the days before the opening of the wall that France does not fear a reunified Germany, flew to Kiev to meet, praise, and agree with Gorbachev when the prospects of reunification became ominous. He has even mentioned the centuries-old Franco-Russian role in preserving equilibrium in Europe. The US, which had avoided high-level contacts with the DGR as long as Communist rule there was firm, sent its secretary of state to Potsdam in mid-December to suggest that its regime should not disintegrate too fast.

Indeed, at times it looks as if the wartime coalition has been recreated: France, Britain, Poland, the Soviet Union, and a US government anxious not to undermine Gorbachev have all indicated that they oppose a prompt reunification, that they want to have a say, and that they have misgivings about Chancellor Kohl's unilateral pronouncements on confederation and state unity which he delivered on November 28.

Many West Germans resent those misgivings. They point out in interviews and in the German press that they have been loyal members of the democratic West and that a new united Germany would not be at all like Bismarck's empire or Hitler's Third Reich. The Federal Republic is already the most powerful industrial and financial country of the continent. Why would the undoubtedly burdensome addition of seventeen million Germans be a problem for the rest of Europe?

The fact is that West German economic preponderance already causes strains in the European Community, and that two kinds of a reunified Germany would be particularly unwelcome. One would be a reunified Germany within the present structures of NATO and the EEC. The Soviets would not consent to letting, in effect, East Germany simply change camps and become a military outpost of NATO: and the EEC as it is now is too fragile a structure to contain and dilute the clearly preponderant power of one of its members. Indeed, the EEC can be seen as a bargain among states whose larger members—France, West Germany, England, and Italy—have achieved something close to a balance of power.

Whether the Soviets would use force to prevent the East German people from imposing reunification remains an open question: the Soviet leaders acknowledge, these days, that there is indeed only one German nation. But the mere presence of several hundred thousand Soviet forces in the DGR constitutes a warning against what they would see as NATO's annexation of the GDR and provides them with a card that they have sometimes thought of playing in the past, although they have preferred to keep Germany divided. If the cost of maintaining forces in an increasingly hostile Eastern Europe becomes prohibitive, the Soviets could offer reunification to the Germans in exchange for the withdrawal of all foreign forces from German soil and the neutralization of Germany.

But this "solution," which many West Germans might find difficult to reject now, would be unacceptable to the Western powers (as the French and Americans have already made clear). A "neutralized" and reunited Germany would be an unshackled giant that one day might not be neutral; and neutralization would mean not only the end of NATO but also the end of any dream of a purely Western European defense organization (allied to the US), and the end of the drive to turn the European Community into a genuine political organization with strong central institutions and a common diplomacy.

Recent events have indeed cast a shadow over the future of the European Community. As in the early 1960s and during the recession of the 1970s, external events disrupt the process of building the Community because the principal members have divergent responses to the appeals, pressures, and perils of the world at large. Before the revolution of this autumn, feeling had already developed in Brussels that the Federal Republic's enthusiasm toward the Community was waning. Having obtained a single, unfettered market for its goods, and a European monetary system dominated by the Bundesbank (which is thus able to determine the rate of growth and the level of employment of the members), Bonn seemed to wonder whether all developments beyond the present arrangements would not act as unwelcome restraints on German freedom of action. And there was already a debate about whether the Community ought to concentrate on strengthening its institutions or to remain sufficiently loose to attract new members and to keep to a minimum the differences between its structure and the groups of outsiders (such as the six countries of the European Free Trade Area, EFTA—Austria, Finland, Iceland, Norway, Sweden, and Switzerland) eager to share the benefits of economic integration.

The events of the last three months of 1989 have heightened these tensions. The Community was supposed to coordinate Western aid to Poland and Hungary, but Bonn has taken many unilateral initiatives in this respect, and Kohl did not consult his partners before making his speech on reunification on November 28. The president of the Bundesbank and several ministers have expressed skepticism toward Jacques Delors's three-stage plan of April 1989 for monetary union— which would in effect turn the Bundesbank into a federal European bank.

Above all, will the Federal Republic have the energy and the resources to be both the banker of the Community (as in the past) and the paymaster of Eastern Europe (and especially East Germany, when, paradoxically, only an influx of West German aid might slow down the East German citizens' clamor for unity with the much richer part of the nation)? Will Bonn be so tempted by economic and political opportunities in the East, or so absorbed by its own concerns about unification, that it will cease to be the engine of development of the European Community?

At the European summit in Strasbourg of December 8–10, Kohl reassured his colleagues by agreeing, in particular, to the summoning in December 1990 of a conference on monetary union that he had tried to postpone. But the positive results of the Strasbourg meeting are mainly promises, and it will take time before it becomes clear whether they will be kept.

In the meantime, Franco-German cooperation, which has been the engine of progress in the European Community, has been badly strained. One can also count on Mrs. Thatcher to insist that the "deepening" of the Community—i.e., its extending itself to new issues, such as monetary union and social policy, and the strengthening of its institutions—be postponed, so that it can be "broadened" to embrace new members from the East; and it will be interesting to see what stand West Germany takes on this. But one can already observe that an agreement on the abolition of border controls that France, West Germany, Holland, Belgium, and Luxemburg were going to sign has been derailed by the fear of Bonn's partners that masses of East Germans (and also many of the Federal Republic's Turks) might arrive, adding to their colossal difficulties with immigration.

Recent events raise the issue of the future of European security. This is the sixth problem. Suddenly, after many years of discussion of possible conflict between East and West, the main functions of the two alliances, NATO and the Warsaw Pact, have become the management of military deescalation and the control of the German problem! Each pact provides its superpower with its last chance to control events, and the other superpower with a short of reassurance that events will not get completely out of hand.

But while they may perform a most useful transitional role, both alliances are in poor condition. Several members of the Warsaw Pact are either tempted by neutrality or eager to see Soviet troops leave their territories. And while NATO is in better shape, West Germany has unilaterally decided on drastic cuts of its forces, and there are serious divisions between the Federal Republic on one side and Britain, France, and the US on the other, about the need for short-range nuclear forces whose main function seems, particularly to Germans, to be to kill Germans.

Above all, there is the unresolved question of how to insure the security of all of Europe in a post-cold-war world, in which the US might well be a much less visible military presence on the continent, while even a troubled and reformed USSR would still be a military giant at the gate.

3

For all these fears to be dispelled, a daunting number of things would have to turn out well. To be sure, the pace with which changes are taking place in the East may slow down. But what is needed is a major concerted effort on the part of the countries concerned to regain control of events, not in order to thwart the wishes of people who at long last are regaining their freedom, but in order to prevent the external effects of domestic upheavals from disrupting an international system paradoxically stabilized (and frozen) by the cold war.

So far, one might say, so good. The diplomacy of recent weeks has been intelligently conducted. At Malta, the leaders of the superpowers concentrated on what they still control: arms reductions and mutual economic relations. In Strasbourg, the Twelve pushed the European Community forward. Gorbachev has both reasserted his preference for a divided Germany at present and left the future open. Secretary Baker's Berlin speech of December 12 has skillfully drawn "a new architecture for a new era," with new missions for NATO—which would become a political alliance concentrating on arms control—the EEC, and (Gorbachev's favored instrument) the Helsinki process, i.e., the Conference on Security and Cooperation in Europe (CSCE), which would become a vehicle for promoting both free elections and freer markets. And Chancellor Kohl has now clearly indicated, at least for the time being, a willingness to subordinate the German drive for unity to an international consensus.

It is impossible for so many governments to resolve so many issues at once, but it is not enough to distribute roles among a variety of institutions (and to point out that here as elsewhere international institutions are the indispensable pillars for world order). What is needed is an agreement on the main tasks of an agenda to be carried out in stages—a procedure borrowed from the history and practices of the EEC. All I can do here is sketch some of the principles and the steps that seem required.

We might take as our text the formidably prescient press conference of General de Gaulle on February 4, 1965 (the twentieth anniversary of Yalta)—the one in which he spoke of the German problem as "indeed the European problem," of the German anguish

> created by its own uncertainty about its boundaries, its unity, its political system, its international role, so that the more its destiny remains undetermined, the more disturbing it always appears to the whole continent.

A solution to "the German anomalies," he warned, couldn't come before a radical change took place in Russia, which "must evolve in such a way that it sees its future not in totalitarian constraint" at home or abroad but "through progress accomplished in common by free men and people." Such a solution would not take place, that is, before the end of Soviet domination over Eastern Europe, and before the transformation of the European community into an instrument of political and military cooperation. Any settlement of the German problem "would necessarily imply a settlement of its borders and of its armaments in agreement with all its neighbors" and give Germany a major role in the development of Europe's resources "from the Atlantic to the Urals" and in assistance to the third world.

What matters is, first, recognition both of the German people's right to self-determination and of the international community's collective interest in how and when it takes place; secondly, recognition of the need to act simultaneously on a number of fronts: economic cooperation, political integration, and military security. Thirdly, agreement, if not on a precise timetable, at least on an overall plan, to be fulfilled in stages. Even though the issues and the uncertainties are such that it will be years before any plan could be fully carried out, a prompt agreement on one plan is the best chance all the principals have both to regain control of events and to channel domestic changes in an internationally peaceful and cooperative direction.

The first stage would take place during 1990. It could entail, first, the conventional arms-reduction agreement that is being negotiated by representatives of the two alliances in Vienna and was discussed in Malta; secondly, the meeting at the end of the year of the EEC conference on monetary union, the launching of the European Development Bank, set up by the Strasbourg summit, and the signing of the agreement between the Community and the six EFTA countries, whose outline was announced on December 7; and thirdly, in agreement with France, Britain, the US, and the USSR, practical measures of cooperation between West and East German ministries—especially in economic matters.

The second stage, beginning after the West German election at the end of 1990, might see the establishment of some "confederal structures" between the two Germanies, the formal recognition by both Germanies of the Polish-German border, and a further transformation of the two alliances through an agreement (beyond that of 1990) that would eliminate Soviet and American short-range nuclear weapons and reduce again the forces of the superpowers on European soil (as well as the force of the European members of NATO and the Warsaw Pact).

This period would also include the launching of the second stage of the Delors Plan on monetary union (the creation of a system of central banks formulating a common monetary policy), after ratification of the amendments to the treaty of Rome (the Charter of the EEC) that the conference on monetary union is supposed to draft. Also during this phase, the European Community would negotiate agreements for association with those East European countries that would want it.

The third stage—probably around 1994—would require institutional reform in the EEC itself: an increase of the budgetary and legislative powers of the European Parliament in Strasbourg, so as to put an end to the Community's "democratic deficit," and the strengthening of the European Commission in Brussels, which is the Community's real international engine but not yet its executive (that function still belongs to the purely intergovernmental Council of Ministers). At about the same time, the third stage of the Delors Plan, calling for fixed exchange rates and a federal central banking system, would begin; and the EEC would sign with all the countries of Eastern Europe the kind of agreement that it is now negotiating with the European Free Trade Association.

During this phase, in the middle of the 1990s, a decisive change would also take place in the structure of the two alliances. The present alliances would be replaced. In the West there would be a West European security organization allied to the US. It could perhaps be based on the currently sleepy West European Union, but it certainly should be incorporated in the institutional system of the European Community. In the East there would be an East European security organization composed of the states that would be willing to abstain from neutrality and cooperate with one another, in alliance with the USSR. In the Western case, this transformation would require no revision of the North Atlantic Treaty of 1949, which is remarkably flexible. Only symbolic or very small numbers of American and Soviet troops would remain on the continent.

At the end of this stage, if the two German electorates so wish, reunification would occur, and the new German Federal Republic would sign an international agreement that would define its military status. This would provide for demilitarization of the territory that is now East Germany and place limits on the levels and the kinds of arms and force which the new state might have.

Finally, the fourth stage would see the establishment, by the end of the Nineties, of a pan-European security system, going beyond the confidence-building measures that the Conference on Security and Cooperation in Europe would have set up in the first three stages to accompany the changes in the alliances. Such a new system would entail a mutual nonaggression pact and a common organization for arms control verification, and a set of bodies for economic and foreign policy cooperation, not only between the Community and the other European countries, but also with the (former) superpowers.

Obviously this is no more than an outline. But a quick agreement on something like it, perhaps at a CSCE conference in 1990, would serve many purposes. It would both confirm and contain the German drive for unity (currently more powerful in East Germany, a territory without any national identity). It would meet the essential security interests of the Soviet Union. It would promote a West European political entity strong enough not to be dominated by a reunited Germany and capable of serving as a source of assistance and an incentive to cooperation among the East European nations, thus helping them to overcome their own old rivalries: for a Europe with a more integrated Western half and a disintegrated Eastern one could be a rather unsafe place.

It would also gradually free Europe from the grip of the superpowers, while preserving a role for them—and by reducing their military burden it would give them a better chance to tackle their respective internal problems of decline. And it would constructively take account of the two most striking paradoxes of the recent post-cold-war period: the Soviet interest in a successful and strong West European Community capable of coping with Germany and of injecting some stabilizing aid in the East, and the Western stake in saving Gorbachev by preventing the disintegration of the Soviet empire from occurring in so disastrous a way as to strengthen the case and the determination of his conservative foes at home.

Dealing simultaneously with such tendencies is a tall order. A number of places are at the mercy of events and explosions, but crowd movements and local demonstrations that may turn violent have less chance of leading to disaster if collective statecraft provides a sense of direction and purpose. It is time to think seriously about the design of the "European common house" imagined by Gorbachev.

10

Reflections on the 'German Question'

Concerns Over German Unity

The 31 May–3 June 1990 summit in the US between presidents George Bush and Mikhail Gorbachev did not resolve the issue of a united Germany's military status. This is not surprising. The positions of the two former antagonists were too different to be easily reconciled, and any such reconciliation will require two things that were missing in Washington and at Camp David: time, and the participation of the German government. Indeed, Germany's neighbours will also want to be heard, for what is at stake is nothing less than the quieting of a wide variety of anxieties concerning Germany's future.

Those of the (ex?) superpowers are clear. The USSR has not forgotten the horrors and sacrifices of World War II, and wants never again to be exposed to a German invasion. It opposes participation of a united Germany in NATO for two reasons. First, it fears that, in the years to come, with the US reducing its forces in Europe, Germany might become the dominant member of the military alliance, and second, after the disintegration of the Warsaw Pact and, essentially, the disappearance of the GDR, a united Germany in NATO would represent the victory of one of the 'blocs' over the other.

The Soviet position is weakened by the fact that Moscow's suggested alternatives are not very convincing. A neutral and demilitarized Germany might turn into a nightmare even for the Soviet Union, whose interest is certainly not to have an economic and financial giant unattached in the middle of Europe, and to face again, sooner or later, the effects of a sovereign decision by that giant to throw off the shackles of imposed demilitarization. As for a 'French solution' for Germany, which would keep Germany in the political but not in the military organs of NATO, it would be almost as bad, for, contrary to what the Soviet champions of that idea seem to believe, it would not necessarily put an end to military collaboration between Germany and its allies. It would, in effect, give to the German armed forces the independence that integration in the supranational, i.e., largely

American command of NATO was precisely aimed at preventing. Finally, membership of Germany in both NATO and the Warsaw Pact, a Soviet idea endorsed by the American historian of the Cold War, John L. Gaddis,[1] would be doubly untenable, for the two memberships would cancel one another, and the Warsaw Pact would have to be artificially revived against the wishes of Czechoslovakia and Hungary.

The Soviet position is also weakened because the main Soviet card, or instrument of pressure, is more a boomerang than a lever. Threatening to keep Soviet troops in East Germany and to slow down negotiations on conventional arms control until a solution satisfactory to the Soviet Union is found is not a good bargaining position, for the USSR would jeopardize the good relations it has with Germany and is trying to establish with the newly liberated ex-satellites in Central and Eastern Europe. Moreover, once Germany recognizes formally its border with Poland, it is likely that the Poles will ask for the removal of Soviet troops from their country, and Soviet forces in Germany will be isolated in a potentially hostile territory. Having—realistically—conceded both the right of Germany to unite, and that of American forces to stay in Europe, the USSR can now only try to get the best possible price for the withdrawal of its own forces that will have to take place sooner or later.

American fears about Germany are different. The American nightmare seems to be—'seems', because officials rarely discuss these things in public—precisely the kind of unattached Germany the USSR half-heartedly appears to want. American obsession with the perpetuation of NATO results both from the conviction that the NATO integrated military structure is the best guarantee against any revival of German militarism, and from the fact that NATO is the one organization to provide Washington with a hold on European developments. The US remains an unhappy outsider so far as the European Community (EC) is concerned, and the Conference on Security and Co-operation in Europe (CSCE), in which it takes part, is too amorphous and too broad to give the US much clout.

The US is in a very strong position—in the short run. The USSR needs conventional arms reductions more desperately than does the US; Germany proclaims its desire to remain in NATO, and France and the UK have endorsed America's stand. However, time, on which President Gorbachev likes to count, may not entirely be on Washington's side. Should the US be too intransigent, and appear thereby responsible for the prolongation of the Soviet military presence in East Germany, will not the German government—especially if it should be different from the present CDU-FDP coalition—begin to waver in its support for an unchanged NATO? Above all, will the US still be the dominant member of NATO if American forces come home in large numbers (either because, despite the deadlock on Germany's military future, a conventional arms-reduction agreement is signed, or because of Congressional decisions), if American tactical nuclear weapons are cut back, and if the whole business of planning a common defence against a Soviet threat in the heart of Europe becomes somewhat moot?

Under such circumstances, will NATO still 'control' Germany, and thus fulfil its second, somewhat hidden function (now rechristened the mission to ensure 'stability')? Is it not the case that the second function depended largely on the persistence of the first—the common defence—and on the division of Germany, and that in the new situation Germany, instead of being contained, might indeed become the dominant member of NATO?

Poland appears to be the country whose public is least enthusiastic about German unity. The issue of German irredentism, i.e., the fear of German claims on land that was once German but became Polish after World War II, is a matter of the utmost importance to a nation whose borders have been moved in all directions, and which expelled millions of Germans after the war. But Germany can, by its own moves, go a long way towards stilling these fears. As for German economic predominance, the Poles, Czechs and Hungarians share the same ambivalence. Germany's public and private resources, technology, and management skills are such that German influence might well become preponderant in a zone that Realists consider a power vacuum, and where the fervent desire to turn to the West after years of artificial domination by Moscow facilitates the spread of German goods and skills. But while they are afraid of excessive German influence and are eager for other investors—from Western Europe, the US and Japan—they are also eager for the benefits that a wealthy Germany can bring. This is one of the reasons for the very tepid support these three countries are giving to Soviet positions on Germany.

Prime Minister Margaret Thatcher's lack of enthusiasm for German unity has been clear. On this point, London and Washington have taken different positions. But Mrs. Thatcher's fears about a united Germany's future do not appear to be different from those of the US. She may have hoped, for a while, that Germany's concern for close ties with the countries of Central and Eastern Europe might push the German government closer to her own position on the future of the EC—opting for an 'open' but looser confederation, rather than pursuing the 'deepening' of integration in the West alone. But Chancellor Helmut Kohl's commitments in support of deepening the EC have left her, once again, if not isolated, at least in a minority among the West Europeans.

France's fears have been much more difficult to delineate. The French government assuredly shares the anxiety of Washington and London about a militarily detached Germany. But the French also worry about the importance a united Germany might have within the NATO of the future, and about the fact that France's military situation, a source of self-congratulation for more than 20 years, has become less than ideal. The absence of France from the military organization of NATO leaves this organization dominated by a 'Washington-Bonn axis', in which Bonn may become the more important partner. France's nuclear independence, which used to be the way in which that country tried to compensate for a variety of West German advantages (conventional and economic), looks far less significant in a world no longer obsessed by considerations of physical security—

except as the deterrent of a most unlikely Soviet nuclear or conventional attack on France. The French also fear an increase of German economic and monetary predominance in Europe, particularly in the East, where their own efforts, concentrated on Poland and Romania, cannot match those of their much more export-oriented neighbours.

Above all, the French worry about the effects of German unity on the EC—and they have contradictory yet convergent fears. On the one hand, they are anxious about a loss of German interest in a further deepening of the Community, insofar as either full monetary union or political institutional reform would place new constraints on the *Bundesbank* and on the German government (whereas a single market and a European Monetary System controlled by the *Bundesbank* are entirely in Germany's interest). Should a powerful Germany decline to accept further restraints and prefer a kind of economic *Weltpolitik* to the narrower horizons of Western Europe, the dream of a strong new West European entity, capable both of being an independent actor in world affairs and of 'containing' Germany, a dream that has become French policy since 1984, would fade away.

On the other hand, the French are also beginning to fear that such a new entity might be dominated by Germany, the country with the biggest population and the most effective economy, no longer hampered by the burden of a rapidly receding past and by its division. The 'balance of imbalances' among four countries with comparable populations—France, West Germany, Italy and the UK—no longer exists. Even if the German governments of the future continue to believe that membership in a tight Community has the advantage of legitimizing German moves in Eastern Europe and the rest of the world, they might feel confident of their ability both to inspire the main policies of the Community (inside and outside its borders) and to preserve sufficient freedom of action in diplomatic and strategic matters—a domain in which neither Bonn nor Paris nor London wants to give up the principle of unanimity. Whether or not Germany becomes reluctant towards a strengthening of the EC, France is beginning to realize that the new Germany will be a giant—and that there is little it can do about this.

It may be worth listing another fear, expressed by some Americans in the Realist tradition.[2] They believe that, multipolarity being more unstable than bipolarity, the removal of the superpowers' grip over the two halves of Europe is likely to exacerbate interstate conflicts and to create the danger of a nuclear Germany. This view is based on the assumption that survival and security, which, for West Germany, were assured by NATO, will remain the dominant concerns of a united Germany that is no longer likely to be constrained by NATO.

The Nature of These Concerns

Is it possible to find formulas that will take care of all these worries? First, it is necessary to establish which are serious.

The fear of a return to the past is probably unjustified. The 'German question' that led to two world wars was caused by the presence in the heart of Europe of a huge nation that could only be contained by a coalition of several other great powers. But what led to war was not simply the dynamics of rival alliances. It was the specific preferences, goals and policies of Imperial and later Nazi Germany: the former's bumbling *Weltpolitik* and full support, in 1914, to the crumbling Austrian ally; the latter's brutally aggressive *Lebensraum* policy and quest for racial domination. And it was the military means as well as the war-like mentality of these two German regimes that led to war. The present-day situation is different; the political, educational and class systems of West Germany have been thoroughly reformed. Realists reply that aggressiveness often results from the security fears inherent in the geopolitical situation of a country—in Germany's case, the fear of encirclement, and of being left out of the division of the spoils by the other countries. Not only is this a rather simple-minded view of the determinants of a state's foreign policy, but it is hard to see why a united Germany would feel particularly threatened, as long as it has close relations with France, the UK and the US, friendly ones with the USSR, and has essentially weaker neighbours around its borders. The Realists' view of the world makes little room for the shift of preferences, from territorial control, military or coercive policies and diplomatic-strategic calculations, to economic and financial influence. While the 'military state' and the 'trading state' may be concepts or ideal-types rather than unalloyed realities, the fact is that for Germany as well as for Japan, unless dramatic changes occur in their security environments, the rewards of economic influence—of being able to provide others with what they crave—are far greater than those of traditional power. The latter are likely to be short-lived, insofar as the quest for control turns neighbours into adversaries and provokes balancing behaviour, whereas the drive for economic influence turns them into clients and breeds 'bandwagoning' behaviour.

To be sure, a hostile Soviet Union could be seen by Germany as a threat requiring military countermeasures. But becoming a nuclear power would only increase Soviet hostility and alienate Germany's allies and partners. The most effective deterrents for German security are likely to be, first, the internal situation in the USSR (a situation sufficiently different from that of Imperial or Nazi Germany to make very far-fetched any analogy between the effects of a backlash of humiliation in the USSR and the results of frustration in the Wilhelmine *Reich* or rage in the post-Versailles Germany). Secondly, there is the Soviet interest in German economic and financial assistance.

This does not mean that lingering fears of German militarism need not be addressed. It should not be impossible for statesmen to find a formula that satisfies both a Germany that has its own security needs, but no desire to return to policies that led to two defeats and to 45 years of division, and those of Germany's partners and ex-occupiers who want guarantees for the future. And it also means that the most serious concern is likely to be the prospect of a Germany, even harnessed inside a 'tight' European Community, that yields to the 'arrogance of power' that has been a characteristic of so many major states in history. Under these circumstances, Germany might behave less like a wise 'hegemon', understanding the need to take account of the interests of lesser powers, than like a selfish player concerned above all with relative gains and insensitive to the claims and fears of others.

The Need for New Defence Organizations

In the realm of security, the best solution is likely to be the one that starts from a rigorous analysis of the needs to be addressed. First, the countries of Western, Central and Eastern Europe will all need reassurance against a re-emergence of the Soviet threat, and against the fact that the Soviet Union will remain the principal military power of the continent. This is a reassurance that may well continue to require some form of American nuclear guarantee and conventional presence. Secondly, the USSR and Germany's neighbours need reassurance against an eventual resurgence of German militarism. Thirdly, mechanisms must be created to resolve disputes among European states, and conflicts resulting from ethnic tensions within some states.

The elements of such a solution might combine a West European Defence Organization, that would be one of the components of the European Community, and a strengthened pan-European Organization set up by the CSCE, with the participation of the US and Canada and of the USSR.[3] If the EC wants to be more than a deregulated common market and become a real entity in world politics (however *sui generis* its institutions), then co-ordinating the defence policies and forces of its members, using the nuclear arsenals of France and the UK as Community rather than purely national deterrents, and promoting co-operation in weapons procurement will all be important elements of the enterprise. Whereas extending NATO all the way to the River Bug (with or without actual membership for the nations of Central and Eastern Europe) would be unacceptable to Moscow, security guarantees to and arrangements with these nations could be undertaken by such a Defence Organization, which would replace the dormant Western European Union and function according to the rules set up by a treaty of the Twelve. These guarantees and arrangements would aim at quieting the fears of the Soviet Union's former protectorates concerning a Soviet return to expansionism. Their fears of a militant Germany could be taken care of by similar guarantees from and arrangements with the USSR.

As for the Organization set up by the CSCE, it would both deal with the settlement of disputes, and supervise agreements on the limits to be put on forces and weapons of its members (in this way, Germany would not be singled out). As two French authors have suggested,[4] part of the agreement might consist in a ban on the stationing of any nuclear weapons on the territory of non-nuclear powers. To be sure, as François Heisbourg has pointed out,[5] the CSCE, where the rule of unanimity prevails, cannot provide collective security. But NATO also worked with that rule, with America's hegemony providing the 'collective good' of collective security.

What about NATO and the US? As indicated above, the US nuclear guarantee to Western Europe and the presence of some US conventional forces will remain, respectively, necessary and helpful. But NATO will be transformed by *la force des choses:* the fading away of the common enemy, the absurdity of a 'forward defence' strategy against a defunct Warsaw Pact, the likely unwillingness of Germany to remain an 'occupied' country with a high density of foreign forces, the disconnection between a military structure dominated by the US and the likely (im)balance of forces between the US and its European allies within NATO, the need for the US to deal with its internal problems, and so forth. Ultimately (it is impossible to be precise as to when: as President Gorbachev has remarked, the talk of schedules and deadlines invites scepticism), the best outcome will be one that is perfectly compatible with the loose North Atlantic Treaty of 1949. It would consist of an alliance between the US and Canada and the new West European Defence Organization, with the task of joint military planning undertaken by a Committee under the jurisdiction of the North Atlantic Treaty Council.

There remains the issue of Germany's economic and financial powers, and of the political benefits that may accrue to Germany as a result. Ideally and theoretically, a West European Federation would be the way to curb the 'excessive' influence of any one member (although there would always be some French people who would fear that Germany would be the Federator, just as General de Gaulle feared that the US wanted to be the Federator in Jean Monnet's design). However, it is most unlikely that the Community will become a 'United States of Western Europe'. The UK, France and Germany do not want to give up what remains of their sovereignty in diplomacy and strategy; the UK and France want to preserve some instruments of national economic and monetary policy (direct taxation, social security); and Germany is not keen on submitting the *Bundesbank* to the political control of other states. The best that can be hoped for is the kind of movement that is now beginning: a monetary union leading to a central bank and a common (if not necessarily single) currency, a co-ordinated diplomacy, a Defence Organization as described above, and a set of institutions in which, on the one hand, parliamentary control will be considerably extended and, on the other, the role of the EC Commission will expand, even in areas still subjected to unanimity. This tighter but not fully federal Community will be able to sign economic agreements with the European Free Trade Association and the countries of East and Central Europe, and the latter might ultimately be allowed to join the Community if they fully accept its institutions, rules and constraints.

Such an entity, especially if these agreements multiply, would offer the best prospects, if not for 'containing' Germany, at least for injecting into German policy a combination of restraint and concern for the long-term interests of others, with whom a consensus will have to be reached. At the same time, it would leave Germany as well as its major European partners with a margin of autonomy, without which a domestic backlash is always to be feared.

Conclusions

Obviously, it will take years to define and carry out the tasks described here. It is up to the Western allies to make the inevitable participation of Germany in NATO, and the almost inevitable withdrawal of Soviet forces from Eastern Europe (including East Germany), acceptable to Moscow. It is up to Moscow, through its own behaviour in Eastern Europe and also in national conflicts at home, as well as through sensible and specific proposals about the 'common European home', to reassure those Europeans, and those American policy-makers and experts, who still see in Soviet proposals a plan to eviscerate NATO, to get the Americans out of Europe, and to remain (through nuclear and conventional superiority) the dominant power on the continent. It is up to Germany to disarm the various anxieties listed at the beginning of this article. At this moment, two conclusions can be reached tentatively and provisionally.

First, the tribulations of the USSR seem destined to drag it into a prolonged eclipse as a world power. Whether *perestroika* and reform progress despite all obstacles, or the Soviet Union disintegrates politically and economically, or a new authoritarian regime tries to restore law and order, the days of the 'Soviet threat' are likely to be over. This is true in the first case because of the very nature of the 'new thinking', and in the second and third cases because of the colossal scope of domestic problems—none of which any diversion towards external aggression, in a nuclear world, could in any way begin to ease or suppress.

Secondly, it would take an extraordinary amount of mischief to turn the new German state into a modern version of the dangerous and unsettling Germany of the past. Neither Germany's partners, nor even its former adversaries in the East, are in any way eager to antagonize or provoke it; and German elites have no desire to return to that past. The habits of co-operation developed in NATO and in the EC, the entanglement of German agriculture, industry and finance in the public arrangements and private deals of the single market, the desire on both sides of the former Iron Curtain for a reunified Europe and a break with a bloody history, all these factors allow one to be at least moderately optimistic, even if the euphoria of 1989 has been replaced by a more sober view of the difficulties head.

Notes

1. See his essay 'Coping with Victory', *Atlantic Monthly,* May 1990, pp. 48–60.
2. See, for instance, the articles by John Mearsheimer in the Summer 1990 issue of *International Security.*

3. For further details, see Stanley Hoffmann, 'A Plan for the New Europe', Chapter 9 of this book; and 'Today's NATO and Tomorrow's', *New York Times*, 27 May 1990, p. E13.

4. Frédéric Bozo and Jérôme Paolini, 'Trois Allemagnes, deux Europes et la France', *Politique étrangère*, Spring 1990, pp. 119–38.

5. Unpublished paper on 'The Common European House', May 1990.

11

The Case for Leadership

"Nothing in history is inevitable, except in the formal sense that, for it to have happened otherwise, the antecedent causes would have had to be different." That remark by E. H. Carr in his 1961 book *What is History?* applies perfectly to the events in Europe over the past year. Soon historians and political scientists will tell us why what happened had to occur. In explaining why the division of Europe and communist rule in much of Central and Eastern Europe both came to a sudden end, we should not too easily assert the necessity of the transformation. Things could have been different. At every point, in every country, choices were made. During the hectic weeks of the late summer and fall of 1989, in each of the communist states of the Soviet glacis, a threatened leadership had to choose between repression and retreat, force and suicide. Only in Romania and in Bulgaria did the Communists succeed in staying in power. It is not enough to say that the satellite regimes in Czechoslovakia, Hungary, and Poland were swept away by their fundamental illegitimacy. That illegitimacy was a permanent condition. What led to their demise were the decisions the demoralized leaders made, their disarray under the challenge of a revived opposition, and their reluctance to use brute force on a large scale once they were on their own.

Similarly, the way in which Germany has marched, or rather run, to its reunification was by no means inevitable. A very different scenario is imaginable in which the pace of events would have been slower and all the other powers concerned about the "German problem" would have tried to guide the change, to subordinate unity to a host of architectural concerns and constructs. Indeed, I suggested such a scheme one year ago.[1] Not only has German unity been accomplished in one year instead of ten, but the role of the other players has been very different from the one I was, in effect, advocating. Choices were made—openly or implicitly—that could have been very different.

This point is of special importance to students of international relations—academicians with their baggage of theories and practitioners with their operational codes. The dominant theory and the customary code stress the decisive importance of the structure of the international system, the way in which the distribution of military, economic, and other capabilities shapes the policies of states. It is high time to get rid of the sterilizing hold this notion has had. As a first cut in analyzing international affairs it has some validity, but not beyond that. In 1989, the capabilities of the Soviet Union in "hard power" terms of military might and economic resources were not significantly lower than before, and the same can be said of those of the United States. What was weaker in both cases (much more in the Soviet one) was what French political scientist Raymond Aron called the capacity for collective action—the ability of the state to extract resources for foreign and military policy goals. The economic system of a state is more important than, and vastly different from, the sum of its material resources. Above all, the goals of the two countries—and again especially Soviet goals—had changed significantly, and both the nature of relevant power and the interplay between such power and goals are far more complex than the "structural" approach to world politics suggests.

What the student of world affairs needs to examine first are two factors that the structural approach has neglected. The most obvious is the role of leadership. In short, leaders matter. European events have been shaped by the decisions of two men, and by the stance of several others. The two men are Soviet President Mikhail Gorbachev and Chancellor Helmut Kohl of the Federal Republic of Germany (FRG).

It was Gorbachev who decided that the USSR would no longer play the hegemonic role in Eastern Europe that his predecessors had forged and preserved by force—even if this meant the demise of communist regimes. This was not an uncontroversial decision; it is, indeed, one that most Western analysts had considered unlikely. It is possible to imagine Soviet leaders other than Gorbachev engaged in attempts to reform the Soviet economy and reduce military expenditures, but determined nevertheless to safeguard the satellite regimes and the USSR's preponderant position in Eastern Europe. Although a sharp reduction in the cost of empire was undoubtedly dictated by the plight of the Soviet economy, a retreat was not. It may be true that Gorbachev did not intend the communist regimes to fall and might have preferred that communist reformers take over. But he was willing to let these regimes fall if such reformers could not be found or could not stem the tide of popular revulsion with communism, and he was determined not to use the massive Soviet forces in the area to hold on.

Gorbachev himself may have been a mere reformer when he came to power in 1985; by 1989, both in foreign and domestic affairs, he was a revolutionary intent on dismantling totalitarianism at home and the whole foreign policy of Joseph Stalin and his successors. It was his decision not to prop up the satellite regimes that deprived them of their legitimacy in Moscow, whose support had compensated for their lack of legitimacy at home. It was Gorbachev who decided not to forfeit German goodwill by using Soviet forces in East Germany as an instrument to blackmail Bonn and to prevent Germany either from reuniting or from remaining in NATO after unity. Gorbachev had weak cards, but it was his decision not to use them at all, or almost not at all. He may ultimately be able to show that his choice will benefit his country. But the returns of the gamble are not in, and not everybody deemed that gamble inevitable. Few people had taken seriously Gorbachev's remarkable article on the United Nations in September 1987; those who did turned out to be right. His speech at the U.N. in December 1988 convinced even the skeptics.

As for Kohl, he had often been accused of lacking vision, of being a skillful politician rather than a statesman, and of being a somewhat reluctant follower of his foreign minister, Hans-Dietrich Genscher, rather than an initiator. Yet after the fall of the Berlin Wall he acted as though the spirit of Konrad Adenauer had suddenly seized him. Kohl was often thought of as a champion of West European integration and of NATO. But he has also been a German patriot, keen on restoring as much German sovereignty as the circumstances allowed, on making the FRG an actor and not an object.

What is striking about Kohl's leadership is his decision to make German unity an issue for the Germans alone. All the key initiatives have come from Bonn. The European Community (EC) was not consulted, even though the absorption of the German Democratic Republic (GDR) amounts to the entry of a 13th member into the Community; Brussels was not always even informed. Both political unification and economic aid have been shaped on Bonn's terms. To be sure, the FRG had to accept the Two plus Four formula; but it was directly with Gorbachev that Kohl negotiated Moscow's acceptance of German membership in NATO, the limitation on the size and nature of German armed forces, and the departure of Soviet forces from East Germany and of the occupying forces from Berlin. Like Adenauer, Kohl proclaims his intention to work for West European monetary and political union and to keep Germany in NATO. But he has in effect presented these courses as sovereign German choices, not as constraints imposed, or even collective options adopted, by a coalition of countries. At every turn, including in NATO summit meetings, he has preempted or evaded external control, while providing what might be called sovereign reassurance about his intentions and destination.

A third feat of leadership, more circumscribed in nature, has taken place since 1984 within the EC through EC Commission President Jacques Delors. While the Community's progress has depended on a series of bargains among its main members, Delors has skillfully prodded them and enlarged the opportunities for further integration.

Still, the picture in Europe today would not be the same without the peculiar leadership of three other actors. President George Bush—or his advisers—have seen to it that all summits in 1989 and 1990 appeared to follow his script and endorse his positions. But images and substance are very different. Basically, he has accepted a much-reduced U.S. role in Western Europe, allowed the EC to be the main actor (after the FRG) in Eastern Europe, and adopted a minimalist policy with three basic aims: helping Gorbachev diplomatically (if not financially), supporting Germany's national aspirations, and saving NATO, the last instrument of America's preponderance in Western Europe. Bush has skillfully taken into account Soviet security interests, German desire for sovereignty in unity, and the need to preserve a West European and a North Atlantic "roof" over the new German house. He has been lucky insofar as the three goals have turned out to be compatible—thanks to Gorbachev and Kohl. But his performance has been that of a supporting player, not a key actor.

French President François Mitterrand appears to have been left somewhat behind by events. After creating an impression of disarray in the fall of 1989 he has allowed Kohl to dominate the scene. The chancellor's failure to inform his partner about his plan for German unity led to a period of Franco-German pique. Mitterrand's own policies remain somewhat inconsistent: the embrace of further West European integration and of NATO does not entirely work well with what remains a highly Gaullist defense policy. The French, worried about France's role in world affairs, nostalgically compare Charles de Gaulle's forceful and eloquent pedagogical leadership with Mitterrand's sparse statements and impressionistic nuances.

As for Margaret Thatcher, nobody can deny that the British prime minister is a forceful leader, but her own strong performance shows the difference between great leadership and wrong leadership. Great leaders exploit the opportunities provided by circumstances, and use their nations' resources to affect the course of history. Great leaders may—as de Gaulle often did—resort to obstruction in order to prevent something they deem contrary to the national interest, but they must first assess correctly whether the obstruction can stick. Thatcher has consistently made it clear that she disapproves of the directions taken by events— deeper integration in the EC, speedy German unity, even the pace of conventional arms control in Europe and changes in NATO's nuclear strategy. Yet she has been unable to affect these events and has preferred being dragged along reluctantly to being isolated. The muted performances, or counterperformances, of Bush, Mitterrand, and Thatcher have left the field to Gorbachev and Kohl, and thus contributed in their own ways to the outcome in Europe today.

Civil Societies

A second factor neglected by the structural approach to international relations is, in a sense, an extension of the previous one. It is the importance of domestic factors in understanding foreign policy, particularly the need to look at the configuration of internal political forces and the relations between what is often called "civil society" and the state. In the 1980s the ability of the East European and Soviet regimes to provide their peoples with the economic benefits they expected had declined or collapsed, and faith in communism had been replaced by cynicism and routine. Moreover, thanks in part to détente, the isolation of these citizens had decreased. Many of them—particularly among the more educated— had become able to compare their condition with that of the West Europeans and North Americans whom they visited or who visited them. Later, in the Soviet

Union, *glasnost* and *perestroika* unleashed a host of political currents, national and ethnic movements, and protests whose quarrels and demands made it difficult to imagine any foreign policy other than one of retrenchment and retreat. The state of the Soviet economy, as well as the discontents it fosters, explains why Soviet diplomacy is so eager to reintegrate the USSR into both the world economy and what its spokesmen often call our "common civilization." In Eastern Europe, it was Gorbachev's decision that doomed communist regimes, but it was the deterioration of the economy and the partial revival of civil society that created the challenge in the first place.

Both in the Soviet Union and Western Europe many observers missed a generational change. In the USSR, Gorbachev was only one member of a new cadre that came to the conclusion that the Stalinist system did not work at home or abroad. And thanks to *glasnost,* they were finally able to put their private thoughts and their public stands in harmony. In Western Europe, meanwhile, a new generation of businessmen, civil servants, journalists, and politicians have acquired the habit of cooperation across barriers. They seem capable of reconciling their national perspectives and their "European" outlook (even in Great Britain). This often distinguishes them sharply from their elders; it explains in great part why, especially on the Continent, Germany's partners did not appear excessively worried by Germany's new prominence, why the German leaders themselves could move toward their national goals without gloating or hubris, and why the German public, especially the young, often appeared ambivalent about unification.

As for the United States, the domestic factors explaining the shift in policy were not generational but structural. Its relative timidity after the years of Reaganesque posturing would be difficult to understand without taking into account a complex set of factors: the size of the American debt, the twin deficits, domestic social concerns, the new importance of economic worries about West European and above all Japanese competition, and the taboo about raising taxes. These factors explain in part the paradox of Bush's foreign policy, which presents the United States as still number one but broke.

"Structure" in the international system has a deceptive simplicity; yet domestic factors are fluid and complex. The structural theory was geared to a world in which states, as discrete actors, sought power or sought to balance power in a game that entailed the possible resort to war. This limited the importance of variations in a state's behavior caused by each actor's domestic regime or politics. Remove that possibility of war or relax those constraints and the nature of the game changes. It is not that the actors will stop seeking power and influence, but rather that the way of acquiring gains, the nature of the desired gains, and the means of provoking international change all will change. In traditional international politics, war provided the most visible and often quickest instrument of change. If war is removed, change in international affairs, or in the pecking order of states, will tend to result either from revolutions or from domestically driven modifications in the goals or in the power of states.

The artificial division of Europe and Germany is gone. But Europe's heterogeneity is blatant. Today, a liberal and capitalist Europe no longer faces a communist one. In their places are a settled Europe and an unsettled one. In the former, nations are either governed by consensus or have well-established political procedures, as well as a host of cooperative channels for interstate interactions. The latter resembles the post-liberation scene in Western Europe 45 years ago. Thus the priorities there are widely different. In the West, the hidden agenda is the digestion of the new Germany; the open agenda is, in Germany, the digestion of the former GDR, and, everywhere, the further development of cooperation along well-laid tracks. In the East, by contrast, the priority is national reconstruction and reform. One side looks toward the future, the other rediscovers its past.

The foregoing points are meant to place a realistic net under the countless exercises in "architecture" for European security after the Cold War by commentators and scholars. Too often, writers have assumed either that the security scene will be the same as before, only at a lower level of danger and with a displacement of a few hundred miles toward the East, or else that the declining weight of the superpowers in Europe is going to bring back the world of competing hostile states that led Europe to so many wars, including two catastrophes in this century. But things are not so simple, nor so grim.

What usually drives statecraft is ambition and fear. Ambitions, in present-day Europe, are largely associated with domestic reconstruction or domestic progress. These, in turn, require a stable and cooperative external environment and, in the eyes of many Europeans (East as well as West), the further development of expansion of the EC.

Current fears are concentrated on the Soviet Union and Germany. Many Europeans see in the Soviet Union—or in Russia, should the USSR disintegrate—a potential threat because of the disproportion between its military might and that of the neighboring European states. For now, any resurgence of Soviet aggressiveness seems remote but internal turmoil could spill over into external diversions, especially if anti-Western, nationalistic, and militaristic forces should prevail in a domestic power struggle. Also, turbulence and conflict in Eastern Europe could provoke new Soviet interventions caused by a fear of spreading insecurity. It is this lingering suspicion of Soviet or Russian moves and capabilities, combined with a fear of the unpredictable effects of a Soviet dissolution, that explains the continuing European attachment to NATO (as well as French and British reluctance to downgrade the threat of nuclear weapons in NATO strategy). It also explains in part why the leaders of the key nations of Eastern and Central Europe want NATO to survive, and why, so far, all these countries want the United States to maintain forces in Europe and to retain its nuclear guarantee to its allies.

The anxieties about Germany are much more varied, and quite contradictory. Some fear a return to a dominant Germany driven to nuclear rearmament by security worries or eager to exploit the "power vacuum" in Eastern Europe. Others fear acts of collusion between the new, strong Germany and the new, weakened Soviet Union, with German foreign policy taking on a more "Eastern" orientation. Such a Germany could gradually empty NATO of its military content, reducing it to a symbolic alliance and rely instead on the Soviet-backed Conference on Security and Cooperation in Europe (CSCE) for collective security. In this conception, a dynamic but naive Germany would let the Soviet fox into the European barnyard. In the opinion of French analyst Pierre Hassner, the price for not having the neutral Germany the Soviets first said they wanted would be a neutralized Europe. The two nightmares are incompatible; but both lead, once again, to a desire to preserve a strong NATO as a barrier to both variants of the "German peril."

In turn, the logic of these fears should lead to a collective Western guarantee to the nations of East and Central Europe to protect them from German revanchism, from a resurgence of Soviet aggressiveness, or from a new variant of the Nazi-Soviet Pact. But practically nobody suggests enlarging NATO membership or expanding the territory covered by the North Atlantic treaty toward the East. Such an extension is deemed unacceptable to the Soviets and would be opposed by France, which is always on guard against any change in NATO's sphere of action.

There are two other fears rampant in Western Europe that would interfere with any such expansion of the Atlantic alliance. One is the fear that the eastern half of Europe will return to the kind of anarchy that people associate with the interwar period and with the concept of Balkanization. Such disorder could result from interstate clashes provoked by antagonistic nationalism (such as that between Romania and Hungary), or from secessionist movements (such as those in Yugoslavia or even Czechoslovakia), or from turmoil in countries that are simultaneously trying to establish democratic, political systems and administer enormous shocks to their economies. As British writer Timothy Garton Ash has warned, the transition from the moralistic unity of anticommunist resistance to pluralistic politics is likely to be made more difficult by the absence of "many elements of civil society" long suppressed by communist regimes. There is a real danger of authoritarian, antidemocratic regimes taking over, as has happened before in Hungary and Poland, if democratic politics cannot "absorb the larger part of the inevitable popular discontents" that drastic economic reform will generate. But what is obvious today is the desire of the rest of Europe *not* to be dragged again into the domestic or external conflicts of Eastern and Central Europe. West Europeans pride themselves on having overcome this dark past at last and for good.

There is another fear found especially but not exclusively in France: It is the fantastical fear of an invasion by outsiders—Muslim fundamentalists and terrorists, starving Africans, refugees from Third World conflicts, or East Europeans in quest of prosperity. Economic and political success usually brings smugness; it also can breed anxieties, including dark suspicions of subversion by evil forces of greed and envy. To many West Europeans, wealthy, capitalist Europe seems like a besieged and coveted island surrounded by hungry pirates that would like to land

and to plunder, or like Rome facing the barbarians. Western Europe's relative demographic decline feeds these phobias, which are based on genuine cultural clashes and worries about national identity. It is the West European fear of having to grant free entry and circulation to a rapidly increasing Turkish population that dooms Turkey's application for membership in the EC. An unspoken but nonetheless real fear of an exodus from Eastern Europe caused by rising unemployment and higher prices is one obstacle to an early entry of Western-oriented countries like Czechoslovakia, Hungary, and Poland into the EC club.

In this vein many Europeans—especially the French—continue to emphasize the North-South dimension of world politics, and the need for greater efforts to reduce the debt of and provide assistance to the developing countries. They are convinced that misery will breed political and economic disasters and produce masses of refugees and emigrants who will knock at, or kick down, the doors of the rich. This explains in part the prudence shown by the West European leaders (except Thatcher) in supporting unconditionally an American military buildup against Iraq that could, in some scenarios, lead to chaos across the Arab world.

CSCE vs. NATO

The debate on European security in recent months has centered on the respective virtues and defects of the CSCE versus NATO, and on the ability of these very different institutions to cope with some of the fears listed earlier. Each camp is better at pointing out the flaws of the other than at proving its own strength. Critics of the CSCE have an easy task reminding us of the failures of collective security. "Nations are loath to sacrifice their *sacro egoismo* on the altar of abstract justice," journalist Josef Joffe wrote in the June 1990 *Commentary*. The critics point to the inconveniences entailed by a vast membership and by Soviet participation in the CSCE: A weak and troubled Soviet Union could wreck the institution, while a strong one could dominate it.

Much of this is true. Collective security, as a commitment to forcibly resisting aggression regardless of the character of the aggressor and of the victim, remains not very compatible with the historic pattern of foreign-policy behavior. Yet today the integrated system of NATO is endangered by the fading away of the common enemy, the collapse of the Warsaw Pact, and developments in the two key countries: The United States plans drastic force reductions in Europe, and Germany has made clear its objections to the presence of short-range nuclear systems on its soil. NATO may thus effectively "contain" neither Moscow nor Bonn (or Berlin). Also, NATO provides no answer to the security problems of the newly free neighbors of the USSR, whether these problems arise from future Soviet threats, German domination, or the pressures that flow from nationalism, minorities, and border questions.

The CSCE has the merit of keeping the superpowers involved constructively in the security issues of a continent whose turbulence could adversely affect them both. It provides one important channel of cooperation between the countries of

Eastern and Central Europe and the West and offers a framework for the negotiation and enforcement of arms reductions and possible procedures for the resolution of disputes. These are tasks that are not within NATO's domain, and will be of considerable importance.

Even the combination of an aging NATO and a strengthened CSCE will not be able to accomplish two other major tasks. The first is to preserve the Western orientation of a united Germany. Germany's legitimate concern with defusing any potential Soviet threat by helping Moscow become a member of the "common European house" should not lead to the emasculation of Western Europe's defenses. It is not simply French paranoia that fears a convergence of America's deep reluctance ever to fight a nuclear war over Europe with Germany's "nuclear allergy." NATO, dominated by the German-American "special relationship," could easily become little more than a clearinghouse. U.S. nonstrategic nuclear forces might be confined to air-based systems in Britain and sea-launched cruise missiles. And if the sense of threat from the East declines further, American forces may be asked to leave the sovereign soil of Germany. Much here depends on the future evolution of German politics: There lies the key to NATO's future substance. Moreover, the U.S. Congress may be unenthusiastic about keeping U.S. troops in Germany if no nuclear weapons are stored nearby. If NATO becomes an empty shell, the Soviets will have attained their goal of a largely neutralized and denuclearized continent. But in exchange Germany might acquire a dominant diplomatic and economic influence in Eastern Europe and a kind of partnership with an economically dependent Russia.

The second task is to further the integration of Central and Eastern Europe—especially Czechoslovakia, Hungary, and Poland—into the rest of Europe. These countries need help in overcoming enormous obstacles on the road to democracy and market economics, and in reducing the risk of nationalistic explosions or exploitation of domestic discontent. The task here is psychological and economic, but it has a military dimension as well. These nations need reassurance both against their Soviet neighbor and against any revival of a German peril—though German economic predominance is far more plausible than the military threat of a Germany that accepts limitations on forces and armaments.

A European Security System

The key to a satisfactory performance of both tasks lies within the EC. On paper, it is easy to imagine that the Community's advances toward monetary and political union will be accompanied by an attempt at setting up, directly or through the West European Union, a defense system for its members. In this system the separation of France's independent strategy and forces from the integrated strategy and forces of its NATO partners would at last come to an end. This separation was not too harmful as long as the old American-dominated NATO functioned well. It would have far worse effects in the new NATO one can now foresee.

In a West European security organization, the British and French nuclear deterrents would be coordinated with the conventional forces of the participants, and joint military procurement would be undertaken systematically. As American leadership in NATO fades, a British-French-German triumvirate would assume the leading role in defense coordination in order to prevent an atrophy of the military dimension of Western cooperation. And this defense system could, if they desire it, provide states in Eastern and Central Europe with a military guarantee. One can also imagine the Community, through its new European Bank for Reconstruction and Development and through the Commission, providing substantial economic aid to these states on the condition—as in the Marshall Plan— that they cooperate with one another. By grouping together they could gradually become more capable of negotiating with the EC agreements similar to those between the EC and the European Free Trade Area. Mitterrand's idea of a confederation would thus be carried out on the economic front, and a reformed or reinforced Council of Europe could serve as a political coordinating body.

These are ways in which functions relinquished by or not appropriate to a fading NATO could be performed. The Atlantic alliance would become, under the vague and flexible 1949 treaty, an agreement between the United States and Canada, on the one hand, and a European defense organization on the other. The nuclear forces of Britain and France and those of the United States (in Britain and at sea) would carry out the necessary deterrent and reassurance roles. At the same time, links could be established among the different parts of Europe without any hasty "broadening" of the EC that would jeopardize its attempt at "deepening" the integration of its 12 current members. Ultimately, if the political and economic systems of Eastern and Central Europe meet the de facto tests the Community has set up for new members, and if these nations are willing to pool and transfer parts of their recently recovered sovereignty, they could join the EC; but in the interim they would not be abandoned.

Still, the factors that could prevent such schemes from moving from paper to reality should not be underestimated. They all return us to the basic problems of leadership, domestic affairs, and European heterogeneity.

First, European security after the Cold War requires the definition of a new relationship between the countries of Europe and the superpowers. American influence on the various European processes will continue to decline—though not vanish—given America's economic and residual military presence, West European needs for reassurance, and West European dependence on U.S. force for the security of its supplies of oil from the Middle East. The security links between Washington and Western Europe will run largely through NATO, even if the organization's makeup and its strategy change. Links between the United States and the rest of Europe are likely to be assured through the EC and the CSCE. But an important variable will be America's prosperity. A recession in the United States would affect Western Europe, probably accelerate the decline of a traditional American-dominated NATO, and undoubtedly limit the willingness and ability of the EC's members to devote to Eastern Europe the amounts of aid and attention that are needed.

Second, the new relationship with the USSR will depend primarily on the outcome of the new Russian revolution. Protracted turmoil, violent conflicts among nationalities, and political paralysis at the top would impede cooperation between the European countries and their troubled neighbor and perpetuate fears of an overflow of violence across borders. The successful establishment of a radically decentralized Soviet confederation—accompanied by Baltic independence—would have exactly the opposite effects. But it is not clear that the United States and its West European allies can affect the evolution deeply, even if they provide considerable economic help.

Third, the linchpin of the various organizations mentioned here will be Germany. The most basic paradox in Europe today is the recovery of full German sovereignty just as the West European economies move toward a single market and later a central banking system with some form of common currency. Yet the single market and a monetary union dominated by the Bundesbank will be net assets for Germany. The united German republic may well be able to attain just enough integration to serve the interests of German farmers, businesses, and services, just enough diplomatic coordination to provide Germany with a seal of European legitimacy, but also enough freedom of diplomatic maneuver to prevent unwelcome constraints in foreign policy and defense.

German governments in the past have remained extremely reluctant to move toward a West European defense system. They have preferred the certainties of NATO as long as the Cold War and the Soviet threat defined the Federal Republic's security condition. Indeed, they may still prefer NATO, with a central role for German armed forces and a convergence between Washington and Bonn on the role of nuclear weapons, to a West European scheme in which they would have to deal with the quite different nuclear doctrines of their two main partners. Nor has Bonn shown more than verbal enthusiasm for a coordinated diplomacy of the Community toward Eastern Europe. At the same time, the talk of German domination of the Community has been excessive: Interdependence in a single market means vulnerability, and influence in the EC has never been proportional to economic power, even for West Germany. But a united Germany could, if its leaders so desired, set limits beyond which they would not accept further constraints and burdens. Moreover, the cost of integrating East Germany is likely to reduce the amount of public assistance and private investment available for the rest of Eastern and Central Europe, as well as for assistance to the poorer countries of the Community and to countries overseas.

Fourth, neither France nor Britain is fully committed to the course suggested here. Under Thatcher, British policy shows both a strong suspicion of Germany and an obstinate unwillingness to deepen the Community in order to limit German freedom of maneuver. What a Labour government would do, given Labour's own divagations on defense, is hard to predict. French policy is not that much more consistent. Defense Minister Jean-Pierre Chevènement presents France as the only nation capable of and willing to fill the security void created by U.S. "fashions" and German antinuclear illusions; yet France's insistence on nuclear independence still impedes any explicit French guarantee to its neighbors or any statement that the deterrence of an attack on them is a vital French interest. Mitterrand, like Kohl, remains unwilling to move foreign-policy coordination from pure intergovernmentalism into a status comparable to that of the EC's foreign economic policy (with qualified majority decisions made by the Council and a major role played by the supranational Commission).

Fifth, the willingness and ability of Czechoslovakia, Hungary, and Poland to cooperate and deal jointly with the EC remains in doubt. Much will depend on their success or failure in creating the "strong, freely elected coalitions" that Garton Ash deems essential for gaining popular support for painful economic reforms. It is too soon to tell whether they will succeed, because the fragmentation of the initial anticommunist fronts should not be seen as proof of a fiasco.

Finally, we are no closer than before to a common West European policy and strategy for what is called in NATO jargon "out of area" issues. The French will continue to deem such issues beyond NATO's jurisdiction. The attempt to have the West European Union deal with Iraq's invasion of Kuwait is a small step forward, but there is no common direction yet. France (and Italy) have shown a desire not to alienate countries in which the government or the public sympathizes with Iraq. Britain is determined to reinvigorate its special relationship with the United States that had shown signs of fading in favor of a German-American one. And Germany remains reluctant to use force abroad. The tendency that prevailed during the oil crisis of 1973—when each of the West European governments had its own strategy and several preferred cutting separate deals with Arab suppliers—has not disappeared. A common policy toward the Arab world, including the Palestinian issue, would require overcoming the pull of historical traditions and the push of competing private interests.

Not only has there been minimal European cohesion, but the crisis also threatens to raise tensions between the United States and its allies. In the short term, America's willingness to deploy vast forces against Iraqi leader Saddam Hussein has allowed the West European countries once again to rely on America to protect their oil supplies. But given its economic difficulties, the United States has raised the old issue of burden sharing with a new sense of urgency (as well as an old sense of self-righteousness). While the allies have responded to the pressure by providing aid to Turkey and other countries hurt by the embargo on Iraq, many Americans have deemed this response insufficient. Their ire, focused largely on Germany, enlarges the cracks among West Europeans. Moreover, the allies' common front with Washington against Iraq conceals serious divergences, both within each of the West European nations and among them, about the possible use of force. That front could collapse should the United States resort to force without a clear provocation in order to expel Saddam from Kuwait or destroy his arsenal and evict him from power.

Thus the problems in constructing a new Europe remain immense. And yet the optimists who bet on historical discontinuity and discount the gloomy precedents of European folly may well turn out to be right. Europe has been a zone of security and stability because of the physical presence of superpowers armed with nuclear weapons. Although the decreasing involvement of those powers, and the retreat of nuclear weapons from the front row of European politics, may provoke the return of long-repressed rivalries and animosities, Europe is likely nevertheless to be, in a troubled world, a "security community," in the sense defined years ago by Karl Deutsch and his associates: an oasis of relative security, stability, and peaceful change.

One reason is a palpable "battle fatigue" about war and violence, especially among the younger generations. This is a factor in the relative restraint shown in the USSR by most of the major contenders in the debate over the country's future. Another is the attraction of prosperity. A priority of wealth over might and a choice of economic influence over territorial control have inspired the policies of Germany and the development of the EC, and their prosperity now attracts the countries to the East. Finally, although there is nothing inevitable about the further deepening of the EC, economic integration and the habit of cooperation among elites profoundly affect the conditions and scope of national independence. Indeed, the greatest peril in coming years may emanate from neither Germany nor the Soviet Union, but rather from an egoistic Western Europe itself—especially if economic growth should stop. Such an inwardly focused Western Europe might be intent only on protecting its assets, unwilling or incapable of substantively helping the developing countries to its south and the struggling nations to its east, and thus turning its fears of external "invasions" and chaos into a self-fulfilling prophecy. But with the help of good leadership, this peril, too, can be kept at bay.

Notes

1. "A Plan for the New Europe," Chapter 9 of this book.

12

Balance, Concert, Anarchy, or None of the Above

The evolution of a reunified but highly heterogeneous Europe, and of its relations with the two great powers that had divided and dominated it, continues to baffle commentators. The year of euphoria is over. The era of confusion and complexity is not. This essay attempts to examine, first, some general issues in the theoretical debate that has been raging for over a year; second, recent events and puzzles; third, the future of the European Community (EC) and of its relations with the countries of east central Europe—especially Czechoslovakia, Poland, and Hungary; finally, European-American relations, that hardy perennial. My main point is that Europe, thanks to a combination of democratic regimes, diffuse threats, and extensive institutionalization, may be on the threshold of a new kind of politics that goes beyond such traditional categories as balancing alliances or alignments, loose cooperative concerts, or junglelike anarchy. Whether Europe will cross this threshold, by extending and deepening its institutionalization, depends on the chief actors inside and outside the continent, but ultimately on the United States and Germany above all.

Issues in the Debate

The theoretical debate that has pitted John Mearsheimer's stark neorealist analysis[1] against his multiple critics has had one merit: it has exposed, in a concrete case, the sterility of neorealism. Mearsheimer's gloomy view of a Europe of states returning to its troublesome past results not from any empirical evaluation of present-day Europe, but from a theory—that of Kenneth Waltz—combining two sets of dogmas. One (the "structural" approach) views international politics as a condition of anarchy in which the distribution of military power in an endless contest for survival and security to a large extent dictates the moves of states. The other contrasts the notion of bipolar stability with the instability of multipolar systems (and describes the new Europe as part of an emerging multipolar system).

This second idea is debatable for several quite different reasons. It is not clear at all that the ideal types of multipolarity and bipolarity fit the current international system, with its different hierarchies of states, depending on the functional domain and the kind of power required in each. Nor is it clear that the end of the Cold War—that is, of highly conflictual bipolarity in the strategic realm—and the acute crisis of one of the superpowers mean the end of the military preponderance of the United States and the USSR. Moreover, even if one characterized the present condition of Europe and of the world as strictly multipolar, one would have to point out, with Stephen van Evera,[2] that multipolarity, in history, has ranged from very unstable to moderate; furthermore, as Raymond Aron showed many years ago,[3] the bipolar system that led to the Peloponnesian War was hardly stable. It is, indeed, impossible to understand the nature of an international system without looking at the character of the leading states. By refusing to do so in order to produce a more economical theory, Waltz and his disciples have not only failed to achieve greater rigor, but produced exactly what they charge their critics with: reductionism. Structure matters, of course. It limits, restrains, and creates both risks and opportunities for the policies of rational actors. But the key questions are: How much does structure matter, and what *is* structure?

Critics of Mearsheimer have, at times exhaustingly, shown how today's Europe and, particularly, Germany differ from the Europe and Germany of 1913 or 1938.[4] I will not do so once more here, but three points, important for both theory and empirical research, deserve emphasis. They all concern the conceptual poverty of neorealism.

First, neorealism's core concepts are misleading. It starts with the notion of anarchy as the key feature of the international political system. But if anarchy means only the absence of central power above the states, it tells us nothing of interest about the countless forms the game of international politics may take (depending, for instance, on who the actors are). If anarchy is supposed to mean a permanent struggle for power, a zero-sum game, the "state of war," then it accurately describes *some* international systems, but not others. (I once referred to two great theoretical and historical types: "state of war" and "troubled peace"; we may, in Europe, witness the birth of a third type altogether.)

The international system of neorealism is a system of states: self-propelled billiard balls endlessly attempting to knock one another out of the field of battle. The world system of today is—if I may refer to myself once more[5]—a complex game played at three levels: a world economy that creates its own rewards and punishments, and provides both opportunities and constraints for the players (not all of whom are states); the states themselves; and, increasingly, the peoples, who intervene insofar as they are unhappy with the effects, inequities, and inefficiencies of the world market, or with the inadequacy of established borders, or with the nature of their governments.

A concept of structure that focuses on the distribution of military power is doubly at fault. On the one hand, it obscures the fact that states, today, do not play only the traditional strategic-diplomatic game—in which such power is indeed either essential for survival and security or important as the gold reserve behind the paper currency of "soft power" used for influencing others, to borrow Joseph Nye's excellent concept.[6] States also play the modern games of economic interdependence. These require very different *kinds* of power, and place sharp limits on the *uses* to which such power can be put. On the other hand, in the traditional arena, the salience of military power depends on the nature of the threats to survival and security. Neorealism (like the cruder versions of realism) posits a kind of existential threat, built into the condition of statehood-in-anarchy. To be sure, theoretically, any independent actor can at any moment be threatened by a neighbor, rival, or partner. In real life, it makes a difference whether one is in, say, the Europe of rival alliances of 1914 and 1939, or the Europe of today, where threats are diffuse, often hard to identify, and not all manageable through armed might.

In the parched landscape of neorealism, states cope with their security dilemma by balancing power (rather than "bandwagoning"), so as to thwart the designs for domination great powers recurrently concoct. Three things are wrong here. One—which Stephen Walt discovered[7]—is that states often balance against perceived threats, rather than against objectively greater power. Also, the repertory of anti-imperial or anti-hegemonic moves, especially in multipolar systems, has often included bandwagoning coalitions around the status quo power, aimed at isolating the would-be hegemon, and at confronting him with overwhelming power should he attack. Finally, the present-day repertory in Europe contains original creations unheard of in neorealist circles. The EC could be seen as a shrewd attempt—an invention of the wily French in 1950 (after the failure of a "traditional" hostile approach to the solution of the "German problem")—to "balance" German power not by building a coalition *against* Germany but by bandwagoning *with* Germany. With respect to Soviet power, the Conference on Security and Cooperation in Europe (CSCE) is only one of the many ways in which, since 1970, western powers have tried to tame the threat from Moscow, not merely by military balancing, but by tying up the Soviet Union in a tangle of agreements that it would not be in Moscow's interest to break. This is, obviously, not classic balancing, and it goes way beyond the ill-defined European Concert of the nineteenth century.

Secondly, the refusal to consider what goes on within states is perhaps the most serious flaw of neorealism. Because independent states are all in the same situation of anarchy, Waltz has dismissed as secondary the differences which the nature of the political regime, the character of the domestic economy, and the specific features of the relations between state and society may make for foreign policy. Yet, international politics is the interplay between the constraints and temptations "structure" provides and the ambitions or needs of the actors. Often, purely domestic factors—interests, ideologies, coalitions, and so on—shape these ambitions and needs, and they can, if the actor is powerful enough, reshape the system itself. This is why the critics of Mearsheimer have underlined the differences between the second and third German Reichs, on the one hand, and the Federal Republic, on the other. Just because Germany remains in the middle of Europe, and is again more powerful (but *not* in all dimensions) than its neighbors, is there really no difference between the revisionist imperial Germany in clumsy search of a world role, the rabid revolutionary Germany of Hitler, and the satisfied, cooperative and world-shy new united republic?

My third point also refers to a glaring gap in neorealism. Just as neorealism downplays the effects of economic interdependence, especially among industrial societies and welfare states, it tends to dismiss the significance of institutional links among them. To be sure, actors continue to be deeply concerned with *national* security and the satisfaction of *national* economic and social goals. Especially in the realm of security, they may remain less concerned with joint gains than with ways of limiting the gains of rivals.[8] But the important fact in present-day Europe is the role of a bewildering array of overlapping institutions, within and through which states seek altogether joint benefits, the balancing of partners who are also potential adversaries, national advantage (by forming institutions in which they have the greatest freedom of maneuver or influence over those which others are better able to manipulate),[9] and a variety of insurance and reassurance policies. One can distinguish at least three important roles these institutions play.

First, within the EC, the density of institutionalized links and the structure of governance have blurred the distinction between domestic and foreign policy and between national sovereignty and federal (or community) powers. At the national level, while elected governments must continue to think first about internal priorities and the satisfaction of domestic interests, the gigantic mesh of the Community limits the extent to which the members can act autonomously and get away with it. Such attempts boomerang, as François Mitterrand's France discovered in 1982–1983, and Great Britain found repeatedly in the 1970s and 1980s. In other words, at that level, the existence of "Brussels" cannot help affecting the way in which governments (if not the Bundesbank) define the national interest and select the instruments and procedures for achieving their goals. At the level of "Brussels," there occurs what lawyers would call a *dédoublement fonctionnel:* the representatives and agents of states, in pooling state sovereignties for joint rules and directives, also behave as (incipient) European statesmen, while the "independent" members and civil servants of the Commission remain marked by their national origins and need to take national realities into account.

Second, in the realm of security, but also in economic affairs, institutions (such as the CSCE, the North Atlantic Treaty Organization [NATO], and the Western European Union [WEU]) and agreements (such as those that link associated states to the EC, and countries of the European Free Trade Association [EFTA] to the Community) reassure their members or signatories against fears that could, if left untended, turn a generally cooperative Europe into, once more, a continent of mutual suspicions and antagonistic precautions. The associates of the EC, left out of its decision-making process but affected by Community regulations and policies, thus, in a sense, receive compensation for being left out. And the various security organizations together reassure the Europeans about the continuing concern of the United States for their fate; reassure the Soviets about the peaceful designs of their neighbors; and reassure the Americans both about the ability and willingness of their European partners to play a major role in their own defense, and about the willingness of the Soviets to provide a fair amount of transparency, as well as to respect the agreements signed in the 1970s and 1980s. Thus, institutions can be life preservers that either save one from drowning or save one from having to drown others to survive. Even in the tragic case of Yugoslavia, the EC has—so far—played a moderating role.

Finally, even when these institutions do not play the roles described above, they can serve as magnets (or should one say: salutary mirages). The east central European states' hopes of becoming EC or NATO members, or of being somehow associated with such institutions is, for the time being, functioning as a substitute for the real thing. So are diplomatic exercises like the Pentagonale, and the negotiation of association agreements between the EC and Poland, Hungary and Czechoslovakia; so is a genuine but undernourished institution like the European Bank for Reconstruction and Development. To be sure, mirages do not last forever, and if the hopes should fade, the consequences might be grim. But precisely because the obstacles to full membership in the most significant and effective institutions are high, and the habits of cooperation among east central European states are weak, it is essential that some institutions serve as magnets, and others as first down payments.

A New Decade, a New Europe

To discuss both the internal problems of Europe and the relations of Europe with the United States, one has to begin with some remarks about what happened in the year since the settlement of the "German question."

The year was one of rude awakenings. The cost of the rehabilitation of former East Germany and the dimensions of the collapse of its economy have far exceeded the expectations of political leaders—and serve as a warning of what would happen if the barriers that separate the EC from the east central European states were suddenly to disappear. In these states, economic reform has been painful: The privatization of state-owned assets has raised innumerable difficulties. Furthermore the economic turmoil of the Soviet Union, on the one hand, and the noncompetitiveness of these countries' industrial goods in the West and the agricultural protectionism of the EC on the other, block export-led growth. As happened in western Europe after the end of World War II, the political coalitions that had formed for the restoration of democracy have begun to split. Yugoslavia has erupted into civil war. The crisis in the Persian Gulf divided the Community and dampened "Europhoria" in the EC; it showed that the old barrier between economic integration and diplomatic-strategic unity is as high as ever. The sudden turn of Gorbachev to the right was another nail in the coffin of utopia.

Yet, one ought to note also that several black dogs failed to bark. Those who feared the East would hold a fatal attraction for the new Germany, pulling it away from its western moorings (largely because of the way in which Chancellor Helmut Kohl bargained all by himself with Gorbachev) have been wrong; what one has witnessed instead is the *Drang nach Westen* of the east central Europeans. German-Polish relations, which Kohl's tactics about the border issue had strained, are on the mend. Despite endless collisions and some violence, and amid general confusion, the USSR has not disintegrated, and survived a major, dangerous, and desperate attempt to restore the old order of the hard-liners. The United States, while drawing on its forces in Europe for the war in the Gulf, has not shown any sign of withdrawing militarily from Europe.

The main uncertainties for the near future result from the difficulties the three main actors in this play have experienced. The Soviet Union, whose moves have, in the past, triggered the solidarity of the United States and of western Europe—a solidarity that made possible not only the containment of the old Soviet threat, but the liquidation of the Cold War on western terms—and, in the late 1980s, led to the reunification of Europe, is obviously going through a particularly stormy phase. In 1989 and much of 1990, a common hypothesis in the United States and in Europe was the gradual integration of the Soviet Union (engaged in a process of economic and political liberalization) into the world economy, into the system of world order the West preferred, and especially into the "common European home." This—as was confirmed by the "G7 + one" London Summit—is still the common goal. But the worsening internal turbulence, the resignation of Foreign Minister Eduard Shevardnadze and the signs of a hardening as well as of a growing influence of the military, have raised unexpected problems. For even if the USSR is in no condition to cause a "clear and present danger," to pose a new military threat in Europe, the fact that it still has troops in eastern Europe (and in former East Germany), and that eastern Europe still constitutes a kind of security no-man's-land, means that a switch from a policy of deliberate cooperation and concessions to a far more suspicious and demanding one could have serious repercussions in a variety of fields. Americans and Europeans have therefore to think about not one, but two unpleasant and unfathomable contingencies—not only the effects abroad of a possible internal disintegration of the last remaining (but only nuclear) multinational empire, but also those of a shift from accommodation to obstruction. Fortunately, the failure of the attempted coup of August 19 makes the latter danger far less likely.

The second main actor is Germany, about which highly contradictory fears have been expressed. Will the new independent Germany try to reduce the burdens and constraints imposed upon the Federal Republic by the EC and NATO and behave more like a national state again—à la Britain or France—or will it now dominate these institutions, thanks to its economic and financial might in one case, its geographic position and the shrinking of the American presence in the other? Would Germany, thanks to its surplus capital, fill the economic vacuum and increase its political influence in east central Europe, or would it become excessively self-absorbed and burdened by the costs of East Germany's absorption, thus stop being the financial engine of the Community, continue to shy away from any *Weltpolitik,* and devote all its energies and available funds to the East German disaster? Equally important are the following questions: Will Germany use a fraction of its economic and financial power not only—as planned—to get the Soviets out of its territory, but also to affect events within the USSR? Will Germany agree both to devote some of this power to the rehabilitation of east central Europe and to do so not as a purely national actor, but as a participant in a Community policy? Will Germany agree to play a larger role outside Europe—even if its allergy to a *military* role continues, after so many years of attempts at repudiating a militaristic past, with the warm endorsement of all its partners!—or will its reluctance to do so doom any attempt at an effective and comprehensive common diplomacy for western Europe? An active Community policy outside the continent may become even more necessary because of what could happen to the third major actor—the United States.

Despite (or perhaps because of) its military triumph in the Gulf, will America's activism abroad remain as great as it was in the past? Much will depend on the still unsettled aftermath of that victory in the Middle East itself. If the prestige of the United States in the area does not suffice to move the Arab-Israeli conflict toward its resolution, if Saddam Hussein succeeds in consolidating his grip on power, external frustration will strengthen the arguments of those who—either because they think the United States is in relative decline or because they want to *prevent* it from declining—believe that America must give priority to its vast domestic problems and concentrate on the weakened underpinnings of U.S. power in the world. During the Gulf war, Americans showed a classic ambivalence between their determination to set the goals and means all by themselves, and their desire to get as wide a participation by others as possible. What was new was not the desire for collective legitimation, but the actual financial dependence on allied contributions, as also the wide preference, which the polls reflected, for what the hero of *A Clockwork Orange* called a "quick in-out": liberating Kuwait, punishing Saddam—and coming home as fast as possible. The decision to leave the rehabilitation of east central Europe largely to the western Europeans and to refrain from large-scale economic aid to the USSR, and the plans for a drastic reduction of American forces in NATO, had already signaled not a retreat into isolationism, but a curtailment in the scope of activism. And yet diplomatic activism remains high.

The Features of the New Europe

If we turn now to an analysis of what might be called the European condition, we could define it as characterized by one ambiguity and two cleavages. The ambiguity, which has provoked almost as much theoretical speculation as the end of the Cold War and the return to multipolarity, lies in the nature of the European Community. After the old, quasi-theological debates (normative and theoretical) between supranationalists and champions of a "Europe of states," between functional federalists relying on the spillover effects of sectoral imbalances and traditionalists stressing the decisive role of interstate bargains, we now have a debate about the respective strength of the member-states and of the Community. Is the latter an emerging federation, with the old nation-states reduced to such domains as culture; atavistic political issues left over from the era of separate paths in the development of the modern state; and what William Wallace[10] calls the ability to shape the balance of national advantages within Europe and on global markets through education and social policy, training programs, research and development expenditures, partnerships with banks and firms, and direct taxation? This would obviously not be an insignificant residue: yet, it would mean that sovereignty would have been either transferred to the European level or pooled in areas as important as monetary policy, interest rates, trade, the movement of goods, people and capital, immigration, agriculture, public procurement. In other words, state autonomy and (insofar as deregulation prevails over the harmonization of existing regulations or the invention of new ones) state scope would have been sharply cut back in behalf of efficiency.[11] On the other hand, one can argue that the reinforcement of the nation-state and that of the Community continue to go together[12]—insofar as the policies and resources of the Community buttress the modern welfare state, redress regional imbalances in countries such as Italy and England, and help modernize the poorer members and provide an income to farmers (at the cost of vast surpluses); insofar as effectiveness, obtainable only at the "federal" level, is essential for the legitimacy of the national regimes; and insofar as no transfer of loyalty and allegiance from the nation-state to the Community has occurred.

Paradoxically enough, both arguments are correct. Both acknowledge the partial surrender of sovereignty. True, one chooses to stress the "federalizing process," the silent yet essential role of the European Court of Justice acting as if the Treaty of Rome were the equivalent of the Constitution of the United States for the Supreme Court, and the more recent moves away from intergovernmentalism in the political governance of the EC (qualified majority vote in the Council, dynamism of the Commission, popularly elected parliament). The other argument stresses the increasing importance of the intergovernmental European Council as the supreme body, and the continuing differences among the "formulas" for state-society relations or in the redistribution policies of the member-states—hence the absence of a single "European model," despite some visible differences between western Europe as an entity and Japan or the United States.[13] The distinction is more a matter of emphasis than a profound disagreement.[14] However, it entails, implicitly, two different forecasts.

To muddy the waters even more, I will state my own position. On the one hand, in analyzing the present, I am closer to the more "sober" view, which finds the nation-state transformed yet preserved, and does not see the relation between nation-state and EC as a zero-sum game (if only because much of what is "lost" by the states is "won" not by the Brussels embryonic state, but by the civil societies of Europe). On the other hand, I think that the federalizing process is likely to proceed, in the domain of the Single Market and in areas that—both because of the logic of sectoral integration and because of interstate bargains—are likely to become Community domains so as to help make the Single Market a reality. The two most important of these connected areas are monetary union and immigration. The former is obviously contentious, since good technical reasons justify either a *single* currency or a *common* currency added to the national ones, and sound political reasons explain why Germany's partners prefer a central bank that would, in contrast to the Bundesbank, define its policies (which affect investment, growth, and employment in their countries) from a Community point of view, whereas Germany prefers a central bank that would in effect be the Bundesbank. But it is most likely that the haggling will result in compromises and, with some delays, the establishment of European central banks and a final central bank. As for immigration, entry and naturalization policies differ profoundly by nation, but the common fears and headaches, and need to establish joint rules at the periphery as barriers within the Community fall, are enough to warrant common policies, or at least coordination of national policies.

The result is likely to be an entirely new entity in world affairs: not a traditional confederation, not a federal union, but a remarkable partnership both among states and between them and common institutions. A transfer (or rather a splitting) of loyalty might even begin if these institutions become more parliamentary and less technocratic. But as long as political life remains predominantly national, because issues of redistribution and national idiosyncrasies (such as, say, the *laïcité* issue in France or the different policies on naturalizing foreigners) dominate it, this transfer will remain limited.

The first of the two significant cleavages is that between the Single Market and its connected domains, on the one hand, and the realm of diplomacy and defense, on the other. A common EC foreign policy that would be more than a series of declarations and deplorations and a common security policy with its own effective institutions (that is, a WEU that would regain some of its original powers—for instance, in the realm of arms control—and would stop being, essentially, a debating society, but could mount common operations both within and outside Europe) seem to be as far away as ever. This is not for lack of agreement on identifying threats. The twelve Community members agree on the residual Soviet threat, caused by Soviet might, and by geography; the possible repercussions of either a disintegrating of the USSR or a return to authoritarian, militaristic rule in Moscow; the threats to oil supplies from the Middle East, on which western Europe has come to rely increasingly; the threat of masses of refugees either crossing EC borders or having to be repelled, should ethnic conflicts escalate within or among east and central European countries, or should unemployment and misery drive the poor out of these countries or out of the Maghreb; the threat of terrorism; and so forth. But a multitude of threats, many of which are hypothetical, concentrates minds far less than a single, unmistakable enemy, and a new security system would not necessarily contain or prevent several of the ones listed here. Above all, the major west European partners have divergent preferences about how to cope with each of these dangers.

Let us limit ourselves to Germany, Britain, and France, the three principal actors here. The first two have a strong preference for the status quo, and the third proposes to replace it with a scheme it probably knows that nobody else truly wants, so that it could—as usual—both preserve a basically comfortable status quo and appear as a foresighted lonely champion of European reform and of the common interest. The United Kingdom continues to see in NATO—that essentially Anglo-Saxon organization—the main institution for the security of Western Europe. Britain has interpreted the EC's disarray in the Gulf crisis as evidence of its impotence in world politics. While London would not object if the west European members of NATO formed a kind of caucus within it, and thus formulated plans for a rapid reaction force that would be able to operate in or outside Europe, the main purpose would be to reinforce NATO (including by extending its scope, via the WEU treaty, which is not limited to Europe). The fact that this notion was rejected by France made it possible for the United States and the United Kingdom to propose a new multinational force structure and a rapid reaction force within NATO, and thus guarantee that NATO will keep its predominance in Europe, and that "out of area" alliances will be ad hoc and interstate, as was the case in the Gulf, where Britain reestablished the "special relationship."

For Germany, the necessary and sufficient framework for its security would be a NATO that provides it with American guarantees, but also with prospects of a greater influence than it had when U.S. forces were abundant and nuclear weapons dominated NATO strategy, in combination with the CSCE. A west European security organization attached to the EC might either drive the Americans out, raise added fears of German preponderance, or put Germany under pressure for military interventions abroad. The Federal Republic has supported the idea of a common security discussion within the EC, but carefully refrained from giving it any substance.

It is France that has interpreted the Gulf crisis as evidence of the need for a diplomatic and security dimension for the Community, and the Europeans' disarray as the effect of its absence. France is now the champion of a reborn WEU linked to the EC, allied to the United States but not reduced to being a branch of or a "bridge" for NATO.[15] The French have objected to the idea of "double-hatted" European forces, at the disposal of both the WEU and NATO, because they see in such a formula a confirmation and an (out of area) extension of America's predominance. They suggest the possibility of contingency planning within an independent WEU, on the basis of a coordination of national forces. But so far, they have not indicated whether and how they would put their nuclear forces at the disposal of such an organization—a reluctance that does nothing to dispel German skepticism. To be sure, if France could get its partners to agree to a scheme that would, in effect, preserve its nuclear autonomy, coordinate west European conventional forces (thus giving France a kind of hold on Germany's), and plan out-of-area actions independently of the United States, Paris would have the best of all possible worlds. British, Dutch, and Portuguese resistance plus German indifference means the preservation of the status quo: a France protected by but not subordinated to NATO in Europe, with purely national nuclear forces and the capacity to act as a quasi-great power abroad when it deems an essential interest at stake. The French emphasize that a common foreign policy must precede a common security organization; this shows that Paris holds little expectation of an early change. Moreover, the divergences among EC members whenever they attempt to take a common diplomatic stand (as in the case of Yugoslavia, where some want above all to preserve the crumbling state's integrity, and others to stress the principle of self-determination) always tempt France to prefer acting as an independent player rather than endorsing the lowest common denominator.

Western Europe's three-way split during the Gulf crisis (with the United Kingdom and France acting as former colonial powers in the Middle East, Germany contributing only money, and the other powers participating in the blockade) and the failure to extend the EC's effectiveness into diplomacy and defense aggravate the second cleavage—between the former Europe of the free (EC and EFTA) and the former Soviet satellites (plus Yugoslavia and Albania). The contrasts are overwhelming, if one compares not only the degrees of ethnic turbulence, the economic and political institutions, the standards of living, and the fate of the environment, but also the degree of cooperation among states in each part of the continent and the amount of institutionalization. In one part, sovereignty is being dismantled and pooled; in the other, it is finally being regained. There has been no western, or west European, "Marshall Plan" for eastern and central Europe. The members of the Community have, deliberately or passively, put "deepening" ahead of "widening." (And while it is true that "widening" would oblige the Community to "deepen" in one respect—by reinforcing its central institutions—it would also dilute the EC's enterprise by introducing states that are quite incapable of accepting the rules and directives of Brussels without either committing economic and social suicide or obtaining countless special exemptions.) Thus the states of east central Europe remain—despite their preferences—outside the EC; outside the European Economic Area Brussels negotiated with the EFTA; and, deliberately, outside Mitterrand's confederation, which is still only a word, and which they dislike because—as the Prague *Assises* in June 1991 made clear—they fear that it would be no more than a "parking place" in which they would be left to linger.[16]

Many of the threats to security listed above affect the countries of the eastern half of Europe even more than the western half. But they remain a security no-man's-land, except for the valuable but limited functions entrusted to the CSCE, which is not a collective security system and has no forces at its disposal. The eastern states have come to appreciate NATO as a deterrent against a resurgent or recalcitrant USSR, and as a "container" of Germany; but they cannot become members of NATO and thus direct beneficiaries of its protection, given clear Soviet opposition to any extension of NATO eastward, and the probable reluctance of the U.S. Congress. Historical enmities or suspicions and stern Soviet warnings make military cooperation among these states doubly difficult. Indeed, one threat that hangs only over some of these states is the Soviet attempt to "sell" to them a bilateral treaty formula that would make it impossible for the signatories to join an alliance or grouping "directed against the other party." In this respect, the absence of a significant WEU, or "WETO," that could provide positive guarantees—or what François Heisbourg calls negative guarantees—to these countries[17] is as serious a hole in the tapestry as the failure to provide them with a substantial amount of public economic assistance in exchange for their mutual cooperation. But the EC suffers from overload, its members' resources are limited or otherwise engaged, and the United States suffers from untended domestic problems and costly Middle Eastern dilemmas. Here as elsewhere, the conflicting pulls of domestic political needs and external imperatives work at the expense of the latter. A revision of the EC's Common Agricultural Policy (CAP) that would allow farm products from east central Europe behind the CAP's wall would create serious troubles with French, German, and other west European farmers. A discussion of security guarantees to countries situated between the limits of NATO and the borders of the USSR would reopen, in the German body politic, some of the wounds of earlier clashes between security worriers (or warriors) and apostles or prophets of peace.

For the time being, an indispensable minimum ought to be done to soften the cleavage between east and west in Europe.[18] It is imperative that the EC devote at least as much energy and money to putting some substance into the idea (if not the controversial word) of confederation as it is putting into its relations with the Lomé countries or with the Maghreb. This would mean extending the European Economic Area beyond the EFTA, opening west European markets to the most exportable products of the east central Europeans, helping the Soviets to increase again their own imports from these countries, and promoting multinational cooperation in the East, for instance by dealing with issues not covered in (trilateral) association agreements, such as energy, transportation, and the environment.[19] And it would be useful to strengthen the still limited institutions of the CSCE, for instance—as the Czechs have suggested[20]—by extending the powers of the Vienna center for the prevention of conflicts over arms control and arms sales, and by creating peacekeeping forces that could intervene either preventively at the request of opposed parties or after a conflict. If the rule of unanimity, and the fear of some CSCE members (such as the Soviet Union and Yugoslavia) of foreign "interference" in domestic affairs, keeps reducing the CSCE's usefulness, the EC—through the WEU—should undertake such tasks. Beyond this minimum, a commitment by the members of the Community to "widening" once certain political and economic conditions are met in Czechoslovakia, Hungary, and Poland—with a target date of, say, the year 2000 or 2002—would be indispensable, and a promise by the members of the WEU to envisage in due course a system of collective security guarantees for European states from the Atlantic to the Soviet border would be useful. (Such a system would make more sense than the European Security Organization that Richard Ullman advocates including the United States and the USSR[21] and modeled on the WEU, for Moscow's and Washington's participation in a collective security system would raise far more questions—particuarly the question of credibility—than would their presence in a diplomatic and confidence-building scheme such as the CSCE.)

The European Policies of the United States

The United States, in 1989 and the first half of 1990, managed with great skill the withdrawal of Soviet power from eastern Europe and its effects. Washington succeeded in reconciling three potentially divergent concerns: preserving NATO, supporting Gorbachev (which required that the retreat not be turned into a rout), and backing Kohl (and therefore the West German drive for quick reunification). Both Kohl's concessions (on the nature and size of German forces, and on the financing of the Soviet exit from East Germany), and NATO's willingness to accommodate Soviet demands for some evidence of its "transformation" as a necessary condition for Moscow's acceptance of a unified Germany in NATO, played their part in the swift and elegant ballet. But having concentrated first on this delicate transition, then, after August 2, 1990, on the Gulf and finally on the issue of help to the Soviet Union, the U.S. government has had little time to think through the future of its relations with Europe.

In this realm, as well as in the EC, there is always the temptation of "disjointed incrementalism," especially in a period without earthquakes, with great uncertainties and diffuse issues. Yet, one ought to be able to do better, especially if one wants to incorporate this area into a global policy of world order. American ambivalence toward west European unity remains as strong as ever. On the one hand, Washington frowns on EC policies in agriculture, or air transport, or space, or on attempts to move toward a west European security system unsubordinated to NATO: too much European unity might be a threat. On the other hand, the resonance of the Mearsheimer analysis in Washington and the belief officials or ex-officials occasionally express that the European allies of the United States, left to themselves, would be once more divided or incompetent or impotent, or all three, and thus oblige America once more to save them, at great cost, from their own mess, suggest that Washington fears European disunity even more than European integration.

Yet both attitudes indicate that the American ambition of omnipotence has not been fully overcome; recent celebrations of a post-Gulf "unipolar world" may well reinforce it. But while it is true that only the United States can mount and win a Gulf-like expedition, even the troublemakers in a world that is full of them are unlikely to provide many opportunities for such displays of mastery; certainly Europe does not appear to be a fertile ground for them. Above all is the nagging issue of American resources for activism abroad, and the question of where the long-term interest of the United States lies: in concentrating, for a while, on internal repairs, or in more benign neglect of the domestic issues in favor of grand diplomacy. Finally, even if one believes that the latter will remain an imperative, the conditions of world politics impose on the United States a new conception and style of leadership: it will have to be multilateral, institutionalized, and in partnership with others. The analysis presented here suggests that the surest way of preventing a return to the past is to favor a continuing institutionalization of European politics, so as to provide for more cooperation, change the context and reduce the intensity of inevitable conflicts, and affect the way in which states define their interests. And this means both accepting—indeed, embracing and exploiting—the redundancy of institutions (instead of attempting to rationalize and streamline them) and trying to overcome the cleavages analyzed above.[22]

For the sake of convenience, I will examine three areas of American-European relations. The first is the traditional domain of *transatlantic relations.* Two main issues matter. One is the management of unavoidable economic friction; the main actors are the United States and the EC. A compromise over agriculture, in the current round of General Agreement on Tariffs and Trade (GATT), is necessary; it is also difficult. The initial positions of both sides were extreme and unrealistic. The Sisyphean nature of the present CAP and the policy's deleterious effects on the peasants of poor countries outside the EC make it untenable in the long run. But domestic constraints will slow down reform; a calendar of change, entailing balanced concessions on both sides, might be the best outcome. Over the issues of access of industrial goods and services from the United States into the Single Market, the general tendency of Community policy, under German and British pressure, has been toward liberalization, away from "fortress Europe." Complications may come from various European resistances to Japanese implantation, but there have also been instances of European-Japanese collaboration and compromises, and European calls for Japanese investments in Europe.[23] The trend seems to be as ambiguous as that in the relationship of the nation-state to the EC: the Community is likely to be both a formidable regional bloc (marked by a constant increase in intra-EC trade) and an international actor, inviting Japanese and American capital in.

The other traditional transatlantic issue requires a drastic turnaround by Washington. The U.S. government is clinging to the dogma of NATO's preponderance in the field of European security; it has sent three warnings in recent months to the members of the Community, telling them that the discussions on a common diplomacy and defense that President Mitterrand and Chancellor Kohl have called for should not weaken or compete with the Atlantic Alliance, but, on the contrary, should strengthen it. The United States has obtained from its partners a recognition of NATO's preeminence. Little has changed, it seems, since the "year of Europe," when Kissinger told the Europeans to subordinate their common concerns to those of the Alliance. The old American ambivalence is particularly manifest in this domain. Washington would like its partners to speak in a single voice, as long as they repeat what the United States tells them. It encourages a revival of the WEU—as long as the latter is a mere subdivision of NATO. This reaction of distrust—in an area where the convergence of interests across the Atlantic is overwhelming—is attributable in part to the fears of European inefficiency and squabbling once the American presence and guidance are removed, to the rather different fear of being unwillingly affected and committed by allied policies unless Washington can be involved in their very elaboration, and to the desire to preserve the superiority of the one common institution that the United States clearly dominates.

It is, however, a shortsighted policy. From a cynical point of view, one might argue that a less pinched American stand, one that would encourage the west Europeans to put some substance into the WEU and to link it directly to the EC, would really be cost-free, since the west Europeans—for the reasons mentioned above—are unlikely to go very far! If, on the contrary, one believes that such American encouragement might actually remove a major reason for Germany's reluctance toward the WEU (the fear of antagonizing and pushing out the United States) and propel the British toward Europe in the realm of defense just as earlier administrations had prodded it toward the Common Market, this redefinition of the security relationship ought not be feared but welcomed. This is so because, insofar as all the European governments—including, most ardently, those of east central Europe—demand the presence of American troops in western Europe (and the Soviets themselves may see it as a lesser evil than an unchecked Germany), the North Atlantic Treaty and Alliance would in no way be imperiled. Moreover, what threatens NATO is not a "rival" European entity, but the course of events: the decline of America's physical presence and of the nuclear component in NATO's strategy risk turning the integrated command into an empty shell—even if the Supreme Allied Commander in Europe (SACEUR) remains an American. And the fading away of the threat that justified so extraordinary a structure in peacetime will contribute to its erosion. It is difficult to see where, "in area," the new rapid reaction and multinational forces will be used, short of a Soviet attack, and "out of area" divisions among the allies are likely to inhibit their use as much as in the past. As a result, one may well—in the absence of a west European entity—end up with a de facto alliance between a small U.S. contingent (backed by the U.S. strategic nuclear arsenal and British-based Forward Based Systems), a conventional "NATO" under the domination of a Germany for which military-security concerns are no longer preeminent, and an autonomous France: not an optimal result. A revived WEU would entail an end of French separatism and oblige the French government to put its defense and strategy in harmony with its economic policy. It would also both *encadrer* Germany and oblige it to think seriously about defense.

Moreover, the Europeans themselves will best handle many of the threats Europe will face—not merely the nonmilitary threats represented by hordes of refugees, but also the possible fallout from interstate or intrastate conflicts in the eastern half of the continent, or threats the Soviet Union could pose to the security of states in that half. The very diffusion of threats ought to make the west Europeans the main actors in the realm of security now. The alternative to a common west European policy to deal with these problems is not a NATO policy, it is paralysis or fractured reactions; and as French officials have warned, the alternative to a west European security entity—allied with but not subordinated to the United States—is not the pre-1989 NATO, but a renationalization of defense policies. Double-hatting of national units from west European countries, assigned both to NATO and to this entity, ought to be acceptable, given a clear division of labor between the NATO and the European commands—that is, a clear division of issues between these institutions. Otherwise, the United States will soon experience the old European fear of being dragged into conflicts against its preferences, and the French (and other west Europeans) will fear American vetoes of moves that would be in the interest of the Europeans. NATO may still be "the only game in town" today, given the WEU's paleness and the CSCE's nature. But changing conditions make it wise to plan for a new game.

The second set of issues is *the relationship of the Atlantic allies to the East* (eastern Europe and the USSR). The allies need to coordinate their policies toward the Soviet Union, so as to balance the desirable pressure for democratization and for a transformation of the decaying centralized empire into a voluntary union, with the equally necessary support to a central government that is, for all its flaws, still preferable both to the old Stalinist model and to disintegration. Economic assistance should be far better planned than it has been until now: initiatives have been national and sporadic; the United States and the EC ought to prepare them jointly (this would be one way of preventing an eventually too large or autonomous role for Germany here). The same ought to be done—but on a larger scale—to help the three countries of east central Europe; the west Europeans will have to provide the main initiatives and resources, and the Marshall Plan can serve as a model. As for security assurances to these countries, it will also be easier for the west Europeans to provide them than for NATO (see above)—another reason why the United States should encourage a west European defense entity.

The third domain is that of *American-European relations outside the continent.*

If we mean what we say when we talk about a new world order, this is clearly a realm of the highest importance—especially as, paradoxically, the restraints that the superpowers imposed on their clients to avoid collisions (restraints resulting not from the dubious virtues of bipolarity but from the risks of nuclear catastrophe) are not likely to be effective any longer, and the loss of influence and power of the Soviet Union reduces the benefits that the cooperation of the former chief rivals might otherwise have brought.

In some ways, the most difficult issue here is the management of out-of-area crises. One of the partners has the habit of a world role, but decreasing resources. The European "partners" have even more limited ones, because the military establishments of the west European countries are not well geared to large- or even medium-scale external engagements, or, as in Germany's case, are constitutionally prevented from committing themselves. Moreover, disagreements about goals often divide the Americans from the west Europeans, as well as split the latter. In the short run, crisis management will remain a matter of ad hoc coalitions. In the long run, it will—again—be in America's interest to encourage the west Europeans to coordinate their foreign policies and to plan jointly, through a defense entity, possible interventions abroad. The fact that both NATO and the CSCE limit their scope to the continent contributes to the Germans' tendency to restrict their military concerns to the European theater and thus, as Heisbourg notes,[24] condemns the west Europeans, out-of-area, to purely national, low-key actions by only some of them, whereas, as he puts it, the EC's famous principle of subsidiarity would require a collective reaction at the level of the Community.

If crisis management—for many other reasons, as well—risks being unsatisfactory, prevention will have to become the key to world order. This will require a break with the past in two vital respects. The United States, the USSR, and the Europeans will have to coordinate their policies so as to put an end to their exports of advanced military technologies (or of technologies capable of receiving lethal military applications) and to reduce their exports of more traditional, but potentially just as disruptive military equipment. The immediate post-Gulf record is far from encouraging, for two powerful factors converge on "politics as usual": domestic constituencies of businesses and workers (including, for instance, in Czechoslovakia) and the traditional "game" of rewarding one's regional friends. The CSCE could serve as the framework for such an effort, inspired by Cocom. In addition, perhaps under UN auspices, the same countries ought to take part in the establishment of regional arms control and inspection regimes. But dealing with weapons is not enough. A much bigger effort will be necessary to resolve disputes before they erupt into violent crises. What can be done in eastern Europe under CSCE or, as in the Yugoslav case, EC auspices needs to be done, in other troubled parts of the world, under UN auspices, but with the United States, Japan, the USSR, and the west Europeans serving as the secular arm or steering diplomatic group for the UN. Once again, this raises the issue of the European partner.

The problem of European-American relations risks becoming not the tragedy of a return to the cataclysmic past, but the drama of a political vacuum, despite the somewhat chaotic abundance of overlapping institutions. America, the dominant partner of the recent past, may turn more inward; a European partner remains to be constructed. Just as its plate was filled by the menu of the Single Market, the EC has been assaulted by new needs and demands, both for functional and for geographic expansion. Conceived on the assumption of a stable division of Europe, with a continuing if moderated Cold War, the west European *relance* of 1984–1987 absorbs the bulk of the members' energies, just when everything else starts moving all around them. The real threat to Europe's dream of peace and democracy, vintage 1989, is not the neorealist nightmare of collisions among ambitious major actors, but economic chaos, political regression away from democracy, ethnic violence, and a void in cooperation. The real European question mark for the future is not balancing, concert, or anarchy—notions that are all conceptually inadequate—nor is it whether the nation-state in western Europe will survive. It is whether the pooled central power of the Community will be sufficiently strengthened to accomplish two goals: create effectiveness in the realms (defense and diplomacy) where either national autonomy has remained strong, but actual policies based on it have produced more illusions than results, or it has been abandoned to an extra-European big brother whose role is now far less justified; and engage and gradually absorb those countries of east central Europe that would otherwise become disaster areas.

A positive answer requires new policies everywhere: in Washington and Brussels, in London and Paris and Bonn (or Berlin). But the most decisive players—or nonplayers—will be the United States and Germany: Washington, because what is needed is, at last, a shift from primacy to world order, Bonn (or Berlin) because either the temptation of acting again as an ordinary great national power—a temptation that Germany has strenuously resisted so far—or the more likely self-indulgence in self-absorption (Germany behaving as a large Switzerland) would have fateful effects. In the first case, the patient institutional buildup would stop and unravel; in the second, the new 1992 Europe would fall far short of its global challenges and duties. In neither case would we be back in the 1910s or 1930s. But the progress toward a new kind of politics would be thwarted, and the more benign forms of traditional international politics (such as concert and balancing, which anyhow are cousins) might then reassert themselves. Presently, French officials gloomily point to an American will-to-dominate, and to signs of a new German will-to-autonomy. I am more optimistic about Germany than about the United States, whose capacity for long-term planning—manifest in 1947–1949—has suffered a long eclipse, for reasons in which government fragmentation and global complexity play a large part. Still, the time has come for a new bargain, among the leading west European states, and between them and the United States, if they want to shape the future instead of merely letting it happen.[25]

Notes

1. John Mearsheimer, "Back to the Future: Instability in Europe after the Cold War," *International Security*, vol. 15, no. 1 (Summer 1990), pp. 5–56.

2. Stephen van Evera, "Primed for Peace: Europe after the Cold War," *International Security*, Vol. 15, no. 3 (Winter 1990/91), pp. 7–57.

3. Raymond Aron, *Peace and War* (New York: Doubleday, 1966), ch. 5.

4. See the correspondence provoked by Mearsheimer's article, in *International Security*, vol. 15, no. 2 (Fall 1990), pp. 191–199, and vol. 15, no. 3 (Winter 1990/91), pp. 216–222; Stanley Hoffmann, "The Case for Leadership," Chapter 11 of this book; and Richard Ullman, *Securing Europe* (Princeton, N.J.: Princeton University Press, 1991), pp. 139ff.

5. Stanley Hoffmann, "A New World and Its Troubles," in Nicholas X. Rizopoulos, ed., *Sea-Changes: American Foreign Policy in a World Transformed* (New York: Council on Foreign Relations, 1990), pp. 274–291.

6. Joseph Nye, Jr., *Bound to Lead* (New York: Basic Books, 1990), ch. 6.

7. Stephen Walt, *The Origins of Alliances* (Ithaca, N.Y.: Cornell University Press, 1987).

8. See the conclusion of Louise Richardson and Celeste Wallander, "A Comparison of British and Soviet Adjustments to Structural Change in Europe" (Paper for the ISA meeting of March 1991.)

9. For instance, in the Yugoslav crises of June–July 1991, France, Britain, and Italy favored the EC, Germany—at first—the CSCE; France, on the issue of global restraints on arms sales opposes a role for the G-7 and prefers the UN Security Council; the Czechs prefer access to the EC, to Mitterrand's Confederation, etc. . . .

10. William Wallace, "The Changing Role of the State in Western Europe." Paper presented at the seminar, "Europe in the 1990s," sponsored by the Economic and Social Research Council and the Royal Institute for International Affairs; London, March 15, 1991.

11. See Wolfgang Wessels, "The Growth of European Integration and the West European State," Bonn, March 1991.

12. Alan Milward, "Historical Elements of a Return to a Comprehensive Theory of Integration." Paper presented at the seminar, "Europe in the 1990s," sponsored by the Economic and Social Research Council and the Royal Institute for International Affairs, London, March 15, 1991.

13. See Jean-Claude Casanova, "Bourgeoise et Homogène," in Dominique Schnapper and Henri Mendras, eds., *Six Manières d'être Européen* (Paris: Gallimard, 1990), pp. 220–240.

14. See Robert Keohane and Stanley Hoffmann, eds., *The New European Community* (Boulder, Colo.: Westview Press, 1991).

15. See Claire Tréan, "France—OTAN: Le Chat et la Souris," *Le Monde*, May 2, 1991, pp. 1 and 3.

16. Mitterrand undercut his own scheme by: a) stating just before the *Assises* that full membership for Poland, Hungary, and Czechoslovakia in the EC would take dozens of years, and b) proposing, at first, a Confederation that would include the Soviet Union but not the United States. Havel and his central and eastern European colleagues made it clear: a) that the United States (and Canada) should also be included, and b) that, in such a case, the CSCE sufficed!

17. François Heisbourg, "From a Common European Home to a European Security System," see Chapter 2 of Gregory F. Treverton ed., *The Shape of the New Europe*, (New

York: Council on Foreign Relations Press, 1991), pp. 35–58. Heisbourg suggests that, for instance, France would promise not to use Hungarian territory for military purposes, provided no other country uses it in such a manner.

18. See the excellent suggestions of six west European foreign policy institutes in *The Community and the Emerging European Democracies,* by Gianni Bonvincini et al, June 1991 (published in English by RIIA).

19. See Elizabeth Guigou, "Les Européens et Leur Destin," *Politique Internationale,* no. 51 (Fall 1991), pp. 313–328, at p. 318.

20. *Le Monde,* May 5–6, 1991, p. 4.

21. Ullman, *Securing Europe,* ch. 4.

22. See Frédéric Bozo and Jérôme Paolini, "L'Europe entre elle-même et le Golfe," *Politique étrangère,* Spring 1991.

23. See Michael Borrus and John Zysman, "Industrial Strength and Regional Response: Japan's Impact on European Integration" (Paper for the Council on Foreign Relations project on 1992 and the Shape of Europe, March 1991).

24. Heisbourg, Chapter 2 of this book, pp. 35–58.

25. For similar conclusions, see Helen Wallace, "Which Europe for Which Europeans?" Chapter 1 of Gregory F. Treverton, ed., *op cit.,* pp. 15–34; and Jenonne Walker, "Security in Post-confrontation Europe," *Beyond the Cold War: Current Issues in European Security,* no. 3 (Woodrow Wilson International Center for Scholars, Washington, D.C., 1990).

13

Goodbye to a United Europe?

1

When the leaders of the twelve members of the European Community signed the Treaty on Monetary and Political Union in Maastricht in December 1991, the project of a United Europe, which began in 1950 under the inspiration of Jean Monnet, seemed to be making spectacular progress. A single currency, a common monetary policy, and an independent central bank were to be established in stages before the end of the century, thus bringing to its logical conclusion the design for a single European market that had been proposed in the mid-1980s.[1] The powers of the Community were also to be extended to deal with a broad range of policies concerning health, consumer protection, the environment, crime, immigration, labor relations, diplomacy, and defense. Even though Britain had refused both to accept the new social provisions of the treaty and to join the full monetary union, agreement on so vast an expansion of community activities was hailed as a great success.

Yet the signing of the Maastricht treaty marked the beginning of a serious crisis, which has led to a new wave of pessimism about Europe's future, both on the Continent and in the US. The pessimism comes from a variety of different troubles. Every Western European economy is stagnant, the result both of the worldwide recession and the huge costs of German unification. Partly as a result, the main European governments are concentrating on their domestic difficulties and programs. Two other sources of the European malaise may be more difficult to deal with in the long run. One is often referred to as the Community's "democratic deficit," the much-resented distance between the bureaucracies that administer the EC and the European voters who are affected by it. Perhaps the deepest problem of all concerns the relation of the traditional nation-state to a new United Europe.

The ambitious plans that are now falling apart were the product of another recession—the one that hit Western Europe after the oil crisis of 1973 and resulted in years of "Europessimism," fluctuations in exchange rates, and stagnation in the development of the Community. Even Britain's entry into the EC didn't help, since the British spent, in effect, ten years—between 1974 and 1984—renegoti-

301

ating the terms on which they had been admitted. In 1978, the French President Valéry Giscard d'Estaing and the West German Chancellor Helmut Schmidt took the initiative to set up a European Monetary System (EMS) that would create monetary stability by narrowing the range of exchange rate fluctuations among the members' currencies. This seemed one of the more striking European successes of the postwar period. Devaluations and reevaluations of currency were not ruled out, but they became increasingly rare. Britain, which had at first stayed out, finally joined the EMS in 1990. The EMS was to be the basis on which a full monetary union, ultimately with a common European currency—an objective toward which Jacques Delors, the president of the EC's Commission, had been working for years—was going to be built.

Progress toward monetary union, as defined at Maastricht, required that the members' economic and fiscal policies would converge with regard to inflation, interest rates, deficits, debts, and currency stability. The treaty set up guidelines that participants in the enterprise were to meet, and, as has been the case during the 1980s, these corresponded to the preferences and policies of the German Bundesbank. Maastricht was supposed to continue the process by which both Britain and (after the grand reversal of the Socialists' economic policy in 1983) France pursued economic strategies, including high interest rates, that aimed at monetary stability and at reducing inflation. Even when the American recession began to reach Europe, these policies continued.

But German reunification, beginning in 1989, destabilized the EMS. Chancellor Kohl's decision to establish a one-to-one exchange rate between the Deutsche mark and the Ostmark and to accept wage parity between the workers of the Federal Republic and the far less productive workers of the former Democratic Republic led to enormous reductions in income, employment, and production in the East, and obliged the German government to transfer huge amounts of public funds there. Kohl's reluctance to raise taxes resulted in large borrowing and a big deficit; the rise in Germany's inflation (which had preceded unification) worsened. The independent Bundesbank reacted by raising its interest rates by six percentage points in five years in order to combat inflation. But this obliged Germany's partners in the EMS to raise their own interest rates in order to prevent an outflow of funds from their countries to Germany and to preserve the stability of their own currencies, the result being lower economic growth and higher unemployment.

In Britain and France, politicians, economists, and businessmen (such as Jacques Charvet, the head of Peugeot, in France) began to question the wisdom both of sacrificing growth to sustain artificial exchange rates and of following the dictates of the Bundesbank, which had become the de facto European Central Bank, yet acted only according to its view of the German national interest. Also the international money markets, computerized and deregulated, began to sell gigantic amounts of currencies that appeared overvalued, such as the peseta, the lira, and the pound. The central banks that tried to defend their currencies by purchasing large amounts of them on the market simply did not have the reserves to succeed in doing so. The daily turnover in currency markets reached $900 billion, while the reserves of the G7 nations amounted to less than a third of this sum.

In early September 1992, the European governments failed to agree on an official currency realignment that would have slightly adjusted the value of currencies in relation to the market. The French objected because of possible negative effects on the difficult campaign to get the French public to vote for the Maastricht treaty, the British because they insisted, in vain, that the Germans reduce interest rates. This led to the uncontrolled devaluation of the pound, the lira, and the peseta, and to Britain and Italy's withdrawal from the EMS after the Bank of England's failure to support the pound even after spending half of its reserves.[2]

The EMS is not dead. With much help from the Bundesbank, the French were able to resist the markets' onslaught on the franc, and thus to keep their currency within the margins of fluctuation required by EMS. As long as EMS is alive, there is a chance for monetary union, but it is clear that Britain, now embarked on a policy of reduced interest rates and monetary autonomy, will not rejoin it in the near future. Nor will Italy, Greece, and Spain, among others, meet the "convergence criteria" set up by EMU. There will be increasing pressure on the Bundesbank, particularly from the French, to lower German interest rates so that these rates can be lowered in France and elsewhere, and the way opened to more growth and reemployment.

If the Bundesbank resists French pressures, the French politicians who argue against any further sacrifice of the French economy on the altar of monetary stability will gain influence. Moreover, the entire experience has strengthened the position of those in Germany who oppose the Maastricht treaty, believing that the dilution of the power of the Bundesbank in a European Central Bank, accompanied by a disappearance of the German national currency, would be a mistake. Thus, even a European Monetary Union limited to the stronger currencies among the twelve EEC nations remains at the mercy of the recession. If the recession prolongs the agony of East Germany's merger with West Germany, which is the cause of the Bundesbank's reluctance to lower interest rates, and one of the causes of the unemployment crisis in France,[3] the chances of organizing a European Monetary Union will be slim. But should the Bundesbank become more lax, Germany's own ability to meet the criteria for economic convergence would be even more compromised. The great step toward a monetary union planned at Maastricht now appears to have been premature.

What the financial crisis has shown is the impossibility of bringing about monetary union without a close coordination of national economic policies—and the fact that, at present, there is a huge discrepancy between a single, deregulated market set up and monitored by the Community and the tax, labor, monetary, and other economic policies that are still in the hands of the national governments. When these governments are determined to pursue the same type of economic policy—as was the case of France and Germany in the 1980s—the EC can make progress; but when the governments are incapable of pursuing the kind of policy preferred by the Bundesbank (as with Italy) or rebel against it (as with Britain), such progress stops.

Resuming the quest for monetary union will require that the governments of Western Europe put their respective economic houses in order. But if they concentrate on politically difficult domestic issues, such as lowering unemployment, they are likely to give less attention to all the other aspects of European unification, and indeed to become all the more impatient with them.

The governments of the EC's "big four" have all turned inward. Of these countries, Italy has always been the most strongly and sentimentally enthusiastic about European unification—but also the least capable of enforcing the rules and directives of the EC because its government has been so disorganized and inefficient. Its regional institutions are sometimes more competent, but Italy is the one country whose regions have no representation in Brussels.[4] Moreover, the current apocalyptic crisis in Italian politics, which has undermined the entire postwar political leadership and the constitutional system, will only reinforce the need to concentrate on domestic matters. To shift from an increasingly corrupt system of unaccountable public enterprises and patronage to a new, reformed Italian administration will be painful and tricky. Under prodding from a public that has long been complicit and cynical but finally has become fed up, such a shift will have to be carried out by the very people who have become targets of popular wrath, the beneficiaries of the old order. A successful economic reform might allow Italy to rejoin the European Monetary System and to put itself in shape for the European Monetary Union—but this would be an immense task, in view of Italy's debts and deficit.

The British concentration on domestic affairs and hostility to Europe extends beyond John Major's government, which decided that British growth must prevail over European monetary cooperation. Along with most conservatives, Major believes that the Thatcherite victory over trade unions has to be protected from the proposed EC labor charter with its liberal provisions on such matters as union rights and powers and factory conditions, which are abhorrent to British employers.

The genteel resentment of Britain's postwar decline—relative not only to France but even to Italy—which was so evident in the 1960s and 1970s, and which had been among the sources of Mrs. Thatcher's appeal, has not disappeared. It has only been supplemented by an awareness of the dark sides of Thatcherism (the gap between the richer and poorer parts of England) and of its failures (in industry or education), and by the discrediting of once sacred institutions, including the monarchy. None of this has made the British keener to participate in the EC. Nostalgia for Britain's "finest hour," in 1940, and for the days of empire, is still there. The special concessions Major had obtained at Maastricht, as well as the monetary crisis of last September, seem only to have strengthened the British tendency to want to have the advantages of being in the European "club" and the single market, but only as long as they do not clash with American policies and the British sense of distinctiveness. Britain's enthusiasm for extending the EC to the newly liberated countries of Eastern Europe derives largely from the old and constant British desire to turn the Community into little more than a free trade area with as few common rules and policies as possible.

The new French government has, by contrast, renewed France's strong commitment to the EC, to the European Monetary Union, and to a common European security system. The prime minister, Edouard Balladur, by his statements and appointments has subtly constrained his "boss" Jacques Chirac, who is expected to run for president in 1995, and has been known to veer opportunistically from statements of shrill nationalism to proclamations of good Europeanism. Balladur's mission is to manage the economy, with its three million unemployed, in such a way as not to undermine Chirac's chances in 1995, and this concern will determine his attitude toward the EC. If the EC can be used to provide tangible benefits for France (a reduction of interest rates by the Bundesbank, for instance), it will be applauded. If it tries to impose sacrifices on French farmers, because of the preference that most EC members (including Germany, if not German farmers) have for a GATT agreement on freer agricultural trade, even at the expense of a very small part of the French peasantry, the EC will be resisted. It is most unlikely that the government will accept a compromise that would cost Chirac, a former minister of agriculture, the votes of France's farmers, most of whom vote for the right but were against Maastricht.

As for Germany, it will hold many elections next year—local, state, and federal—and its government will have to deal above all with an electorate whose mood has been soured by the most serious recession in the postwar era, by the flood of refugees who have sought asylum (and against whom the growing far-right movements have turned their violence), and by the nasty revelations of the Stasi files in the East, which have worsened the climate of suspicion and resentment. The psychological gap between the West Germans, proud of their economic performance and of their ability to confront and repudiate the Nazi past, and the East Germans, accused of having bad working habits and a bad conscience as well, has not been closed. The many insecurities that afflict the public of a country whose internal tensions have, in the past, spelled trouble for much of Europe, are now central concerns of Germany's tired and divided government, which has only one year and a half to go. The government's main party, the Christian Democrats, has been slipping badly in the polls and in votes in state elections.

The overriding need felt by leaders throughout Western Europe to concentrate on domestic difficulties and to try, during a time of economic troubles, to cope with widespread public impatience with politicians, their stilted language, unfulfilled promises, and scandalous behavior, helps to explain why the Maastricht treaty may become a dead letter. So do the decline, except in England, of "established" parties (in France last month, the Socialists and the moderate right got only 57 percent of the vote) and the rise of extremism in Italy, France, and Germany. Instead of the common European policy on asylum called for by the end of 1993, new German legislation unilaterally declares that refugees who come to Germany from its eastern and southern neighbors do not deserve asylum.

As for a common European foreign policy and defense, nothing has done more to tarnish the prestige of the EC than the disastrous tragedy in Yugoslavia. The most "activist" of the EC members, Germany, prematurely pushed for recognition of Slovenia and Croatia. Germany has been the most indignant about Serbian crimes in Croatia and Bosnia, while remaining the one state that is constitutionally unable to fight outside its borders. (Hence the limited significance of the Franco-German Army Corps.) Those countries that can fight, such as Britain and France, have had no desire to go beyond humanitarian involvement. The EC's impotence and its eagerness to dump Yugoslavia on the UN reflect, once again, its members' overriding domestic political preoccupations.

2

Such a conclusion may seem unfair, since diplomacy and defense, unlike agriculture or the single market, are still matters in which the EC members can act only when they are unanimous. But here we come to the third kind of crisis. The machinery of the EC has become increasingly complex and opaque. One of the reasons why the majority of the Danes and almost half of the French said no to the Maastricht treaty in 1992 was that the text was nearly incomprehensible. Drafted after the heads of state and government had left Maastricht, it was written by and for lawyers and bureaucrats and required legal experts to explain it.

The more clarification was provided, the more it became apparent that with the extension of the Community's competence came a vast tangle of procedures—cases in which decisions can be taken by a two-thirds majority, cases requiring unanimity, cases in which a two-thirds majority can decide because of a unanimous decision to allow it to do so—creating an almost impenetrable maze. Few Europeans really understand how the EC works. It has a dense network of committees on which bureaucrats serve both as national agents and European civil servants, and an extremely cumbersome machinery. The Commission, charged with taking initiatives and applying decisions, is made up of supposedly independent leaders appointed by the members. The Council, composed of government representatives, is a legislative body, quite distinct from the Parliament in Strasbourg, whose discussions, budgetary deliberations, and "co-decisions" on some matters with the Council are barely comprehensible to the public.

Hence the widespread lament about a "democratic deficit." The Council is the chief legislator, while the popularly elected Parliament has only very limited powers. The Commission, set up by the governments but basically not accountable to them or to the Parliament, is the main organ for taking initiatives and drafting regulations. The almost three hundred measures that were needed to create by 1993 a single market for goods, services, capital, and people were drafted by the Commission, submitted by it to the Council, which turned them into three hundred directives and regulations; these were then discussed by the Parliament, and referred to the member countries for enforcement by the national bureaucracies.

Such a setup is obviously very different from that of a federal democracy. During the negotiations over political union, not only the UK and France but the EC Commission opposed any dramatic increase in the Strasbourg Parliament's powers. The UK and France wanted, of course, to preserve the Council's preeminence because they can use it to assert national interests. But why was the Commission hostile to giving more power to the Strasbourg Parliament as well? The parliamentarians were said to be given to ceaseless, irresponsible talk. But how can they be expected to be anything else if they have no real powers?

Even more serious is the problem of the relations between the EC's institutions and national institutions. National parliaments in the EC countries, where parliamentary government is the norm, feel doubly dispossessed. Everywhere in Western Europe, it is the executive—i.e., the cabinet—that initiates the main legislative acts and sets the course for the nation. Quite unlike the system in the US, parliaments have only the choice between overthrowing the cabinet (and thus often risking their own dissolution) and accepting the cabinet's proposals. The transfer of an increasing number of state functions to Brussels has already reduced the sphere in which national parliaments can act and under the Maastricht treaty they would be reduced even further. These functions, moreover, are to be carried out not by a supranational parliament, but by the representatives of the national executives.

Quite understandably, a backlash has occurred. In amending the French constitution so as to make it compatible with Maastricht, the French Senate insisted that EC legislation be submitted to the French Parliament. But it also said that the French Parliament could do no more than pass "resolutions" approving or disapproving the EC's decisions, which often take the form of complex package deals, negotiated in Brussels, that cannot usefully be dealt with by a simple parliamentary resolution. If similar resolutions are passed by parliaments in other countries this would lead to paralysis rather than to a closing of the democratic gap.

An attempt was made at Maastricht to appease such fears of dispossession by invoking the principle that the Community should deal only with what cannot be handled "effectively" at the national level. But of course much of politics is itself a struggle among people with conflicting views precisely about the level on which decisions should be taken. This "principle of subsidiary," borrowed from Catholic thought, is of no help: it does nothing to make the EC more democratic, and could do much to provoke a constant tug of war between the national states and the EC.

The Byzantine complexity of the whole structure will be aggravated by the increasing heterogeneity of the EC, which will grow even further if new members join. One now hears talk of a "flexible Europe" in which all members will have to sign the same charter, but exceptions, transitory periods, and special provisions will be granted to those who otherwise wouldn't or couldn't join. Denmark, for instance, has obtained a special deal aimed at making a "yes" vote in the forthcoming referendum more likely. Under it, Denmark accedes to the Maastricht treaty but not to most of its provisions. The more Byzantine the structure, the less democratic it will be.

Two proposals are being made to deal with the democratic deficit. There could be a second house of the Parliament, composed of delegations from the national parliaments. This would associate these delegates more closely with what goes on in the EC. However, this arrangement would only intensify and duplicate a flaw of the present system: the Parliament is elected not so much as a truly *European* assembly, but as a collection of *national* deputies, who run, in their respective countries, on purely national slates, and campaign not on European but on national issues. A truly European assembly would presuppose not nationwide slates of candidates but slates elected by smaller constituencies, and composed not only of natives, but of people of different nationalities.[5] This would be a second way of dealing with the democratic deficit—if, and only if, the election of such an assembly was accompanied by a major expansion of its powers. Indeed, without such an increase, neither method would resolve the issue.

Most of the European governments have been reluctant to increase the Strasbourg Parliament's powers and to change its makeup not only because they are the major beneficiaries of the "democratic deficit" but because both reforms would clearly turn the EC in a federal direction. The reforms would thus dissipate the deliberate ambiguity that has characterized the Community since the beginning and has allowed it to proceed despite the different conceptions that exist among and within its members about its goals. Is the EC destined to become a federal state, more or less on the American model, or is it to be a particularly active regional organization, governed by its members? In other words, is the purpose of the enterprise a transfer of any other regional organization that has ever been organized? It is a unique experiment, but its very uniqueness has provoked a profound doubt and distrust about the relation of the Community to the national states and public. The debates on Maastricht in Denmark, France, and now Britain have brought such feelings to light. Their sources are not difficult to understand.

First, in recent years, the activities of the Brussels bureaucrats have expanded, often in somewhat absurd ways, literally regulating ways of making cheese. As a result, Europeans tend to believe that Brussels already dictates, as Jacques Delors imprudently predicted, 80 percent of what affects their daily lives. But in fact Brussels firmly controls little more than agriculture, the elimination of regulations that hamper competition and trade among Community members, and trade with countries outside the Community. The EC does not try to establish uniform standards and rules. As long as certain minimum standards set by the

Community are observed (for instance for health and safety or environmental protection) each state is simply obliged to recognize as valid the standards and regulations set up by each of its partners. The public, suffering from unemployment and connecting it to high interest rates, tends to blame the EC for what are, basically, still national policies. The Maastricht treaty, for all its verbiage, was a modest treaty (even insofar as EMU is concerned, in view of the conditions and stages specified in the treaty), but it was overpromoted as a major advance.

This made the discontented members of the public—who blamed layoffs and cuts in subsidies on the single market and on reforms in the EC's bloated agricultural policy—even more suspicious of the next stages. Even if the EC's procedures were more democratic, it would be a target of expressions of social and economic unhappiness: in every democracy, it is the government and the bureaucracy that are held responsible for events or trends they often can't control. In fact, the powers given up by European states have not all been transferred to the EC's institutions; many have gone to the private investors and speculators who are central to the European economy and to world finance. Indeed, the single market is a boon to industry and especially to multinational enterprises. They have exerted far greater influence on the recent development of the Community than the labor unions, which have been weakened by the recession. This in turn strengthens the objections of those who believe that the duly elected representatives of the various member countries are no match for the combined power of unelected European bureaucrats and businessmen.[6]

Secondly, the relation of the nation-state to the Community is not everywhere the same. For many years, the French, who dominate the Brussels bureaucracy, saw in the EC a vehicle for French influence and for imposing restraints on the power of West Germany. Today, and for good reasons, the fear of Germany dominating the Community has replaced (as also in Denmark) the old fear of an unshackled Germany outside the Community. Especially after unification increased the relative weight of Germany among the Twelve, the Federal Republic's economic and financial might has made the EC an instrument of German influence. It has done so both through Bonn's willingness to dispense funds to (and thus obtain business from) the poorer members of the Community, and by using its influence to maintain a decentralized EC whose institutions resemble those of the Federal Republic far more than they resemble those of France.

It may seem excessive to say that, in the EC, what Germany wants, it gets, especially since the German government remains determined not to want anything that would cost it the external support it deems indispensable. Basically, however, Germany does get much of what it wants, and what it doesn't want doesn't get done. The European Community has been central to the rise of Germany. It has lifted Bonn step by step from its constricted and shriveled sovereignty of 1949, to its full legal sovereignty in 1990.

For Britain, which never even began to win its bet on finding new channels of influence through the Community (largely because of its own ambivalence), and for France, which has found the post–cold war world far less hospitable than the "order of Yalta" it once so vigorously denounced,[7] the Community is beginning to look much less desirable. For Britain it seems more like a cage from which the country is trying to liberate itself. For France it is worth staying in the EC as long as Germany is in it, but the French have increasing doubts about who is the guard and who is the captive. Hence the appeal, during the French referendum campaign over Maastricht, of those who said they were not "against Europe," but only against "Maastricht's Europe." They argued for a different kind of Europe that would extend farther East *and* allow for greater French independence at the same time.

This nostalgia for independence results not only from a geopolitical fear of being diminished. It springs from a third and more ideological or mythical consideration, powerful both in France and in the UK. Both are countries in which the nation has been created by, and remains inseparable from, the state—in contrast to the national history of Germany and Italy. The British ideological tradition, revived by Mrs. Thatcher, associates the notion of parliamentary sovereignty within the United Kingdom (however empty of substance it is in reality) with that of Britain's external sovereignty, i.e., its power to act without constraint in Europe.

France's Rousseauistic, Jacobin, and Republican tradition, evoked by De Gaulle and, in 1992, by the Gaullist Philippe Séguin, the new speaker of the National Assembly, combines France's claim to external sovereignty with its insistence on the domestic sovereignty of the people (another potent myth). Most of the governments of the Twelve have, pragmatically, treated external sovereignty quite differently—as a bundle of powers that could be traded off and pooled. In most EC nations the institutional setup of the Community has diluted the strength of parliamentary or popular sovereignty at home. But in France and in the UK, much of the public remain attached, in a Danish commentator's phrase, to a view of sovereignty as "something like virginity": it is not divisible.[8]

Nations like France and the UK, where the state is seen as the source of rights and duties, and as the source of the nation itself, can only interpret the distinction which the EC encourages between the nation and the state (whose powers are now shared with the EC) as a dangerous and disturbing trend. The distinction points, indeed, to a European state, but one without a European nation, since there are still no European mass media, parties, interest groups (except in business), or public. The establishment at Maastricht of a common European citizenship is only a formal first step. Without such a European nation, many feel, so to speak, denuded, for the national state is losing power, but the European would-be state, uncomfortably straddling nations with diverse traditions and interests, seems incapable of defining a common policy in matters as vital as defense and diplomacy, as the failure in Yugoslavia shows.

In France and the UK, by contrast with Germany, the state was seen and embraced as the founder and guardian of the nation. Its weakening and replacement by a weak multinational pseudo-superstate only increase fears about national identity. The same fears are already inflamed by the influx of "others," such as immigrant workers and refugees, or by the "Americanization" of popular culture, or by the decline of traditional ways of life, whether of British miners, French peasants, or small shopkeepers throughout the continent. The Community had been celebrated as a way, the only one perhaps, to preserve "European distinctiveness," particularly from American pressures and cultural influences, but of course the bureaucrats in Brussels could never do this. It is not surprising that in the 1992 debates on Maastricht, the treaty's opponents blamed the EC for every threat to national identity, for yielding to American policy over GATT or to American television imports, as well as for opening borders to more immigrants (a charge that had little basis in the treaty).

Countries like France and the UK, whose identity was shaped early and whose people see the nation as a long-defined and completed entity, have far greater difficulty accepting the implications of an ever-expanding Community than, say, Germany, which like the US, although in a very different way, tends to see itself as unfinished and continuously developing. The Germans' almost permanent uncertainties about German identity somehow make it easier for them to endorse a European identity which is equally uncertain and unfinished. French and British certainties about their national past and character are being shaken, and the EC is seen as one of the culprits.

This does not mean, in either case, that the policy of European integration will be abandoned: there is no turning back. But resistance to integration, fed by the EC's institutional flaws, is likely to increase as the EC's powers expand. So will the gap between the European governments, for whom joint action (or inaction) has become second nature (especially since it is often unchecked), and their citizens, who wonder where their governments are taking them and who benefits and who loses, from the march to an unknown destination. Western Europe today is a collection of bruised nations, whose states have traded visible and distinctive power for diffuse collective influence.[9] It is not surprising that so many Europeans find it difficult to identify with a "Europe" that remains a purely economic and bureaucratic construction and shows few signs of becoming a nation.

Notes

1. See Robert O. Keohane and Stanley Hoffmann, editors, *The New European Community* (Westview Press, 1991).

2. I have relied on the account in David Cameron's still unpublished paper, "British exit, German voice, French loyalty: defection, domination, and cooperation in the 1992–93 ERM crisis," March 1993.

3. There are other causes: the world recession, of course, the unstoppable decline of traditional industries in the mid-1980s, the need to be competitive abroad (a need made more acute by deregulation and the policy of tying the franc to the mark), which led to large-scale layoffs in a country where labor costs are high.

4. See Paul Ginsborg, "Lo stato italiano: transformazione o transformismo," *La Rivista dei Libri*, March 1993.

5. Only the Italian Communists have put distinguished foreigners on their list in elections to the European Parliament.

6. See Nicholas Hildyard, "Maastricht: the Protectionism of Free Trade," *The Ecologist*, Vol. 23, No. 2 (March–April 1993).

7. See S. Hoffmann, "French Dilemmas, and Strategies in the New Europe," in Joseph Nye, Robert Keohane, and Stanley Hoffmann, editors, *After the Cold War* (Harvard University Press, 1993).

8. Ulf Hedetoft, *Sovereignty, Identity and War in 90s Europe*, Department of Languages and Intercultural Studies (Aalborg: Aalborg University, 1993), especially pp. 14–38.

9. See Wolfgang Merkel, *Integration and Democracy in the European Community: The Contours of a Dilemma*, Working Paper 42 (Madrid: Instituto Juan March de Estudios e Investigaciones, 1993).

About the Book and Author

Bringing together all of Stanley Hoffmann's significant essays on the development and difficulties of European integration, this collection highlights the intractability of the divisions that plagued the European Union from its very beginning. Just as the process of integration has displayed the same ambiguities, hesitations, and failings over the years, so have Hoffmann's general preoccupations and emphases remained constant.

These essays provide a view of evolution and change as well as an examination of the crises and turning points in the history of European integration. Hoffmann chronicles the ebb and flow of the process from the time of Charles de Gaulle's challenge to Jean Monnet's conception of supranational integration through the 1970s "period of stagnation" and on to the 1992 single-market program and the Maastricht Treaty.

Scholars will welcome the opportunity to have Hoffmann's analyses—most long unavailable—within one volume. Students will find Hoffmann's consistent and cohesive vision an invaluable guide to understanding the evolution of European union.

Stanley Hoffmann is C. Douglas Dillon Professor of the Civilization of France at Harvard University, where he has taught since 1955. He has been chairman of the Center for European Studies at Harvard since its creation in 1969. Born in Vienna in 1928, Hoffmann lived and studied in France from 1929 to 1955. He has taught at the Institut d'Études Politiques of Paris, from which he graduated, and at the École des Hautes Études en Sciences Sociales.

At Harvard, he teaches French intellectual and political history, the development of the modern state, U.S. foreign policy, the sociology of war, international politics, ethics and world affairs, and modern political ideologies.

His many books include *Contemporary Theory in International Relations* (1960), *The State of War* (1965), *Gulliver's Troubles* (1968), *Decline or Renewal? France Since the 1930s* (1974), *Primacy or World Order: American Foreign Policy Since the Cold War* (1978), *Duties Beyond Borders* (1981), *Dead Ends* (1983), and *Janus and Minerva: Essays in the Theory and Practice of International Politics* (Westview, 1986). He is coauthor of *In Search of France: The Fifth Republic at Twenty* (1981), *Living with Nuclear Weapons* (1983), *The Mitterand Experiment* (1987), and the forthcoming *Taming Cold Monsters* (with Michael Joseph Smith). He also coedited *Rousseau on International Relations* (1991) and coedited and coauthored *The New European Community* (1991) and *After the Cold War* (1993). He contributed two autobiographical chapters to the book of essays in his honor coedited by Linda Miller and Michael J. Smith, *Ideas and Ideals* (Westview, 1993).

Index